Self-Esteem and Positive Psychology

Christopher J. Mruk, PhD, is a professor of psychology at Bowling Green State University Firelands College in Ohio, where he has received the college's Distinguished Teaching and Distinguished Scholarship awards several times. Dr. Mruk was trained in general psychology at Michigan State University and in clinical psychology at Duquesne University. His publications include two books and over two dozen book chapters and articles in the areas of clinical, existential-humanistic, and positive psychology. Dr. Mruk also is an associate editor of *The Humanistic Psychologist*. Prior to his academic appointment, he spent time working in a number of mental health positions, including supervising a methadone rehabilitation program in Detroit, MI; serving as a crisis intervention specialist in Lansing, MI, at one of the nation's first two comprehensive psychiatric emergency service facilities; functioning as a staff psychologist for a community mental health center in Monessen, PA; and directing a counseling center at St. Francis College in Pennsylvania. Today, Dr. Mruk continues his clinical work by consulting at Firelands Regional Medical Center in Sandusky, Ohio.

Self-Esteem and Positive Psychology

Research, Theory, and Practice

Fourth Edition

Christopher J. Mruk, PhD

SPRINGER PUBLISHING COMPANY

NEW YORK

Springer Publishing Company, LLC
11 West 42nd Street
New York, NY 10036
www.springerpub.com

Acquisitions Editor: Nancy S. Hale
Composition: diacriTech

ISBN: 978-0-8261-0898-2
E-book ISBN: 978-0-8261-0899-9

13 14 15 / 5 4 3 2 1

The author and the publisher of this Work have made every effort to use sources believed to be reliable to provide information that is accurate and compatible with the standards generally accepted at the time of publication. The author and publisher shall not be liable for any special, consequential, or exemplary damages resulting, in whole or in part, from the readers' use of, or reliance on, the information contained in this book. The publisher has no responsibility for the persistence or accuracy of URLs for external or third-party Internet websites referred to in this publication and does not guarantee that any content on such websites is, or will remain, accurate or appropriate.

Library of Congress Cataloging-in-Publication Data

Mruk, Christopher J.
 Self-esteem and positive psychology : research, theory, and practice/Christopher J. Mruk. — 4th ed.
  p. cm.
 Rev. ed. of: Self-esteem research, theory, and practice. 3rd ed. 2006.
 Includes bibliographical references and index.
 ISBN 978-0-8261-0898-2 — ISBN 978-0-8261-0899-9 (ebook) 1. Self-esteem. 2. Positive psychology.
I. Mruk, Christopher J. Self-esteem research, theory, and practice. II. Title.
 BF697.5.S46M78 2013
 155.2—dc23
                                   2012044270

Special discounts on bulk quantities of our books are available to corporations, professional associations, pharmaceutical companies, health care organizations, and other qualifying groups.

If you are interested in a custom book, including chapters from more than one of our titles, we can provide that service as well.

For details, please contact:
Special Sales Department, Springer Publishing Company, LLC
11 West 42nd Street, 15th Floor, New York, NY 10036-8002
Phone: 877-687-7476 or 212-431-4370; Fax: 212-941-7842
E-mail: sales@springerpub.com

Printed in the United States of America by Gasch Printing.

Contents

Preface

The fourth edition of this book is different from the others in a number of important ways. First, the request to write it came to me as a surprise. While talking with Nancy S. Hale, the editor of this edition, I was asked if I would be willing to write a fourth edition. Initially, I was disinclined because I was working on a draft for another book. In addition, my students often complain about authors and publishers who simply add a few words to an existing text and call it a new edition for marketing rather than for academic purposes. I certainly did not want to be guilty of such an exploitative practice. However, Nancy's reasoning was difficult to fault. In addition to the usual minimum criterion of at least 10% new material that Springer Publishing Company has required for a new edition in the past, she also made another more powerful point I could not refute.

Nancy pointed out that the last chapter of the third edition focused on demonstrating how there is an important relationship between the fields of self-esteem and positive psychology, but that this connection was not yet appropriately recognized in that field. Thus, the chapter focused on creating a conceptual link between the fields. Since then, she carefully pointed out, considerable progress has been made in this regard and now there is a demonstrable recognition of self-esteem in positive psychology. Perhaps, Nancy suggested, the third edition had something to do with that new development. In any event, it was clear to me that what I call the "second generation" of positive psychologists do seem to be recognizing the value of self-esteem, so her point was well made.

Now even general undergraduate textbooks in positive psychology routinely include self-esteem as a topic (Baumgardner & Crothers, 2009) and at least one even includes my theory of self-esteem in a chapter on positive selfhood (Carr, 2011). In addition, people have been writing about self-esteem in relationship to positive psychology since the last edition (Mruk, 2008a, 2008b, in press). Thus, when Nancy finally pointed out to me that my choice was to either let the book recede in significance because part of it was outdated or to rewrite the book so as to reflect these new and exciting realities, her argument prevailed: I set aside the other projects in order to revise and update the book in this and several other ways.

Chapter 1 still concerns defining self-esteem, but was substantially rewritten for three reasons. First, since the last edition, I noticed some important connections between the ways in which John Milton (1642/1950) used the term in its earliest days and various problems concerning how self-esteem is defined today. It turns out, for example, that his original rendition of the concept appears to be much more closely tied to the two-factor approach to defining self-esteem that is the basis of this book, rather than to the more common "feelings of worth" approach that is popular today. Second, the changes in positive psychology just mentioned mean that there is no longer a need to defend incorporating self-esteem into positive psychology. Thus, it is now possible to work this theme into the body of the text throughout the book, in addition to focusing on positive psychology at the end. Finally, defining self-esteem as a balance of competence and worthiness has received professional attention in the United States and Europe during the past few years, meaning that it is now possible to concentrate on showing how this two-factor approach constitutes a legitimate tradition of research, theory, and practice.

Chapter 2 remains largely focused on methodological issues facing those who work on self-esteem. However, now that the two-factor approach is an established view, I tend to emphasize the value of a research approach called "integrated description" that is capable of bringing together qualitative and quantitative work in the field. Chapter 3, which concerns research findings, was revised to update the review of work in the field during the past several years. For example, the book now includes new findings concerning work on the importance of self-esteem in relationships that did not appear in previous editions. Chapter 4 remains largely intact, although I streamlined the presentation of major historical and contemporary theories of self-esteem and the types of enhancement programs they generate. As before, Chapter 5 continues to present my theory of self-esteem. However, some additional clarification has occurred, such as clarifying the point at which self-esteem problems become clinically significant.

Next, since the previous edition, the self-esteem program presented in Chapter 6 has been researched and used by others in the United States and in Europe. Students in Eastern and Middle Eastern countries have contacted me about it for their graduate work as well. Because I wanted to preserve the researchability of the program, its step-by-step nature has been retained. However, I did make two small but notable changes. First, I gave a name to the program: It is now called "Competence and Worthiness Training," or CWT, in order to reflect the two-factor definition of self-esteem. Second, I have included more references supporting the clinical efficacy of this existentially oriented positive therapy in order to address the call for "evidence-based" treatments that has become important today. Finally, as mentioned earlier, Chapter 7 has been extensively revised: Instead of arguing *for* a place in positive psychology as I did in the previous edition, now I focus on describing the *existing* space self-esteem actually occupies in that field and where to go next.

It should also be noted that this edition involved adding over 50 new references. In order to do that without substantially lengthening the book, it was necessary to shorten, move, and remove a good number of unnecessary or dated quotations and citations. I have endeavored my very best to be accurate in this regard. Thus, if an error occurs in this edition, it is a function of accident, not intent.

Over the years, I have taught and trained psychologists, counselors, nurses, social workers, educators, and others in academic and applied settings. Such interdisciplinary work has convinced me that all good therapists bring certain "common factors" to the table and that no single discipline is comprehensive enough to do it all alone. Thus, this edition continues to be oriented toward a range of audiences. As before, academics and researchers will probably find Chapters 2 through 5 most interesting because they cover research and theory. Clinicians and other practitioners are likely to find themselves drawn more toward Chapters 4 through 6 because they address how self-esteem works in relation to problems of living and how to help people cope more effectively. Chapters 1 and 7 should be of equal interest to both groups because defining self-esteem may be the most crucial issue in the field right now, and the relationship between self-esteem and positive psychology is likely to grow in the future.

Finally, it might be helpful to say a word about writing style. Moving all the way from research, through theory, and then to practice for an entire field is an unusual approach: Most books emphasize only one or two dimensions of a topic. However, I know as a researcher and clinician that the best practical tools come from a theory that is based on good research. Thus, I try to find a "middle path" in style and tone that is compatible with key needs and expectations of academics or researchers as well as practitioners or educators. The result is an attempt to proceed in a logical, systematic fashion that begins with research issues and findings, that then moves through theories (including my own approach), and that ends with practical applications, including possibilities for the future.

Acknowledgments

It usually takes more than one person to write a book, even though most of the credit (or blame, as the case may be) falls on the author. First and foremost, of course, is my wife, Marsha Mruk, who lovingly shows the patience to put up with the challenges associated with being a "book widow" once again. As always, thanks go to my original family consisting of Steven, Veronica, and Joseph Mruk, my brother, mother, and father, respectively; to my second family, which includes Dee Mruk, Tina Bradshaw, and Pam Pawloski; and to my married family, especially Virginia, Carl, and Sylvia Oliver.

Friends who helped smooth out the process this time include Scott Churchill, Joan Hartzell, Pete and Marsha Kowalski, Robert Noe, and Frank and Mary Ann Salotti. Karen Page Osterling, my colleague at work and personal copy editor for both of my books in all their editions, continues to play a key role in my writing. Others include two psychological colleagues and friends. The first is Edward O'Brien, who is a kindred self-esteem soul and sometime coauthor with me in the field. The other is William Balzer, who often helps me find a balance between quantitative and qualitative positions. And then, of course, there are my mentors: Tony Barton and Connie Fischer, who will never be forgotten for the goodwill they consistently extended to an often struggling graduate student.

Finally, I remain indebted to the staff of Springer Publishing Company for their interest and help over the past two decades. In addition to Sheri W. Sussman's continued support, this time Nancy S. Hale is given credit for the possibility of a fourth edition, which at the time of this writing may be the only one in the field. Of course, a word of thanks always goes to Dr. Ursula Springer, who stands as something of a David facing the Goliath of gigantic for-profit publishing houses in her dedication to bringing scholarly work to psychology and related fields. Last, but closer to first than to least, it is important to thank all the clients whom I cannot name. However, common practice does allow me to acknowledge former students, and this time I would like to mention Mia Bartoletti and Travis Skelly for their willingness to engage in discussions that help reveal more of the subtle and lived dimensions of self-esteem. Thank you all!

1

The Crucial Issue of Defining Self-Esteem

Although seldom mentioned by those wishing to understand self-esteem, the single most important task one faces while venturing into this rich territory may concern the need for clear definitions. Beginning at this point is especially important when dealing with this field because social scientists define self-esteem in at least three different ways. For example, one major definition connects self-esteem to a person's general success or "competence," particularly in areas of life that are especially meaningful to a given individual. A second and most commonly used definition is based on understanding self-esteem as an attitude or feeling concerning a sense of worth or one's "worthiness" as a person. The third approach involves defining self-esteem as a relationship between these two factors. In this view, it is only an individual's competence at dealing with the challenges of living in worthy ways that gives rise to healthy, positive, or authentic self-esteem. Although the least well known of the three, this book aims to demonstrate how such a two-factor approach (Tafarodi & Swann, 1995) offers insights, possibilities, and applications concerning self-esteem and its value not found in work based on the other definitions.

The opening chapter is devoted to defining self-esteem this way because clear, operational definitions are a hallmark of good science, including social science. Each of the other chapters not only addresses an important topic in the field, but also marks a step in what I hope is a logical and empirically supported progression that steadily moves from research on self-esteem, through major theories about it, to practical applications that are compatible with both existential and positive psychology. Thus, Chapter 2 identifies the important research issues in the field. Next, we attempt to identify and summarize the major findings concerning self-esteem that have emerged over time. Chapter 4 examines the leading theories of self-esteem that seem to consistently attract attention. Then, we consider the comprehensive two-factor model of self-esteem that is the heart of this book. Based on this theory, Chapter 6 presents a detailed, step-by-step enhancement program called Competence and Worthiness Training (CWT), which has been shown to increase authentic self-esteem in an evidence-based fashion. Finally, the book ends with a chapter that discusses how this program, as well as authentic self-esteem in general, stands as a part of what is now being called positive psychology. In the end, the book attempts to be true to its title: taking the reader through the research, theory, and practice of self-esteem from its beginning as a field to its current place in modern psychology, one that now includes positive psychology.

THE IMPORTANCE OF DEFINING SELF-ESTEEM

We begin with defining self-esteem because different definitions lead to different types of theories, research findings, and practical applications. Since self-esteem is one of the oldest topics in psychology, it is not surprising to find that the work generated using one definition tends to become mixed with material found by another. To compound matters, the need for operational definitions is always great when dealing with "subjective" phenomena, such as self-esteem, because they are difficult to observe, measure, or test. Today, the result of not paying sufficient attention to the types of definitions available manifests itself in at least three unfortunate ways: confusion about what is meant by self-esteem, unsubstantiated claims made about practices aimed at increasing self-esteem, and exaggerated criticisms questioning the importance of self-esteem. In order to address this situation, it is necessary to focus on what is meant by self-esteem from the outset. This approach involves the process of examining the development of the major definitions of self-esteem, evaluating their respective strengths and weaknesses, and then selecting the one that seems to best describe what is meant by the term "self-esteem."

The context for the following investigation is surrounded by the vitality of this topic. For example, if history is an indication of significance, then self-esteem easily stands out as an important subject. After all, William James (1890/1983) introduced the topic to social science more than a century ago in what is often regarded as the first American textbook on psychology, thereby making self-esteem one of the oldest themes. Similarly, the breadth of a subject or how much attention it generates is another good indicator of importance. Even a cursory database search of PsycINFO will reveal that scholars, researchers, and practitioners have written a massive amount of material on self-esteem to date. For instance, in early July of 2012, a PsycINFO key-word search of self-esteem in the title of a work resulted in 9,078 publications. The term was also identified in 29,744 abstracts and a search in "All Fields" resulted in 37,314 references to the term. The latter number is nearly a third larger than the one produced by the same method in the last edition of this book only 6 years earlier. The fact that the number seems to grow substantially each time the database is updated certainly supports the position that self-esteem is a basic, if not fundamental, topic in the social sciences. Indeed, Rodewalt and Tragakis (2003) stated that self-esteem is one of the "top three covariates in personality and social psychology research," following negative affectivity and gender (p. 66).

Finally, the ability to endure controversy may be seen as another general indicator of vitality, and self-esteem appears to be resilient in this regard as well. Indeed, we shall see that self-esteem shows itself to be one of those relatively rare topics for which even heated controversy only seems to stimulate more interest in the subject, as indicated by the numbers cited above. In short, self-esteem is just as likely to be an important subject in the 21st century of psychology as it was in the last.

Today there are several sets of reasons that self-esteem deserves continuing attention. One of them is that self-esteem appears to be among those relatively few dimensions of human life that stretches across the full spectrum of behavior, much like the topics of development, personality, or identity. At one end of the continuum, for instance, low self-esteem is often mentioned in regard to various clinical phenomena, such as depression or anxiety. Leary and MacDonald (2003) noted that studies overwhelmingly show that when compared to people with high self-esteem, those with low self-esteem experience more negative emotions, affect, or states across the board. Examples include anxiety, sadness and depression, hostility and anger, social anxiety, shame and guilt, embarrassment, loneliness, as well as general negative affect and neuroticism (pp. 404–405).

Even more to the point, O'Brien, Bartoletti, and Leitzel (2006) pointed out that low self-esteem is identified as either a diagnostic criterion for, or associated feature of, some 24 mental disorders in the fourth edition of the *Diagnostic and Statistical Manual of Mental Disorders* (American Psychiatric Association, 2000). Indeed, if it is true that some 15% of Americans meet criteria for a diagnosable mental health condition in a given year (Regier et al., 1993), and if self-esteem is involved in many more conditions such as those mentioned above, then it is evident that self-esteem is of considerable social significance. After all, in addition to those who directly suffer from self-esteem problems, others around them often encounter the "fallout" of low or unhealthy self-esteem as well. The result is that problems associated with self-esteem probably touch most of us either directly through personal experience or indirectly through such things as the pain of a loved one, negative self-esteem–related behavior that is directed at us, or at least some of the general costs associated with providing mental health care.

In addition to clinical issues, self-esteem and problems with it are also important for what may be seen as the middle of the human behavioral spectrum. For example, we shall see that self-esteem appears to play a role in being able to manage one's life in ways that are competent and worthy while facing developmental and other challenges of living. These challenges occur in everyday life and take place in ways that are sure to affect us all, such as dealing with failures, facing losses, and overcoming setbacks (Epstein, 1979; Jackson, 1984; Mruk, 1983). Finally, self-esteem also seems to be a factor at the other, more positive end of the spectrum. For instance, studies clearly demonstrate links between self-esteem and happiness, well-being, and optimal functioning (Diener & Diener, 1995; Kernis, 2003a), all of which are important themes in positive psychology.

A second set of reasons for looking at self-esteem anew concerns events that seem to be creating important changes in the field. This development means that it is necessary to appreciate something of the field's history. William James introduced the concept of self-esteem, but then academic psychology made a strong shift to the behavioral position, which eschewed phenomena involving consciousness or experience and instead focused on observable behavior (Harter, 1999; Mruk, 1999). The concept of self-esteem was then embraced by those with more clinical and applied interests, especially psychodynamic thinkers. For example, Alfred Adler (1927) saw self-esteem as a way of overcoming a deep sense of inferiority, which he thought was related to much of human behavior, both positive and negative. Karen Horney (1937) went so far as to declare "war" on neurosis and envisioned healthy self-esteem as the solution to many, if not most, psychological and behavioral problems. During the 1950s, Robert White (1959) focused on the developmental implications of self-esteem, particularly in relation to mastery and competence.

Then in a way somewhat akin to a Cambrian explosion, self-esteem suddenly erupted back onto the psychological stage in the mid 1960s. This period was led by such figures as Carl Rogers (1951, 1961) and Abraham Maslow (1964, 1968), who explored self-esteem from a humanistic perspective. Thus, the importance of self-esteem was connected to such things as self-actualization and living a full or authentic life. Stanley Coopersmith (1959, 1967) began to look at self-esteem from a learning theory point of view and attempted to observe and even measure self-esteem in controlled situations. Morris Rosenberg (1965) introduced a major research tool with the creation of a 10-item, easy-to-administer, self-esteem scale that became the "gold standard" for assessing self-esteem. Indeed, this instrument may have been used in as much as a quarter of all the (considerable) research that existed on self-esteem up to the 1990s and beyond (Tafarodi & Swann, 1995). Finally, during this rather amazing period in the development of the field, Nathaniel Branden introduced self-esteem to popular culture through a best-selling book, *The Psychology of Self-Esteem* (1969).

During the late-1980s to mid-1990s, two converging forces worked together to push the field of self-esteem into a much larger social arena. One of them originated with a group of academicians and politicians largely based in California. Among other things, they emphasized to the general public the possibility of a link between individual self-esteem and major social problems, including substance abuse, welfare, and teen pregnancy. As Smelser (1989) said, "The well-being of society depends on the well-being of its citizenry. . . . many, if not most, of the major problems plaguing society have roots in the low self-esteem of many of the people who make up society" (p. 1).

Perhaps in response to the Zeitgeist of the time, maybe as a result of the high profile from which this group benefited, or simply because it seemed to make so much "common sense," this position generated a broad base of political and social support. For the first time, self-esteem work received considerable financial backing and interest. This support allowed the field to involve other areas, especially the educational setting (Beane, 1991; Damon, 1995). At the same time, self-help and popular psychology markets joined the self-esteem bandwagon and spread interest in the topic to an even wider audience, including the popular media. The results of this concatenation of events included such things as a dramatic increase in programs aimed at enhancing self-esteem in school settings, a greater parental interest in fostering self-esteem, and a significant rise in the number of books and discussions on self-esteem across the board. In short, the old but quiet field of self-esteem achieved social significance culminating in what is now commonly known as the "self-esteem movement."

However, popularity is a double-edged sword. In addition to obvious benefits, such as more research funding and more people working in the field, bringing a scientific concept to the public forum also exposes it to scrutiny and, sometimes, negative forms of attention. The most important of these appears to be the development of a second, countervailing social force operating against self-esteem that took the form of a backlash against the topic. Early signs of what might be called "self-esteem bashing" or even an "anti-self-esteem movement" began to appear in social commentaries with eye-catching titles such as *The Trouble with Self-Esteem* (Leo, 1990) or *Education: Doing Bad and Feeling Good* (Krauthammer, 1990), that appeared in popular news magazines. Such criticism of self-esteem spread to various segments of the popular media during the remainder of the 1990s (Johnson, 1998; Leo, 1998) and still persists today (Gottleib, 2012), although in somewhat muted form.

At the same time, a more substantial line of scientific work criticizing the merit of self-esteem research and practices arose in professional literature. For example, the psychologist Martin Seligman (1995b) said in a book on child rearing that by focusing on self-esteem, "parents and teachers are making this generation of children more vulnerable to depression" (p. 27). William Damon (1995) criticized self-esteem work in the educational setting even more strenuously when he called it a "mirage" for those who work with children, and "like all mirages, it is both appealing and perilously deceptive, luring us away from more rewarding developmental objectives" (p. 72).

Perhaps the most significant and influential scientific work of this type was led by Roy Baumeister. Although once a strong advocate supporting the importance of self-esteem for understanding human behavior (Baumeister, 1993), a turning point seemed to occur just a few years later. In a highly reputable scientific journal, Baumeister, Smart, and Boden (1996) suggested that high self-esteem appears to be associated with certain undesirable forms of behavior, most notably egotism, narcissism, and even violence. These negative correlations were collectively presented as the "dark side" of self-esteem. Other scientifically oriented work also criticized the importance of self-esteem in similar ways (Emler, 2001). Although we will find that this so-called dark side may be understood in a very different way, the phrase caught the negative eye of the popular media and press. The result was an atmosphere that was far less receptive to self-esteem work than ever before in the history of the field. In short, the combination of poignant empirically based criticism from within, coupled with a reversal of fortune in the popular media from without, worked together to challenge the very foundations of self-esteem, let alone increasing it. In fact, some even questioned the merit of pursuing self-esteem altogether (Crocker & Nuer, 2003, 2004) and advocated its abandonment.

Fortunately, science can be unrelenting in its pursuit for knowledge and little dominates the picture for long. At the turn of the 21st century, the same self-correcting power of the scientific method that exposed the dangers of overgeneralizing the value of self-esteem also placed the claims of those who criticize it into question. The result of this progressive process is that over the past few years a number of research and theoretical advances have occurred in the field that make it absolutely necessary to examine the topic anew. For example, some recent work focuses on emerging findings concerning the existence of several types of self-esteem. Low self-esteem still seems to be strongly associated with unhealthy forms of behavior, such as depression and anxiety. However, another type, often called defensive self-esteem, might be connected to more socially disturbing behavior, such as narcissism, bullying, or the dark side mentioned earlier. Similarly, now people differentiate between high self-esteem, which can just be a score on a test, and healthy, genuine, or authentic self-esteem, which is correlated with highly desirable personal and interpersonal phenomena (Deci & Ryan, 1995; Kernis, 2003b).

In addition, developmental work seems to be making considerable progress in terms of understanding the antecedents of self-esteem (Harter, 1999; Trzesniewski, Robins, Roberts, & Caspi, 2004), something that Coopersmith (1967) called for decades ago. Perhaps even more important, the critical look at the field has not only led to re-examining old theories, but has also stimulated the formation of powerful new ones, such as terror management theory, sociometer theory, and two-factor theory, all of which we will explore in detail later. In other words, recent events in the field are so important that they must be considered when thinking about self-esteem from this point onward.

The third and final group of related reasons for taking another look at self-esteem is that new positive forces are now at work in the field that are creating exciting possibilities. Some of these developments arise from within the field. For example, it is already well established that there is a relationship between self-esteem and happiness that even critics of self-esteem are forced to recognize (Baumeister, Campbell, Krueger, & Vohs, 2003). Research also points to an important relationship between self-esteem, authenticity, and optimal functioning (Kernis, 2003a, 2003b). Similarly, the two-factor approach has been shown to be capable of increasing healthy or authentic self-esteem in ways that are measurable in both clinical and general population settings (Bartoletti, 2008; Hakim-Larson & Mruk, 1997).

Most recently, the emergence of the field known as positive psychology is beginning to focus on these and other topics related to self-esteem. In fact, where the previous edition of this book argued that positive psychology needed to make room for authentic self-esteem, this one builds on the growing place self-esteem now occupies in that field. For instance, self-esteem is now clearly recognized as a topic in positive psychology. This topic is now discussed in positive psychology textbooks (Carr, 2011), in work concerning the relationship between self-esteem and happiness that is relevant to both fields (Baumgardner & Crothers, 2009), and in ways that are relevant to positive therapy (Linley & Joseph, 2004; Mruk, 2008b). In short, attempting to clear up confusion, making an effort to address an issue that spans a broad spectrum of human behavior, responding to new developments in the field, and integrating one stream of work with another are good reasons to re-examine self-esteem in a new edition of this book. Having delineated the context, we may now turn back to the first task and take a closer look at the importance of defining self-esteem.

THE MAJOR DEFINITIONS

In one sense, we all know something about what self-esteem "really is" because it is a human phenomenon. However, as Smelser (1989) observed, "We have a fairly firm grasp of what is meant by self-esteem, as revealed by our own introspection and observation of the behavior of others. But it is hard to put that understanding into precise words" (p. 9). In other words, like many common-sense understandings, there are serious limits to such knowledge that become apparent as soon as we begin to examine them more closely.

A simple but revealing way to explore this problem is to ask almost any reasonably mature group of people to do the following exercise. At the beginning of a class or discussion, ask each person to write down his or her own definition of self-esteem. Then, invite the group members to either read their definitions aloud or to hand them in to be read aloud. As the information comes in, write the key components of each definition down so that they can be examined publicly. After that is done, ask the group to develop a single definition of self-esteem. Participants usually see the point almost immediately: What seems so familiar and easy at the beginning of the activity quickly shows itself to be quite complex or difficult at the end. Typically, people tend to be struck by the diversity of definitions. For some, it may even seem as though there are as many ways to define self-esteem as there are people trying to do so. However, the group will also notice that, although different, several definitions appear to be of some value in that they suggest, capture, or describe an important aspect of the phenomenon few wish to discard.

If the group spends enough time with this exercise, participants also begin to notice that definitions can be grouped on the basis of key characteristics. For example, one person might see that some depictions focus on values, such as self-respect. Another might point out that other definitions center on the affective dimension of self-esteem and how it involves a feeling of worth. Someone else may be struck by how it is that some of the definitions emphasize cognitive factors, such as the attitudinal components of self-esteem. An astute individual may even notice that particular definitions focus attention on the behavioral aspects of self-esteem, such as being more independent or assertive. The lesson, however, really begins to solidify when they are asked to defend the definitions they developed while the others in the group offer critique.

Two things usually become quite apparent by the end of this activity. The first is that developing a good definition of self-esteem is difficult, because people tend to emphasize different aspects of it when they put their thoughts into words. The other is that how one defines self-esteem is a crucial issue, because definitions have power: They help shape what we see and what remains hidden. In addition to being a good pedagogical tool, the reason the exercise is mentioned here is because *it is a microcosm of what actually seems to happen among writers, researchers, and clinicians in the field* (Smelser, 1989; Wells & Marwell, 1976). Unfortunately, what typically seems to be so clear to beginners often appears to be forgotten by experts, for it turns out that some researchers define self-esteem in one way, others define it differently, and many simply take the term for granted and don't offer a particular definition at all. The result is that the concept loses specificity: People may talk about self-esteem, but often little communication occurs.

Thus, there are several good reasons to consider why defining self-esteem is a crucial first step when investigating this phenomenon. First, definitions open up pathways of understanding, in part because they name things. "Naming" shapes perception and, therefore, much that follows. In this sense, every major definition is important because each one shows us some things about self-esteem that can only be seen from that particular point of view. At the same time, of course, definitions also create limits. Although each particular definition opens up a way of looking at a phenomenon, it closes off other perspectives that can lead to different insights or understandings. Phenomenologists call this aspect of human perception "perspectivity" (Gurwitsch, 1964), which means that it is necessary to fully appreciate the ways in which each approach or definition both reveals and conceals.

Second, even though we are limited in this fashion, we must choose a direction in beginning any kind of a journey, even one of understanding. Thus, it behooves us to select the best definition possible. The problem in this field is that there is much variation in this process. Indeed, there are so many ways to proceed that confusion is the rule, not the exception. Even worse, whereas novices know that taking the time to define terms operationally is a scientific first step, it is surprising to find that experts often do not: "Of the thousands of entries listed in ERIC on some aspect of self-esteem, only a few are listed as targeting its definition" (Guindon, 2002, p. 205). A consequence of this condition is what Smelser (1989) calls a "definitional maze" (p. 9) concerning self-esteem.

One way to deal with such a problem is to examine the major definitions of self-esteem that are in use to see whether or not any of them proves itself superior to the others. For instance, in one of the earliest attempts to deal with this situation, Wells and Marwell (1976, p. 62) organized definitions of self-esteem on the basis of two psychological processes: evaluation (which emphasizes the role of cognition) and affect (which prioritizes the role of feelings) as they pertain to self-esteem. The result was a typology of definitions that consists of four ways of defining self-esteem. The first and most basic definition is to simply characterize self-esteem as a certain attitude. As with any other attitude that is held toward a given object, this one can involve positive or negative cognitive, emotional, and behavioral reactions.

They found a second type of definition to be based on the idea of a discrepancy. In particular, it is the discrepancy between the self that one wishes to be (the "ideal" self) and the self that one currently sees oneself as being (the "real" or "perceived" self) that matters. The closer these two percepts are, the higher the individual's self-esteem is said to be. Conversely, the wider the gap between the two, the more self-esteem is thought to suffer. A third approach focuses on the psychological responses a person holds toward himself or herself rather than attitudes alone. Such global indicators of self-esteem are usually described in terms of positive or negative affect about the self or feeling accepted versus rejected, and so forth. Finally, Wells and Marwell (1976) maintained that self-esteem is understood as a function or component of personality. In this case, self-esteem is seen as a part of the self-system, usually one that is concerned with motivation, self-regulation, or both.

A newer approach to organizing definitions is based on identifying general or common aspects of self-esteem. Using this method, Smelser (1989, p. 10) developed a classification system based on which of three basic components a given definition emphasizes. To paraphrase, one is cognitively oriented and involves describing what type of a person one is in terms of specific descriptive characteristics, such as power, confidence, and agency. Another is more affective and concerns an emotional process that involves attaching general positive or negative quality to the perception or experience of one's self. The third focuses on an evaluative process that compares one's current level of worthiness to an ideal or standard. He went on to note that definitions also vary as to whether they focus on self-esteem as a global or situational phenomenon. That is, some definitions see self-esteem as being reasonably stable over time, whereas others regard self-esteem as being responsive to situational and contextual influences, which means that it fluctuates. This aspect of self-esteem is seen in such phrases as "trait versus state" self-esteem (Leary & Downs, 1995), "stable versus unstable" self-esteem (Greenier, Kernis, & Waschull, 1995), or "global versus situational" self-esteem (Harter, 1999).

Unfortunately, neither developing typologies nor identifying basic elements can offer us the one thing that is needed most: a clear statement concerning what self-esteem is as it is actually lived by real human beings in real life. Although typologies reduce the number of definitions with which we must contend, they offer us no criteria for identifying one as being more valid than another. Similarly, while identifying common elements is a necessary step toward developing such a definition, it is also important to work them into an integrated, comprehensive form; otherwise, the elements simply constitute a list. Clearly, then, we are in need of another method.

The approach that we use to reach this goal consists of two steps. First, we examine the three definitions of self-esteem that seem to run throughout the depth and breadth of the field. This activity involves analyzing the theoretical strengths and weaknesses of each one to assess their potential usefulness. The second step takes us into the lived character of self-esteem or how it is actually experienced in everyday life. Then, it should be possible to evaluate the definitions and find out whether one of them stands as superior to the others existentially as well as theoretically.

At first glance, it might seem as though identifying major definitions, significant findings, or leading theories of self-esteem is an arbitrary process. However, using time as a criterion to "measure" such things is one of the most useful and accepted ways of identifying important themes in a field. Time is helpful in this task because the field of self-esteem is old enough to have undergone several scientific shakeouts. In other words, once a definition, finding, theory, or technique is formed, later researchers tend to re-examine such work in the process of replication. In doing so, the particular item in question is confirmed, modified, or discarded on the basis of current evidence or understanding. Those that withstand scrutiny over a long period of time and yet remain relatively intact may at least be considered to be *persistent* or reliable enough to be useful, although certainly not necessarily valid.

Another test offered by time concerns power rather than duration. Definitions, findings, theories, or techniques that are able to stimulate meaningful research and give rise to entire schools of thought over time demonstrate another valuable characteristic, namely *significance*. Of course, items of scientific discourse that are both persistent (i.e., enduring) and significant (i.e., generative) are likely to warrant the status of existing as a "standard" in the field. The three approaches mentioned in the introductory paragraph meet these criteria, so let us examine and evaluate them in turn so as to identify the one to be used and why.

Self-Esteem as Competence

Time and history are good places to begin when looking at previous work, so it seems most appropriate to start with the oldest psychological definition developed by William James (1890/1983, p. 296) more than a century ago. While describing the qualities of the self, he said,

> So our self-feeling in this world depends entirely on what we *back* ourselves to be and do. It is determined by the ratio of our actualities to our supposed potentialities; a fraction of which our pretensions are the denominator and the numerator our success:

$$\text{thus, Self-esteem} = \frac{\text{Success}}{\text{Pretensions}}.$$

This definition offers a number of things worth considering. First and foremost is that James defined self-esteem in terms of a type of behavior, namely, action that results in success. We can call this type of action "competence" because it involves exercising one's abilities and skills effectively. Second and equally important, James noted that self-esteem also involves "pretensions," which today are better understood as aspirations, including one's desires, goals, hopes, and dreams. Thus, work on self-esteem that stems from this definition tends to focus on particular forms of success, namely those that are related to an individual's identity.

James presented this aspect of self-esteem in a well-known analogy with which it is easy to identify. "I, who for the time have staked my all on being a psychologist, am mortified if others know much more psychology than I. But I am contented to wallow in the grossest ignorance of Greek" (James, 1890/1983, p. 296). James went on to emphasize the point by noting that the situation could be completely reversed for someone who identified with Greek instead of psychology. Thus, when we say that a definition of self-esteem is based on competence, we also maintain that it is a certain type of competence that matters: It is one that must be demonstrated in areas of life that matter greatly to an individual in terms of his or her sense of self. James strongly conveyed this vitality of self-esteem by the word "staked," which is to say that success or failure in such an area is tied to nothing less than our basic values, identity, and hopes as a person. Also note that from this definitional perspective, it is quite possible to be very successful and yet have low self-esteem. For example, being successful in areas that do not matter to a person in terms of his or her identity would have no positive impact on self-esteem.

Finally, James' expression offers two more valuable insights into self-esteem when it is seen this way. One is that, like a steady ratio, the self tends to be fairly stable, which means that self-esteem can be seen as a trait. The other is that, like all ratios, numbers can be changed, which is to say that self-esteem is also dynamic. On one hand, for example, self-esteem may reach a fairly steady level and become relatively stable. On the other, it is also possible to modify self-esteem by increasing the frequency of success, decreasing the degree of aspiration, or shifting attention to other meaningful areas of life in which one is more competent and, therefore, more likely to succeed.

As mentioned earlier, self-esteem became an important theme in the psychodynamic tradition after James abandoned psychology. Freud's (1914/1957) original discussion of self-regard is limited to understanding it as a function of narcissism that occurs when meeting ego ideals. However, Adler (1927) greatly expanded this notion into a general theory of motivation and Horney (1937) made self-esteem a central clinical concern. White's (1959, 1963) work is probably the most articulate psychodynamic expression of self-esteem and it is explicitly based on competence. He began by noting that both classical analysis and behavioral psychology suffer a central contradiction when it comes to their theories of motivation. In one way or another, both models are based on drive reduction theory. In other words, people become motivated when a need is not met because it disturbs homeostasis, which generates a negative tension or distress. That stress, in turn, motivates behavior by directing it toward an incentive or goal that is seen as capable of satisfying the need, thereby reducing the tension and re-establishing the steady state of homeostasis. From this point of view, all basic needs appear to work in this fashion.

However, White pointed out that the problem with homeostatic theories of motivation is that they have great difficulty accounting for a set of behaviors that seems to do just the opposite. For example, although properly fed, young animals, such as cats and dogs, seem to disrupt the steady state generated when basic needs are satisfied (homeostasis) by engaging in highly energetic activities, such as play. Children will experience boredom if left in unstimulating environments for long. Adults will even give up comfortable lives to explore unknown regions. Such behaviors, he argued, are also need-based but cannot be explained in terms of tension reduction because the organism actually seeks out activities that stimulate the sympathetic nervous system, create new tension, and may even involve risk to life and limb. Consequently, he concluded, "it is necessary to make competence a motivational concept; there is a *competence motivation* as well as competence in its more familiar sense of achieved capacity" (White, 1959, p. 318). Satisfying this need through the mastery of developmental tasks and experiencing other successes in childhood result in feelings of "effectance" and a sense of self-respect. In White's (1963) words, "self-esteem . . . has its taproot in the experience of efficacy" (p. 134).

The most recent manifestation of seeing self-esteem largely in terms of competence does not come from a psychodynamic perspective, but it does take us to what might be the ultimate expression of this definition. Crocker and Park (2003), for example, began their work on self-esteem by basing it squarely on James' definition when they said that, "Our central proposition is that people seek to maintain, protect, and enhance self-esteem by attempting to obtain success and avoid failure in domains on which their self-worth has been staked" (p. 291). They went on to build a model of self-esteem based on contingencies of worth that both regulate and motivate behavior. Like James, in this view, people seek out activities and situations that are meaningful to them in terms of their identities. Since who they are and how they feel about themselves depend upon success and failure in these areas more than others, people shape their lives around them in various ways. If it is true that self-esteem is based on success and failure in this fashion, and if it is true that people must have self-esteem, then in some sense, we are bound to these particular areas of life. Some people may even become so invested in success in these areas that they become driven, or in more extreme cases, even enslaved by them.

In other words, instead of being a positive developmental and motivational force, Crocker and Park (2003, 2004) took the competence model to its final conclusion and pointed out that self-esteem could actually motivate people to seek success and avoid failure in ways that are harmful to themselves or to others. They referred to this aspect of self-esteem as the "problem of pursuing self-esteem" (Crocker & Park, 2004) and went on to list its many costs. On one hand, potential problems of self-esteem when it is defined this way include such things as taking too many risks or being driven by the need to succeed at all costs, including the use of aggression or force. On the other, those without the skills necessary for success may react by lowering expectations, avoiding risks, or damaging relationships by defending themselves against losing self-esteem when honesty and openness would serve the relationships much better. These authors even discussed how various clinical problems could result from an unhealthy pursuit of self-esteem connected with a drive toward perfection. Eating disorders are one such condition.

In sum, we can reach at least four conclusions about defining self-esteem primarily in terms of success. First, individual competence is the key to self-esteem from this point of view, because being successful over time requires the ability to acquire and use skills relevant to domains of life that are tied to one's sense of identity. This vision of self-esteem allows us to appreciate how unique individual self-esteem is for each of us: We care deeply about success and failure in areas that are personally significant to us based on our particular constellation of abilities, history, circumstances, and interests. Second, this approach certainly merits the status of a major school of thought and work in the field of self-esteem. After all, seeing self-esteem in terms of competence not only was the first way to conceive of it, but it is still very much alive over a century later.

Third, there are considerable advantages to this approach. For example, by understanding self-esteem in relation to success and failure, we can connect self-esteem to such things as basic needs, human motivation, and self-regulation. Such an approach is useful when, for instance, attempting to understand why people can seem so driven to succeed, so fearful of failure, and so defensive when their ego or sense of self is threatened. In other words, this type of definition shows that self-esteem does, indeed, have a potential dark side and gives us insight about unhealthy ways of pursuing self-esteem. Finally, we also see that there is a glaring problem with this approach to self-esteem that cannot be ignored. If self-esteem is defined in terms of competence, then it is contingent on success and failure. Because success never lasts forever and because failure is always possible, this view of self-esteem means that it is as much a liability as an asset, perhaps even more so, depending upon the degree to which one feels vulnerable in a given domain of life. Indeed, having reached this conclusion, Crocker and Park (2003, 2004) advocated the position that it may be more rational to give up the pursuit of self-esteem than to engage in it. They might be correct if this way of defining self-esteem is the only one available.

Self-Esteem as Worthiness

Morris Rosenberg (1965) introduced another way of defining self-esteem that led to the development of the next major school in the field. This definition is also the one that is most commonly used today. He defined it in terms of a particular type of attitude, one that is thought to be based on the perception of a feeling, a feeling about one's "worth," which is to say one's character or value as a person. Hence,

> Self-esteem, as noted, is a positive or negative attitude toward a particular object, namely, the self. . . . High self-esteem, as reflected in our scale items, expresses the feeling that one is "good enough." The individual simply feels that he is a person of worth; he respects himself for what he is, but he does not stand in awe of himself nor does he expect others to stand in awe of him. (pp. 30–31)

The distinguishing characteristic of defining self-esteem this way is that it is seen primarily as affective in nature: In this case, self-esteem is based on a particular feeling, one of being worthy or what I often refer to as worthiness. This emphasis on evaluative mental processes and affective experience, rather than on behavior and its outcomes, means that self-esteem can be seen in terms of the psychology of attitude formation.

Of course, forming attitudes about the self is more complex than doing so for anything else, largely because the perceiver is also the object of perception (Wylie, 1974). However, social scientists are reasonably familiar with the formation of attitudes, how they work, and, especially, how to measure them. Indeed, the chief strength of this approach to defining self-esteem is that it allowed social scientists like Rosenberg to develop scales and other instruments to assess self-esteem. The ability to quantify and measure self-worth in this way opened the door to a wide range of research possibilities. For instance, this approach makes it possible to rate individuals and groups in terms of various categories, such as high, middle, and lower levels of self-esteem.

The primary advantage of such instruments may be that they give us the opportunity to explore connections between self-esteem, various levels of it, and a wide range of characteristics or behavior, such as depression, anxiety, neuroticism, happiness, academic success, and so forth. Scales can and have been used to assess the self-esteem of large groups of individuals, such as high school students (Rosenberg, 1979). Indeed, this approach even makes it possible to compare the self-esteem of entire demographics, such as Caucasian, African American, and Hispanic populations, or even Americans in general (Twenge & Crocker, 2002). Thus, it should come as no surprise that the majority of empirical research in the field is based on this way of defining self-esteem.

Rosenberg's definition may seem to suggest that self-esteem plays something of a passive role in behavior: After all, from this point of view, self-esteem is the result of something else, namely, a process of evaluation. However, others who see self-esteem as a function of individual worth understand it as a much more active and dynamic process. For example, cognitive psychologists, such as Seymour Epstein (1985), give self-esteem an active, even central, role in the life of the self. In this case, feelings of worth are essential for one's identity and, therefore, self-esteem plays a crucial role in regulating behavior. Such an approach may even see self-esteem as a lynchpin, because a good portion of the entire self-system is to help to protect and enhance the feeling of worth.

Others who operate from this definitional perspective also see self-esteem performing similar functions in an interpersonal context. For instance, in another chapter, we will see that Leary's and Downs' (1995) work on Sociometer Theory demonstrates how feelings of self-worth help govern social behavior, much like an emotional compass that helps us find a socially functional path. New research looks at self-esteem as a central variable in forming, maintaining, enhancing, and ending relationships (Mruk, in press). When seen in these ways, self-esteem is part of the emotional glue that holds personal identity and social relationships together. Thus, like competence-based definitions, understanding self-esteem in terms of worth also gives it powerful emotional and social motivational implications.

As with competence-based definitions, the weakness of this approach is made obvious by considering what happens when it is carried too far, when there is nothing to balance it. In this case, self-esteem can be taken to mean *merely* feeling good about one's self. For example, the powerful critique of the work on self-esteem offered by Baumeister et al. (1996) is based on such a (shaky) version of the definition. They said, "Although some researchers favor narrow and precise concepts of self-esteem, we shall use the term in a broad and inclusive sense. By *self-esteem* we mean simply a favorable global evaluation of oneself" (p. 5). In later work, Baumeister et al. (2003) modified this definition somewhat, but for them self-esteem is "literally defined by how much value people place on themselves. . . . Self-esteem does not carry any definitional requirement of accuracy whatsoever" (p. 2).

It is easy to see how such a weak definition of self-esteem would mean that it can be associated with positive characteristics, such as dignity, honor, conscientiousness, and so forth. However, such a loose definition also makes it possible to associate self-esteem with negative phenomena, including egotism, narcissism, or aggression, because this type of behavior can make one feel good about one's self, at least temporarily. When seen as a mere positive feeling or as only a positive view of one's self, it is no wonder that self-esteem can be said to have a dark side. The result of defining self-esteem in such an open-ended way is more confusing than clarifying.

Recognizing that the most common way of defining self-esteem is to understand it as a judgment or feeling of worthiness or worth can help us to understand another important problem in the field. Although "common sense" suggests that self-esteem is important because it plays a major role in human behavior, social scientists have been puzzled by the general lack of empirical support for such a position. Even those who are sympathetic to self-esteem work note this condition. For example, when reviewing the literature concerning the social importance of self-esteem for a study commissioned by the State of California, Smelser (1989) said, "The news most consistently reported . . . is that the associations between self-esteem and its expected consequences are mixed, insignificant, or absent" (p. 15). Emler (2001) did an independent report examining the correlations between self-esteem and behavior in England and reached similar conclusions. Finally, Baumeister et al. (2003) conducted a highly structured review of self-esteem literature done in a given period and found that, "With the exception of the link to happiness, most of the effects are weak to modest. Self-esteem is thus not a major predictor or cause of almost anything" (p. 37).

This line of work leaves us with several possibilities to consider. One of them is that self-esteem is not a particularly significant phenomenon. If so, then we should move beyond discussions about self-esteem. Another possibility is that even if self-esteem is significant, it is too difficult to untangle it enough to tease out clear relationships between self-esteem and behavior. If this position is correct, then we must await new methodological breakthroughs as Smelser (1989) or Wells and Marwell (1976) recommended. Of course, it could also turn out to be that, as some conclude, self-esteem is more of an outcome than a cause (Seligman, 1995a). In this case, we should look for the variables that affect self-esteem instead of focusing on self-esteem per se. Finally, if any of these possibilities are true, we must conclude that work on self-esteem, which "probably represents the largest body of research on a single topic in the history of all of the social sciences" (Scheff & Fearon, 2004, p. 74), has been an abysmal waste of time.

However, it is also possible that just as defining self-esteem in terms of competence leads to one kind of scientific dead end, so does seeing it largely in terms of worth or worthiness. If this position is correct, then many of the difficulties that we just mentioned may actually be the result of unidimensional ways of defining and understanding self-esteem, and not a problem with the concept or phenomenon itself. To be sure, such a realization would not mean that all the problems involved in researching self-esteem or measuring its significance will be solved. Nevertheless, it is necessary to consider this alternative for two reasons. First, there may be a more effective way of defining self-esteem that clarifies such matters and that opens up new pathways in the field. Second, if such an approach does show that self-esteem is an important aspect of human behavior in spite of methodological complexity, then failing to consider it is a serious error, one that constitutes scientific "bad faith."

Self-Esteem as Competence *and* Worthiness

Fortunately, one more definition of self-esteem seems to have withstood the tests of time as indicated by the fact that a distinct body of work has developed around it: It is a two-factor approach that defines self-esteem in terms of a relationship between competence and worth or worthiness. Nathaniel Branden (1969) may have been the first to offer such a definition when he said that,

> Self-esteem has two interrelated aspects: it entails a sense of personal efficacy and a sense of personal worth. It is the integrated sum of self-confidence and self-respect. It is the conviction that one is *competent* to live and *worthy* of living. (p. 110)

Working from this position, it is possible to maintain that human beings have a fundamental need to feel worthy but can only achieve that goal by acting competently when making decisions, especially those that involve facing the challenges of living. Competence, in this case, means facing reality directly and then making rational decisions. Branden also specified that rational decisions are based on goals that are personally significant, are life affirming, and are such that they do not compromise one's integrity as a person either in design or in execution. Because we are faced with making decisions so often in life, and since there is no guarantee as to their outcomes, self-esteem may be seen as a precious psychological resource that can be won or lost when seen from this point of view. If so, self-esteem is something that needs to be carefully managed at all times.

Tying competence to worthiness in this fashion distinguishes this view of self-esteem from mere success because, from this position, competent behavior must be tied to worthwhile actions in order to matter for self-esteem. In other words, one cannot be good at bad things and merit authentic self-esteem. Conversely, connecting a sense of being worthy to competence in this way also means that just feeling good about oneself does not necessarily reflect self-esteem: Such a feeling must also be rational, which is to say based on appropriately corresponding behavior that demonstrates one's worth as an individual. In other words, authentic self-esteem must be earned.

Perhaps because Branden offered more philosophical than empirical support for his definition, it did not receive the kind of attention in the field as did the others. Even worse, the book in which the definition appeared became a best seller, something that the scientific community often regards as "popularistic" and, therefore, is easily ignored or dismissed. However, this approach has been generating empirically oriented work on self-esteem since the early 1970s. For instance, this third force in the field is described as a "dual model" of self-esteem (Franks & Marolla, 1976), a "two-factor" theory (Tafarodi & Swann, 1995), and a "multidimensional approach" (Harter, 1999; O'Brien & Epstein, 1988). Viktor Gecas (1971) may have been the first researcher to follow this path when he investigated factors affecting self-esteem in adolescence. After exhausting other possibilities, he finally found that only a two-factor approach accounted for the variables that were necessary for his adolescent population to experience self-esteem: They were independent enough to recognize the importance of personal accomplishment (a form of competence) and yet still young enough to seek some form of parental approval or acceptance (a form of worthiness). When both factors were present, so was self-esteem.

Later, while reviewing two-factor or multidimensional work, Gecas (1982) noted that, "Common to these subdivisions is the distinction between *(a)* self-esteem based on a sense of competence, power, or efficacy and *(b)* self-esteem based on a sense of virtue or moral worth" (p. 5). He also went on to explore how each factor involves different psychological and social processes. For example, the competence dimension of self-esteem is connected to performance, whereas virtue is grounded in values, particularly those that concern one's own worth as a person. Finally, like Branden, he also pointed out that competence and worthiness intertwine in regard to self-esteem: It is the relationship between these two factors that creates self-esteem. In other words, the reciprocal interaction of these two factors working together makes self-esteem a unique phenomenon.

We will see that the multidimensional approach is also very much alive in empirically oriented research today. However, it is profoundly disappointing to see that such material is often missing in the reference sections of more "mainstream" work done from the perspectives of the other two definitions. The absence of the two-factor approach is conspicuously characteristic of the work that criticizes self-esteem research for its "weak," "conflicted," "heterogeneous" findings. Yet, time and time again it has been shown just how inadequate and ineffective unidimensional approaches to defining self-esteem are in theory and in research.

Tafarodi and Swann (1995), for instance, examined Rosenberg's Self-Esteem Scale and found that its questions actually load in two directions. Some items seem to assess factors that are associated with worthiness, which was the original intent. However, others clearly tap into competence even though the instrument was not designed to do that. Noting that researchers have been aware of the need to consider two axes of self-esteem, they took the position that, "Rather than experiencing ourselves as simply positive or negative, we experience ourselves as globally *acceptable-unacceptable* (referred to here as *self-liking*) and globally *strong-weak* (referred to here as *self-competence*). Together these dimensions are held to constitute global self-esteem" (p. 324). The term self-esteem, then, may be seen as an efficient way of talking about an interaction between these two variables. In short, self-esteem "may simply be an expedient of discourse, in the same way that one speaks of the *size* of a person's build rather than the person's (constitutive) height and girth" (p. 337).

Furthermore, those who work within this school often note that the two-factor approach has the potential ability to bring two major streams of the field together much more effectively than do the other ways of defining or understanding self-esteem. For example, competence and worthiness work well together conceptually. On one hand, "Self-competence, as the valuative experiences of one's own agency, is closely linked to motivational concepts such as effectance. . . personal causation. . . and striving for superiority. It is the self-valuative result of acting out one's will on the world—of being effective" (Tafarodi & Vu, 1997, p. 627). Thus, competence involves the types of behavior that James talked about and has the conceptual room to accommodate such things as Bandura's (1997) notion of self-efficacy, which concerns one's beliefs about one's own competence. On the other hand, self-liking "is the valuation of one's personhood—one's worth as a social object as judged against internalized social standards of good and bad. This social worth dimension of self-esteem figures prominently in accounts of the genesis of the ethical self" (Tafarodi & Vu, 1997, p. 627). Here we see the potential to incorporate the worthiness-based affective components of self-esteem, including those seen in Rosenberg's concern with attitudes and feelings of worth in regard to self-esteem.

In addition to the possibility of bringing two very well-established lines of existing work on self-esteem together, the two-factor approach to self-esteem also takes the field in new directions. For instance, one possibility concerns the relationship between culture and self-esteem. Tafarodi and Swann (1996) found that whereas both individualistic and collectivist cultures appreciate the need for people to demonstrate competence and to feel worthy, each one tends to emphasize one component of self-esteem over the other, namely, the one that is most characteristic of the general social orientation of the culture. Other areas of research that characterize this school include investigating such things as how self-competence and self-liking affect success and failure over time (Tafarodi & Vu, 1997); how a dual model accounts for major types of self-esteem (Mruk, 1999; Tafarodi & Milne, 2002); and how to use a two-factor definition of self-esteem to effect change in the clinical setting (Bartoletti, 2008; Hakim-Larson & Mruk, 1997). All of these themes and more will be pursued in the following chapters.

Finally, it is helpful to realize that much of the work that is based on understanding self-esteem in terms of competence and worthiness does not necessarily use the phrase "two-factor" or "dual." For example, although still emphasizing these two general sets of factors, the term "multidimensional" is sometimes used to distinguish the work from that which is based on only one or the other of the two unidimensional definitions. While Susan Harter (1999) used the terms "self-esteem" and "self-worth" interchangeably, for instance, her multidimensional approach to self-esteem clearly includes competence in various domains of life and feelings of worth in regard to others as its two primary components. Similarly, modern methods of measuring self-esteem eschew the unidimensional approach to assessing it. For example, the Multidimensional Self-Esteem Inventory developed by O'Brien and Epstein (1988) measures several dimensions of self-esteem that reflect primarily competence and others that do the same for worthiness.

In addition, there is another richer but even more complex way in which there are dual factors in the two-factor approach. At one level, it may seem that this view only involves identifying competence and worthiness as the two factors that are involved in self-esteem. But virtually everyone in this school recognizes that the relationship between competence and worthiness is also a central feature of this approach. Perhaps the term "three-factor model" is more accurate in this regard (competence, worthiness, and their dynamic reciprocity). However, for consistency's sake, it is not beneficial to alter the name of the approach. Suffice it to say that although this dimension of the two-factor approach is often underappreciated, it may arguably be the most important part of the definition: It is the relationship between competence and worthiness that actually creates or generates the psychological phenomenon we call self-esteem in the first place. So as not to be theoretically naive, of course, it is also necessary to point out that this strength is also the chief weakness of this approach to self-esteem: Multidimensional models are more complex than unidimensional ones, and that characteristic complicates the research process.

THE ORIGINAL DEFINITION OF
SELF-ESTEEM AND SELF-ESTEEM IN EVERYDAY LIFE

The final task of this chapter is to examine the three standard ways of defining self-esteem in the hope that one stands out as more accurate (valid) or at least more comprehensive (descriptive) than the others. By now, it should be fairly clear that defining self-esteem primarily in terms of either competence or worthiness alone offers no advantage because they both seem to have reached a serious impasse, perhaps even a dead end. After all, success is never guaranteed and is always fleeting, even when it is achieved. Therefore, basing self-esteem largely on competence means that the individual must live in a constant state of vigilance, a state of being that entails looking out for and acting against a threat when it occurs, sometimes in ways that are destructive. If this view of self-esteem is followed to its logical conclusion, then Crocker and Park (2003, 2004) are quite correct: The pursuit of self-esteem is far too "costly" and we should be studying ways to get rid of it rather than means of enhancing it.

Similarly, understanding self-esteem in terms of feeling good about oneself without connecting such a belief, attitude, feeling, or affect to reality through the expression of appropriately corresponding behavior is also a lopsided way of understanding self-esteem. As we have seen, Baumeister et al. (1996, 2003), Damon (1995), Seligman (1995b), and others pointed out that such a "feel-good" approach can only result in confusing authentic self-esteem with things like narcissism, egotism, conceit, and other undesirable or "dark" states. One very good reason to investigate the concept of self-esteem based on a relationship between competence and worthiness, then, is that otherwise there is simply no reason to go any further with work based on unidimensional definitions.

The second reason to define self-esteem in terms of competence and worthiness is more appealing. This way of understanding self-esteem is inherently more comprehensive than the others, which means, among other things, that it offers different possibilities, such as standing as a stronger platform upon which to integrate the disparate literature of the field. Tafarodi and Vu (1997, p. 627) use an analogy concerning the difference between rectangles and the lines that form rectangles to help understand the relationship between competence and worthiness, and why it is so important for self-esteem. Seeing self-esteem only as a single factor, such as mere lines on a page, will never result in forming a space or a shape. However, identifying lines as length and width and then putting them in relationship to each other creates something much more substantial, in this case a rectangle and the space it defines. In other words, competence and worthiness together define the "semantic space of global self-valuation" (p. 627). Defining the "thing" we call self-esteem in terms of competence *and* worthiness rather than either term alone allows us to view the phenomenon more completely and, therefore, puts us in a better position to understand it more fully.

In addition to providing a more powerful conceptual understanding of self-esteem, there are two other ways that thinking about self-esteem as a relationship between factors is helpful. One of them is seen in regard to the earliest uses of the term. The concept of self-esteem appears to have been introduced to English-speaking peoples by the great writer and poet John Milton in the 17th century. His earliest use of the term can at least be traced to an essay that he wrote defending his work from what he, and others, felt was unwarranted criticism. In that piece, Milton (1642/1950, p. 565) identified "self-esteem either of what I was, or what I might be, (which let envie call pride)" as a legitimate reason to stand up for oneself in regard to unjust accusations. Notice that there are two components to his use of the term. The first is that identity is involved in regard to self-esteem, in this case terms of his character as a person, including such matter as honor, dignity, and self-respect, which he called pride in a healthy sense. The other is that by writing a reasonable response to critics, Milton competently dealt with his challenge in a worthwhile fashion: He faced it directly, which is to say authentically. The point is that, from the beginning, the term self-esteem was meant to convey something about respecting value or worth and about having the courage or ability to stand up for it when necessary.

The way that Milton goes on to use the term in *Paradise Lost* reveals these aspects of self-esteem more clearly. In a section that involves the protagonist discussing worthy pursuits with an angel, Milton (1667/1931) wrote,

> Then value: Oft times nothing profits more
> Then self esteem, grounded on just and right
> Well manag'd; of that skill the more thou know'st,
> The more she will acknowledge thee her Head,
> And to realities yield all her shows. . . (p. 256)

Here, we see that self-esteem expresses two factors and a connection between them. First, the concept of "just and right" certainly pertains to positive values and their importance for living a good life in the authentic sense. Second, self-esteem appears to involve competence, namely, the skills necessary to conducts one's life in relation to that which is just and right.

In other words, it appears as though self-esteem was first used to describe a particular way of dealing with the challenges that life brings to each and every human being. Although we seldom face those of a biblical nature, many of them involve matters of right and wrong (worth) and doing them justice by taking appropriate actions (competence). In short, the two-factor approach seems to be very consistent with Milton's original sense of the term. Note that this view of self-esteem has some powerful implications for those who wish to rant about the dark side of self-esteem, but we will deal with those issues later.

As substantial as that argument is, social science requires evidence as well as theoretical validity, which means that we must go one step further. Although the methods used to research self-esteem as it is lived in everyday life are discussed in the next chapter, it is necessary to bring some of the results forward here so that we can take a position on which definition of self-esteem has more empirical value. Fortunately, a surprising number of studies have investigated self-esteem in this way. Epstein (1979) is one of the pioneers of rigorous experiential work in this area. For example, in *A Study of Emotions in Everyday Life*, he asked female and male participants to track daily experiences for a month and record in some detail the ones that enhanced or lessened their self-esteem. In brief, he found that there are two types of experiences that people report as being particularly thematic in this regard. I call these and other such poignant self-esteem experiences "self-esteem moments."

Epstein found that situations capable of generating success or failure in areas of life that are important to a given person constitute one set of powerful self-esteem experiences. The other type concerns those that involve being accepted or being rejected by others, both of which seem to pertain to one's sense of worth as a person. Others have done work that comes to similar conclusions. For instance, Tafarodi and Milne (2002) asked 244 students to respond to a retrospective measure of life events on two separate occasions, some 4 weeks apart. Their results correspond to Epstein's, with failure affecting participants' sense of "self-competence" and negative social events affecting their reports of "self-liking."

In addition to demonstrating that competence and worthiness are linked to self-esteem, other work indicates that it is actually the relationship between competence and worthiness that creates self-esteem. For example, in a study titled "Experiences That Produce Enduring Changes in Self-Concept," Epstein (1979) asked a total of 270 college participants to describe in writing "the one experience in their lifetime that produced the greatest positive change in their self-concept and the one experience that produced the greatest negative change in their self-concept" (p. 73). The analysis of this data, which were gathered from almost equal numbers of men and women, identified that there are three types of such experiences that occur most often in adulthood. They are having to deal with a new environment, responding to a problem that requires the person to acquire new responses, and gaining or losing significant relationships. Once again, we see competence and worthiness in action.

Using a smaller number of subjects but studying them much more in-depth, I examined another class of self-esteem experiences that appear to change self-esteem at deeper, more existential levels. The participants were reasonably well-diversified in terms of age, gender, and socioeconomic status. They were asked to describe in detail a time when they were pleased with themselves in a biographically crucial way and a time when they were displeased with themselves in that fashion (Mruk, 1981, 1983). Then, they were interviewed extensively about these powerful self-esteem moments.

The experiences spontaneously chosen by all the subjects can be described as encountering a situation that challenged them to deal with what could be called a strong approach-avoidance situation, but one with unusually powerful biographical implications that tied the entire situation to important dimensions of their personal histories and identities. This dimension of the situation called into question who the people knew themselves to be at deep levels, particularly ones that had caused difficulty for them in the past. That is, each subject was faced with a situation where, on one hand, they desperately wanted to do what they believed to be the "right thing" (notice the connection to Milton here), but where their ability to do so was historically problematic or filled with inauthentic decision making or behavior. To use James' language, these self-esteem moments take place in situations where one's self-esteem is genuinely put "at stake" by a challenge of living in a way that calls one's very identity as a decent person into question.

One example involved an older woman with a traditional sense of gender who had to choose between complying with a male supervisor's request to give up her current duties for others or to take a stand and argue vigorously against changing positions based on the fact that she liked her job and did not want the new duties. On the surface, the immediate problem is a relatively simple one of compliance versus risk-taking. Interviewing and analysis revealed, however, that she had a long history of complying with authority figures, particularly males, and especially her father, sometimes even to the point of abuse. In her life, then, such decisions inevitably led to an inauthentic outcome, namely, merely complying instead of standing up for what was "just and right," and feeling terribly unworthy as a person when so doing.

Another example concerned a much younger man who had a clinically significant fear of public speaking. In the past, he always avoided situations in which speaking publicly was necessary, sometimes at a cost of considerable psychological pain and missed financial opportunities. However, this individual also had a strong commitment to his career and work. Then, one day life suddenly challenged him on both levels when his career and personal development came together in a situation that required him to either defend his work in public forums or lose any hope of staying in the field that he loved the most.

In these two examples, the individuals faced their particular challenge of living and handled them in a way that was appropriate for a mature adult. After facing the challenge authentically by doing that which was "just and right," both participants experienced a meaningful increase in their self-esteem that lasted well into the future: Each of them demonstrated competence at living in ways that were worthy of a decent, healthy, or authentic human being. We will examine each step of this process later on, but it is important to note here that facing such existential dilemmas does not always end on a positive note.

One negative example involved a woman who had a life theme of loneliness around the holidays connected with the fact that her entire family died when she was young. One holiday season, she was facing the possibility of terrible isolation yet again. At that moment, a certain colleague made advances toward her. She did not care for the individual in any special way and was also aware that the circumstances were such that fellow workers would know of any intimate contact. Even so, the thought of being alone again seemed too overwhelming and the immediate possibility of comfort seemed too appealing to resist. Giving in to these biographic forces in an inauthentic mode of care, she compromised herself with the colleague, much to her own chagrin.

Similarly, a young man had a negative biographic theme that involved neglecting his physical well-being in certain situations. He subjected an already injured body to additional stress rather than allowing himself the time to rest, because doing so would have meant thinking about the loss of an important relationship he could not bear to face. Unfortunately, this decision led to the development of a chronic illness and continual pain. In both instances, the person took what at first appeared to be the easy way out, failed to face the challenge of living authentically, and then subsequently suffered negative consequences, especially inauthenticity and a concomitant loss of self-esteem. We will also examine the stages involved in this type of response at the appropriate time. However, right now the point is that we do seem to be able to find evidence supporting the position that self-esteem involves competence *and* worthiness at the lived level, sometimes even in ways powerful enough to have a transforming effect on people.

AN EXISTENTIALLY BASED TWO-FACTOR DEFINITION OF SELF-ESTEEM

The two-factor approach to defining self-esteem seems to be more theoretically valid because it may be more robust than either of its single-factor counterparts, because it seems closer to the original definition of the term, and because it appears to be empirically descriptive at the lived level. Therefore, there is only one more task that needs to be completed before taking this way of defining self-esteem to the field. This step involves fleshing the definition out so that we can see what is meant by competence and worthiness, as well as how their relationship works to create self-esteem in positive or in negative ways.

Phenomenological psychologists often use what is called the "general structure" of an experience, process, or phenomenon (Giorgi, 1971, 1975) to complete this process. A general or fundamental structure is a succinct description of all the elements that are necessary to give rise to a given human phenomenon or experience. It also describes how the individual components work together to create the phenomenon at the lived level. When properly done, such a complete and dynamic description also makes an excellent definition of a phenomenon because it is more substantial than a mere abstract concept. Because fundamental structures are only found in the "real" world of everyday human experience, something phenomenologists call the "life world," their descriptions must emerge from data generated at this level. The investigation that I conducted into more poignant self-esteem moments presented earlier also led to the development of a fundamental structure, and it has been refined over time (Mruk, 1981, 1995, 1999, 2006). As it is used in this book, then, *self-esteem is the lived status of one's competence at dealing with the challenges of living in a worthy way over time.*

One of the valuable things about succinct descriptions of human phenomena offered by fundamental structures is that they show what is both necessary and sufficient for a particular human phenomenon or experience to occur. Thus, it should be possible to unfold such a description in a way that reveals the inner workings of the phenomenon, as well as its basic components. The lived structure of self-esteem consists of five key elements, which can be unpacked in the following fashion. The first one, "status," concerns states of being. The word was chosen to represent this aspect of self-esteem because status implies something that is present, reasonably stable, and yet still open to change under certain conditions. One's economic, social, or marital status is an example of this condition. In this sense, each of us tends to live a relatively stable degree, level, or type of self-esteem that we characteristically bring to the world. The word "lived" is added to status to express that existential fact that self-esteem, when defined this way, cannot be avoided: It is grounded in the past, can become alive in the present, and follows us into the future in one form or another. Of course, like other dynamic conditions, sometimes self-esteem is lived in a way that is more important in regard to particular situations than others, such as the ones that have been identified as self-esteem moments.

Competence, of course, is a familiar term. It is often used in this field to refer to an individual's particular set of physical, cognitive, and social skills or abilities. However, it is also important to realize, as developmental psychology does, that competence is also a process, one that involves mastery. Thus, it takes time and practice to learn how to master the tasks of life. Competence, which includes a sense of efficacy in any given situation, is important for self-esteem because individuals deal with the various challenges of living on the basis of two things: what specific skills are available to them at a given time in their lives and their level of maturity as an individual, particularly their degree of authenticity or sense of self and individual responsibility.

Sometimes the challenges of living are small, or at least normal, such as learning to walk, growing up, and acquiring the survival skills that are necessary in a particular culture. However, we also are likely to encounter much larger challenges, such as finding and maintaining meaningful relationships, earning a living, raising a family, and so forth. In addition, at other times, life presents us with challenges that are especially powerful because they mobilize who we are at the deepest or most authentic levels.

In all three cases, the word "challenge" is appropriate because, by definition, a challenge involves facing a task that has an uncertain outcome, taxes us in terms of our current abilities, and stands as an opportunity to reach higher levels or fall back to lower ones in ways that suggest either gains or losses.

The concept of worth, worthy, or worthiness is important in describing the structure of self-esteem because it expresses the fact that self-esteem does not occur in a vacuum. Rather, it is tied to the value or quality of our actions. In this sense, there is a relationship between worthiness and what the Greeks called virtues, which, we shall see in the last chapter, is an important connection between self-esteem and positive psychology. Competent behavior tends to result in positive feelings and poor performance often creates negative ones. However, worthiness is more difficult to understand because it is based on meaning, not measures, connected to that which is "just and right." Although social scientists are often reluctant to speak in this way, certain actions are worth more than others because they are more virtuous. For example, "doing the right thing" generates healthy or authentic self-esteem because such actions are both competent and worthy, whereas failing to do so indicates a lack of competence, a lack of a sense of that which is "just and right" or worthy, or both.

In relationship to self-esteem, then, competence is needed for worthiness because only certain types of actions have such a positive meaning. However, worthiness also balances competence because not all things that one does effectively are necessarily meritorious. Accordingly, talking about competence or worthiness without stressing their relationship could mean that we are not talking about healthy, genuine, or authentic self-esteem at all. After all, competence without worthiness can result in negative acts of human behavior, such as lying, stealing, or injuring others for personal gain; and feelings of worthiness without doing something to earn them is narcissism. Again, the relationship between competence and worthiness is at the heart of self-esteem, just as we saw earlier in the analogy of a rectangle offered by Tafarodi and Vu. Because they are equal partners, the only way to show the particular nature of the relationship between competence and worthiness using lines and figures is to point out that one form captures such balance: that of a square. Since this analogy is a bit more complete, it will also play a major role in presenting the theory of self-esteem that is the heart of this book and its approach to enhancing authentic self-esteem.

Time is the last component in the fundamental structure of self-esteem and it pertains to this phenomenon in several ways. First, it takes time to develop a stable form of self-esteem because, in the largest sense, it is the result of a developmental process that involves facing many challenges of living, both large and small. Second, time is also that which carries us into the future, which is to say toward self-esteem moments that have yet to come to us as adolescents, as adults, and as older people. This aspect of the relationship between time and self-esteem means that time is both an adversary and a friend when it comes to self-esteem. The bad news is that when we fail to act in ways that are competent *and* worthy, we suffer a loss of self-esteem and experience corresponding pain of one type or another. The good news is that when we do rise to the challenge of being "just and right" and actually demonstrate our competence and worthiness in this fashion, then we have the opportunity to affirm, to regain, or even to increase healthy self-esteem. In either case, time is important to the fundamental structure of self-esteem because it shows us that self-esteem is something that deserves our attention throughout the entire life cycle.

By now it should be clear that defining self-esteem as a relationship between competence and worth or worthiness is more comprehensive than basing it on either competence or worthiness alone. Similarly, there is reason to believe that this approach also better reflects the intent in Milton's original use of the term than is found in the other definitions. Finally, it should seem plausible that defining self-esteem in terms of these two factors (three, if one counts the relationship as a factor) may be more accurate at the lived level, which is the basic source of data for understanding human behavior. In the following chapters, I hope to show that understanding self-esteem as a balanced relationship between competence and worthiness helps deal more effectively with important problems in the field, such as measuring self-esteem, increasing authentic self-esteem in both clinical and nonclinical settings, and understanding the connections between the field of self-esteem and positive psychology.

2

Self-Esteem Research Problems and Issues

Like most investigations into human behavior, understanding self-esteem involves dealing with several major research problems and issues that are associated with the phenomenon. Understanding something about them is a helpful step toward developing a reasonable framework for evaluating the many findings that characterize the field today. The first set of issues concerns self-esteem as a specific phenomenon. For example, what is the difference between self-esteem and related concepts, such as self-regard, self-respect, self-acceptance, self-love, self-confidence, self-efficacy, or self-image? How is self-esteem connected to these things? Although no one has all the answers to these questions, it is important to appreciate their presence in the field because they help to create the definitional maze that Smelser (1989) noted in Chapter 1.

Another more complex layer to appreciate is that all self-related phenomena are connected to a much larger philosophical and scientific set of questions that arise when investigating matters involving such things as consciousness, identity, the self, and meaning (Diggory, 1966; Harter, 1999; Jackson, 1984; Leary & Tangney, 2003; Wells & Marwell, 1976; Wylie, 1974). Of course, it is not realistically possible to address these matters in a definitive way in this or any other book. After all, philosophy has tried to deal with them for at least 2,500 years (Miller, 1992). However, we do need to find a way of standing in the face of such complexity so that we do not become lost in it.

THE MAJOR PARADOXES OF SELF-ESTEEM

The second set of issues, of which there are at least five, result from attempting to apply the scientific method to something like self-esteem. Bednar, Wells, and Peterson (1989) suggested understanding one of these issues as a paradox, and I think that analogy applies to them all because, in each case, they can be seen in two rather dichotomous ways, which can create confusion in the field.

Is the Function of Self-Esteem to Maintain the Self or to Expand It?

Although there are exceptions, the majority of those who research and otherwise investigate self-esteem approach it in terms of a need, motive, or dynamic connected to the general psychosocial process of self-regulation (Bednar et al., 1989; Branden, 1969; Leary & Downs, 1995; Mecca, Smelser, & Vasconcellos, 1989; Pyszczynski, Greenberg, Sheldon, Arndt, & Schimel, 2004b; Sheldon, Elliot, Kim, & Kasser, 2001; Sheldon & Kasser, 2001; Wells & Marwell, 1976). However, there are two very different ways of understanding the role that self-esteem plays in regulating the self and behavior that run throughout the field.

On one hand, self-consistency and self-maintenance theories and related work see the primary function of self-esteem as helping to regulate behavior in order to provide a steady, stable, or consistent sense of self and identity. In this case, a primary purpose of self-esteem is to buffer the self against stress. This protective mechanism helps the individual find ways of coping with the slings and arrows of life so as to maintain a sense of self-sameness and continuity both personally and interpersonally. In this sense, self-esteem acts as a shield (Coopersmith, 1967; Newman & Newman, 1987). On the other hand, an equally powerful set of theories and supporting work, often called self-expansion or self-enhancement theory, views the basic function of self-esteem as enabling the self to develop, to grow beyond its current limits, and to even actualize unique possibilities. In this case, self-esteem allows the individual to tolerate the anxiety associated with destabilization of the self that comes with taking the risks necessary to reorganize the self at a higher level and also reinforces positive expansion when it occurs (Deci & Ryan, 1995; Kernis, 1995; Rogers, 1961; Ryan & Deci, 2003, 2004).

It may be surprising to find that, more often than not, self-esteem researchers assume one position or the other. However, a simple dichotomous approach to the question of whether self-esteem is related primarily to self-maintenance or to self-enhancement, or however these processes may be framed, is extremely misleading because it greatly oversimplifies matters. A more descriptive approach is to allow the paradoxical nature of self-esteem to stand as one of its basic characteristics. After all, if both camps offer good evidence for their positions, rather than attempting to determine which is "right," it may well be that self-esteem works both ways. If so, a comprehensive model will have to find some way of incorporating both motivational structures and regulatory functions into its framework without contradicting itself.

Is Self-Esteem a Trait or a State?

For a good while, self-esteem was understood to be a single and relatively stable global characteristic, something like personality or intelligence, which gave it the form of a trait. As such, it was possible to think of self-esteem largely in terms of general types, typically high, medium, and low. Yet, more recently, researchers began noticing that some people's self-esteem appears to fluctuate considerably between different situations, within the same type of situation, or even in general (Greenier et al., 1995; Kernis & Goldman, 2003). Thus, it is important to see self-esteem in terms of states as well as traits. In other words, instead of understanding self-esteem as ranging on a continuum of high to low levels, it may also be necessary to see self-esteem as ranging from being relatively stable to unstable as well.

The result of this development is that there are distinctly different types of self-esteem, but they can no longer be arranged or ordered along a simple continuum of high to low, which has been the classical model. Instead, types and levels can be thought of as two intersecting or overlapping continua. The paradox in this regard concerns the question, how can self-esteem manifest itself as a trait much of the time and yet fluctuate as a state in this or that situation, sometimes even remarkably so? This paradox is especially active in the literature concerning testing or measuring self-esteem (Harter, 1999). Any model of self-esteem that claims to be comprehensive must account for how it is that global self-esteem tends to be reasonably stable, how state-related self-esteem tends to be situational, and how fluctuation can occur.

Is Self-Esteem a Developmental Product or a Process?

Another paradox related to the previous one concerns the issue of whether self-esteem is primarily the product of development or an open-ended developmental process. On one hand, it can be said that self-esteem develops in a certain direction or to a certain point and then stays relatively consistent thereafter (Trzesniewski et al., 2004). If so, then it is important to emphasize the developmental antecedents of self-esteem as Coopersmith (1967) suggested. This work is likely to concentrate on such things as the forces of temperament, environment, reinforcement, circumstances, choices, and how they work together to result in an individual's type and level of self-esteem.

On the other hand, we have also seen that it is very possible to change self-esteem through such things as normal development and acutely positive or negative self-esteem moments throughout adulthood (Epstein, 1979; Harter, 1999; Jackson, 1984; Mruk, 1983). In this sense, self-esteem seems to be more of an ongoing developmental theme, issue, or process. Understanding this aspect of self-esteem has practical as well as theoretical and research implications, because if self-esteem processes are fixed rather than flexible, then there is little point in attempting to change it.

Is Self-Esteem Primarily a Psychological or Sociological Phenomenon?

Bhatti, Derezotes, Kim, and Specht (1989, p. 60) pointed out that there are two basic ways of researching self-esteem, namely, from a psychological or from a sociological perspective, each of which has important research, theoretical, and practical consequences. Historically, the psychological approach to the self and self-esteem focuses largely on the intrapsychic developmental processes, the role of the individual in the creation of the self through decision making, and the specific forms of behavior associated with self-esteem, such as individual mastery, success, and achievement, which are largely competence based (Adler, 1927; James, 1890/1983).

However, it is interesting to note that, starting at nearly the same time, a more sociological approach to the self also began to develop loosely based on the Cooley–Mead tradition in sociology (Cooley, 1909; Mead, 1934). Here the self is held to be a largely interpsychic phenomenon that develops in a social context. As such, the focus is on how others react to us, how we react to their reactions, and how over time those processes lead to the development of a sense of personhood as well as one's relative worth. Such a sociologically based view of self-esteem can easily be seen running through the work developed by Rosenberg (1965, 1986), Smelser (1989), and even some positive psychologists who tend to emphasize the worthiness component of self-esteem (Hewitt, 2002).

The paradox that self-esteem may be primarily seen as a psychological or social phenomenon plays itself out in other areas as well. For example, when clinical psychologists study self-esteem, which is a topic they deal with more intensely than most in their work, the methods of introspection, case study, and interview seem most likely to be used. In contrast, sociologically oriented researchers tend to employ surveys, develop group norms, and attempt to establish correlations between various demographic variables, such as race, gender, and socioeconomic status. Social psychologists may be seen as somewhere between these two perspectives on self-esteem and often do more controlled work. However, it is usually based on reasonably young, usually healthy, upwardly mobile college students who constitute a rather unique, and perhaps not particularly representative, sample from which to generalize.

Finally, one of the most important manifestations of this paradox occurs in an area that is becoming increasingly thematic in this field: the role culture plays in regard to self-esteem. Some researchers, for example, maintain the position that self-esteem is a basic human need and therefore cross-cultural in nature (Sheldon et al., 2001; Tafarodi & Swann, 1996). However, others feel that self-esteem is important largely in individualistic cultures rather than collectivistic ones (Crocker & Park, 2004; Hewitt, 2002). The point is that such factors as starting from different positions, having separate priorities, and working with different methods all serve to create a bewildering, sometimes contradictory, range of hypotheses, data, and findings in the field. Any comprehensive theory of self-esteem must at least address these issues, as difficult as they may be.

Is Self-Esteem an Independent Variable or a Dependent Variable?

The final issue might be the most perplexing paradox of all from a scientific point of view. Yet it may be the most important one because of its practical as well as theoretical implications. This one concerns the matter of whether self-esteem is significant because it has an impact on behavior or whether self-esteem is only a by-product, the result of something else. On one hand, as Kitano (1989) said, "From a sociocultural perspective, it is a dependent variable, that is, self-esteem is the result of a person's ethnic, social class, or gender group" (p. 318). On the other hand, "Self-esteem is also used as an independent variable—that is, as the 'cause' of behavior" (p. 318).

The relationship between self-esteem and academic achievement is a good example of this paradox in action. From one perspective, helping children to feel good about themselves could be a priority because a positive sense of self should enhance the odds of higher performance, while negative self-experience should detract from one's ability to succeed. From the other position, however, achieving the higher scores could be emphasized because success and mastery could lead to self-esteem whereas failure detracts from it. The paradox is that self-esteem seems to work both ways. As Harter (1999, p. 219) said, the "directionality" of self-esteem may vary as cause or effect between or even within situations. Controversies understanding the connection between self-esteem and behavior, it will be recalled, are some of the driving forces for popular as well as professional criticisms concerning work on self-esteem. Any theory that fails to deal with the thorny but crucial issue of causality cannot be considered to be comprehensive.

By now it should be clear that dealing with the paradoxes of self-esteem is an overwhelming challenge if we think about it based on unidimensional thinking. However, the two-factor approach has not yet been put to the task. Thus, it remains to be seen whether we can integrate these seemingly oppositional issues more effectively when operating from this definitional foundation.

PROBLEMS ASSOCIATED WITH ASSESSING SELF-ESTEEM

Much of the empirical work on self-esteem involves testing someone's self-esteem, measuring self-esteem across various samples, or assessing self-esteem in relation to other variables, such as depression, anxiety, life satisfaction, and so forth. Therefore, it is important to address the fact that it is difficult to develop a good (i.e., reliable, valid, and useful) instrument to measure this human characteristic. Unfortunately, although there are dozens, if not hundreds, of self-esteem instruments available, few are worth considering, because the majority of them succumb to problems in one or more areas described in the following sections. These design issues can also be used as criteria for determining whether or not a particular instrument is a good one.

The first factor to consider in developing, using, or evaluating a test or measure is to make sure that the instrument measures the right things and that it actually assesses what the test claims to assess, in this case, self-esteem. Our work on defining self-esteem lets us know, for example, that it is usually thought about in terms of a sense of competence, a feeling of worth, or both. Therefore, one thing we need to do when examining an instrument is determine the definition of self-esteem upon which it is based. The problem is much more complex than one of merely stating a definitional preference, because most existing instruments were constructed to measure self-esteem as a unidimensional phenomenon. However, if self-esteem is composed of two factors instead of one, instruments that are not designed with multiple components in mind may be largely incapable of yielding high-level results in principle as well as practice. Fortunately, Harter (1985), Tafarodi and Swann (2001), and O'Brien and Epstein (1988) developed approaches to measuring self-esteem that were based on multiple domains of life that reflect both factors. Thus, we must consider the possibility that multidimensional tools may be the best ones capable of actually measuring self-esteem in principle as well as in practice.

The dynamic nature of self-esteem is another issue with which test designers must contend. Remember, self-esteem is a phenomenon that may be seen as being global or situational in nature because we live out a certain basic level of self-esteem most of the time, but it may fluctuate in certain situations. The simplest example of how this factor affects a testing situation is when the subject has recently experienced a failure or success, relational gain or loss, and so forth, as such events can affect self-esteem test scores. Similarly, certain domains of life may be more relevant to one individual's level of self-esteem than to another's.

Even researchers who design unidimensional measures are aware of this situation. For example, later in his career, Rosenberg (1986) talked about "baseline" (overall or global) self-esteem and "barometric" (domain-specific or situational) self-esteem (p. 127). Unfortunately, most self-esteem tests are too general to tell us about the particular areas of life that are important for a given individual's self-esteem. This testing challenge is a difficult one to overcome because it requires identifying specific and appropriate domains that can contribute to, or that have an effect on, self-esteem before constructing the instrument and then building them into the test. Very few instruments have achieved this level of sophistication, especially those in wide use.

Next, there appears to be a fairly standard set of criteria that good instruments must employ concerning their normative base. First, the selection processes for finding subjects from which to obtain norms must be random so that the test does not reflect a bias for any group. Second, the subject pool must be stratified so that the normative sample is genuinely representative of the general population of those who will be examined with the assessment tool once it is developed. Third, the size of the normative sample must be large enough so that the test can be used with a wide range of individuals and backgrounds. For example, if we are interested in assessing self-esteem for the general population, then the normative samples must also be sensitive to age, gender, culture, and so on. Unfortunately, the history of developing self-esteem tests is such that individual researchers often construct their own scales for specific rather than general populations (Wells & Marwell, 1976), which give the results little generalizability.

In addition, various developmental factors affecting self-esteem pose a normative challenge. For example, Pope, McHale, and Craighead (1988) and Harter (1999) pointed out that developmental age needs to be included in normalizing a self-esteem test, especially in regard to younger people. For instance, it is likely that a 10-year-old has different self-esteem issues than a 16-year-old or a 30-year-old and using the same set of norms to evaluate all individuals is simply inappropriate. The problem of developing norms is compounded by the fact that many tests do not even report how, and sometimes even whether or not, they were standardized in relation to any particular criteria (Sappington, 1989).

Another well-known problem with most psychological tests is that they are subjective: We must use an individual's report of his or her own experience, behavior, or character to draw conclusions about that person. The responses of even the most well-meaning subjects are likely to be filtered by all kinds of factors usually involved in self-perception, not to mention the additional problems that can occur when an individual is anxious, angry, suspicious, or mentally ill. Even under the best circumstances, for instance, self-esteem tests are vulnerable to the "ceiling effect," or the tendency to see oneself in a positive light when reporting about oneself. The most common form of this problem may be that people tend to rate themselves more favorably on positive qualities, and less unfavorably on negative ones, than they are likely to actually merit when compared with external standards (Wells & Marwell, 1976). As we shall see, this issue becomes extremely important in regard to assessing self-esteem, because few instruments are capable of detecting such factors as cognitive rigidity, defensiveness, narcissism, and antisocial tendencies, all of which distort self-perception. These and other characteristics can adversely affect test results, usually in the form of false positives for higher levels of self-esteem.

Similarly, self-esteem tests are also vulnerable to what social psychologists call the "social desirability" effect (Baumeister et al., 2003). Such an effect is extremely important when dealing with self-esteem, because in addition to elevating scores in general, the desire to be seen in a positive light by others may generate other false positives (Greenier et al., 1995). This issue is especially important in assessing self-esteem because certain forms of it are associated with people who do not have mental health conditions but who do suffer some from unstable, fragile, or defensive self-esteem. Some of them are very sensitive to being seen in a critical light and resist it consciously or otherwise. Instead of reporting such insecurity, however, they may deny it or even overcompensate for such perceived shortcomings on a test. The result is that not only are their scores elevated, but they are simply wrong.

Whether clinically significant or not, in addition to creating difficulties in terms of developing good norms, problems concerning clinical and nonclinical forms of defensiveness are especially acute in the practical setting. In other words, instruments that do not have scales or other devices designed to detect the many forms of defensiveness mentioned above are sure to cause researchers and clinicians alike to miss an entire range of serious self-esteem problems as well as overestimate levels of high self-esteem. Probably the best way to deal with the issue is to develop defensiveness scales, such as those of the Minnesota Multiphasic Personality Inventory-2 (Butcher et al., 2001). Although such an exhaustive approach is not practical, it is reasonable to expect a good self-esteem test to at least alert us to the possibility of excessive exaggeration, self-deception, and defensiveness. Sadly, few tests even come close to being helpful in this regard.

Even if a self-esteem test addresses all of the issues mentioned earlier, we still have to know whether, and to what extent, a given instrument is valid. Although written decades ago, the review by Wells and Marwell (1976) still does an unparalleled job of examining the technical difficulties involved in developing self-esteem tests. Their work described how self-esteem measures can be evaluated against three traditional indicators of test validity. The highest type of validity such an instrument can have, of course, occurs when test items or tasks predict a particular outcome accurately. Unfortunately, such "criterion validity" is unlikely to occur with self-esteem tests, in part because it is such a complex phenomenon.

Content validity is another approach and is based on whether the test questions are connected to self-esteem in some logical way. For instance, it should be possible to define what kinds of behaviors or attitudes are most likely to be associated with high and low self-esteem, and then design questions that ask about them. This type of validity increases with the thoroughness of the questions: The more the test covers the whole range of factors thought to reflect self-esteem, the greater the validity of the instrument. Unfortunately, most self-esteem assessment instruments are unidimensional, which makes achieving this form of validity difficult. Furthermore, even when both competence and worthiness are covered, brevity often takes precedence over comprehensiveness because short tests are less expensive, easier to administer, and require little interpretation compared to using longer ones.

Construct validity, or "the degree to which certain explanatory concepts or constructs account for performance on the test" (Wells & Marwell, 1976, p. 153), is another way to achieve some degree of validity in self-esteem testing. This type of validity is based on the connections between a particular self-esteem test and the theory or definition of self-esteem that a researcher or clinician is using in his or her work. If the theory is well constructed and if the test questions embody the major components of self-esteem that are expressed by the theory, then the measure has logical integrity or theoretical validity. Not surprisingly, such face validity, as it is often called, is by far the most common one in this field. Unfortunately, such tests are usually transparent and easily manipulated by the subject. In short, finding good, which is to say reliable, valid, and accurate, ways of assessing self-esteem is much more challenging than meets the eye. Very few instruments meet these criteria, even the ones that are used most widely today, such as the Rosenberg Self-Esteem Scale (1965).

SPECIAL PROBLEMS GENERATED BY STUDYING SELF-ESTEEM SCIENTIFICALLY

The next group of problems faced by self-esteem researchers occurs when we try to investigate this phenomenon scientifically. Proponents of so-called popularistic or self-help approaches to self-esteem do not have to deal with these knotty issues. For social scientists, however, there are certain methodological problems that invariably arise in self-esteem research due to the presence of two scientific paradigms used to investigate higher levels of human behavior, especially those that involve consciousness. A few major social scientists try to grapple with this condition by reviewing the type of work that has gone on in the field to date. The most thorough and comprehensive may be that of Wells and Marwell (1976), whose entire book is devoted to the subject. Rather than attempt to duplicate this classic, I will refer to it as the leading authority of the issue of the methodological complexity of investigating self-esteem, although *The Social Importance of Self-Esteem* (1989) by Mecca et al. updated some of this information. In general, the list of methods used to study self-esteem is fairly typical of the social sciences as a whole. Self-esteem has been studied introspectively (Epstein, 1979), with case studies (Bednar et al., 1989; Pope et al., 1988), through interviews (Jackson, 1984) by surveys and tests (Rosenberg, 1965), and through experimentation (Coopersmith, 1967; Tafarodi & Vu, 1997), to name a few.

One rather classical way of understanding such methodological diversity in the social sciences, particularly in psychology, is to organize methods in terms of increasing degrees of objectivity (measurability). The result may be seen as a type of methodological pyramid, as shown in Figure 2.1.

According to this arrangement, the most experientially oriented or subjective (qualitative) methods are placed lowest on the hierarchy and the most measurable or objective (quantitative) ones are placed at the top, with the experiment standing as the epitome of the scientific method. Let us move quickly through this pyramid in terms of the strengths and weaknesses of the various methods as they are used for researching self-esteem, so that we then can examine the range of methods from a different, more revealing angle afterward. Although experienced readers are likely to see the first part of this section as a basic review, some of them may also be surprised by the implications of the second part of this examination.

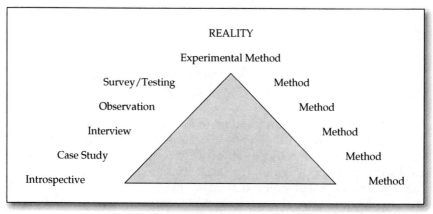

FIGURE 2.1
The traditional methodological pyramid.

Introspection

James (1890/1983) used this approach to study self-esteem more than a century ago. Examining one's own experience by describing and reflecting on it is the first method social scientists used to investigate self-esteem. However, many consider this approach to be so subjective that it is often not taken seriously today. One major problem is that classical introspective research depends on one individual's perception of his or her own experience and such subjectivity is difficult to replicate or validate. Nevertheless, it is instructive to note that we have seen some of James' early findings based on this technique turn out to be worthy of consideration over a century later in terms of defining self-esteem and understanding its major dynamics. Thus, we must conclude that although introspection is at the bottom of the traditional research hierarchy, it is not without value at least as a source of insight.

Case Study

This method, which includes clinical case study, is another "soft" technique that is often overlooked but is not without value. For example, the method has clinical significance today because it allows us to investigate problems that a given individual may be having with self-esteem. This approach also helps us to explore the relationship between self-esteem and psychological functioning by noting regularities or variations that occur between subjects, albeit small in number. In fact, some approaches to enhancing self-esteem in the clinical setting rely on case study evidence as the main source of support for their therapeutic efficacy (Bednar & Peterson, 1995). In the end, case study is an integral part of good clinical training. However, it is important to appreciate the limitations of this method as well: Because of small sample sizes, it is difficult to generalize such research from a small number of subjects to people in general.

The Interview Method

Interviewing subjects is higher up the pyramid because this method can correct some of the weaknesses inherent to introspection and case study. For instance, structuring the interview in advance helps to make it more reliable. In addition, an interview can be recorded and transcribed so that trained evaluators have access to the data, which reduces some subjectivity. We will even see that it is possible to use interviews to advance research in this field, particularly when they are coupled with other methods, such as tests (Scheff & Fearon, 2004). Even so, the major limitations of doing research this way include the fact that sample sizes are still relatively small because interviewing takes time. Therefore, establishing cause-and-effect relationships through the method is difficult.

Observational Methods

Because it is not possible to see self-esteem directly, laboratory- and field-based observational methods are not used often in researching self-esteem. However, some important work in the field is based on direct observation of children, which includes asking parents, teachers, and even peers to evaluate the behavior in relation to self-esteem (Coopersmith, 1967; Harter, 1999). In addition, this method also can be used in the therapeutic setting, where a clinician actually may ask a child's parents and teachers about domains where the child is experiencing success or difficulty and then make observations of client behavior in those areas (Pope et al., 1988). Such information is often helpful to clinicians, but it is expensive, time consuming, and still limited in terms of its ability to tell us about such things as whether self-esteem causes or effects behavior.

Correlational Method

Much of the work on self-esteem involves the use of surveys and tests as ways of gaining access to the phenomenon. These instruments offer an especially attractive way to study self-esteem, because once a test is developed, it can be used to establish correlations in many ways. For instance, we use such measures to assess an individual's self-esteem in relation to clinical behavior, academic performance, and personality functioning. High versus low self-esteem is the most frequent type of comparison made in this regard, but researchers have focused on behavioral correlates of medium and unstable or defensive self-esteem as well (Kernis, 2003b). Measures based on statistical significance are useful in the clinical setting but have also been helpful to positive psychologists studying such things as the relationship between self-esteem and happiness, optimal performance, and well-being (Baumgardner & Crothers, 2009). However, it is still important to keep in mind the difficulties associated with developing good instruments for assessing self-esteem mentioned earlier. Another difficulty is that even when correlations are found, the old adage "a correlation does not a cause make" is still at play: Correlations can reflect coincidences as well as causes.

Experimental Research

Finally, we come to the top of the pyramid, where the experimental method is usually placed. According to Wells and Marwell (1976), there are two basic types of experiments used to research self-esteem and both of them usually involve some pre- and postmeasures of self-esteem. This early finding still appears to hold true today. The most straightforward format is to set up an experiment so that subjects are engaged in an activity in which they believe their performance or ability is crucial in determining whether a successful or unsuccessful outcome occurs. However, the experimenter actually controls the results, meaning that success and failure can be manipulated so that their effects on self-esteem can be measured. Baumeister (1993) used such a technique in his earlier work when he was still advocating self-esteem as an important variable.

The other format differs in that subjects are given information about themselves or their personalities either just before or while attempting a task or activity. In this situation, information is manipulated so that, for instance, a low self-esteem subject hears positive comments about himself or herself and a high self-esteem subject receives negative personal feedback instead. Research on terror management theory (Pyszczynski, Greenberg, & Goldberg, 2003), work that investigates what is called implicit (unconscious) versus explicit (conscious) self-esteem (Devos & Banaji, 2003; Dijksterhuis, 2004), and work from the two-factor perspective (Tafarodi, Tam, & Milne, 2001) often use this technique.

The strength of this method is that it allows us to test for causal links between self-esteem and other phenomena or behavior. For example, a self-esteem enhancement program that has this kind of evidence to support its use is more valid than one that does not. However, we also know there are some real difficulties in applying this method in self-esteem research. For one thing, our ability to generalize from controlled conditions of a laboratory situation to real life is limited. As a result, Scheff, Retzinger, and Ryan (1989) concluded that it is "especially disheartening that the experimental studies have tended to be inconclusive . . . because these studies are conducted in laboratory settings, the extrapolation of results to real situations is uncertain. Such studies may lack what is called 'ecological validity'" (p. 167).

Similarly, there are constraints on how far one can take this method in areas that are most important to understand, such as the relationship between self-esteem and troubled behavior. Epstein (1979), for example, pointed out some of these limits when researchers want to examine emotionally significant human phenomena in the lab setting.

How does one investigate love in the laboratory, or threats to an individual's ego that produce such high levels of anxiety as to produce enduring changes in personality? Obviously, for both practical and ethical reasons, such states cannot be studied in the laboratory. (p. 50)

Partly because of the high value we place on the experimental method to help determine causality, the difficulties this approach presents for the field create an unfortunate side effect: It results in a lack of the type of evidence that critics of self-esteem work most desire, which only adds fuel to their fires.

THE PROBLEM OF SCIENTIFIC PARADIGMS AND RESEARCHING SELF-ESTEEM

Examining the methodological diversity in this field suggests that each approach offers a way of finding out valuable information about self-esteem. In fact, every method has generated a significant stream of self-esteem research and findings. Yet, we also saw that each approach has serious limitations, which, among other things, makes it difficult to achieve any type of consensus in the field. Indeed, some early self-concept experts suggest that investigating this class of phenomena using the scientific method is essentially a hopeless task (Diggory, 1966). Others regard the methodological difficulties in researching self-esteem as reflecting the limits of our quantitative sophistication at the time and, therefore, call for "improved" statistical methodologies as the best hope (Smelser, 1989).

Consequently, today there is a general recognition from both sociologists and psychologists studying self-esteem that the field is in a state of methodological flux. A key issue seems to concern difficulties establishing clear, quantifiable, causal connections between self-esteem and behavior. Scheff et al. (1989), for instance, examined six major reviews of the methodological issues facing such research. Four of them reached a negative conclusion about the possibility of resolving the problems effectively, but two were hopeful. Scheff and colleagues concluded that,

In our opinion, the implication of all six of the general reviews is not that the field is healthy but that it is in a state of crisis, and has been for some time. . . . Perhaps what is needed is a new paradigm more closely connected with the particular problem of self-esteem. (p. 177)

No doubt, self-esteem bashing has even made this situation more acute. Yet, a crisis for one methodological paradigm can be an opportunity for another (Kuhn, 1962), and one way to see this possibility in terms of self-esteem work is to turn the traditional methodological pyramid on its side.

Instead of a simple traditional methodological hierarchy, a literal shift in perspective results in a continuum of methods, as shown in Figure 2.2.

Figure 2.2 shows that scientific methods actually have a range of characteristics that act more like a continuum rather than a pyramid when applied to understanding human phenomena like self-esteem. To the right of the midpoint, for instance, we encounter a focus on external realities and their measurements, which is characteristic of the natural sciences and traditional psychology. This approach begins with observation and progresses toward an increasing degree of "objectivity" (measurability) that culminates in the experimental method. Such a progression in quantitative sophistication helps us to understand the natural world by observing properties, measuring characteristics, and discovering cause-and-effect relationships, often in that order. Since people exist as objects in this world, it stands to reason that the methods of natural science may be applied to us as well.

However, it is also true that human beings are unique in that we are conscious and self-aware. Thus, we also live in a world of experience and meanings, as well as one consisting of physics and biology. The methods to the left of the midpoint reflect a human science paradigm that is better able to access such invisible internal realities because the focus is

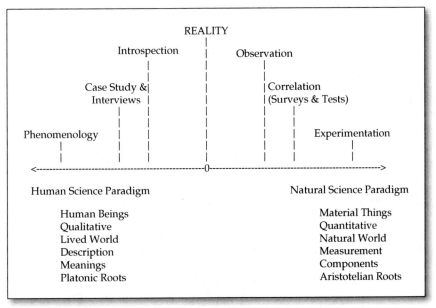

FIGURE 2.2
A methodological continuum.

on the participant's experience, the lived reality in which it occurs, and its meaning. These qualitative methods are also characterized by degree of progressive sophistication. Each move to the left of center represents an increase in the descriptive richness offered by a method and culminates in the more rigorous techniques of classical phenomenological psychology.

It is interesting to reflect on the metaphorical implications of the terms "left" and "right," because in a real sense they are perfectly balanced mirror images of one another. For example, it may be no accident that the left side of the diagram is "softer," more inclusive, or idealistic in the Platonic sense; whereas the right side connotes a certain "harder," more realistic, or Aristotelian approach (Mruk & Hartzell, 2003). In addition, we have seen that simple dichotomies do not work well when trying to understand the paradoxes and complexities of human behavior, so it is important not to regard one paradigm as being good and the other as bad.

Instead, the important question concerning scientific method and these two paradigms is whether one technique is more suitable to a particular task than another. For instance, if we want to know whether a self-esteem enhancement program is effective, the methods of the measurement-oriented natural science paradigm make good sense: In this case, it is important to identify outcomes in terms of such quantitative indices as degree of statistical significance. Similarly, if the goal is to understand how self-esteem is actually lived by real people in everyday life, the qualitative methods are more effective in principle as well as practice: They are better equipped to access the lived world more directly and more completely.

PHENOMENOLOGICAL METHODS

We have already investigated traditional methods for researching self-esteem from the paradigm of psychology practiced as a natural science, so let us now examine the qualitative paradigm by looking at the methods used by modern existential-phenomenological psychology. There are several reasons to examine this approach as a case in point. For one thing, it is difficult to dismiss the value of paying attention to the qualities of experience in this field. For example, Harter (1999) reminded us that even if we wished to dismiss such "fuzzy" or subjective aspects of self-esteem as "non-scientific," we cannot do so because self-esteem and its components "do represent a phenomenological reality for individuals" (p. 192). Although more objective models of explaining behavior may be preferable, "the challenge is to develop models that identify the specific antecedents of different outcomes while preserving the critical role of self-representations as phenomenological mediators" (Harter, 2003, p. 635). Devos and Banaji (2003) made a similar point when discussing an individual's immediate, nonreflective reaction to various events. Such phenomenological experience, they noted, is an important factor even in experimental situations, but is usually not taken into account by researchers who do such work.

Unfortunately, many people confuse the term "phenomenology" with its medical meaning, which concerns the description of symptoms, or with mere subjective experience, which is actually something called "phenomenalism." The word is being used in this book as a technical term that refers to an entire approach to psychology that starts with individual experience. This method is designed to end with understanding the basic human structure of an experience as well as its meaning for people in general, and reaches this goal in a very rigorous fashion. Giorgi's work (1971, 1984) is especially helpful in this regard, perhaps at least in part because he was first trained in traditional empirical psychology. His presentation of the method began by pointing out what phenomenological psychology is not to be mistaken as being. For example, modern phenomenological psychology is not mere introspectionism because we want to investigate the structure of a given experience, not just a particular incidence of it. Individual experience, I like to say to my students, is a good starting place, but unless we are working in a clinical setting, a sample of one limits the generalizability of results to a very small space. What would be the significance of the research if, for example, the subject whose experience was used turned out to be emotionally upset at the time it was described, was under the influence of a drug then, or happened to be in a psychotic state?

Thus, although it is true that phenomenological research starts investigating a person's experience of something by having him or her describe it, that procedure is only the first step. Phenomenological inquiry is interested in understanding both how an experience or phenomenon is lived concretely in a person's life *and* what makes a certain type of experience even possible in the first place. Instead of merely analyzing the components of an experience as we might with content analysis, phenomenology attempts to describe what and how the components of a phenomenon or experience interact with each other to create the possibility of a given phenomenon or experience in the first place.

Giorgi also made it clear that, contrary to some characterizations, such qualitative methods are not "anti-scientific." Both methodological paradigms are based on some form of rigorous description, whether it involves words or numbers. For one thing, qualitative methods can actually be quite formal as we move from the center and toward the extreme left of the continuum. For another, this approach attempts to understand more of how an experience actually unfolds than merely observing or measuring it might produce. The fact is that many of the things that are most human, and therefore most important for psychology, involve meaning, and meaning is hardly quantifiable. As Giorgi (1971) said,

> Traditional psychology has avoided the major psychological issues by either ignoring the peculiarly human phenomena or by reducing them to such an extent to fit the strict scientific method that they were no longer recognizable. From a phenomenological viewpoint measuring a phenomenon is not the same as determining its meaning. These are two separate perspectives that must be balanced in every research. (p. 14)

A related misconception Giorgi noted is that phenomenological psychology is sometimes thought to be largely speculative. Like natural science methods, however, qualitative work can be done as a step-by-step approach and is based on a set of rules to follow. The most important of these is that research must remain faithful to the phenomenon, an objective that is captured by the phenomenological adage of making sure that a phenomenon is described in a way that allows it to show itself "from itself in the very way in which it shows itself from itself" (Heidegger, 1927/1962, p. 58). In other words, we cannot simply create a description or impose one we prefer on a phenomenon because in order to reach qualitative validity, a phenomenological description must be consistent with the experience upon which it rests.

This criterion for the validity of results also means that phenomenological psychology is not antidata, which is another misconception. In fact, the descriptive power of this approach may be capable of handling more diverse forms of data than its natural scientific counterpart, a feature that is particularly important for dealing with the diverse methods and findings concerning self-esteem. Similarly, Giorgi (1984) stated that phenomenological psychology is not antitraditional, "Rather it is willing and able to dialog with traditional psychology" (p. 14) which, we will see, may be another important criterion for validity. I happen to find Giorgi's approach to phenomenological psychology the most scientific of qualitative methods because of its step-by-step process. This approach allows others to duplicate work and refute, modify, or validate it. His method also offers the possibility of developing a body of work by different authors on the same topic to which others may add later. However, in all fairness, I must point out that although I was trained in traditional psychological methods as an undergraduate, Giorgi was one of my graduate teachers. Thus, I will not speak for others interested in qualitative methods.

Of course, the nature and merits of psychology envisioned as a human science versus those of psychology practiced as a natural science, which is to say traditional psychology, is a topic that is discussed in great depth. Those who are interested in understanding more of this approach are invited to do so by investigating Giorgi's work (already cited), as well as that of

Heidegger (1927/1962), Husserl (1954/1970a), Gurwitsch (1964), Merleau-Ponty (1945/1962), and many others. My basic point is really quite simple: There is a limit to researching self-esteem, or any other human phenomenon for that matter, by insisting on the methods of the naturalistic paradigm. But there are also serious limits to the human science paradigm, the chief of which may be that it is difficult to show clear or simple cause-and-effect relationships this way. What is needed, then, may be an approach that breaks though the limits created by insisting on one or the other as being scientific.

METHODOLOGICAL ADVANCES IN RESEARCHING SELF-ESTEEM

Fortunately, advances are being made in terms of applying qualitative methods to studying self-esteem. Epstein (1979), for instance, took issue with the appropriateness of doing artificially constructed experimental research on self-esteem. His alternative is an ecological one that may be done in two ways. The first is to manipulate self-esteem in what he called "natural laboratories," where it is possible to introduce experimental manipulations on naturally occurring experiences associated with self-esteem. However, the technical difficulties and ethical constraints of this alternative are limiting. As he said, "We had previously studied sport parachuting as a natural laboratory for the study of anxiety. . . . Unfortunately, natural laboratories can be found for only limited phenomena. For other events, we turned to self-observation of experiences in everyday life" (p. 51). His point is that having subjects report on their own self-esteem experience in a way that is relatively structured and that occurs right after an appropriate event increases the relevance or value of such data and results.

In Chapter 1, we saw that another version of Epstein's ecological approach is to have students track self-esteem over time. The technique may be used for any period, which means that it is possible to conduct longer-term studies of what happens to self-esteem in an individual's life, something that is greatly lacking in this field. One advantage of researching self-esteem in this fashion is that the paradoxes mentioned earlier are more likely to show themselves as they are actually lived, which gives us the opportunity to study them more fully. Another reason to use such qualitative methods is that these data can be more "objective" than may meet the eye. For example, Epstein (1979) made the important observation that self-reports usually reflect experiences or reactions that occur over longer periods of time, a process that results in multiple observations. Traditional laboratory research, by contrast, does not.

Indeed, traditional, empirical, controlled studies only give us what amounts to a snapshot of reality, and a rather artificial one at that. As Epstein (1979) said, "On this basis alone there is reason to suspect that laboratory findings, as customarily obtained, are often low in replicability and generality, and cannot therefore establish strong relationships with findings obtained on other occasions by other means" (p. 52). It is also worth noting that he fully recognized the limits of using self-report as data. However, he still found himself forced to conclude that given the weaknesses of laboratory research on meaning-based or meaningful human behavior, research based on self-reports should not be so readily dismissed, as more traditional psychology tends to do when it comes to such findings.

In general, the qualitative approach is capable of putting us in much closer proximity to the link between self-esteem and behavior as it actually occurs in real life. For instance, Tafarodi and Milne (2002) asked 244 participants to record negative experience over a 4-week period and to fill out the Life Events Record at the beginning and at the end of that time. Those records were then analyzed by judges who were trained to look for the effect of negative experiences on self-esteem. Similarly, Scheff and Fearon (2004) take the fascinating approach of combining both qualitative and quantitative techniques. This work involved asking participants to take a standard self-esteem test and then interviewing them about how they answered the questions. This technique resulted in a measurable evaluation of self-esteem *and the reasons for it*, because discussing the meaning of each response with participants takes us to the one place more traditional or objective methods cannot go: the lived world of meaning. Clearly, just because the qualitative approach is experiential rather than experimental does not mean that qualitative work is methodologically undisciplined. Rather, they each simply have different strengths and weaknesses.

Phenomenological psychologists tend to investigate real-life human experiences, such as emotional states, decision making, and thinking (Aanstoos, 1984; Costall & Still, 1987; Dreyfus & Dreyfus, 1986; Giorgi, 1970, 1975, 1984; Wertz, 1984). Like quantitative research, the basic form of this method involves what can be thought of as a stepwise process. Typically, the researcher begins by identifying the phenomenon to be studied and then finds suitable participants for the investigation. The study might simply be a retrospective look at experiences or it could involve a host of contrived (experimental) situations or manipulations designed to elicit or test responses. Data are usually generated by asking subjects for an initial description of the experience or event and often involves using interviews to clarify and expand on the material. Each description and its related interview can be transcribed to stand as a single body of data. This narrative or "extended protocol" of behavior is then examined for meaning units which are often identified by looking for turning points or the emergence of new themes in the narrative.

These results, in turn, are used to develop a description of a given subject's experience as a single or situated instance of the phenomenon, which is to say how it is lived by a particular subject at a particular time.

Next, these individual records of the phenomenon are examined for regularities that occur between subjects. The recurring themes that arise from this step are identified as being basic to the phenomenon and are known as its essential or constitutive elements. Finally, these components, and the relationships between them, are worked into a resulting phenomenological description that covers all the variations reported in the data and is usually identified as the fundamental structure of the phenomenon.

The final product of the method, or its results, is the general structure. It captures that which is necessary and sufficient to give rise to the phenomenon for any given individual at any particular time. Just as the researcher must maintain scientific objectivity while using traditional methods, it is important for the qualitative researcher to do so as well. In this case, scientific objectivity involves disciplined attention, especially something called "bracketing," which requires the social scientist to suspend his or her own judgments and preconceptions as much as possible during each step of the process.

Of course, like their natural science counterparts (Howard, 1985), human science researchers recognize that in all cases the best research method is the one that is most suited to working with the particular phenomenon in question. When studying experience, this axiom means that the method must be flexible as well as rigorous, because experiences are more fluid than experiments. These two characteristics of the phenomenological method allow it to be faithful to the phenomenon and its investigation, wherever they may lead. Finally, it should be noted that I used this method to analyze the self-esteem moments discussed in Chapter 1 that led to the fundamental structure and definition of self-esteem presented there. More of that work later.

Jackson's (1984) *Self-Esteem and Meaning: A Life Historical Investigation* probably represents the most in-depth and articulate discussion of the value of using qualitative methods to research self-esteem in this way. In dealing with the problems and limits encountered when researching self-esteem from the natural science paradigm Jackson noted that,

> The problem seems rather to lie in experimentation itself. . . .
> Self-esteem is not a determinate process like the ones studied in
> the physical sciences; its nature lies rather in its subjective char-
> acter and in its ever-changing manifestations and implications.
> Confronted by a phenomenon so elusive and so dynamic, the
> experimental method is, as it were, overpowered. (pp. 4–5)

He went on to discuss that high-level human phenomena tend to incapacitate the experimental method because they revolve around meanings, not measures. We saw, for instance, that self-esteem is literally filled with meaningful implications concerning our worthiness as individuals whenever we face a challenge of living, especially existentially power-ful ones. No ethical experiment could hope to completely capture such richness.

More recently, Scheff and Fearon (2004) presented a similar argu-ment when critiquing methods that use static techniques to study dynamic processes such as those associated with self-appraisal, self-feeling, and the like. They concluded that, instead, studies based on discourse with subjects, and not just their measurement, might "help new conceptions of self-esteem, and generate important and testable hypotheses" (p. 87). In short, it seems unlikely that meaning can be broken down into observ-able parts: Although their sum may turn out to be correct in number, it is always less than the lived realities people actually experience.

INTEGRATED DESCRIPTION

In all fairness, I must say that qualitatively oriented researchers have seri-ous weaknesses as well. Sometimes, for instance, they focus so much on meaning that they become just as biased as their natural scientist coun-terparts in insisting that one approach is intrinsically superior to another. Also, much of what passes for qualitative work done from a human sci-ence paradigm seems to suffer from an overemphasis on one of two things. First, the work may emphasize personal experience to the extent that it becomes difficult to replicate. This type of activity is merely phenomenal-istic and constitutes a database of one. Second, such research can also be so excessively postmodern that it is based largely on argument, not data, much like literary criticism. In other words, good qualitative work also requires rigor. We must be faithful to the phenomenon, as it were, and self-esteem seems to be telling us that both scientific paradigms are necessary if we wish to describe and understand it scientifically.

One way of reaching a balanced goal is to use a form of the phenom-enological method I refer to as "integrated description" (Mruk, 1984, 1994, 2010). This approach is based on Giorgi's scientifically rigorous vision of qualitative research in that it is a step-by-step procedure that can be dupli-cated by others, just as the scientific method requires. However, unlike much qualitative work, integrated description also requires the use of quantitative material found through more traditional methods, so that the qualitative findings can be tested and validated, which is another hallmark of science. Consequently, the result is a more comprehensive analysis than using only one paradigm can hope to achieve.

Thus, integrated description is a two-stage research process. First, it is necessary to identify the general structure of a phenomenon by using a replicable, preferably step-by-step, version of the phenomenological method, such as Giorgi's approach. Then, it is possible to proceed to the second, or integration, phase, which involves validating the results of the first stage in at least one of two ways, preferably both. One is to identify key findings in the quantitative research on the topic and then determine whether they can be accounted for in terms of the fundamental structure without violating its integrity. In this case, the degree to which such findings can be placed within the basic description without contradicting its components tells us something about the conceptual (construct) validity of the general structure. In an attempt to satisfy quantitative standards of traditional psychological methods, the second technique is to test predictions based on the general structure. For example, if the general structure suggests certain things are likely to influence self-esteem, such as increasing a person's competence and worthiness, then we ought to be able to test that hypothesis quantitatively. If the results turn out to be positive, then we can claim to have met the standards of evidence-based methodologies that are necessary for establishing predictive validity. Qualitative research that demonstrates both types of validity is extremely desirable because it meets the standards of both paradigms.

Although developed and refined in order to research self-esteem, it is important to realize that the method of integrated description may be applied to any number of human phenomena. For instance, if we were interested in doing an integrated description of troubling experiences such as depression, I would first attempt to find out what it means to be depressed by asking participants to describe their experiences and then develop a general structure of the phenomenon in a step-by-step fashion. Next, I would examine more traditional research on depression and show where those results fit into the structure. For example, because depression involves bodily sensations and states, I would have to show where and how the biology of depression comes into play in being depressed. Yet, depression also affects perception, so I would elaborate the description further by including findings on thinking patterns typically associated with depression. Furthermore, because depression often affects a person's relationships with others, it might be helpful to show how the fundamental structure of depression is lived interpersonally as well.

The result would be a more comprehensive picture of depression than more simplistic approaches, such as seeing depression only as a "chemical imbalance" or a mere "lack of meaning," because both views would be accounted for in the integrated description. Then, we could examine the resulting understanding of depression to develop hypotheses to help treat it more effectively and test them. Although medications and cognitive therapy are standard treatments today, for instance, we still do not understand why they fail as often as they do. Perhaps an integrated description of depression and its treatment would help us to help those who stop medications prematurely or who give up the attempt to do the cognitive restructuring necessary to change thinking patterns. Note that the same approach could be used for other troubling experiences, such as anxiety, or perhaps even schizophrenia. The same case may be made for positive psychology, as the method of integrated description could be used for investigating such things as joy, happiness, love, or any other positive human experience.

Lest we wax too highly on possibilities offered by integrated description, it is also important to recognize that using information generated from both paradigms presents a difficult challenge. For one thing, integrating qualitative and quantitative work is demanding: It requires being trained in both approaches and analyzing a broad range of material generated by both paradigms. For another, the results are likely to please neither the hard-core, empirically oriented, number-crunching social scientists, nor their "touchy-feely," experientially oriented, postmodern counterparts.

Even so, as Giorgi (1971, 1984) pointed out, there are ways these paradigms can balance each other. For instance, whereas psychology as a natural science focuses on measuring behavior, the human science approach deals with the meaning of behavior. Similarly, where the natural science paradigm looks for determined or causal reactions, the human science approach attempts to account for "free" or intentional ones. Finally, where one method seeks identical repetition of a measure or outcome to reduce uncertainty, the other does so by searching for essential themes that are consistently present in a given phenomenon. In short, human beings live simultaneously in external (natural) and internal (human) worlds, both of which must be described if we are to be understood. Only something like integrated description avoids an inherent paradigmatic trap, which suggests that this approach may help us to achieve some degree of the "consensus" that Wells and Marwell (1976) claim is so important in this field.

THE QUESTION OF VALIDITY AND SELF-ESTEEM RESEARCH

We now have an idea of what some qualitative research looks like in terms of its method and the approach being used in this work. However, it is also important to examine how the question of validity applies to the study of self-esteem. Although I do not wish to belabor the point because the focus of this book is on self-esteem and not the philosophy of science, it is important to understand some things about the complexity of the issue of validity in this field and many others, especially when dealing with such a question as to whether something like self-esteem is a cause or an effect of behavior.

Wells and Marwell (1976) and Jackson (1984), respectively, may represent the quantitative and qualitative approaches in regard to examining the question of validity and self-esteem in considerable detail. Interestingly, they both concluded that validity is not so much a matter of absolute truth but of available proof. In other words, a primary value of the scientific method is that it helps to eliminate possibilities and thereby reduce uncertainty to increasingly manageable levels. Tryon (1991) referred to this aspect of science as "uncertainty reduction." It is also important to realize, of course, that this process never has to stop. I think this characteristic is one of the profound beauties of the scientific method broadly defined.

One good way to deal with the concept of validity is to ask, as Jackson (1984) did, *"validity for what?"* (p. 216). If the goal of research is, for instance, to measure self-esteem in a person, then the quantitative method is valid because it is very capable of dealing with crucial dimensions of the task, such as developing norms, creating scales, assessing self-esteem, and comparing it within or between individuals or groups. If, however, we are interested in investigating how self-esteem is alive in the world of everyday life, then qualitative methods are more valid both in principle and in practice.

Jackson (1984) captured this dimension of research when he pointed out that when it comes to researching self-esteem, it is important to keep in mind that the subject of study pertains to experience that is meaningful to the individual being studied. Self-esteem and other things like it occur "in a system of relations that is unique and irreducible in each separate instance. Such knowledge cannot be captured by a method that breaks it down into standard components" (p. 217). In other words, the problem with the experimental method we encounter with something like self-esteem is that the method is "designed to perform exactly this kind of reduction. *It is aimed at washing out the very information which we seek—namely, information about unique and specific constellations of personal meaning"* (p. 217).

If Jackson is correct, and I think to a large extent he is, then we must also add that self-esteem research needs to be concerned with information from both the qualitative and quantitative approaches for two good reasons. First, human beings exist in both ways: We are quantitative objects in the world just like any other physical body, so all the laws and methods that apply to such entities also apply to us. Still, we are also conscious entities that are embodied in physical form and only qualitative research methods are capable of accessing this crucial dimension of behavior. Second, if it is true that the field is in need of consensus, and again I think it is, then we cannot avoid the reality that the psychology of self-esteem is filled with both types of research and findings: We cannot dismiss either set of such work simply because they do not fit with our methodological or paradigmatic preferences.

The final question becomes, then, what are the criteria by which qualitative indicators may be said to have validity? Historically, qualitative validity is based on evaluating whether a finding is consistent with an explicit conceptual framework or theory. Such correspondence is based more on the rules of logic than on numbers, so we should expect to be held accountable in this way. Therefore, fidelity to the phenomenon, or being descriptively accurate, is an important criterion in phenomeno-logical research (Heidegger, 1927/1962; Marcel, 1964). For example, this type of validity is found in the degree to which a given description of the fundamental structure of a particular phenomenon actually reflects that phenomenon as it is experienced by real people in real-life settings.

The difficulty with this form of validation is, of course, how do we make sure a fundamental structure is actually fundamental? To para-phrase Husserl (1901/1970b), for this we must return to the facts them-selves. If a particular description leaves out something important about a phenomenon, or if it does not account for a major finding concerning an experience, then the validity of that description is weakened. In short, the overall validity of a two-factor general structure of self-esteem depends on its ability to show that it can accommodate what is known about the phenomenon through quantitative as well as qualitative work.

Note that I used this procedure in defining self-esteem. For example, we found that two of the basic definitions demonstrated problems with this type of validity because they left out one essential component or the other. By the same measure, the third definition of self-esteem had greater validity because both the components were accounted for in that descrip-tion and the linkage between them was identified. This set of factors was also found to be more faithful to the original use of the term self-esteem and to the lived character of self-esteem in everyday life. Taken together so far, the two-factor approach appears to capture the definition more accurately than the unidimensional approaches. Of course, determining just how well the fundamental structure derived from this definition also involves evaluating how well it is capable of integrating the major quan-titative findings of the field, but that criterion will be addressed in the next chapter.

Finally, it is important to keep in mind that, in all science, validity is more of a process than an event. In other words, validity involves discourse: Researchers in both paradigms dialog with their respective colleagues through their work and over time come to some form of agreement as to whether something may be taken as "true" or not. On one scientific hand, for example, Wells and Marwell (1976) pointed out that even when dealing with instruments, which are so important in quantitative work,

> Validity is not something that an instrument 'has,' but a qualita-tive attribution made to it through investigation, negotiation, and persuasion. . . . Very briefly put, validity is a joint property of a measurement or observational technique, an interpretive frame-work, and a scientific audience. (pp. 155–156)

On the other and more qualitative scientific hand, we see that Jackson (1984) and others understand validity as a process. It is one based on argument, dialog, and "the method of converging indices" where some form of agreement, or at least understanding, is achieved over time (p. 219). In short, regardless of paradigmatic preference, validity turns out to be a process that involves reaching a degree of consensus based on the best evidence available at the time. Scientific validity, then, is always a matter of degree. Why should it be different with self-esteem?

Much more could be said about validity and self-esteem research. For example, I could talk about the "plausibility" of a theory, which is the type of credibility that comes when ideas are useful in an applied or practical setting, regardless of whether they can be "proven" in the ordinary sense (Wells & Marwell, 1976). However, we are not so much concerned with explicating the scientific method as with understanding how it can be used to research, understand, and enhance authentic self-esteem.

By way of sum, then, four things appear to stand out at this second stop in our journey through the field. First, we see that qualitative and quantitative methods have been applied to the topic for a long time. Next, it is clear that there is a large body of qualitative and quantitative research currently available on the subject. Third, the field suffers from a need for some type of "consensus" (Wells & Marwell, 1976). Finally, a method that is capable of integrating qualitative and quantitative findings may help reach this goal. It is my position that the two-factor approach and integrated description allow us to make progress in this direction and I hope to demonstrate that in the next several chapters.

3

Major Self-Esteem Research Findings

The purpose of this chapter is to develop a working familiarity with many of the major findings about self-esteem, particularly those that are clinically relevant, as they are highly relevant to the applied nature of this book. In addition, the findings can also act as the building blocks for a comprehensive theory of self-esteem, which is to say one that is capable of integrating them into a meaningful whole. As before, the general criteria for identifying key findings are based on persistence and significance. Also note that there are now tens of thousands of studies that pertain to self-esteem. Given the length of this chapter, it may stand as one of the most comprehensive reviews in the field.

One problem in dealing with the findings is that most of them are based upon definitions of self-esteem that we found lacking. Nevertheless, they constitute the bulk of this field and some of them do reveal important things about self-esteem in spite of this limitation. Research using the two-factor approach is of particular interest for obvious reasons. Some of them were presented in Chapter 1 when introducing this approach, others will be mentioned in this chapter, and more will be presented in Chapter 5 when the two-factor theory I offer in this book is fully presented.

PARENTAL FACTORS AFFECTING SELF-ESTEEM

Genetic Predispositions

One of the newer trends to appear in the field of self-esteem is the study of possible genetic influences. Developmental psychology has been interested in how genes affect the emergence of such things as temperament and personality for some time now, and its research methods have become quite sophisticated. Neiss, Stevenson, and Sedikides (2003) reviewed this small but growing body of literature in relation to self-esteem. In general, they concluded that genetic influences account for 30% to 40% of the variance among self-esteem levels in siblings. According to this work, nonshared environmental factors, such as play, school, peers, work, and so forth, account for the largest portion of the variance and shared environmental factors explain a relatively small amount.

More specifically, biology appears to bring with it certain predispositions, such as energy level, basic temperament such as the well-known "big 5" personality factors, and certain physical, social, and cognitive abilities (or the lack of them). This work suggests that one's degree of extraversion, which is known to have a strong genetic component in regard to personality and happiness or subjective well-being (Baumgardner & Crothers, 2009), may pertain to self-esteem. Such a disposition to actively engage one's environment, for instance, could make a difference in how often or how vigorously one accepts challenges related to the acquisition of competence in school or initiates such things as relationships in adulthood. Of course, it is important to remember that most developmental work on genetics understands their influence in terms of possibility, not destiny. That is, the genetic component of behavior is thought to provide a biologically based range of potential, not a specific degree or amount.

A range has upper and lower limits but where one is located within that space varies, as it also depends on such nongenetic factors as circumstance and choice. Lyubomirsky (2001) makes much use of this fact in her hedonic theory of happiness, which is important in positive psychology. In the case of self-esteem, for example, if an individual is fortunate enough to be born into a family or culture that appreciates his or her particular constellation of characteristics and abilities, then a good person-environment fit is likely to occur. This situation is fortuitous in that it should help foster such things as being valued as a person and acquiring competence in many skills necessary for success. If one is not such a genetic or environmental lottery winner, so to speak, then one's self-esteem story is more likely to be complex, perhaps even difficult. The point is that although we should not make too much of genetic predispositions, they cannot be ignored.

Parental Support (Involvement)

Carl Rogers (1961) was among the first to emphasize the importance of positive parenting and self-esteem through his notions of unconditional and conditional parental regard. Unconditional positive regard describes the type of parenting characterized by recognizing that a given child is a unique person and involves helping him or her grow in ways that reflect individual values, interests, and so forth. Conditional parental regard pertains to the general practice of encouraging and supporting the child largely when he or she complies with the values and interests of the parents. Parental involvement was one of the first antecedents of self-esteem to show up in empirical work (Coopersmith, 1967) and still does today.

Usually, supportive parental involvement is presented as a positive force. For example, Gecas (1971) found that support from mother correlated more with developing a sense of worth in children, whereas support from father seemed to be tied more to the development of competence. He also noted that middle-class fathers tend to spend more time with their children than working-class parents, which increases opportunities for supportive engagement. Burger (1995) found that parents who encourage their children in the process of acquiring various skills offer more positive support than those who do not. Other work noted the importance of support by the effects of its absence. For instance, parents who are described as being indifferent toward their children, as well as parents who are absent frequently or absent for long periods of time, tend to have children with lower levels of self-esteem (Clark & Barber, 1994; Coopersmith, 1967; Rosenberg, 1965). Moreover, this effect may be particularly important for male children (Miller, 1984).

Parental "Warmth" (Acceptance)

Mere involvement does not seem to be enough. Rogers (1961) said that unconditional positive regard is an important general parental characteristic for building healthy self-esteem. However, Coopersmith (1967) found empirical support for the more specific parental practices of warmth and acceptance. This dimension of parenting is still recognized among those who work in self-esteem today (Bednar et al., 1989; Pope et al. 1988). Specifying the behavioral components of such a stance is difficult, but the term *acceptance* is used most often to describe a parent's willingness to see a child's strengths *and* weaknesses, potentials *and* limitations. Such acceptance is "warm" in that it is balanced, not blind, which means that mere approval is not enough and may even harm authentic self-esteem. The key to healthy or positive acceptance is to embrace children in ways that facilitate their ability to explore and engage the world in order to maximize such things as intrinsic values, mastery, self-awareness, and so forth, all of which are related to self-esteem (Kernis, 2003a).

This factor can also be illustrated by studying what happens when acceptance is absent. For example, Kernis (2003a) noted that a lack of warm or loving acceptance is detrimental to self-esteem. He found that when individuals suffer a deficit in this area, they often become more likely to base their sense of worth on extrinsic rather than intrinsic factors, which increases vulnerability and decreases happiness. Similarly, Crocker and Park (2003) found that students who place much of their worth on academic performance suffer a greater loss when they do not get accepted into graduate school than those who value other aspects of their person more highly. Finally, it should almost go without saying that parents who are harsh and derogatory or who practice such things as name calling and love withdrawal can have a negative effect on self-esteem (Kernis & Goldman, 2003).

Parental Expectations and Consistency

Mere involvement and simple acceptance do not necessarily lead to the development of authentic self-esteem because they can convey the mistaken impression that self-esteem is automatic, not earned. Clearly defined expectations and well-maintained limits are parental attitudes and behaviors associated with developing positive self-esteem in children (Coopersmith, 1967). Setting high but not impossible expectations, for instance, involves providing clear standards that help the development of the skills necessary to achieve competence. Setting goals and holding reasonably high behavioral standards also lets children know that certain forms of behavior are desirable, good, or "worthy" and, therefore, to be aspired to and strived toward. Such expectations also define the limits of behavior and help children make the important discovery that some forms of behavior are unacceptable or even unworthy, which may be just as important in healthy development.

Establishing and maintaining limits is important because failing to do so is destructive to self-esteem in the long run. For example, a long line of developmental literature shows that parental over-permissiveness is related to negative behaviors, such as impulsivity and aggressiveness. The same literature, which can be found in almost any standard text on child development (Newman & Newman, 1987; Sigelman & Shaffer, 1995), indicates that overly severe limits or those that are too harshly reinforced are also problematic. For instance, such practices may engender the development of anxious and restrictive behavior, rather than spontaneity and engagement with life.

Parenting Style

Treating children respectfully by acknowledging their essential humanity when dealing with them is another positive parental attitude associated with the development of self-esteem. Research on parental styles of discipline, for instance, suggests that rather than being authoritarian or permissive, the authoritative approach to parenting is more conducive to developing self-esteem in children (Coopersmith, 1967; Rathus, 2007). For instance, parental willingness to discuss matters and negotiate conflict, but not at the expense of violating certain basic standards of behavior, such as respecting the rights of others, is conducive to the formation of self-esteem. Of course, few people are naive enough to believe that one must always be democratic or authoritative. Rather, it is a matter of which discipline style one uses most often or of being a "good enough" parent (Winnicott, 1953). Kernis and Goldman (2003) noted that the mother's parenting style may be particularly important. However, Leary and MacDonald (2003) may have said it best when they summarized what research has to say about the relationship between parenting style and self-esteem: "Thus, parents who are approving, nurturant, and responsive tend to produce children with higher self-esteem than parents who are disapproving, uninterested, and unresponsive" (p. 413).

Other Parental Factors

There is a small but consistent stream of research beginning with Coopersmith (1967) suggesting that birth order can have an effect on self-esteem. All things considered, being firstborn slightly enhances the possibility of developing positive self-esteem, as does being an only child. Although there is no simple causal relationship between birth order and self-esteem, the general understanding seems to be that first and only children receive more attention from and interaction with parents than those who arrive later.

Finally, it stands to reason that modeling may also be a factor that pertains to the development of self-esteem, as it is with many other aspects of childhood. In other words, the old adage of "do as I say, not as I do" that parents often present to children appears to have some truth to it. For instance, Coopersmith (1967) studied children in laboratory-based or controlled situations where such phenomena could be observed. He was among the first to document a positive relationship between self-esteem levels and related behaviors in mothers and their children. Bednar et al. (1989) made considerable use of this factor by pointing out that parents actually *show* (i.e., live out, demonstrate, present by example) their children the route to self-esteem (or the lack of it) by how they handle their own challenges, conflicts, and issues. As they said, "The impact of parents' behavior upon the child's self-esteem is undeniable; given the immaturity of children, however, parents' expression of their own resolution of the self-esteem question is far more influential than what they teach verbally" (p. 257). Of course, it is very important to remember that models can work both ways: Many children are exposed to parents' unhealthy ways of coping with the challenges of living as well.

Summary

Although parents or primary caregivers are the first ones to bring these kinds of social factors into play, it is especially important to remember two things as we move on. First, these social forces never leave us. As Harter (1999) said,

> Across numerous studies with older children and adolescents, as well as college students and adults in the world of work and family, we have found that the correlations between perceived support from significant others and self-worth range from 0.50 to 0.65. (p. 175)

In short, basic human warmth, encouragement, respect, and support are necessary to the development or maintenance of self-esteem over the course of a lifetime. Second, no single family or social factor is overwhelmingly significant. After all, some children with "great" parents turn out to be quite poor in terms of their self-esteem and behavior, whereas many children with poor parenting turn out to be high self-esteeming individuals who demonstrate many desirable characteristics and behaviors.

This problem of weak statistical correlation is common in developmental psychology literature. For example, even basic texts on developmental psychology point out that the work on linking attachment style to adult relationship formation is statistically present but not very strong (Sigelman & Shaffer, 1995). Similarly, the emerging research on resilience shows that even when there are strong correlations between negative developmental environments and negative adult behavioral patterns, there are plenty of exceptions (Vaillant, 1995; Werner & Smith, 1992). Such factors are more accurately understood as being predisposing and interactive rather than causal or deterministic. They are *among* those conditions that increase (or, by their absence, decrease) the likelihood of healthy self-esteem. Instead of being dismayed by the weakness of the correlation between self-esteem and family factors as some critics lament, perhaps we ought to be thankful for it. The indeterminate nature of these variables means that the absence or diminishment of any one of them does not necessarily doom people to a lifetime of low self-esteem.

SELF-ESTEEM AND VALUES

In general, research seems to indicate that we cannot escape dealing with a relationship between values and self-esteem if we want to understand either self-esteem or its link to motivation and behavior. For example, it is clear that although people exhibiting high or low self-esteem obviously differ from each other, what they actually value concerning self-esteem is similar. As the "expectancy" literature on self-esteem would have it, "Both groups want to feel good about themselves" (Brockner, Wiesenfeld, & Raskas, 1993, p. 220). The difference seems to be in what each of these groups tends to expect about their respective chances of having positive feelings about themselves. For example, both groups of people value being successful, but they often have different expectations of how likely they are to prevail in this regard. Thus, the strategies they employ for filling in this part of the self-esteem picture differ markedly.

People with high self-esteem usually feel competent enough to take the risks of failure associated with success because they feel worthy enough to sustain a loss or setback. Therefore, they tend to set their sights high from the beginning and give their best efforts. Those with low self-esteem, by contrast, are often just as concerned with avoiding the loss of self-esteem as with gaining more. As a result, they tend to use what is called "self-handicapping" and other self-protective strategies, even as they go about trying to be successful (Snyder, 1989; Tice, 1993). Although perhaps a self-fulfilling prophecy, focusing on reasons one is likely to fail or holding back from trying one's very best seems to allow people with low self-esteem to better prepare for failure and reduce disappointment if it occurs, thereby preserving their self-esteem. Thus, both groups clearly value feeling good about themselves but differ in how they go about the process.

Social Values

Another set of findings concerns the way more socially derived values affect self-esteem. Historically, there has been debate between two aspects of this relationship (Rosenberg, 1979). The "stratification hypothesis" links self-esteem to general social groups such as socioeconomic class. The "subcultural hypothesis" sees self-esteem as being more closely connected to primary social groups, such as the neighborhood. Like many controversies in the social sciences, the answer to the question of which view is right is "both" because each set of factors is active. For example, researchers recognize a consistent, albeit weak, link between self-esteem and general social class in the expected direction (Coopersmith, 1967; Mack, 1987; Rosenberg, 1965; Schneiderman, Furman, & Weber, 1989; Twenge & Campbell, 2002). At the same time, those researchers agree that social factors within a subcultural group are more influential in determining a member's particular self-experience than the general social values of the larger society: These "local" values are formed earlier, experienced more directly, and reinforced more often, so they tend to have a stronger impact. The family and the neighborhood are seen as being a particularly powerful source of self-esteem-related values if people stay in touch with their roots over time.

Self-Values

In addition to having social values similar to people who are close to us, we also have values that are of particular interest to us as individuals. These self-values, as they are called (Pope et al., 1988), involve "the conceptions of the desirable that represent the individual's criteria for self-judgment" (Rosenberg, 1965, p. 15). They are important for self-esteem because self-values are connected to one's identity, which, in turn, creates a relationship between self-esteem and behavior as noted by James over a century ago. However, these values concerning that which is good and desirable are based more on direct, meaningful, and personal experience than are social or sub-cultural values. In other words, self-values are more individual because they arise intrinsically from the self and thereby affect us more directly. These self-values also help give us a sense of self-sameness or identity as a unique person, regardless of social class or background.

Research also shows that certain types of experiences can change self-values in ways that affect identity, self-esteem, and behavior. For example, Epstein's (1979) research suggested that "there are certain experiences that can be a turning point in an individual's existence" (p. 73). In this case, 270 subjects were asked to fill out forms that required them to describe such an experience and rate it according to various scales. This information was then analyzed to develop a typology of experiences, leading Epstein to conclude that "significant changes in self-concept are produced by three broad kinds of experience, namely exposure to a new environment, being required to make new responses, and establishment or loss of significant relationships" (p. 79).

Similarly, we saw in Chapter 1 that self-esteem seems to be affected by value conflicts within the self that manifest in certain types of challenges (Jackson, 1984; Mruk, 1983). This phenomenon typically happens in situations where people hold one basic self-value to be important but also find that it is simultaneously opposed by another deeply held belief. For instance, an individual can hold independence as a self-value worthy of aspiration, but the same person may also value security so much that he or she actually becomes dependent in relationships. Such value conflicts shape identity and create lively self-esteem stories that Jackson (1984) calls "central conflicts" and that I call "self-esteem themes."

The worthiness dimension of self-esteem means that it always involves values. Otherwise, how would we know what is worthy in the first place? However, researching values is challenging work. For one thing, values are difficult to measure, observe, or even define. In addition, the problem of relativity is always attached to values. Although learning theory and post-modernism (Gergen, 1991) tempt us to say that all values are culturally relative, it is dangerous to maintain that culture alone determines what is worthy. If we did that, for example, then we would also have to say that people could be worthy (i.e., "good") bullies, sexists, racists, or Nazis, and the like, as long as their primary social group promoted such values. Such a relativistic position is deeply disturbing to many and, as we shall momentarily see, may even be contradicted by emerging research from several respected perspectives.

Although proving their existence is a daunting task, evolutionary psychology (Leary, 2004) has shown that sometimes cooperative values have more use than competitive ones, so it might be argued that such values as self-sacrifice and cooperation are more "worthy" of emulation than mere selfishness based on biology itself. It is also possible to think in terms of the humanistic position, which is that human beings are innately disposed toward a hierarchy of good or healthy intrinsic values that is also grounded in our nature, not culture. After all, Rogers' (1961) concept of an innate tendency to grow and Maslow's notion of actualization as a natural tendency are both rooted in biology, although critics of this approach often forget this important fact. In addition, some cross-cultural work indicates that there are at least four things most human beings value, and self-esteem is one of them (Sheldon et al., 2001).

Although this aspect of the "value dimension" of self-esteem is always going to be controversial at some level, it is still essential to recognize the importance of values in work on self-esteem. For example, values, it can be argued, may lie at the heart of the worthiness component of self-esteem. After all, values were a part of Milton's original definition (that which is "just and right") and values help us identify what to feel good about in ourselves as well as in others. Finally, although it may seem as though values are relative, there seems to be a connection between self-esteem and positive psychology that suggests otherwise. We will see that, among other things, this approach focuses on researching basic human values called "virtues." These almost universally valued characteristics, which include such admirable qualities as courage and authenticity, are understood as being "deep" human structures (Peterson & Seligman, 2004). As such, they play an important role in human life that cannot be easily dismissed as being merely relative because they appear to transcend time, place, history, and culture around the world. We shall return to this topic when discussing the relationship between self-esteem and positive psychology in Chapter 7. For now, it must be said that there is little doubt that values are actively involved in acquiring and maintaining self-esteem.

SELF-ESTEEM AND SOCIAL FACTORS

Gender and Self-Esteem

Rosenberg noticed a possible interaction between gender and self-esteem as early as 1965 and more recent findings support it. For example, Epstein (1979) found that when females were asked to report on experiences related to self-esteem, they "reported more experiences involving acceptance and rejection, particularly acceptance, than males, and males reported slightly more experiences involving success and failure than females" (p. 62). However, he also noted that, although statistically significant, the difference was small. O'Brien and Epstein (1988) extended this work into the area of testing and measuring self-esteem and found differences in responses based on gender to be significant enough to require separate norms for males and females. Gender also seems to influence self-esteem to some degree even in childhood (Pallas, Entwisle, Alexander, & Weinstein, 1990). For example, Block and Robins (1993) reported that relating to others in positive ways enhanced self-esteem in women, but higher levels of independence and detachment are more highly correlated to self-esteem in men. As they said, "in crasser terms, females are socialized to get along in society and males are socialized to get ahead" (p. 920). At least until the turn of the century, the consensus was that the influence of gender runs in the expected direction, albeit modestly so.

Like others, Harter (1999) found that there is a drop in self-esteem during adolescence that affects both genders. However, females seem to experience a greater decline than males, particularly in the domain of self-esteem associated with satisfaction concerning one's physical appearance. Harter also discovered that one group of females appears to suffer a particularly large drop: those whose gender identification is strongly based on what might be called "traditional femininity." More androgynous females, by contrast, do not typically experience such a marked decrease in self-esteem.

Harter (1999) also noted that this finding calls into question some other work on self-esteem and gender. For example, much attention was given to the idea that women suffer low self-esteem in general because of discrimination, a lack of "voice," and other factors (American Association of University Women, 1991; Sanford & Donovan, 1984). However, Harter very strongly made the point that it is a particular subset of women who experience these difficulties, not women in general. Only those who live a type of femininity that fosters dependence on social approval and limits their ability to be assertive are the ones who seem to be vulnerable to this condition. This combination may create difficulties for achieving a healthy sense of competence earned through success, thereby forming a real self-esteem dilemma if both factors are needed for genuine self-esteem. Such dynamics may be at work in the findings that suggest that teen pregnancy may be associated with low self-esteem as well (Emler, 2001).

Similarly, it must also be pointed out that pushing men toward competence may be just as detrimental because it may diminish their access to sources of worthiness: Being too "macho" often results in a lack of healthy social acceptance or support. For example, some work indicates that males who are unemployed may suffer damage to their self-esteem (Waters & Moore, 2002). Other work suggests that the gender difference seems to be much less prominent (O'Brien, Leitzel, & Mensky, 1996), perhaps reflecting some cultural shifts in this area, at least in America. In short, it may be best to conclude that culture influences self-esteem in terms of gender more than gender influences self-esteem, and that both genders need competence and worthiness to have healthy self-esteem.

Racial, Ethnic, and Economic Factors Affecting Self-Esteem

The questions of whether and how racial, ethnic, and economic forces affect self-esteem have been a part of the field for decades. The basic issue first seemed resolved by Rosenberg and Simmons (1971), who did a large research project involving 1,917 students in urban schools, many of whom were African Americans. They reported that, contrary to popular assumptions at the time, African American children do not have lower self-esteem than Caucasian children. Indeed, they examined 12 other studies done on this topic from 1963 to 1970 and found that "while the results probably do not justify the conclusion that blacks have higher self-esteem than whites, the weight of the evidence certainly does not seem to support the general conclusion that their self-esteem is lower" (p. 8). Later, Twenge and Crocker (2002) undertook a large meta-analysis of race, ethnicity, and self-esteem. They confirmed the basic finding, but went beyond it to other groups. "From highest to lowest self-esteem scores, the groups are ordered as follows: Blacks, Whites, Hispanics, American Indians, and Asians" (p. 377). They also examined the question of how to understand these major self-esteem findings by considering four different explanations.

The first one is based on the concept of *internalized stigma*, which is based on the notion of the "generalized other." It suggests that if society as a whole looks down on an entire group, then people in that group should do the same because they have internalized that generalized other in constructing their identities. *Stigma as self-protection* is an explanation that sees self-esteem as buffered from the effect of discrimination by selective comparison. In this case, an individual who is a member of a minority group that is the subject of discrimination may discount failure in a particular domain by attributing such an event to external causes, such as the social forces of discrimination, instead of internal ones, such as a lack of ability, thereby protecting the self. The *positive racial identity hypothesis* suggests that self-esteem could be higher in a minority group because that group focuses largely on its positive qualities, which elevates its status at least in their own eyes.

Finally, the *cultural differences hypothesis* maintains that certain aspects of cultural identity, particularly whether it is based more on the individual or the group, could account for the data. In this case, groups that value individualism would be likely to emphasize such things as personal performance, especially success, which would be reflected on measures of self-esteem that detect such a variable. Conversely, groups that downplay the role of the individual would also tend to de-emphasize personalizing success, which could depress scores on the same measures. Twenge and Crocker then compared each hypothesis with the data and found that, with little question, the cultural difference hypothesis seems to be the only one that is able to account for all the findings. In other words, the central variable that runs through each group in the expected direction is the degree to which its culture emphasizes the individual. In the case of race or ethnicity, the results appear as they do because, as a group, African Americans tend to emphasize the role of the individual slightly more than Whites. Whites, in turn, emphasize this quality more than collectively oriented minorities. Although the other explanations may have value at certain times, they are not as scientifically parsimonious as this one.

Self-Esteem in Relationships

In more recent years, considerable attention has been given to self-esteem in the context of relationships. One study examining this body of work identified 10 themes that characterize this area (Mruk, in press). In general, it was found that the role of low self-esteem in relationships stands out as a research priority that has generated a considerable body of findings that any comprehensive work on self-esteem must consider.

For example, people with low self-esteem tend to underestimate the degree to which a partner perceives the former's positive qualities (Bellavia & Murray, 2003). In addition to working very hard cognitively to diminish positive affirmations about themselves, they are also more likely to be sensitive to signs of disapproval from others. Both such tendencies reinforce negative self-beliefs and low self-esteem (Sciangula & Morry, 2009). Similarly, those who suffer low self-esteem seem inclined to engage in self-protective measures, such as avoiding conflict in relationships and distancing themselves from their partners, rather than effectively dealing with problems, which is necessary for relationship maintenance or growth (Sommer, 2001).

Downey and Feldman (1996) referred to this type of phenomenon as "rejection sensitivity" and pointed out that it can lead to more negative forms of self-protection with more damaging results, such as blaming, criticizing, or even derogating the partner. In addition, people with low self-esteem appear to be more open to relationship-disrupting behaviors, such as flattery from others, than those with high self-esteem who seem more secure in their relationships and express less interest in such flirtation. There is even some evidence linking low self-esteem and the likelihood of using violence in an attempt to manage relationships under certain conditions, especially when alcohol is involved (Stinson, Logel, Zanna, Holmes, & Cameron, 2008). All of these things act to reinforce low self-esteem in a strong, dynamic fashion.

Acceptance has been shown to be connected to self-esteem, so it is reasonable to expect acceptance to play a role in the way that self-esteem functions in relationships. For example, Cramer (2003) found an association between self-esteem, relationship satisfaction, and degree of acceptance (which, in turn, affects self-esteem) in romantic relationships. Harter (1999) reported that those who suffered difficulties in the area of social acceptance from parents, peers, or teachers, for example, tend to have lower self-esteem in social domains. Those who study what is called "relationship-contingent self-esteem" make the point that a lack of acceptance may manifest itself in a number of ways, such as a strong need to be accepted by others or being more sensitive to rejection (Knee, Canevello, Bush, & Cook, 2008), both of which have negative implications for self-esteem.

Similarly, attention is given to the relationship between attachment style and relationships, with self-esteem acting as a moderator (Park, Crocker, & Vohs, 2006). Self-expansion theorists, as they are called, note that being accepted helps individuals to take the types of risk that are necessary in a relationship for it to grow and develop in ways that foster self-actualization (Aron, Ketay, Reila, & Aron, 2008). The lack of acceptance may even be more powerful. Leary (2008) found that being excluded typically creates a much larger drop in self-esteem than being accepted by others increases it. Self-esteem even appears to play a role in sexual behavior and satisfaction (Menard & Offman, 2009). Zeigler-Hill, Campe, and Myers (2009) found that sexual standards are in some way connected to self-esteem: In general, women tend to have higher sexual standards than men in sexual partner selection, higher even than men with high self-esteem.

All things considered, one conclusion often reached by researchers investigating self-esteem in relationships is that the dynamics of self-esteem act as a self-fulfilling prophecy in them (Baldwin, 2006; Berenson & Downey, 2006; Leary, 2008; Murray, 2008). Those with low self-esteem are very vulnerable to moving into a negative self-fulfilling relational cycle: After all, people with low self-esteem seem to need relationships more than others, perhaps to make up for a lack of a sense of inherent worth. However, they often engage in self-protective behaviors that diminish the chances for a relationship to form or deepen, thereby increasing chances for loneliness, conflict, or rejection. In contrast and in support of this self-fulfilling view, people with high self-esteem seem to engage in the opposite behaviors, such as taking the risks for initiating a relationship or allowing themselves to be vulnerable in order to resolve a conflict and thereby nurture the relationship. Berenson and Downey (2006) call these behaviors "rejection-prevention strategies." In other words, high self-esteem also seems to work as a self-fulfilling prophecy, but this time one that moves in a positive direction.

Culture and Self-Esteem

A relatively new development in the field concerns the relationship between culture and self-esteem, and now this work includes cross-cultural studies. Like much cross-cultural work, the dominant theme seems to be making comparisons between individualistic cultures, or those that emphasize independence and the role of the person in social life, and collectivistic societies, which focus more on interdependence and communal social structures for identity construal (Pettijohn, 1998, p. 67). At this point, there appear to be two schools of thought on the general relationship between culture and self-esteem (Mruk, in press).

On one hand, there are those who maintain that a conception of self-esteem based on either competence or worthiness is a largely Western phenomenon. For example, Hewitt (2002) saw self-esteem as a social construction, something that arises out of contemporary culture to meet contemporary needs, particularly in America. He argued that even the term self-esteem is relatively new and then went on to "deconstruct" it as a "linguistic space" that is created to help individuals make sense out of emotional reactions that involve the self. Similarly, Crocker and Park (2004) pointed out that self-esteem, or at least pursuing it, is a "particularly American phenomenon, born of the nation's founding ideologies" (p. 405), especially our emphasis on the importance of the individual, the history of the Protestant ethic, and the idea of a meritocracy. Then, they compared this cultural orientation with a Japanese cultural emphasis on the group, an incremental or continuous approach to personal improvement, and the importance of relationships rather than personal achievements. They concluded by supporting the position that culture determines the importance of self-esteem.

On the other hand, Tafarodi and Swann (1996) investigated the issue of the relationship between self-esteem and culture at some length. They also recognized the possibility that self-esteem may only be a Western concept or phenomenon, which would mean that it is not a basic human need. However, when they reviewed several studies on self-esteem in collectivistic cultures, namely several Eastern societies, it was found that when self-esteem is defined in terms of two factors (competence and worth) rather than one, self-esteem seems important in collective cultures as well. Tafarodi and Swann concluded that the differences found in individualistic versus collectivistic self-esteem can be accounted for by what they named a "cultural trade-off."

The trade, of course, occurs in terms of emphasizing one component of self-esteem over the other. What appears to happen cross-culturally from this perspective is that both factors are always present, but a culture may load self-evaluation in one direction more than the other. Such a trade-off would be consistent with the individual focus of one culture and the communal orientation of another. Thus, in a highly individualistic culture, we would expect to find people evaluating themselves in ways that emphasize their competence through such things as personal success or achievement, as Crocker and Park noted above. At the same time, it would also be reasonable to expect people in a culture built on communal or collective structures to focus more on a sense of one's value in relation to others, which tends to emphasize worthiness more and which may also account for Crocker's and Park's findings mentioned above.

Similarly, Pillemer, Ivcevic, Gooze, and Collins (2007) found that individual achievements are often emphasized by North Americans when recalling memories concerning the self, but their more communally oriented Japanese subjects focused much more on interpersonal and group membership experiences or events. Kwan, Bond, and Singelis (1997) found that both American and Hong Kong samples rated self-esteem as being important for life satisfaction. However, the latter also rated the quality of their relationships with others, or "relationship harmony," as equally important for happiness and the former did not. Such findings also are compatible with the notion of a trade-off, because in collective cultures interpersonal harmony is seen as more valuable and more worthy than in individualistic ones.

Moreover, Brown, Cai, Oakes, and Deng (2009) found that failure produced less stress in those with high self-esteem in both American and Chinese samples, suggesting this function of self-esteem transcends culture. Finally, of course, Sheldon et al. (2001) offer some surprising evidence supporting the position that self-esteem is a basic human need and, therefore, cross-cultural in nature. They began by examining major need theories and developed a list of the 10 most frequently mentioned needs. They are autonomy, competence, relatedness, physical thriving, security, self-esteem, self-actualization, pleasure-stimulation, money-luxury, and popularity-influence. Then, they asked people to identify experiences that were satisfying for them to see if any of the needs were more universal than others at the lived level. Interestingly, "self-esteem, relatedness, and autonomy emerged in a three-way tie at the top of the list" (p. 329). Competence was rated fourth.

This type of work indicates that self-esteem is a very basic human need, especially if one considers relatedness as a form of worth and competence as involving autonomy as well as ability. One of the most fascinating aspects of this study is that this finding occurred across highly individualistic cultures, such as Americans, and in very collectivistic ones, such as the Korean culture, *just as should be the case if we are looking at a basic human need.* Thus, it is important to realize that just because cultures appear to differ in terms of emphasizing competence or worthiness as a more focal interest, all human beings seem to recognize the value of both factors, which is also consistent with the two-factor theory as a universal approach.

THE SOURCES OF SELF-ESTEEM

Stanley Coopersmith (1967) was one of the first to study the sources of self-esteem and identified four: power (the ability to influence or control others), significance (being valued by others as shown by their acceptance), virtue (the adherence to moral standards), and competence (successful perform-ance in regard to a goal). Epstein (1979) pointed out that if success is involved in self-esteem, then the possibility of failure also must be active. Hence, he described four similar sources, but characterized them more dynamically: Achievement is balanced by setbacks and loss, power is offset by power-lessness, acceptance is coupled with the possibility of rejection, and moral self-acceptance must also include the possibility of shame or guilt. There is so much convergence between these two independent lines of work that the results stand out as a basic finding according to the criteria we are using. Thus, it is helpful to clarify them.

Acceptance Versus Rejection

Although varying with age, acceptance (or, conversely, rejection) affects our self-feeling through our relationships with parents or caregivers, sib-lings, peers, friends, spouses or partners, co-workers or colleagues, and so on throughout our lives. But there are other words that describe this source of self-esteem. For example, Harter (1999) made the same observa-tion but used the term "relational self-worth" in her work. I prefer "being valued" in my clinical work because that phrase describes something of the significance of what goes on in an accepting relationship or in positive social interactions in general. In any case, no matter how it is expressed, acceptance is a source of self-esteem because when we are valued in this way, our worth as an individual is recognized or affirmed by others and we respond to it in a positive way.

It is also important to realize that there are many ways that accept-ance and rejection can be alive in relation to the development and main-tenance of self-esteem. For instance, care, nurturance, and attraction are important features of acceptance, but respect, fondness, and admiration are often more common or appropriate in a professional relationship. Similarly, there are several modes of being rejected, such as being ignored, devalued, marginalized, used, mistreated, or abandoned, which may negatively affect self-esteem (Epstein, 1979). Even as adults, who has not experienced the increase in self-esteem that comes with a new positive relationship, such as love, or the decrease that usually accompanies an interpersonal loss involving betrayal or abandonment? In all cases, we are dealing with interpersonal events concerning whether or not one is valued by others.

Virtue Versus Guilt

Coopersmith's (1967) definition of virtue, which is the adherence to moral and ethical standards, is close to Epstein's "moral self-acceptance" and O'Brien and Epstein's (1988) notion of "moral self-approval." I tend to use the phrase "acting on beliefs," but I do not wish to add terms to the field when plenty of good ones are already available. We will use Coopersmith's term "virtue" because it implies that there are higher values or standards of behavior to follow in order to merit consideration as a worthy person, rather than simply measuring up to some culturally relativistic code of conduct. Virtue may also be closer to the way in which Milton used the term in regard to that which is "just and right."

Failure, in this domain, of course involves such things as shame and guilt, particularly what existentialists call "authentic guilt." The lived connection between being virtuous and self-esteem was identified earlier when we examined the findings about values and self-esteem in certain types of self-esteem moments: Each time we *act* virtuously, or in a way that is recognized as adhering to a reasonable standard concerning what is desirable, healthy, or "good," we also find ourselves as already *being* more worthy because our actions express ourselves in these situations. Each time we fail to respond in this way also affects self-esteem, but in a correspondingly negative or inauthentic way. Although much of psychology seems to have forgotten about concepts like virtue, we will encounter this dimension of self-esteem in more detail when we examine the relationship between self-esteem and positive psychology in Chapter 7.

Influence Versus Powerlessness

Power is the word that both Coopersmith (1967) and Epstein (1979) chose to describe one's ability to manage or direct one's environment. However, in this case, I will use the word "influence" to describe this source of self-esteem and break with tradition for two reasons. First, power over one's environment may capture something of how this kind of behavior is actually lived, but other people can be a part of one's environment, too. However, it is difficult to embrace the idea that a person who acts on his or her environment to meet individual ends while negatively affecting others is actually tapping into an authentic source of self-esteem. In addition, the word may be too strong to describe the full range of possibility concerning this source of self-esteem. Although power can be used to describe a way of relating to others, it does not capture more subtle aspects of interacting with others effectively, such as gentle or loving persuasion.

Second, there may be a gender-based problem with the term "power" in that it can be too forceful to be genuinely descriptive. For instance, I have found in working with both academic and clinical self-esteem enhancement groups that women often object to this term. When asked why, the most commonly offered response is that, for them, power carries too much of a negative connotation, as in "power over someone" or "the abuse of power." When I ask what term they would prefer, the word "influence" is recommended most often, perhaps because it is more gender-free or maybe even because it is simply more descriptive and, therefore, more accurate. In any event, the ability to interact with the environment, including others in it, in a way that shapes or directs events, is a form of competence that is relevant to dealing with the challenges of living. Success in this area leads to a sense of having some "say so" or "voice" in life and is often called "empowerment," which is a more helpful concept to many. Conversely, too many failures tend to engender a sense of inadequacy, incompetence, or even helplessness, depending on how frequent or severe the failures happen to be, all of which bode ill for self-esteem.

Achievements Versus Failures

Coopersmith (1967) used the word "competence" when talking about a source of self-esteem. However, that term is too broad for our purposes because it is also used to describe one of the two basic components of self-esteem. Epstein (1979) chose the word "success" to describe this class of possibilities, but it suffers from being too general. For example, we can say that it is good for a person's self-esteem to be "successful" in regard to any of the other three sources of self-esteem. I use the term "achievement" because it avoids these problems and because it is more accurate in describing this particular source of self-esteem. After all, it is not just any kind of competence or success that matter in terms of self-esteem. We all know, for example, people who are successful in this or that area of life but who also have obvious problems with self-esteem. Moreover, achievement carries with it a much stronger personal connotation than does mere success.

Indeed, starting with William James, a whole string of self-esteem theorists and researchers point out that success must be in a domain or area that matters to the individual in terms of his or her identity before it has any value for self-esteem. For example, brushing one's teeth is not a particularly significant act for most of us, but it may be a great personal achievement for an intellectually or physically challenged individual. There also appears to be a set of extraordinary personal achievements that affect self-esteem in an extremely powerful way. For instance, the research by Epstein (1979), Jackson (1984), and Mruk (1983) indicates that when we reach a goal that requires dealing effectively with problems or obstacles that also have personal or biographical significance, we demonstrate a higher level of competence at dealing with the challenges of living.

Competence and Worthiness as the Two Basic Sources of Self-Esteem

There is one more important point to explore concerning the sources of self-esteem. It concerns what is called "variability," or how individuals can use these four sources in different ways to obtain self-esteem. Coopersmith (1967) maintained that individuals may develop healthy levels of self-esteem by being successful in just one or two areas, particularly if these domains of life are approved of by their primary reference group: "We should note that it may be possible for an individual to attain high self-esteem by notable attainment in any of the four areas. This might occur even where attainment in the other areas was mediocre or even poor" (p. 38).

Bradshaw (1981, p. 7) offered an economic analogy based on the concepts of income and savings that describes how this view of self-esteem works. He viewed all the experiences that may enhance self-esteem in life as a reserve of potential self-esteem "income." Which type of experiences an individual chooses to use as a "deposit" to place in this self-esteem "account" does not matter in this model because all of them go to the same place. Only the strength or frequency of the "income flow" determines the degree or level of our self-esteem. Failures can be seen as detracting from self-esteem, much like a debit in an account. But, blocking any one route is not necessarily a problem because others can be used to compensate for such a development. Only the total amount matters.

This position creates an important contradiction that must be resolved. On one hand, it appears as though self-esteem can come from any of the four sources of self-esteem. On the other, we saw in Chapter 1 that basing self-esteem on only one factor is a theoretical and behavioral dead end. How are we to make sense of this apparent contradiction?

One way is to understand the various aspects of the problem in the light of the fundamental structure of self-esteem. Success and achievement are clearly tied to competence, but they are not sufficient to create self-esteem because we have seen that unbalanced competence only creates a state of contingency, not authentic self-esteem. One can even be competent at very negative or even morally repugnant behaviors because that combination clearly contradicts the worthiness component of the two-factor definition. Turning to worthiness as a sufficient source of self-esteem is no solution either. For one thing, acceptance does not give us the skills that are necessary to master the ordinary tasks of life, let alone its challenges. For another, the fundamental structure of self-esteem shows us that worth must be earned. Otherwise, we would have to include narcissism as authentic self-esteem, and research clearly indicates that they are different (Campbell, Rudich, & Sedikides, 2002).

The most scientifically parsimonious way to resolve this situation is to stay with the "facts themselves," which we saw in the fundamental structure as involving a relationship between competence and worthiness. This framework allows us to see that influence and achievement involve some degree of mastery and skill, which means that they are connected to self-esteem through competence. Acceptance and virtue are connected to being worthy to others or acting in ways that are regarded as worthy, so they are tied to that component. However, we also know that competence and worthiness must balance each other in order to create self-esteem. Thus, it is *not* the case that one may have authentic self-esteem through any particular source or any random combination of the four possibilities. Instead, it is quite clear that authentic self-esteem requires accessing either influence or achievement *and* acceptance or virtue: Although it may seem like there are four sources of self-esteem at first glance, a deeper analysis shows that there are only two, and that both competence and worthiness must be accessed in order for one to have authentic self-esteem.

THE PARADOXES REVISITED

In Chapter 2, we described several key self-esteem research issues as para-doxes because certain aspects of self-esteem stand out when viewed from one angle and their opposite emerges when seen from another. Although not every issue may be resolved, current research offers a higher degree of understanding than in the past, and a two-factor approach may allow us to reconcile such dilemmas by understanding them as something akin to the well-known "figure-ground" phenomenon that is found in the psy-chology of perception.

The Function of Self-Esteem Is to Maintain *and* to Expand the Self

When describing this paradox in Chapter 2, it was said that the connec-tion between self-esteem and behavior is most often talked about in terms of needs. For instance, Gecas pointed out that "The motivation to main-tain and enhance a positive conception of oneself has been thought to be pervasive, even universal" (1982, p. 20). The same position can be found among those who represent an evolutionary point of view. For example, Leary and Downs noted that "In a discipline with few universally accepted principles, the proposition that people are motivated to maintain and enhance their self-esteem has achieved the rare status of an axiom" (1995, p. 123). The most convincing research on this issue may be that of Sheldon et al. (2001), who did a large cross-cultural study examining major human needs mentioned earlier. Even those who are critical of self-esteem admit that, at least in social psychology, understanding self-esteem as a need is "axiomatic" (Crocker & Park, 2003).

Except for those who see self-esteem strictly as a result rather than a cause of behavior, such as Seligman (1990), most researchers seem to see self-esteem as a basic need that centers around what is called "self-regulation." This term is used to describe such things as the management of the self, identity, and related personal as well as interpersonal behavior. On one hand, some researchers emphasize self-regulatory processes aimed at stabilizing or maintaining the self, which is described as the self-protective function of self-esteem (Leary & Downs, 1995; Mecca et al. 1989; Wells & Marwell, 1976). Even Baumeister et al. described this aspect of self-esteem as providing "a stock of positive feelings that can be a valuable resource under some conditions" (2003, p. 37), such as when protecting the self under stress.

Others understand self-esteem as providing a similar function in regard to relationship stability (Sciangula & Morry, 2009). Leary (2004), for instance, found that people experience a drop in self-esteem when they engage in behavior that is likely to result in social rejection or exclusion, and that such a drop in positive self-feelings prompts individuals to engage in restorative behaviors. Both self-maintenance and self-consistency theories, which play large roles in this area, focus on the protective self-regulatory function of self-esteem in the interpersonal context and each is accompanied by a good body of supportive work (Mruk, in press).

On the other hand, another group presents equally impressive research supporting the position that the regulatory function of self-esteem is more future than present oriented. Such self-expansion or self-enhancement theories, as they are often called (Aron, Ketay, Riela, & Aron, 2008; Brown, Collins, & Schmidt, 1988), emphasize the developmental function of self-esteem. This type of motivational picture of self-esteem was seen in psychodynamic literature in terms of White's (1963) work on competence and has always been a part of the humanistic tradition (Maslow, 1954/1970).

Today researchers present more empirical evidence for how it is that self-esteem helps allow us to expand the self through personal and interpersonal risk-taking. For instance, we mentioned work that found that those who have high self-esteem tend to engage in behavior that makes the self more vulnerable, rather than protecting it, in order to initiate, nurture, or heal relationships (Berenson & Downey, 2006). This dimension of self-esteem allows us to better tolerate the anxiety involved in accepting a challenge, exposing ourselves to potential rejection, or putting our own needs aside in order to address those of another in a significant relationship so that it may continue to grow and develop over time.

Instead of focusing on what could be seen as a dichotomy, a third approach may be able to integrate both the protective and the actualizing functions of self-esteem. One of the earliest researchers to understand self-esteem as having two functions that balance each other said that, "As aspects of the self-esteem motive, self-enhancement emphasizes growth, expansion, and increasing one's self-esteem, while self-maintenance focuses on *not* losing what one has. The two engender different behavioral strategies" (Gecas, 1982, p. 21). Epstein (1980, 1985) went further and placed these two functions of self-esteem at the center of his entire self-theory. In this case, these processes dynamically work together to provide the self with the protection needed to maintain consistency, but in a way that also allows it, under certain conditions, to loosen up enough to take risks and then reorganize at a higher level.

More recently, work on self-determination theory (Greenberg, Pyszczynski, & Solomon, 1995), sociometer theory (Leary & Downs, 1995), and terror management theory (Pyszczynski et al. 2003) tie self-esteem to both regulatory functions because that would be the most adaptive possibility. The evidence suggests that the function of self-esteem is to help regulate personal and social behavior in both ways, which indeed makes self-esteem a very important need.

In sum, it seems fairly clear that there is considerable agreement among researchers that self-esteem is needed in order to maintain a stable, consistent sense of self and connections to others, *and* is necessary to allow the self to grow or expand in these ways as well. Self-handicapping strategies, negative thinking patterns, and self-protective relational behaviors such as withdrawal are common forms of defensive behavior most often identified with maintaining the self and regulating behavior in ways that provide a sense of stability as well as consistency. Reasonable risk-taking, a sense of self-efficacy, positive cognitive appraisals of self and others, and prosocial behaviors that foster the development of meaningful relationships are most frequently associated with growth and expansion (Mruk, in press). Instead of a paradox, the need for self-esteem and the regulatory function it serves may be more like the two sides of a coin: Both are always present, but at any given time one is usually more active or visible than the other.

Self-Esteem as Traits *and* States: Basic Types and Levels

Historically, most of the work on self-esteem distinguishes between its various types, particularly "high" or "low" self-esteem. Now we know that the self-esteem picture is much more complex than simple typologies could accommodate. For example, now there appear to be several types of self-esteem, each of which can manifest itself in one of two ways, called levels. We begin with low self-esteem because this unfortunate condition has been studied the most.

Low Self-Esteem

We have already seen that low self-esteem is associated with many general negative affective and behavioral states. After studying self-esteem for over three decades, Rosenberg and Owens (2001) identified low levels as being connected to hypersensitivity, instability, self-consciousness, lack of self-confidence, threat vigilance, lack of risk-taking, general depression, pessimism, loneliness, and alienation. However, research also shows that although not without consequence for well-being, far less debilitating nonclinical characteristics are often associated with low self-esteem as well. For example, Campbell and Lavallee (1993, p. 14) found people with low self-esteem more often utilize self-protective strategies in order to maintain their current level of self-esteem. They identified several of them, such as avoiding taking risks (which makes raising self-esteem through achievements difficult to do), focusing on one's own negative qualities (which tends to make self-perception and experience less pleasant or worthy, but stable), and minimizing attention to one's self (which may limit various interpersonal and relational opportunities).

In addition, it was also found that such individuals often demonstrate a lack of clarity concerning their identity and are more sensitive to self-relevant social cues. "In other words, the self-presentational styles of people with low self-esteem are not self-derogatory but self-protective, cautious, and conservative" (Campbell & Lavallee, 1993, p. 14). Another general characteristic of low self-esteem is a tendency to readily engage in negative thinking patterns by "overgeneralizing" mistakes, negative events, and the like (Kernis, 2003a). Self-handicapping strategies and a tendency to resist positive information about themselves in favor of focusing on negative feedback were found to be other characteristics commonly associated with low self-esteem (Campbell, 1999; Epstein & Morling, 1995; Tennen & Affleck, 1993; Tice, 1993; Wood, Giordano-Beech, Taylor, Michela, & Gaus, 1994). Finally, we saw that people with low self-esteem tend to engage in protective relational behaviors, such as withdrawal, in order to protect themselves when the relationship is stressed (Sommer, 2001).

However, as any clinician knows, low self-esteem also seems to exist at another deeper or clinical level as well. For example, low self-esteem is a diagnostic criterion or associated characteristic of nearly two-dozen mental disorders, including "dysthymic disorder, major depression, anxiety disorder, eating disorders, sexual dysfunction, pathological shame, suicide attempts, and an array of personality disorders in both children and adults" (Leary & MacDonald, 2003, p. 412). In addition, there are other situations that often become a clinical problem involving low self-esteem, which may or may not carry a particular diagnosis. One of them is the effect of trauma.

Abuse during childhood is worth spending some time with as an example of how more severe levels of low self-esteem can become clinically significant in this way. One of the more impressive studies supporting the position that sexual abuse has powerful developmental, behavioral, and clinical implications for a developing person is found in the work of Swanston, Tebbutt, O'Toole, and Oates (1997). This study is one of the earliest to involve a well-stratified sample of reasonably good size (86 participants) that was compared to a similar control group that did not experience abuse. Subjects were also followed for a 5-year period, which gives the work longitudinal strength. In addition to confirming the general finding that many sexually abused children suffer increased rates of several types of mental health problems, it also found that the impact of the abuse may continue to take a toll on self-esteem over time.

One useful way of understanding the effects of abuse in relation to self-esteem and its relationship to behavior is found in Finkelhor's and Browne's (1985) model of traumatization. This view identifies four "traumagenic dynamics" that are associated with the "categories of psychological injury experienced by children who have been sexually abused" (p. 605). They are sexual traumatization (learning age-inappropriate sexual behavior), betrayal (feelings of depression, hostility, or isolation associated with the abuse), powerlessness (described as anxiety, a decreased sense of personal efficacy, and an increased risk of victimization in the future), and stigmatization (a sense of self-blame or shame).

Note that at least two of these dimensions, power and stigma, are related to competence and worthiness, respectively. Thus, the two-factor model offers a relatively direct pathway to understanding how it is that abuse may take a serious toll on self-esteem and its development. Of course, it is also important to note that, just as with any traumatic event in general, which particular problem develops, or whether one even develops at all, depends on a host of variables. They include such things as the identity of those involved, the frequency and severity of trauma, one's age and level of developmental maturity, the degree of social support present, one's particular personality, and resilience. Nevertheless, it is clear that one of the most damaging potential effects of childhood abuse is how it may affect self-esteem.

High Self-Esteem

Originally and for many decades, high self-esteem was almost invariably associated with desirable positive abilities and characteristics, something that helped it to become a major psychological concept in the developmental as well as clinical literature. However, contemporary research suggests that not all forms of high self-esteem are positive, a condition that now generates considerable confusion both within and outside the field.

We saw this dimension of self-esteem collectively referred to as its dark side, which complicates the older view.

On one hand, most of the positive characteristics traditionally associated with high self-esteem are still affirmed. It is even possible to differentiate them into two general types: those that help maintain the self and those that assist the self to grow and develop or expand. The maintenance function of self-esteem that has received most empirical support concerns its capacity to act as a buffer. For example, even Baumeister et al. (2003) admitted that the evidence supports understanding high self-esteem as a protective factor: one that helps people to deal with stress and to avoid anxiety, which, in turn, helps them to engage in more adaptive responses. Furthermore, research on terror management theory offers considerable empirical support for the importance of self-esteem in managing ordinary anxiety and even existential anxiety about death (Greenberg et al., 1995; Pyszczynski et al., 2003). In short, the "anxiety buffer hypothesis" about high self-esteem, as it is often called, is confirmed.

The enhancement function of self-esteem also has received considerable support both from research on self-esteem and from positive psychologists. For example, there is a positive statistical relationship between high self-esteem and happiness (Baumeister et al., 2003), thereby making high self-esteem generally desirable. Similarly, the "hedonic" quality of high self-esteem makes it attractive: People with high self-esteem simply feel better about themselves, their relationships, the future, and about life in general than do those with low self-esteem (Baumgardner & Crothers, 2009). High self-esteem is also associated with preferable personal and interpersonal characteristics and behavior, such as job performance and problem-solving, especially under conditions that require initiative and persistence (Baumeister et al., 2003; Dubois & Flay, 2004). Moreover, high self-esteem is also associated with extraversion (Leary & MacDonald, 2003), autonomy (Kernis, 2003a; Leary & MacDonald, 2003), and authenticity (Kernis, 2003b).

In addition, there is empirical support linking high self-esteem to various types of other healthy behavior and states. For example, we have already seen how high self-esteem is associated with positive relational phenomena. Some work also connects positive self-esteem to such prosocial things as higher moral standards (Leary & MacDonald, 2003), better educational behavior (Harter, Whitesell, & Junkin, 1998), and greater interest in one's physical well-being and health care, especially in regard to such things as maintaining lower levels of cholesterol and limiting alcohol consumption (DeHart, Tennen, Armeli, Todd, & Afflect, 2008). Finally, high self-esteem may even have long-term benefits. "Higher levels of self-esteem similarly have been found in other research to prospectively predict growth in socioemotional functioning among younger, preschool-age children ... and, at the other end of the developmental continuum, decreased likelihood of mortality among older adults" (Dubois & Flay, 2004, p. 416). Clearly, then, high self-esteem is linked to the good life.

However, research also indicates that there are less than positive, and even distinctly negative, characteristics associated with high self-esteem when it is broadly defined that must be dealt with in any comprehensive theory. For example, people with high self-esteem have been shown to sometimes place success over well-being and to demonstrate more in-group favoritism than others (Baumeister et al., 2003; Crocker & Park, 2003). They may blame others for their own shortcomings in relationships or engage in downward social comparisons that put others down personally (Crocker & Park, 2004; Harter, 1999). Some higher self-esteem individuals appear to think more of their value to others in relationships than is actually deserved and they may overvalue the contributions they make in group situations (Baumeister et al., 2003).

In addition, high self-esteem has been associated with some genuinely negative conditions, such as defensiveness (Crocker & Park, 2004; Epstein & Morling, 1995; Greenier, Kernis, & Waschull, 1995; Jordan, Spencer, Zanna, Hoshino-Browne, & Correll, 2003; Kernis, 2003a) and narcissism (Baumeister et al., 1996; Campbell et al., 2002; Crocker & Park, 2003; Sedikides, Rudich, Gregg, Kumashiro, & Rusbult, 2004). Finally, high self-esteem has also been implicated in some types of genuinely anti-social behavior and even violence (Baumeister et al., 1996; Salmivalli, Kaukiainen, & Lagerspetz, 1999).

In sum, once again, we see that research on self-esteem has expanded considerably and has done so in a way that shows the limitation of thinking in terms of simple types. In this case, the concept of high self-esteem must be broken down into two groups: one that is associated with the positive phenomena mentioned above, and one that is associated with more problematic or even negative things. Authors are beginning to use such terms as healthy self-esteem (Branden, 1994) and optimal self-esteem (Kernis, 2003b) to describe the former, and the latter have been identified as forms of pseudo self-esteem (Branden, 1969), defensive self-esteem (Coopersmith, 1959), or fragile self-esteem (Kernis & Goldman, 2003). I prefer the term "authentic self-esteem" for the healthy high self-esteem and "defensive self-esteem" for negative elevated forms, and will discuss the reasons behind this approach later.

A Word About Medium Self-Esteem

At one time, there was active discussion of something called medium self-esteem in the field. For example, Coopersmith (1959, 1967) viewed this type of self-esteem as the result of not having had enough exposure to the developmental factors that lead to high self-esteem in order to reach it, but of at least receiving enough exposure to such factors so as to avoid having low self-esteem. Others regard medium self-esteem as a distinct type with its own unique characteristics (Block & Thomas, 1955; Cole, Oetting, & Hinkle, 1967; Weissman & Ritter, 1970). Unfortunately, work on this type of self-esteem has not grown rapidly.

However, the situation may need to change for at least one important reason that is revealed by the assessment literature. By design, most measures are constructed so that they assess three basic groups: people with low self-esteem, individuals with high self-esteem, and everyone else; the latter of which happens to be the vast majority. If we truly wish to understand self-esteem in terms of the real world, then it is important to keep medium self-esteem in mind. In this book, we will regard medium self-esteem as being a low level of high self-esteem in the way that Coopersmith advanced because it is more positive than negative and because some degree of medium self-esteem probably pertains to most of us in general as a normative phenomenon.

Rethinking Types of Self-Esteem: Levels as Well as Types

As previously indicated above, self-esteem has long been divided into two basic types, but now it is also possible to see each of them as having two different levels. One consists of milder manifestations of a given basic type and the other involves more extreme or clinically significant behaviors and states associated with the same basic type. For example, in classical research on self-esteem, low self-esteem is seen as mild or severe and high self-esteem can be seen as being medium (normal) or high. More recently, however, much research has focused on the fact that these basic types and levels may fluctuate or change under various conditions. Harter and Whitesell (2003) found that for some people, self-esteem is relatively stable, but for others it varies considerably over time or in different situations. Campbell (1999) noted that other factors, what he called the "clarity" of one's self-concept, could affect the stability of self-esteem. Thus, it is also necessary to bring the possibility of states and changes in states into this picture.

Apparently, some individuals with uncertain, weak, or ill-defined self-concepts (identity) are much more susceptible to negative feedback or failure. This increased vulnerability may, in turn, affect their level of self-esteem in a way that makes it unstable or at least very dependent on external factors that may change quickly. In addition, there is an emerging stream of research that suggests any type of self-esteem may have conscious as well as unconscious components in terms of the way information about the self is processed by any given individual. In this case, it is possible for one's "explicit" self-esteem, which is one's conscious experience of his or her self-esteem, to be the same as *or* different from one's "implicit" self-esteem, which is one's unconscious experience of one's self-esteem

(Devos & Banaji, 2003). According to this view, for instance, one person could have high levels of both explicit and implicit self-esteem, whereas another could be high in one and low in the other. To make matters even more complex, these levels may fluctuate, sometimes in as few as 25 seconds (Dijksterhuis, 2004).

The range and variety of research on the levels and types of self-esteem are broad but fascinating because they reveal all kinds of issues and possibilities concerning the dynamics of self-esteem. Although some people may find this work on self-esteem confusing, it actually reflects progress in the field because we are finally approaching the point of having enough data about self-esteem to look for underlying patterns and structures. Greenier et al. (1995), Kernis and Goldman (2003), and Kernis (2003a) have done some of the most comprehensive analysis of this material to date. This work allows us to better understand what was originally called defensive self-esteem (Coopersmith, 1959), which appears to have two levels as well.

Defensive Self-Esteem

For many years now, work has been done on various manifestations of self-esteem that seem to have one thing in common: It is too fragile to be genuinely high, but often looks high initially and is always accompanied by a degree of vulnerability that results in some form of vigilance. Researchers often emphasize different aspects of this type of self-esteem and name it accordingly. Hence, we encounter work on what is called, in alphabetical order, contingent self-esteem (Crocker & Park, 2003), incongruent self-esteem (Devos & Banaji, 2003), paradoxical self-esteem (Tafarodi, Tam, & Milne, 2001; Tafarodi & Ho, 2003), pseudo-self-esteem (Branden, 1969), unstable self-esteem (Kernis & Goldman, 2003), and so on. Since all of these variations involve a form of vulnerability that requires the individual to be ready to defend against perceived threats to his or her self-esteem, I refer to this type and all of its manifestations as defensive self-esteem.

Kernis (2003a, 2003b) made significant progress in this area. He began by categorizing each type, level, or configuration of related self-esteem patterns according to whether it is "fragile" (vulnerable in at least one obvious problematic fashion) or "secure" (relatively steady and healthy). He then found that most of the distinctions made between levels or types of self-esteem actually occur in pairs when set in this framework. Using this approach, it is possible to organize the research on many variations or combinations of self-esteem types and levels in the following way: Defensive high self-esteem, which is really not high at all, may be seen as the fragile counterpart to secure self-esteem; incongruent mixtures of explicit/implicit self-esteem, where one aspect is markedly different from the other, occur in contrast to high explicit/high implicit self-esteem, which is congruent; contingent self-esteem is set against true self-esteem; and unstable high self-esteem stands opposite of stable high self-esteem.

In each case, the term that comes first represents a particular form of weak or problematic self-esteem and the second one describes a more solid or healthier self-esteem counterpart. Going one step further, Kernis went on to realize that "optimal" self-esteem could be characterized by combining the self-esteem qualities found on the secure side of the pairs. Thus, optimal self-esteem can be seen as being secure, high both explicitly and implicitly, stable, and true or authentic.

Self-Esteem and Authenticity

Of course, authenticity has been a part of existentialism and humanistic psychology since their beginnings (Tageson, 1982). However, until now this aspect of self-esteem has not received much in the way of empirical support, mainly because accessing experiential dimensions of personal well-being is problematic. Fortunately, progress is also being made in this regard. For example, Koole and Kuhl (2003) noted that researchers are now able to study authentic self-experience and authenticity in general. They went on to say that such work verifies that high self-esteem "that is genuine, true, stable, and congruent with implicit self-esteem is linked to various indicators of authentic functioning, which include self-insight, unbiased processing, autonomous goal striving, and an open way of relating to others" (p. 43).

Although authors vary somewhat on what actually constitutes authenticity, the most basic definition involves a particular combination of awareness and action. The more the individual is aware of his or her own intrinsic motivation, for instance, the more able the person is to engage in autonomous, authentic, and satisfying action, should he or she be willing to take responsibility for the risk involved in making such choices. Self-determination theory builds much of its position on research that supports a link between functioning in these ways and psychological well-being (Ryan & Deci, 2003). We have already seen some correspondence between self-esteem moments and authenticity (Jackson, 1984; Mruk, 1983). Indeed, experimentally oriented research on existential themes, such as authenticity, autonomy, and self-esteem, has solidified to the point where it justified the need for an entire handbook on the topic (Greenberg, Koole, & Pyszczynski, 2004). Moreover, later, we shall see that authenticity is also of interest to positive psychology (Peterson & Seligman, 2004).

In order to capture the research concerning types and levels of self-esteem, as well as their relationship to authenticity, I suggest thinking of the following arrangement. Any comprehensive approach to self-esteem must deal with three types of basic self-esteem: high, low, and defensive.

In addition, it is important to recognize that each of them has two levels, one clinically significant and the other not, although that does not mean it is problem free. In this framework, low self-esteem ranges from mild to severe, high self-esteem ranges from medium to authentic, and such issues as fragility, contingency, instability, and the like characterize defensive self-esteem, which also may be divided into mildly and severely problematic levels. We will return to this way of organizing the research on the varieties and characteristics of self-esteem patterns in Chapter 5, where we attempt to integrate the major findings of this chapter into a general model of self-esteem based on competence and worthiness.

Self-Esteem as a Developmental Product *and* Process

Trzesniewski et al. (2004) conducted a meta-analysis that examined the rank-order stability of self-esteem using 50 articles that involved nearly 30,000 subjects. They concluded that

> Overall, the findings support the view that self-esteem is a stable individual-difference construct. Test-retest correlations are moderate in magnitude and comparable to those for personality traits; across all age groups, the mediation correlation (unadjusted for measurement error) was 0.47. (p. 167)

This group also found that the developmental course of self-esteem is fairly predictable. In other words, self-esteem does seem to be a factor that is at least as consistently present as other personality traits, which makes it a developmental product of some type. In other words, it is appropriate to consider self-esteem as something of a basic trait.

In addition, Orth, Trzesniewski, and Robins (2010) followed self-esteem through the developmental trajectory from young adulthood to old age in a longitudinal study. Several of their findings are noteworthy. First, self-esteem appears to gradually rise from young adulthood to old age in both men and women, although women's self-esteem was lower earlier in adulthood. The peak occurs around the 60s and starts to gradually drop off thereafter. Next, Whites and Blacks were similar until old age, when the latter declined at much faster rates. Third, higher levels of education appear to be associated with higher levels of self-esteem. Finally, changes in socioeconomic status and physical health are strongly associated with age-related declines in self-esteem.

Susan Harter (1999) seems to have studied the overall development of self-esteem longer and in more depth than any other researcher to date. For example, she traced the development of self-esteem through Piaget's developmental structure (Rathus, 2007). At each step of the way, she obtained empirical measures of self-esteem using aged-based assessment scales she and her colleagues developed. Harter found that although each of us goes through the stages in an individual fashion, a general trend emerges. First, early forms of self-esteem develop to fairly high levels in most children, perhaps because of the child's inability to see much beyond his or her own point of preoperational view. Then, self-esteem levels or drops off somewhat as children move into middle childhood, probably because their concrete operational cognitive development makes possible more realistic comparisons and appraisals.

Next, many people experience a significant drop in early adolescence, which may reflect adjustments to puberty and the structure of school systems. Self-esteem then seems to increase steadily throughout late adolescence and in a person's 20s. Finally, self-esteem appears to remain fairly high and stable for the next several decades and then eventually tends to decline with age. In summarizing the longitudinal work done on self-esteem mentioned thus far, it is again clear that self-esteem can be seen as a product created by the outcome of various developmental forces associated with age.

Yet, there are at least two ways of making a convincing argument for understanding self-esteem as an ongoing process as well. One is that the particular areas upon which we tend to evaluate ourselves change over time. For example, although Harter (1999) tracked self-esteem over most of the life cycle, she also found it was necessary to modify the domains of self-esteem her scales assessed depending on age. Scholastic competence is relevant up through the early college years, for instance, but is replaced by job competence later on, which reflects a change in priorities and opportunities associated with adulthood. Other domains were altogether dropped and some new ones were added, which shows variability in self-esteem. Significantly enough, only our concern with our physical appearance ran throughout the entire life cycle. For the most part, then, we are bound to have new opportunities to gain or lose self-esteem throughout the entire life cycle.

Second, considerable work also indicates that certain situations can alter self-esteem. For example, changes in self-esteem have been examined in relation to treating such problems as substance abuse, anxiety, depression, and so forth (O'Brien & Epstein, 1988). We also saw that self-esteem is flexible enough to undergo significant global change in relation to powerful self-esteem moments (Epstein, 1979; Jackson, 1984; Mruk, 1983). Finally, other work supporting the process nature of self-esteem can be found in programs that are aimed at modifying it (Bednar & Peterson, 1995; Frey, Kelbley, Thomas, Durham, & James, 1992; Hakim-Larson & Mruk, 1997; Pope et al., 1988).

In short, it may be said that self-esteem is a process that begins early in life and then becomes a fairly stable developmental product. However, because of its regulatory function to help expand the self as well as protect it, the process nature of self-esteem reveals itself time and time again throughout the life cycle, especially when attempting to master key developmental tasks or when facing certain challenges of living. In other words, self-esteem is lived as a state as well as a trait, and fortunately so. Otherwise, change would not be possible.

The "Self" in Self-Esteem Is Both Psychological *and* Sociological

One matter that may have come to partial resolution concerns the issue of whether self-esteem is primarily a psychological or a social phenomenon. Most work now sees the self as resulting from both forces acting together over time to construct the self. Epstein (1985) was one of the first to advance this model in the field with his notion of a "self-theory." However, Susan Harter may have done the most comprehensive job of describing how people come to have a theory of self and how that understanding moves through the various stages of development in relation to self-esteem. She said, "Our species has been designed to actively create *theories* about our world and to make *meaning* of our experiences, including the construction of a theory of self. Thus, the self is, first and foremost, a *cognitive construction*" (2003, p. 613). Basically, the self-theory starts out as a crude potential that is hardwired into the brain and becomes modified by experience, much as Piaget suggested with his classical concepts of schema and adaptation. Over time, patterns are recognized, connections between them are created, and the brain grows in its capacity to organize them into basic understandings of the world, self, and others.

As development continues, regularities in self-experience begin to occur, thereby creating a sense of self-sameness or "self." Other developmental and social processes, especially the ways in which others react to us through "reflected appraisals" (Cooley, 1909; Mead, 1934), help to stabilize this emerging self in a way that allows identity to form. This entire process undergoes continuous growth and modification as the body, mind, abilities, and social relationships become more mature or sophisticated over time. This process never stops until we die. The result of this constellation of integrated biological, psychological, and social processes is what we call a "self," which is not reducible to any one or two of the components. Hence, in the larger picture, the psychology–sociology distinction no longer makes much sense (Michel & Morf, 2003).

It is easy to see the connection between both psychological and social forces when using the two-factor approach. For example, Gecas and Schwalbe (1983) researched self-esteem primarily from a sociological point of view, but soon noticed that individual psychological forces play just as powerful a role in the development of the self. As they said, "In short, human beings derive a sense of self not only from the reflected appraisals of others, but also from the consequences and products of behavior that are attributed to the self as an agent in the environment" (p. 79). More contemporary work such as Harter's and the entire constructionist position in the social sciences understand the "self" in self-esteem as both psychological *and* social. The relationship between the psychological and social contours of the self is one of intimate connection that may best be described in terms of the perceptual metaphor of figure and ground mentioned above. In this way, not only are they linked, but they actually give rise to one another, just like competence and worthiness are needed to form self-esteem.

One possible exception to understanding the self in this way is found in a school of humanistic psychology. The transpersonal branch of this perspective consists of those who hold the position that the capacity to transcend the self, perhaps even spiritually, is an essential feature of being human. Such an understanding would literally take the concept of worthiness to a different, perhaps higher, plane because it would mean that certain values stand above all others. Unfortunately, there is no way to resolve this issue scientifically, but a comprehensive approach to the research, theory, and practice of self-esteem must at least mention it. Finally, even though I have taken a stance on the issue, the problem of whether self-esteem should be seen as a basic psychological need or as a cultural phenomenon is still the subject of debate. Once again, if self-esteem turns out to be a basic structure, then we can generalize quite far, although the two factors may be emphasized differently in various cultures. If self-esteem is not so fundamental, then our work is largely limited to cultures that emphasize the individual or that move in this direction over time. Either outcome is acceptable to the two-factor approach.

Self-Esteem as a Variable?

The findings concerning the last research paradox focus on a most crucial but equally complex question: whether self-esteem is an independent variable, a dependent variable, or something else, such as a mediator. This dimension of self-esteem is important because it is connected to the question of causality or, more specifically and importantly, the issue of whether self-esteem is a significant psychological phenomenon that makes a difference in life or not. The answer to this question is crucial because if self-esteem is not worth pursuing then we should, indeed, give it up. By the same token, however, if self-esteem does turn out to be important, we should vigorously strive to enhance it in positive ways.

For nearly 100 years, the link between self-esteem and behavior was so widely assumed in the field that people did not pay much attention to it: They "knew" self-esteem was an important variable in human behavior as a matter of common sense. In the 1990s, however, people began examining the strength of that relationship in earnest and some found it so lacking that they questioned the value of the concept altogether (Baumeister et al., 1996; Emler, 2001; Seligman, 1995b). Now we know that one important reason for such confusion is that much of the research done on the relationship between self-esteem and behavior occurred on the basis of defining self-esteem in terms of only one of its components. Such work cannot establish a cause-and-effect relationship *in principle*. After all, partial definitions are bound to generate insignificant results because lopsided beginnings usually lead to skewed endings.

Instead of insisting on the impossible, it is more useful and valid to look at this issue in another way, one that involves a more sophisticated understanding of human behavior than is possible with models based on simple or lineal causality. The earliest and most common approach is to see the dynamics of self-esteem as a type of self-fulfilling prophecy. Coopersmith (1967) said, "Although there are undoubtedly variations in the origins of a cycle from self-esteem to anxiety, the model of a cyclical, self-reinforcing, self-propelling sequence seems appropriate once either state has been established" (p. 133). We also saw that contemporary work on the way self-esteem functions in relationships often uses the same mechanism to understand how self-esteem functions in this context.

Others use more advanced information processing metaphors to explain the relationship between self-esteem and behavior. Here, self-esteem is seen as a form of feedback that plays a critical role in determining behavior: It is "a special type of information that can describe, evaluate, or influence performance: in our case, human behavior" (Bednar et al., 1989, p. 91). This more cognitive view sees self-esteem serving a regulatory function in the self-system that is not uncommon in research concerning complex adaptive systems (Johanson, 2009). In this case, the focus is on understanding how something as complicated and dynamic as the self system can come to recognize patterns and achieve stability based on them, but also change enough to make adaptive responses when necessary. From this perspective, it makes good sense that once we develop a certain type or level of global self-esteem, we tend to operate in ways that are consistent with it so as to maintain a sense of self-sameness over time. However, in order to survive, complex adaptive systems cannot be static: They must retain enough flexibility to adapt to new situations when they arise or to grow when circumstances favor furthering development.

Similarly, it is possible to understand how events influence behavior, and vice versa, through a process of exchange known as "reciprocal determinism" (Rathus, 2007). This concept does not figure predominantly in discussions concerning the link between self-esteem and behavior, perhaps because it does not fit well into a mindset that focuses on lineal causality. However, it should. After all, other extremely empirical scientists, such as geneticists, often use the concept of reciprocity to understand how genes work with environmental factors to produce all types of physical, behavioral, and developmental phenomena (Hernandez & Blazer, 2006).

Harter (1999) took a more developmental track on the mediating character of self-esteem on the basis of her research on depression in adolescence. In this framework, the link between self-esteem and behavior is based on the direction of self-esteem, or whether it is functioning as a cause or as an effect for a particular individual in relation to a specific situation. For example, for one person, a given failure or rejection could lead to a temporary or minor drop in self-esteem. For another, the same situation could trigger some depression, which, in turn, might also lead to a subsequent drop in self-esteem and thereby open the way for a severe depression or even suicidality. For yet a third individual, the same event could have little or no effect on self-esteem at all. Harter found that what determines in which direction self-esteem will flow depends upon a key factor not often discussed in traditional research: the situation's meaning to the individual.

Jackson (1984) pointed out that experimental work aimed at establishing simple or one-way statistical causality in regard to self-esteem is doomed to failure. Most of the experimental work done in this field, for instance, involves setting up a situation where someone is asked to solve a problem or to compete in a contest where some type of treatment is introduced, usually unknown to the subject. In one case, it might be verbal cueing that is manipulated; in another, rigging the contest so that failure is certain; and in a third setting, distraction might be added to the situation, and so forth. However, if it is true that a situation must *mean* something to an individual before self-esteem becomes mobilized, let alone affected, then subjects must be personally connected to the situation and its outcomes for the experiment to be relevant to self-esteem. Yet, Epstein showed us in Chapter 1 that it is difficult for experiments to achieve such status in ethical ways.

Finally, it has been pointed out (Mruk, in press) that clinical work concerning self-esteem may be underappreciated in scholarly and academically oriented material on this topic. Much research on this topic is based on using college students who stand as a convenient sample for many researchers, particularly those who do work from a social or social psychological perspective, as this work tends to occur in more academic rather than "real life" settings. Interestingly, this selection factor may actually distort research on the significance of self-esteem in a way that minimizes its value because this population is generally young, usually healthy, comparatively affluent, and often living in an unusually low-stress or stable environment compared with much of humanity in general.

In sum, at this point in the development of the field, it is possible to conclude at least two things about the status of self-esteem as a variable affecting behavior. One is that the two-factor model may be better equipped to deal with this issue because competence is often measurable and it must be balanced by worthiness in order to "count" in relation to self-esteem. Such restrictive criteria alone may help with the often lamented problem of statistical significance among traditionally oriented social scientists because it narrows the type of behavior that researchers would examine to a particular class of experience: those that involve developmental, personal, and existential challenges of living. This increase in specificity could eventually result in clearer research and findings. Second, meaningful research linking self-esteem and behavior must be just that: based on the meaning involved in the behavior, not just its measurement. This aspect of self-esteem requires using methods that are capable of dealing with this dimension of behavior rather than avoiding them. We will return to examining the relationship between self-esteem and behavior after completing the development of a comprehensive, meaning-based, two-factor theory of self-esteem in Chapter 5.

PRACTICAL RESEARCH FINDINGS: ENHANCING SELF-ESTEEM

Assessing and Measuring Self-Esteem

It was mentioned in Chapter 2 that the state versus trait and product versus process issues were also alive in the assessment of self-esteem. In addition, we saw in the section on research problems associated with measuring self-esteem that most such measures are unidimensional and, therefore, inadequate in principle if self-esteem is multidimensional as the two-factor model maintains. One advantage of assessing self-esteem based on multiple dimensions, then, is that it avoids some of the problems associated with unidimensional measures. For example, some multidimensional measures assess both global self-esteem and how self-esteem pertains to various domains of life in which self-esteem plays an especially important role. As Harter (2003) said,

> It has become increasingly important to the field to distinguish between self-evaluations that represent global characteristics of the individual (e.g., "I am a worthwhile person") and those that reflect the individual's sense of adequacy across particular domains, such as one's cognitive competence (e.g., "I am smart"), social competence (e.g., "I am well liked by peers"), athletic competence (e.g., "I am good at sports").... Conceptualizations and instruments that aggregate domain-specific self-evaluations

(e.g., Coopersmith, 1967) have been found wanting in that they mask the meaningful distinctions between one's sense of adequacy across domains. (Harter, p. 612)

Even Rosenberg saw the need to deal with the global versus situational issue in its broadest sense later in his career when he said, "It is particularly important to distinguish between global and specific self-esteem because the relationships reported in the literature between self-esteem and other variables are often weaker than might be expected" (Rosenberg, Schooler, Schoenbach, & Rosenberg, 1995, p. 143). However, his own 10-question instrument fails in regard to assessing specific domains and instead only measures a global one.

There are dozens, if not hundreds, of self-esteem measures to consider in assessing self-esteem. However, Guindon (2002) found that four of them are used most often. They are the Self-Esteem Scale (SES) (Rosenberg, 1965); the Self-Esteem Inventory (SEI) (Coopersmith, 1981); the Tennessee Self-Concept Scale (TSCS) (Roid & Fitts, 1988); and the Piers-Harris Children's Self-Concept Scale (P-HCSCS) (Piers & Harris, 1969). Other frequently used instruments include the Culture Free Self-Esteem Inventory (CFSEI) (Battle, 1992); the Minnesota Multiphasic Personality Inventory's Self-Esteem Scale (MMPI-2) (Butcher et al., 2001); the Perceived Competence Scale for Children (PCSC) (Harter, 1985); the Adult Self-Perception Scale (ASPS) (Messer & Harter, 1986); the Multidimensional Self-Esteem Inventory (MSEI) (O'Brien & Epstein, 1988); and the Self-Liking/Self-Competence Scale (SLSC) (Tafarodi & Swann, 1995).

We have just seen that unidimensional measures are inadequate, which narrows the list down to a handful. Similarly, we understand self-esteem in terms of competence and worthiness, which reduces the list even further. These requirements result in a limited set of instruments: limited, but good in that they are capable of "measuring the right thing," as discussed in Chapter 2. They include the MMPI-2, the MSEI, the PCSC/ASPS, and the SLSC, each of which has its own strengths and weaknesses. Of these instruments, the MMPI and the MSEI include at least one scale that enhances validity because it is designed to reveal patterns that suggest inconsistent, inflated, or deceptive responses. Such measures are crucially necessary when assessing self-esteem because of the ceiling effect already noted. In addition, such scaling helps to reveal whether or not psychological rigidity is present, both of which may pertain to such things as fragile or defensive self-esteem. Unfortunately, the MMPI is difficult to use because of its length, expense, and clinical nature, which can raise ethical issues when the focus is on research or on non-clinical populations. In short, we turn to the MSEI as the single most effective *and* practical test to evaluate self-esteem when it is defined in terms of a relationship between competence and worthiness.

Findings Concerning Enhancing Self-Esteem

Because this book aims to move from research through theory to practice, the last task we face in a chapter that focuses on identifying major findings concerning self-esteem is to look at work that concerns changing self-esteem in a positive direction. This area is one of the newest in the field, but for those of us who are interested in change or working with self-esteem clinically it is also the most exciting. As before, the findings presented here are qualitative and quantitative but always based on persistence, significance, or both.

The Importance of Acceptance and Care

We saw from the findings concerning parental and social factors affecting self-esteem that how we are treated by others is likely to affect our development. Although such factors may diminish somewhat with age, we never lose the capacity to respond to the way that others reflect our worth to ourselves (Cramer, 2003). Parents are replaced by friends, spouses, coworkers, and even bosses, who accept or reject us in ways that hold meaning for self-esteem, particularly in regard to our sense of worth. What people seem to think of our appearance also matters in this way to some extent throughout the life cycle. Acceptance and being accepted, then, should be a part of any decent self-esteem enhancement program.

This technique may even be seen as the most basic one because it is tied to the development of self-esteem in the first place and because most systematic attempts to enhance it include acceptance as an important part of the process (Bednar et al., 1989; Coopersmith, 1967; Epstein, 1979; Sappington, 1989). In fact, whether envisioned humanistically as providing "unconditional positive regard," psychodynamically as a "working alliance," or cognitive-behaviorally as "building rapport," this technique has been found to be one of the "common factors" essential to the therapeutic process in general (Arkowitz, 1997). In addition, appreciating the value of the individual suffering from self-esteem problems can itself be a powerful therapeutic experience, mainly because he or she is usually more familiar with rejection than acceptance, thereby making it doubly helpful.

Providing Consistent and Positive (Affirming), but Genuine, Feedback

Whether seen as offering corrective emotional experiences, healthier reflected appraisals for self-construction, consistent affirmation of one's inner self, or as a way to introduce feedback change into a system in order to change it, giving positive information about themselves to people is a standard technique for enhancing self-esteem. There are good reasons and some supporting evidence for this practice (Bednar et al.,

1989; Bednar & Peterson, 1995; Bhatti et al., 1989; Frey & Carlock, 1989). As Bhatti et al. (1989) summed it up, "Many experts suggest focusing on positive rather than negative behavior to begin building self-esteem" (p. 54). No matter which standard approach to self-esteem one uses, positive feedback can make a difference.

There are, however, two caveats to be aware of when applying such a technique. First, humanistic psychology states that such feedback must be "authentic," which is to say based in reality and not phony praise. Second, some cognitive research indicates that there might be value in providing positive feedback in a way that is slow but steady rather than fast or sudden. The understanding for this practice is that the self-system is designed to be and to remain stable, even when its overall character is negative or painful. Trying to change things too quickly is likely to be disruptive, so the system is likely to resist through the use of such things as self-handicapping, withdrawal, or some other defensive response that discounts the information (Bednar et al., 1989; Bednar & Peterson, 1995; Epstein, 1985; Marigold, Holmes, & Ross, 2007). The same type of finding emerged in relation to enhancing self-esteem for some people in regard to their relationships (Marigold et al., 2007). Consequently, small doses of positive feedback are likely to be more effective than larger ones because they are more likely to be non-threatening enough to slip into the self-system in a way that may gradually alter it over time.

Generating Positive Self-Feedback Through Cognitive Restructuring

No matter what one's theoretical position, it is important to realize that we use some form of feedback to ourselves, such as "self-talk" and the information we receive about ourselves from others, to help make sense of things. The well-established technique of cognitive restructuring is the most empirically supported method of intervening at this level. This approach is generally characterized by three basic steps: learning how to identify problematic habits of thought, labeling them as such according to some nomenclature of common problems or mistakes, and then substituting a more rational or realistic response for each occurrence until such patterns are replaced by healthier, more realistic ones.

Several authors provide extensive lists of terms describing the problematic thinking patterns that cause inaccurate perceptions, maladaptive behavior, and unnecessary personal and/or interpersonal pain (Burns, 1980, 1993a; Freeman, Pretzer, Fleming, & Simon, 1990; Leahy, 2003). These techniques work on increasing self-esteem in several ways. First, they interrupt the normally smooth-flowing links between thinking, feeling, and acting in negative ways that create and that maintain low self-esteem in the first place, thereby creating the possibility for something new to happen. Second, being able to demonstrate some control over behavior allows the individual to feel more worthy, if not more competent, which is conducive to self-esteem. Third, with practice, new habits of perceiving, thinking, experiencing, and acting set up a more virtuous cycle that helps self-esteem move upward toward higher levels or types.

Increasing Self-Esteem by Using Natural Self-Esteem Moments

We saw that some cognitive, humanistic, and existentially oriented self-esteem researchers investigated how self-esteem is lived in real life. Among other things, this work indicated that self-esteem can change spontaneously, particularly during periods of transition (Epstein, 1979; Harter, 1993) or at certain crucial turning points (Jackson, 1984; Mruk, 1983), both of which involve what I call challenges of living. A logical extension of such findings is to apply them to the task of enhancing self-esteem. In other words, if we can identify these situations as they are occurring or are about to occur, then it might be possible to intervene therapeutically and perhaps even turn them into positive self-esteem moments.

One thing that most clinicians advocate in this regard is to help people increase their awareness of the role that self-esteem plays in their lives (Bednar et al., 1989; Frey & Carlock, 1989; Hakim-Larson & Mruk, 1997). Such interventions usually involve raising consciousness and providing support when someone is facing or preparing to face a challenge of living that affects self-esteem. To help increase awareness, therapists often encourage clients to keep a journal and write about their self-esteem, as well as what affects it (Epstein, 1979; Fava, 1999; Frey & Carlock, 1989; Hakim-Larson & Mruk, 1997; Sappington, 1989). We will also see that positive psychology includes a place for journal writing when discussing what is known as positive therapy in Chapter 7.

Increasing Self-Esteem Through Modeling

It has been more than a century since William James suggested that successes and failures are crucial factors in determining self-esteem. Psychology has learned a good deal about helping people tip the scale to the favorable side since those early days. Modern learning theorists, for example, talk about self-efficacy (Bandura, 1997; Maddux & Gosselin, 2003), which concerns a person's beliefs about how he or she is likely to do in a given situation based on a number of variables, such as past performance on similar tasks.

Coopersmith (1967) and Bednar et al. (1989) noted that "showing by doing" seems to be helpful for two reasons: First, modeling is often useful when trying to learn complex activities. We cannot help but to model our parents, older siblings, peer groups, and teachers, and we learn all kinds of things in doing so, not all of them good. Second, modeling occurs in clinical situations as well. For example, a good facilitator or therapist will demonstrate techniques for handling conflict or other difficult situations in ways that promote self-esteem, often by attempting to be authentic (Bednar et al., 1989; Mruk, 1999). In addition, many clients with low self-esteem have had few opportunities to model a person who is reasonably competent *and* worthy, so the clinician becomes especially important as a model. Indeed, clients probably learn more from the clinician in this way than the clinician ever realizes.

Enhancing Self-Esteem Through "Empowerment": Increasing Problem-Solving Skills

Most self-esteem enhancement programs include the idea that self-esteem helps us to cope more effectively with life's challenges, both small and large (Bednar et al., 1989; Pope et al., 1988; Sappington, 1989). Above all, coping well means that a person is able to influence the situations of life or is capable of dealing with its problems with a reasonable degree of competence. Assertiveness training is one such technique. However, while these skills may be acquired at any age (Alberti & Emmons, 1982), they often involve up to 8 weeks of structured practice (Rakos, 1990).

A more general way to help increase self-esteem is to teach people how to solve problems more effectively and efficiently (Bednar et al., 1989; Pope et al., 1988). Teaching people problem-solving skills is an effective technique that may be applied to a large range of difficulties and challenges. The process usually begins with learning how to break up problems into manageable steps, each of which can be practiced and evaluated until learning occurs (D'Zurilla & Goldfried, 1971; D'Zurilla & Nezu, 2001). The steps typically include learning how to recognize that a problem exists, being able to identify possible responses and their likely outcomes, knowing how to select the best alternative given a particular situation, and having the ability to develop a realistic plan to reach that goal. The process of learning these skills is facilitated by a good teacher, a non-threatening environment, appropriate reinforcement, and supervised practice, all of which are fairly standard practices in problem-solving work.

Several positive things can happen for self-esteem once this skill has been acquired. First, knowing how to better solve problems increases an individual's chances of being successful, and we saw that certain types of success are a source of self-esteem. Second, the technique is flexible enough to allow us to target a particular area that is especially troublesome to an individual and to then help the person develop a realistic problem-solving strategy that is based on maximizing his or her strengths while minimizing their weaknesses. Indeed, "individualizing" (Fischer, 1986) training in problem-solving skills may be the ideal way to address specific individuals with particular self-esteem themes. Thus, increasing competence through better problem-solving skills can be done in ways that are sensitive to age, gender, culture, and so on.

Enhancing Self-Esteem Requires Practice

The last factor to be included in any self-esteem enhancement program affects all the others, so perhaps it is the most important. In spite of popular books to the contrary, the evidence shows that enhancing self-esteem in a lasting way requires considerable time and work. There is no effective "1 minute to authentic self-esteem" program. There are several reasons for this fact, of course, but they can be summed up most succinctly by pointing out that self-esteem problems take a long time to develop. They usually involve deeply ingrained habits of perception, experience, and behavior, all of which are well-cemented by the time we reach adulthood. These self-esteem habits shape our world in ways that are both subtle and complex, meaning that change requires considerable unlearning as well as new learning, both of which take time. In the final analysis, then, self-esteem is increased through hard work and practice. In the end, there is simply no escaping this basic existential fact.

Format Factors for Enhancing Self-Esteem

Although it would not be proper to term the next factor as an enhancement technique, there is some consensus about what we might call "format factors" to consider for enhancing self-esteem in the clinical or psycho-educational settings. These factors are important because they offer professionals the ability to be flexible in helping others. One is to build a program around the traditional one-to-one relationship between client and clinician (Bednar et al., 1989; Harter, 1999; Mruk, 1999). A key advantage of this self-esteem encounter is that it focuses on identifying and understanding a particular individual's self-esteem themes, strengths, and weaknesses in considerable detail. The therapist and client may then target appropriate ones as central therapeutic projects.

Another advantage is that the process can go on for longer periods of time, meaning that it should be possible for both therapist and client to actually see change as well as create it, which is always encouraging. Also, more seriously ill patients or clients with more deeply embedded self-esteem problems often require more focused attention that can be offered in such a setting. On the negative side, we know that this intensive, often long-term format requires considerable resources in terms of clinical expertise, time, and money, and, most of all, is limited to the interpersonal factors created by only two people.

The other major design format is through the group setting, which is positive in a number of other ways (Bhatti et al., 1989; Burns, 1993a; Frey & Carlock, 1989; Mruk, 1995, 1999). For one thing, groups may be designed to meet the needs of various populations, as this format may be tailored to a number of audiences. In this case, most of the general rules for clinical groups apply, such as screening clients carefully before admitting them to such a group (Vinogradov & Yalom, 1989). The group should consist of a leader who acts as a therapist, facilitator, and teacher and should range from 8 to 12 participants. It is also possible to involve male and female co-therapists to lead the groups, something that is beneficial to certain clients. Groups may also be designed to emphasize growth instead of remediation, which means they can be used with non-clinical populations as well. In fact, such psychoeducational groups may be ideal for general use, prevention, or even "coaching" because they can be adapted to serving a broad range of people and ages (Frey & Carlock, 1989).

In addition, groups are usually more cost effective, which is important when seen in the light of today's mounting health care crisis, because they can be used to address larger numbers, especially those who have limited income (Hakim-Larson & Mruk, 1997; O'Brien et al., 2006a). This format may also seem less threatening to people who are put off by the idea of psychotherapy or to those who are simply interested in bettering themselves and not having someone "dig around in their heads."

The group format can do some things better than the individual setting (Vinogradov & Yalom, 1989) because the rich mixture of perceptions and reactions that comes from being around several different people more closely approximates the conditions of real life than does the individual treatment setting. For instance, a group situation usually presents a greater variety of "safe challenges" or here-and-now opportunities to try out new pro-self-esteem behaviors, such as communicating more effectively or being more assertive. Groups also bring more of the social factors affecting self-esteem into play, such as offering more opportunities for positive feedback, acceptance, and healthy modeling. Finally, groups can offer a sense of camaraderie and support that are hard to duplicate in individual formats: Seeing how others suffer from low self-esteem and witnessing their struggle to gain it can be helpful in many different ways.

Summary of the Techniques

It might first appear as though these tools for enhancing self-esteem that emerge from examining the literature on this topic may not seem like much in the way of results. However, they are actually quite valuable because these tools are the *most valid techniques we have for enhancing self-esteem today*, suggesting that they can be used with some confidence and clinical credibility. In short, it is possible to mount an evidence-based argument for using any or all of them, though some, such as cognitive restructuring and problem-solving, are more easily supported in this way than others.

Major Self-Esteem Theories and Programs

As we approach the midpoint of this look at self-esteem, it is time to examine the major theoretical approaches to understand it, as well as the leading approaches to enhance self-esteem. This step should offer valuable insights and guidelines for developing a more comprehensive and systematic two-factor approach based on the fundamental structure of self-esteem presented in Chapter 1. However, an important word is necessary before beginning this work. Selecting and reviewing theories is always a challenging task in a field that has many of them. It is virtually impossible to present such material without offending someone through an act of omission (leaving someone or something out), commission (saying something with which the author disagrees), or interpretation (which can never be perfect). Like many authors, I have had the opportunity to experience all these phenomena in regard to my work. Thus, it is with great care that I struggled to decide which approaches to present and how to condense their rich and powerful ideas into a few pages. I can only say that although I have tried my best to select representative work and to present it accurately, I apologize in advance for these inevitable shortcomings that are sure to occur when facing such a challenge: The hope is that readers will find these ideas and practices stimulating and promising.

GENERAL PERSPECTIVES ON SELF-ESTEEM

The Jamesian Tradition

We have already examined James' basic approach, but the fact that it is very much alive in the literature today (Crocker & Park, 2003; Harter, 1999) suggests that we need to deepen our understanding of it. James began talking about self-esteem by pointing out that each person is born into a set of possible social roles or identities created by factors such as history, culture, family, interests, and circumstances. Over time, we find ourselves becoming invested in some of these "selves" more than others, a process that creates certain priorities in our lives. Gradually, we also develop an overall sense of how well or poorly we live up to these expectations, which results in an "average feeling tone" about ourselves called self-esteem (James, 1890/1983, p. 292). As James said,

> So we have the paradox of a man shamed to death because he is only the second pugilist or the second oarsman in the world. That he is able to beat the whole population of the globe minus one is nothing; he has "pitted" himself to beat that one; and as long as he doesn't do that nothing else counts. He is to his own regard as if he were not, indeed, he *is* not.

> Yonder puny fellow, however, whom everyone can beat, suffers no chagrin about it, for he has long ago abandoned the attempt to "carry that line," as the merchants say, of self at all. With no attempt there can be no failure; with no failure no humiliation. So our self-feeling in this world depends entirely on what we *back* ourselves to be and do. (p. 296)

This citation is used to point out the major characteristics of thinking about self-esteem when it is seen largely in terms of competence. One chief feature of this definition is that it is very dynamic. By using such words as "pitted" (which involves being challenged), "carry" (which concerns maintaining a certain status), and "back" (which requires taking action), James placed self-esteem at the heart of much human behavior. By making it so contingent on success and failure, self-esteem also takes on many motivational qualities associated with basic needs. For example, when we are deprived of self-esteem or when it is threatened, this approach predicts that we would change our behavior to acquire or defend it. This type of motivational dynamic is especially characteristic of the psychodynamic approach to self-esteem found in Adler's (1927) drive toward superiority and White's (1963) concept of effectance mentioned earlier.

The good news of this model is twofold. First, self-esteem motivates us to try to master the challenges of life, particularly those that have implications for our identities. As such, self-esteem may be regarded as a crucial developmental process and force. Second, if self-esteem is like a ratio that is dependent on our successes or failures, then change is inherently possible. In fact, James' definition even suggests that there are several ways to alter the ratio in a direction that is favorable for self-esteem: We may change it by increasing success in crucial areas, by decreasing failures in them, or by finding new areas in which we have a better chance of being successful to base our identities upon. Theories of self-esteem that emphasize success in regard to comparisons between an ideal and actual self are often based on this approach. Of course, making self-esteem largely dependent on success also has serious limitations, as we saw with Crocker and Park's (2004) critique of contingency approaches in general.

The Social Learning Tradition

In Chapter 2, we saw that another early approach to self-esteem involved emphasizing its interpersonal character through the Cooley–Mead tradition, which emphasizes the process and power of social learning. This school was further developed by Harry Stack Sullivan (1953) when he applied it to practical problems in his interpersonal approach to psychiatry. With more empirically oriented work on self-esteem initiated by people such as the sociologist Rosenberg and the social learning theorist Coopersmith of the mid-1960s, this perspective became well established in the field.

After defining self-esteem as "a positive or negative attitude toward a particular object, namely, the self" (p. 30), Rosenberg (1965) focused his attention on the social factors affecting self-esteem. He began by pointing out that understanding self-image or self-esteem as an attitudinal phenomenon created by social and cultural forces is an approach, as we saw, that makes measuring self-esteem relatively easy. In addition, attitudes are often connected to emotions and behaviors. Thus, it is reasonable to postulate that because emotions and behaviors stem from the self, attitudes about the self are quite capable of giving rise to various affective and dispositional inclinations. In short, self-esteem also has motivational implications from this point of view. Indeed, so intimately connected are these forces that Rosenberg (1965) went on to identify self-esteem, or one's attitude of personal worth, as a "pivotal variable" (p. 15) because it works for or against us in any number of situations.

> High self-esteem, as reflected in our scale items, expresses the feeling that one is "good enough." The individual simply feels that he is a person of worth; he respects himself for what he is, but does not stand in awe of himself nor does he expect others to stand in awe of him. . . . Low self-esteem, on the other hand, implies self-rejection, self-dissatisfaction, self-contempt. The individual lacks respect for the self he observes. The picture is disagreeable, and he wishes it were otherwise. (p. 31)

In short, the presence or absence of such perceived worthiness disposes one toward positive or negative experience and behavior.

Rosenberg went on to explore the way in which self-esteem (or the lack of it) is created: It results from a process that involves values and discrepancies. According to this view, individuals have self-esteem to the degree they perceive themselves as matching up to a set of central self-values. These core values concern what individuals have learned to be worthy of emulating, aspiring toward, or attaining through the process of socialization (Rosenberg & Simmons, 1971). Tying self-esteem to such central concepts as values and the process of acquiring them through socialization makes this approach deeply social.

At about the same time, Coopersmith (1967) was doing work on self-esteem that was also based on worthiness and social learning. However, his concern was more practical in that he aimed to develop "a conceptual framework that might serve as a guide in investigating self-esteem, or a tool for altering it" (p. vii). After doing 8 years of empirically oriented research on the subject, Coopersmith (1967) concluded that self-esteem has "great significance—personally, socially, and psychologically. It is therefore disconcerting that so little is known about the conditions and experiences that enhance or lessen self-esteem" (p. 1). Consequently, instead of comparing groups and developing norms, he focused on understanding how self-esteem is learned, ways in which it could be nurtured, and what might be done to modify it.

Although Coopersmith did not go farther than offering suggestions for increasing self-esteem, we shall see that three of them have stood the test of time. The first one focuses on assessing how well or poorly an individual is faring in all the basic sources of self-esteem. This formal assessment covers four areas of life especially germane to self-esteem. In no particular order, the evaluation should identify: areas of life in which the individual makes meaningful achievements or fails to do so; where he or she demonstrates desirable influence and where not; where the person tends to comport himself or herself virtuously as well as where the struggle to do so is important; and where the individual feels accepted, cared for, or loved by others as well as where not. Only such a thorough assessment lets us know where attention is needed and what we have to help in that endeavor.

Next, he built on the findings that children with high self-esteem tend to have families that set clear limits and expectations. Therefore, Coopersmith (1967) suggested that structured therapeutic situations might be more effective in increasing self-esteem than unstructured approaches. Finally, he strongly advocated modeling as a central therapeutic device. Realizing that different people will benefit from different types of models, he also offered a general rule for selecting the individual to model and what is to be modeled: It "may be that the style of response is more critical than the particular action. Thus the individual may observe how an effective individual deals with anxiety, resolves ambiguities, and makes decisions" (p. 263). Although Coopersmith did not investigate the efficacy of these modes of intervention, they are clear extensions of social learning theory and practice.

Whether conceived of socially or psychologically, the social learning approach to self-esteem emphasizes defining it in terms of worth or worthiness; researching self-esteem based on empirical work; and changing self-esteem by modifying social practices associated with childrearing, education, or clinical practice. On the positive side of the ledger, these qualities give the social learning perspective on self-esteem considerable appeal because it implies that we can and should do something about raising self-esteem for many people. However, we also saw that defining self-esteem largely in terms of worthiness also leads to certain important problems, such as weak results, poor statistical strength, and confusing self-esteem with dark psychosocial phenomena.

The Humanistic Tradition

Self-esteem has been an important theme in the humanistic approach to understanding human behavior from its beginnings. Indeed, both Abraham Maslow and Carl Rogers regarded self-esteem as a basic human need that plays a key role in both development and behavior. Although perhaps a mixed blessing, Branden (1969) presented a largely humanistic picture of self-esteem appealing enough to make it a popular topic for the first time in its history. In this case, self-esteem is seen as a basic human need that is tied to our highest capacities: reason, choice, and responsibility.

> Man experiences his desire for self-esteem as an urgent impera-
> tive, as a basic need . . . . So intensely does a man feel the need of
> a positive view of himself, that he may evade, repress, distort his
> judgment, disintegrate his mind—in order to avoid coming face
> to face with facts that would affect his self-appraisal adversely. . . .
> If and to the extent that men lack self-esteem, they feel driven
> to *fake* it, to create the *illusion* of self-esteem—condemning them-
> selves to chronic psychological fraud—moved by the desperate
> sense that to face the universe without self-esteem is to stand
> naked, disarmed, delivered to destruction. (p. 110)

When seen from this point of view, self-esteem is a need that drives human behavior in two ways. First, we must learn that we have such a need and then we must stumble through the challenges life brings until we learn how to manage it rationally. In other words, we learn about competence and worthiness through our highest human faculties: Reason is capable of helping us make intelligent decisions, a process that is reinforced by the fact that we live with the consequences of our actions. Living rationally involves hard work but also brings certain powerful positive feelings that are worthy enough "in principle" (Branden, 1969, p. 111), to keep people heading in a psychologically healthy direction. However, it is important to appreciate that this process is often a dif-ficult one because it involves making mistakes and finding the courage to face them.

Second, in addition to motivating us in such a positive, rational, and actualizing direction, Branden also pointed out the other side of this coin. Failing to know one's self fully or making poor choices also have powerful consequences: Such a life is subject to all sorts of psychosocial ailments. In other words, if one is cut off from legitimate sources of self-esteem (or, more properly, if one cuts oneself off from them), then the need for self-esteem motivates one to search for substitutes. Branden called the result of this deficiency "pseudo self-esteem," which is manifested in such things as ordinary unhappiness, then to acute misery, and in some cases even to genuinely destructive personal or antisocial social behavior.

In a later book, Branden (1983) clarified the dynamic nature of self-esteem by specifying two conditions. First, he identified four basic "pillars" of healthy self-esteem: the degree of an individual's conscious awareness; one's integrity as a person; the willingness to accept responsibility for one's decisions; and self-acceptance or being honest about the kind of choices one makes. The relationship between these foundational processes is that one supports the other. Of course, such a dynamic structure that means failure in one area also has consequences for others. For instance, a lack of awareness about the need for self-esteem makes it more difficult to understand how important it is for us to make choices that affirm our integrity as a person. A low degree of integrity means that our actions become incongruent and lessen our ability to engage in honest struggle. Failing to take responsibility is a self-deception of the greatest sort because it limits our ability to see, let alone correct, our self-esteem mistakes. Finally, the inability to accept ourselves leads to the possibility of self-neglect. Thus, self-esteem "is often a struggle of heroic proportions" (Branden, 1983, p. 19). Eventually, Branden (1994) added assertiveness and purposefulness as additional pillars.

Finally, it must be noted that, although very richly detailed, the early versions of the humanistic perspective on self-esteem, such as those found in Rogers, Maslow, and Branden, are not accompanied by a significant degree of empirical support.

MAJOR CONTEMPORARY EMPIRICALLY BASED
THEORIES OF SELF-ESTEEM

Epstein's Cognitive Experiential Self-Theory

Although cognitive psychology has not been a part of the history of the field for long, it has been instrumental in terms of integrating many of the psychological and social influences, as we saw in Chapter 3. In general, cognitive theories use information processing concepts, such as pattern recognition, feedback, reciprocity, and other computational images, to describe complex adaptive systems, such as ecosystems, weather systems, economic systems, and, in this case, individual self-systems and related behavior (Johanson, 2009).

Seymour Epstein's cognitive experiential self-theory is one of the first cognitive theories of self-esteem and still stands as representative of this approach. This theory is based on the notions of information (experience), organization (concept formation), representation (a system of concepts arranged hierarchically), and the process of development. These central concepts and their related processes allow human beings to organize information about the world, self, and others into what Epstein (1985) called "personal theories of reality."

Epstein (1985) characterized human development as a brain-based process that allows us to make sense of the patterns around us as we grow and develop. Those that concern how the world works, which includes other people and their behavior, are used to create a general "world theory" that helps us to understand that part of life. Events, experiences, and patterns concerning how we respond to the world, especially to others in it, and the positive or negative feedback we receive about our behavior lead to the creation of a basic "self-theory." Like all theories, personal theories make sense out of data in ways that allow us to develop hypotheses. Over time, we test, learn from, and revise them until new data or experience comes along that requires further modification. The self-theory, then, is

> A conceptual tool for fulfilling life's most basic psychological functions, namely, to maintain a favorable pleasure/pain balance over the foreseeable future, to maintain a favorable level of self-esteem, to assimilate the data of reality within a stable, coherent, conceptual system, and to maintain favorable relationships with significant others. (p. 286)

Finally, such personal theories are practical in that they are "prescriptive," which is Epstein's way of saying that they help us to identify our needs and to find ways of satisfying them that are most likely to be successful given the particular time, culture, and circumstances in which we live.

Self-esteem, which is defined as a need to be "loveworthy" (Epstein, 1985, p. 302), occupies a special place in this system. On one hand, once self-esteem reaches a reasonable degree of stability, it acts as the force that holds the self-theory together so that it may provide a consistent basis for identity. For example, low self-esteem begets behavior that primarily seeks to maintain itself by keeping life and its experiences fairly steady in a myriad of ways, such as by employing personal and interpersonal self-protective strategies. Medium and high self-esteem involve different assumptions and priorities but work in the same way.

On the other hand, change is a part of reality and must be accommodated by complex adaptive systems as well: If it is not to become outdated, a good theory must be open to modification and even expand or grow when necessary to accommodate new information. Thus, the other function of self-esteem is to help provide the capacity for taking risks necessary for growth or to effectively adapt to changes. When successful, enhancing and expanding the self in these ways feels good: Therefore, it is reinforcing and motivating. Thus, this theory not only recognizes the paradoxical nature of self-esteem but also actually depends on it. Epstein (1985) said, "As a fundamental preconscious postulate, self-esteem has profound effects on behavior and emotions. Accordingly, the regulation of self-esteem is of critical importance to the individual" (p. 303).

Later, Epstein modified his theory of self-esteem so as to give more attention to information processing at different levels, one that is called "rational" and the other that is named "experiential." These two systems "are not simply different ways of reacting within a single system, but are conceived as two separate systems for adapting to reality" (Epstein & Morling, 1995, p. 10). One system is conscious and easily accessible to the individual. Therefore, it involves what is called "explicit" self-esteem. The other is largely unconscious but often very powerful, and is thereby termed "implicit" self-esteem. Consequently, this theory allows for the possibility of different complex types of self-esteem and the more traditional ones. For example, one might have high explicit and high implicit self-esteem or low explicit self-esteem and low implicit self-esteem, either of which would be fairly stable. However, according to this view, it is also possible to have high explicit but low implicit self-esteem, which is likely to be more unstable. This material is relevant to some of the patterns associated with defensive self-esteem as presented in the previous chapter. However, such work does not conflict with the fundamental structure, so there is no reason to pursue it further.

Harter's Developmental Approach

It was mentioned earlier that in the field of self-esteem, as elsewhere, the gap between psychological and social views of the self is closing. Harter (1999) effectively brought the two together in regard to self-esteem by using modern developmental psychology to show how behavioral competence (the Jamesian tradition) works with social approval (the social learning tradition) to create self-esteem. When studying self-esteem in adolescence, for example,

> Our findings reveal that both James' and Cooley's formulations, taken together, provide a powerful explanation for the level of

self-worth . . . the effects of these two determinants are additive. At each level of social support (representing the average of class-mate and parental approval), greater competence in domains of importance leads to higher self-worth. Similarly, at each level of competence in domains of importance, the more support one garners from classmates and parents, the higher one's self-worth. (p. 182)

As we can see, although Harter defines self-esteem as self-worth, her work is clearly based on two factors, because domains of competence that are of particular importance to an individual combine with various sources of social approval a given person seeks to result in basic or global self-esteem.

Harter went on to recognize that domains of activity important to one's sense of competence change with life. She also found that the social support or approval one seeks or experiences moves with time as well, for instance, from primary caregivers to teachers, peers, friends, spouses or partners, coworkers, and so forth as we age. The relationship between domain competence and approval or support is additive, meaning that self-worth or esteem consists of a summative interaction between the two factors at any given time. In envisioning self-esteem this way, Harter also connected self-esteem to many other developmental processes in power-ful ways.

Self-esteem, then, starts out in relation to many behavioral domains and reflects those that are most important during a particular period of life. Approval takes a similar developmental course. However, some time during middle childhood, cognitive capacities mature to the point where individuals develop an overall evaluation of themselves referred to as glo-bal self-esteem and it becomes another element in the additive picture of self-esteem. At this point, what happens in the domains and what occurs in important relationships continue to influence self-esteem, but now self-esteem may also influence what happens in the domains or relationships. Harter (1999) identified this type of reciprocal causality as "directionality," and thereby sees self-esteem as a "phenomenological mediator." In later work, Harter (2003) also noted that this process of mediation is particu-larly powerful in terms of organizing a person's perception, experience, and behavior. Such a view stands in stark contradiction to that of those who see self-esteem as a mere "epiphenomenon" (Seligman, 1990).

Harter's approach is especially powerful developmentally because she ties the interaction of competence (domains) and worth (relation-ships) to the processes of cognitive maturation and social growth. For example, Harter explicitly connected her theory of self-esteem directly to the cognitive structures of the self as they unfold according to the stages and steps seen in neo-Piagetian developmental theory (Sigelman

& Shaffer, 1995). Among other things, for example, she made it clear that there are distinctions between how self-construal occurs for individuals functioning at the preoperational, concrete operational, and formal operational levels. She also developed separate assessment instruments designed to address these developmental processes for childhood, adolescence, and adulthood.

One result of emphasizing social and psychological processes is that the multidimensional approach enabled Harter to trace the development of self-esteem throughout the entire life cycle, which is an extraordinary achievement. Although all the processes cannot be presented here, it is important to note that she found that there is predictability to the types of domains of behavior and social feedback that may be most significant for self-esteem at a given age, just as one might expect from a developmental perspective (Harter, 1999, p. 119). For instance, there are only five domains of self-concept that have relevance for the development of self-esteem in early childhood, but there are 12 in late adulthood. Some, such as peer acceptance, drop out of significance by early or middle adulthood, but others, such as concerns about mortality, appear at that time. Indeed, only the domain of physical appearance stays with us throughout the life cycle in regard to self-esteem: Apparently, the fact that we are social creatures means that we can never fully escape the way others respond to how we look. Like it or not, the reaction of others always matters to us at some fundamental level, probably in terms of our social desirability or worth as a person.

Harter also made it clear that there is a tremendous degree of individual variation in this process. For example, academic competence can be achieved in writing, math, social science, physical science, shop class, and so forth. Social support or approval from parents is especially important in childhood, but other sources also become important, such as grandparents and teachers. The result is that there is a myriad of developmental possibilities for each individual and all of us must make our own unique way through them. This condition makes assessment crucial, and it begins with identifying the various domains of life that are developmentally tied to each major phase of life, such as childhood, adolescence, and so forth. Then, it is necessary to construct an instrument capable of assessing self-evaluation in each relevant domain as well as a general evaluation of one's global self-esteem. The final step requires creating a large enough sample of subjects to determine what is normative at each major time in life.

The fact that she and her colleagues have developed such instruments for childhood, adolescence, adulthood, and late adulthood stands as a tribute to the range of this approach. However, it also has power. For example, this model of self-esteem and its measures have been used to research problems with self-esteem and depression in adolescents (Harter & Whitesell, 2003). In addition, it is also possible to use these assessment devices in the applied setting and tailor treatment to the needs of a given individual, regardless of where they happen to be in life (Shrik & Harter, 1996).

An Existential View: Terror Management Theory

Terror management theory (TMT) is based on the work of Ernst Becker and places self-esteem at the intersection of two primary human motivations. One source of motivation concerns an irreducible, biologically based desire to live, to expand, and, if possible even to flourish. The other is tied to the problem of living with the awareness that we must all die and that it can happen at any moment. All living things die, of course, but the development of consciousness changes this natural condition in human beings by creating a paradox: The same characteristic that distinguishes our species as unique also creates a specific and terrible awareness of death that is ultimately terrifying. If left unchecked, this theory holds that consciousness of the inevitability of death would be so overwhelming that it could only result in paralytic fear. As Hobbes (1651/1994) said, life is "solitary, poore, nasty, brutish, and short" (p. 76). Thus, human beings require something that will buffer them from existential angst in a way that allows them to live to the fullest while also facing reality: That something is self-esteem.

According to this view, human beings contend with the terror of death through the same capacities that created the problem in the first place: our abilities to think, organize, communicate, and do all of that in a social context. With culture came the possibility of developing systems of belief that transcend the death of an individual and give life meaning. This system of thoughts, beliefs, values, and conventions allows us to avoid the paralytic terror that awareness of death would otherwise create.

> Our species "solved" the problem posed by the prospect of existential terror by using the same sophisticated cognitive capacities that gave rise to the awareness of death to create cultural worldviews: humanly constructed shared symbolic conceptions of reality that give meaning, order, and permanence to existence; provide a set of standards for what is valuable; and promise some form of either literal or symbolic immortality to those who believe in the cultural worldview and live up to its standards of value. (Pyszczynski et al., 2004a, p. 436)

Being connected to a group, family, or community is helpful in warding off terror, but only some form of immortality is capable of triumphing over death, so belief systems that include such a possibility hold great attraction. From the beginning, then, cultural belief systems, such as religion and related practices, evolved to organize behavior in a way that gives it meaning, *especially in the face of death.*

However, for such a rationale to work, the individual must sustain it through beliefs and actions that affirm the values and standards of a particular transcendent worldview, otherwise the entire system crumbles and terror may reign. TMT maintains that the way to regulate behavior so that it supports a given worldview and allows the individual to feel protected from terror is through the development of self-esteem. In other words, "self-esteem is a sense of personal value. . . . It is the feeling that one is a valuable contributor to a meaningful universe—a sense that one's life has both meaning and value" (Pyszczynski et al., 2004a, pp. 436–437). Thus, self-esteem helps the individual transcend the terror of death by living with others in a shared community of morals, beliefs, and practices that are thought to extend beyond the dark door. This sense of connection and protection only occurs by internalizing the various standards of a "sacred canopy," as Berger (1967) so artfully said, which gives the world and life the appearance of being comprehensible, orderly, and meaningful instead of overwhelmingly chaotic and threatening.

At the same time, these standards act as the pathway to self-esteem: They are, in fact, the contingencies for self-worth. The internalized social standards concerning that which is good, desirable, and worthy act as measures for assessing how one is faring in the journey toward immortality. The more a particular individual regulates his or her behavior in accordance with a given religious, cultural, or philosophical belief system, the more meaningful the person's life becomes and the better they feel about themselves, both of which push the terror of death away from consciousness. Conversely, the more people stray from these standards, the less protection they have and the stronger the anxiety of death becomes. These forces, in turn, are thought to drive the individual back to the comfort of the canopy by complying with its standards and practices.

When seen this way, self-esteem is useful in regulating social and individual behavior. For example, acting in accordance with accepted social values generates a sense of competence and worth, but when individuals behave in ways that threaten the worldview of a particular group or culture, existential anxiety resurfaces and lowers self-esteem. This anxiety may be reduced by re-engaging in socially sanctioned, worthy behaviors. Thus, culture provides protection against the terror of death by showing us how to transcend it and self-esteem helps to regulate behavior in a way that sustains such worldviews. The result of these two forces, belief and regulation, is a self-sustaining process that makes life bearable. In short, in TMT, people need self-esteem "because self-esteem provides a shield against a deeply rooted fear of death inherent in the human condition" (Pyszczynski et al., 2004a, p. 437).

The authors of TMT and others have conducted or reviewed dozens of studies concerning this "anxiety-buffering" function of self-esteem. Typically, they show how increasing an individual's awareness of mortality also increases the person's anxiety in ways that the theory predicts, thereby generating empirical support for it (Pyszczynski et al., 2004a). However, adherents also acknowledge the criticism that there are biologically based motives and drives in many organisms that contradict the need to reduce tension, anxiety, or terror, especially in human beings (Ryan & Deci, 2004). For example, risk-taking or the process of exploration actually takes us closer to the possibility of dying, which seems to contradict the theory. TMT attempts to solve this problem by offering a "dual role" for self-esteem. To paraphrase, self-esteem acts as a drive toward the type of growth and enrichment that comes with a search for meaning and stems from a self-preserving need to avoid what would otherwise be an incapacitating anxiety (Greenberg et al., 1995, pp. 82–83). In the end, TMT concludes that "The pursuit of self-esteem is thus neither a good thing nor a bad thing but rather, a part of the system that human beings use to both regulate their behavior and cope with their existential situation" (Pyszczynski, Greenberg, Sheldon, Arndt, & Schimel, 2004b, p. 464).

The Evolutionary Approach: Sociometer Theory

Evolutionary work in the social sciences is gaining considerable scientific attention. Although TMT may be certainly characterized in that fashion, its existential tone distinguishes it from another, strictly evolutionary approach to self-esteem called sociometer theory (ST). As Heatherton and Wyland (2003) pointed out, this theory begins with the assumption that human beings "have a fundamental need to belong that is rooted in our evolutionary history" (p. 39). To appreciate the power of this position, it is only necessary to remember that, as a species, our early ancestors had little in the way of biological equipment to assist in survival. In comparison with other animals, our teeth are dull, our sense of smell is poor, our claws are fragile, our night vision is pathetic, and we only have two legs: When push comes to shove, under these conditions, it is a wonder that we survived at all. Thus, it is not surprising that human beings turn to each other to facilitate survival. Consequently, one of the most threatening things for us to experience is to be cut off from the group. This event not only could hasten death but also could stop genetic transmission that is even more important in an evolutionary context. In other words, not only are groups necessary for human survival, but also their importance far outweighs that of the individual.

According to ST, there is considerable evolutionary survival value in minimizing the threat of becoming marginalized, isolated, or in some other way excluded from the group. To adapt to this situation, biological specialization evolved to help regulate behavior in a way that reduced the risk of being cut off from others. Hence, self-esteem evolved as an adaptive mechanism designed to function as a "psychological module that monitors and responds to events that are relevant to interpersonal acceptance and rejection" (Leary, 2004, p. 374). In other words, self-esteem emerged as a type of "sociometer," as ST calls it, one that is responsive to such things as social cues, interpersonal relationships, and social status indicators that signal the possibility of rejection or exclusion.

Of course, there are other social modules that have evolved to fulfill special functions, such as the attachment–separation modules of infancy, a bonding module associated with parenthood, and so forth (Leary & Downs, 1995). But all of them tend to do three things. One is to scan the environment for relevant cues, especially threatening ones. For the most part, such monitoring is a background process, much like our ears may be attending to a conversation while we drive an automobile, although our eyes are much more intensively engaged with the tasks at hand. Next, when a threat is detected, the module is tied to enough other brain-based processing agencies and modules to evoke a strong affective response, such as suddenly being alarmed by the siren of an emergency vehicle and attending to its potential location. Finally, the detection of a threatening stimulus and a strong response to it lead to changes in behavior designed to effectively deal with the emergency, such as breaking off conversation and pulling to the side of the road.

Thus, the sociometer automatically scans the environment for signs of trouble and alerts us to possible threats or opportunities by evoking our feelings about ourselves in unpleasant or pleasant ways. When self-esteem is threatened or drops, it motivates the individual to regulate behavior so as to prevent rejection or perhaps even increase the changes of positive affiliation. In this way, self-esteem helps us avoid behavior that is likely to get us into trouble and also enhances socially desirable behavior that could improve our chances of getting important needs met, especially the biological imperative of passing along genes that is so characteristic of evolutionary work. Because it is an internal neurologically based module we carry with us, the sociometer may even regulate behavior in the absence of other people. For example, in situations where others are not present, the sociometer becomes generalized enough for us to consider what others would do if they saw our behaviors at these times, which, in turn, helps us regulate our behaviors in socially acceptable ways.

So far, this understanding of self-esteem may seem to regard it as an important but very situational phenomenon or state. However, the theory compares the sociometer with a gauge to illustrate how it also functions as a general phenomenon or trait.

> In addition, what is commonly called trait self-esteem—a per-
> son's typical or chronic level of self-esteem—is also relevant to
> the workings of the sociometer and interpersonal self-regulation.
> If we think of the sociometer as a meter or gauge that assesses
> relational value, trait self-esteem may be conceptualized as the
> resting position of the sociometer in the absence of incoming
> interpersonal feedback. (Leary, 2004, p. 381)

This aspect of ST is also used to account for types and degrees of self-
esteem as well as differences in behavior associated with them. For example, people for whom the "resting point" of the gauge is high because
of their developmental history should generally be reasonably confident,
fairly spontaneous, relatively open, and able to take risks more freely than
others, all of which are advantageous and often associated with high self-
esteem. However, people whose needle is already set to a lower point
to begin with must be more cautious lest it fall farther. In this case, they
would tend to monitor social situations more critically, hold back on initiative, or be more anxious than their counterparts who are higher on the
sociometer.

In addition, the metaphor of a gauge allows ST to account for various self-esteem problems in this way. For example, Leary (2004) noted
that one common type of "miscalibration" occurs when the sociometer is
set too low. In this case, the individual is likely to be overly sensitive, pay
undue attention to negative social cues, brood about events longer than
necessary, and perhaps even become depressed. Conversely, the resting
point of the sociometer can also be too high, which means that people may
act as though they have more social value than they actually do, as in the
case of narcissism. Here, the person is likely to run afoul of social mores or
damage relationships before he or she takes notice of what is happening.

Still, other meters may be hypersensitive in either direction, which
could result in frequent wide swings from one end of the range to the other
in a way that might be characteristic of fragile or defensive self-esteem. If
some sociometers are too sensitive, others may be "sluggish" in a way that
results in less sensitivity to others, which could result in relationship difficulties. Finally, and most important for an evolutionary theory, the metaphor of a gauge can also be applied to sexual relationships. In this case,
mutual attraction can be seen as moving the needle to higher regions of
self-esteem, thereby promoting social risk-taking, or the interaction may
move the pointer down, such as after an argument, thereby encouraging
the development of better communication skills in the future.

In short, although the evolutionary approach is the newest major
perspective on self-esteem, it certainly brings much to the theoretical and
applied table of the field, just as it does elsewhere in the social sciences.
However, unlike most need-based theories, this one does not understand

self-esteem as a free-standing motive. Rather, ST contends that "most behaviors that have been attributed to the need to maintain self-esteem may be parsimoniously explained in terms of the motive to avoid social exclusion" (Leary & Downs, 1995, p. 129). Self-esteem is central to this theory, then, because it is a key component of a biologically foundational need.

Summary of Findings About Theories

There are many other theories that pertain to self-esteem worth considering. For example, self-determination theory (SDT) offers important insights and considerable research on self-esteem. This approach has been used to criticize TMT and focuses on what is called "intrinsic motivation," which we will show is essential to understanding how self-esteem is tied to authenticity. However, proponents of SDT often cite the study by Sheldon et al. (2001) and their list of cross-cultural goals or values mentioned in Chapter 1 as a central foundation for the propositions on which SDT is based. Yet, self-esteem is often left off SDT's "list" of basic needs, although Sheldon et al. clearly found self-esteem to be among the top three needs. Instead, SDT identifies autonomy, competence, and relatedness as central motivations, and self-esteem is usually regarded as a by-product of these factors. Therefore, this approach and others that include self-esteem as an important, but not necessarily crucial, component of behavior are excluded from the analysis, although some of them, such as SDT, certainly make important research contributions to the field.

The aim of this review was to put us in a position where it is possible to ask the more phenomenological question: What do the general theories of self-esteem show us about developing a good theory about it? Several "findings" emerge in this regard. First, major general perspectives in the social sciences offer unique ways of seeing self-esteem. Second, there seems to be a fairly consistent set of specific self-esteem themes or issues that are addressed in these theories that are also seen in the paradoxes on self-esteem presented in Chapter 2, such as its motivational and developmental dimensions. Finally, although each general theory of self-esteem starts out at the abstract level, they all open up implicit or explicit pathways to changing self-esteem at the practical level, much as good theories should.

MAJOR SELF-ESTEEM ENHANCEMENT PROGRAMS

Like many important fields, this one also involves applied work. Several fully developed programs designed to enhance self-esteem began to appear in the 1980s. Although few in number, it is possible to examine work on enhancing self-esteem using the familiar criteria of persistence and significance. In addition, we will examine only self-esteem enhancement programs that seem to focus explicitly on enhancing self-esteem instead of more general therapeutic goals that may enhance self-esteem en passant, as it were. The first part of this process involves a brief presentation of the basic self-esteem ideas on which a particular approach is based, as well as a discussion of the techniques each one uses to enhance self-esteem. The second part of the analysis is to use this information to identify what is required to make a good (i.e., theoretically sound, practically oriented, empirically supportable) self-esteem enhancement program.

Frey and Carlock: Eclectic Variations on a Humanistic Theme

Basic Ideas

Frey and Carlock (1989) are two clinicians who use a definition very similar to Branden's. "Self-esteem has two interrelated components: the feeling that one is competent to live and the feeling that one is worthy of living" (p. 7). The major mechanism for regulating personal experience is found in the humanistic concept of organismic self-regulation. The main body of this program consists of a large collection of experientially oriented human growth and development activities. In other words, this approach is an eclectic one that uses many ideas and practices from other perspectives. For instance, the development of the self-concept is presented in terms of social learning factors, particularly negative environmental influences or "psychological pathogens" (p. 31) that contribute to self-esteem problems. But the program also includes cognitive concepts, such as self-talk and self-fulfilling prophecies, which are identified as important tools for changing self-esteem.

System and Techniques

Although Frey and Carlock bring an extremely diverse mix of theoretical concepts and experiential exercises into play in their approach, all these ideas and activities are organized into a clear four-stage, systematic process or framework. Moreover, the authors stress that although each phase is a distinct step on the path to enhancing self-esteem, they actually constitute a system in which the whole process is greater than the sum of its parts. Hence, it is necessary to follow the phases in order.

This process of enhancing self-esteem begins with the "identity phase." The reason for such a complex starting point may be that self-esteem is readily tied to identity, as we saw in several of the major theories. "Initially in intervention, an individual with low self-esteem needs to discover his/her own identity. Because of distorted perceptions, such persons rarely have a clear understanding of who they really are" (Frey & Carlock, 1989, p. 181). In addition to learning about oneself in some basic ways, this step allows for the fact that obstacles often block awareness or self-experience that must be worked through to know about ourselves and our self-esteem. Accordingly, several standard exercises are suggested to help individuals engage in self-discovery, such as values clarification activities and the like.

Although the search for identity can probably be expanded indefinitely, at some point it is necessary to shift into the second stage that focuses on developing an awareness of one's strengths and weaknesses. This stage concerns helping clients to develop an appreciation of their assets and liabilities as persons. More stress is placed on the positive than negative because individuals with low self-esteem are usually practiced at ignoring their assets and are often skilled at focusing on their liabilities. Two kinds of therapeutic work characterize this stage. First, the facilitator consistently offers positive feedback each time such an opportunity presents itself. Of course, this feedback must be done on the basis of sincerity (it must be true) and concreteness (it should be clear and specific). The second type of intervention is thought to help people alter the characteristically negative ways they filter information about themselves and allow more accurate information to have a voice in self-perception. This technique involves activities that allow people to acknowledge the positive and the negative and to not exaggerate the significance of the latter or minimize the importance of the former.

The third stage, called the "nurturance phase," is the most complex one. Frey and Carlock use the analogy of planting seeds to describe the relationship of the first two steps to this one. "The first two phases in themselves are not sufficient as newly acquired positive self-esteem can be lost if it is not nurtured. Teaching nurturing helps the person to enhance strengths and use them to minimize weaknesses" (Frey & Carlock, 1989, p. 197). The aim of the nurturing phase, then, is to help the new pro-self-esteem behaviors to take root, so to speak. It is especially important to help people transfer their newly developed awareness of the importance of positive self-esteem to environments outside the supportive but limited atmosphere of the therapist's office or group room. Moreover, these clinicians recognize that this project is difficult under even the best of circumstances. For instance, they point out that some people suffer from home or work environments that are "toxic" (a richly descriptive term) to self-esteem, which makes change even more difficult.

The major thrust of the activities involves dealing with the self-fulfilling dynamics that Frey and Carlock place at the heart of perpetuating low self-esteem. In particular, the negative thinking and behavioral patterns that sustain low self-esteem must be overcome and replaced with more positive ones. Accordingly, they offer a number of exercises and activities to facilitate this development. For instance, teaching individuals to identify their self-esteem needs and to get them met in appropriate ways is a step in the right direction. Similarly, participants are asked to affirm their own positive qualities, as well as those of others, in a supportive group setting. Likewise, the importance of individuals developing their own self-esteem support systems is stressed.

In the final stage, this approach focuses on the importance of maintaining self-esteem after the program is over. In this "maintenance" phase, "One needs to learn how to maintain adequate self-esteem just as it is necessary to maintain a car, house, or an interpersonal relationship if it is to grow and flourish" (Frey & Carlock, 1989, p. 205). There are several important reasons for building such a step into a self-esteem enhancement program. First, Frey and Carlock (1989) see increasing self-esteem as an evolving process, so the work that goes on in therapy is just the beginning. As people or their circumstances change, the ways they get their self-esteem needs met may change too. Thus, "During the maintenance phase, individuals are taught to turn experiences into learning situations, practice facilitative risk-taking, set appropriate goals, forecast desired personal outcomes, and publicly affirm goals" (p. 206). The exercises and activities used to further these aims include learning how to set realistic goals and how to develop appropriate risk-taking strategies.

In addition to developing a systematic approach to enhancing self-esteem, Frey and Carlock (1989) note that there are at least three significant practical issues to consider that are almost always present in helping people change. The first is usually called resistance and concerns dealing with the usual technical problems associated with change in general as well as those explicitly associated with changing self-esteem. Next, they focus on the role of, and need for, assessment in changing self-esteem. They note, for instance, that self-esteem issues vary considerably from person to person, which means the clinician must become attuned to differences in participants, a process that is facilitated by accurate assessment. Finally, they recognize that changing self-esteem is a difficult, long-term project: "The change process, like much of human learning, is erratic. Improvement can be followed by a slight regression, which is in turn followed by improvement. This process repeats itself until some stabilization of changed behavior occurs" (p. 213). Ultimately, then, the entire system is based on persistence and hard work.

Summary

One outstanding feature of this approach to enhancing self-esteem is that the program is broken into clearly defined steps, each one of which includes specific objectives and concrete activities. Moreover, these steps progress in a logical fashion, and the exercises are based on fairly common therapeutic or growth-oriented activities. Finally, it is important to note that this program is flexible, which means that it may be applied in a number of clinical and growth settings.

Increasing Self-Esteem Behaviorally: Pope, McHale, and Craighead

Basic Ideas

The approach developed by Pope et al. (1988) actually focuses on working with children and adolescents, even those who excel academically but still have low self-esteem. The program also addresses the needs of various challenged populations. However, this system is based on social learning theory, which means that change occurs on the basis of general and specific learning principles that apply to all ages. The program begins by defining self-esteem as "an *evaluation* of the information contained in the self-concept, and is derived from a child's feelings about *all* the things he is" (p. 2).

Like most social and learning approaches to self-esteem, this way of understanding it is based on a discrepancy notion: the difference between the individual's ideal self-concept (what one thinks one should be) and the perceived or actual self-concept (how one currently sees oneself), or the "ideal vs. the real" self. Self-esteem problems are seen as resulting from a significant difference between these perceptions, which creates the possibility of two basic self-esteem problems. The first one occurs when the ideal self-concept is too high or unrealistic given the individual and his or her circumstances. The resulting gap between what is desired and what is perceived creates low self-esteem: The greater the difference, the greater the self-esteem problems. This type of low self-esteem is associated, for instance, with overachieving children who do well in school or elsewhere but who still feel unworthy because they fail to meet their expectations, however unrealistic they may be. The second type of self-esteem problem occurs when the ideals and expectations are appropriate for a particular person, but the individual fails to live up to them in realistic ways. For instance, underachieving individuals can suffer a sense of inadequacy that comes with failing to meet reasonable expectations of performance given their actual abilities.

In either case, this enhancement program focuses on working with five domains affecting self-esteem: global (overall) self-esteem, social self-esteem (how the child evaluates himself or herself in relation to others), academic self-esteem (the child's school performance and abilities), how the child sees himself or herself as a valued (or unvalued) family member, and the quality of the child's body image (how a child sees his or her physical appearance and abilities). The goal is to identify areas where self-esteem problems are especially important, then design cognitive-behavioral activities to increase skills either to bring performance up to reasonable standards or to reduce exaggerated standards to allow a reasonable degree of skill or success to be and feel satisfactory.

Because learning is the engine that powers this approach, it is not surprising to find that general learning principles are used to effect change, especially positive reinforcement and modeling. Indeed, even the role of the therapist is couched in a learning framework. For instance, the authors indicate that the clinician must be a supportive teacher and a skilled practitioner. Modern social learning theory also recognizes the importance of certain processes as crucial components of behavioral change. One of them, problem solving, is a pivotal element in this approach: "One of the basic findings of cognitive psychology is that humans possess problem-solving skills. The potential discrepancy between our ideal and perceived self-concepts can be viewed as a problem to be solved" (Pope et al., 1988, p. 11).

In addition to presenting a general strategy for change based on such an orientation, Pope et al. are also concerned with the developmental context of self-esteem. Their program recognizes that there are relatively specific, age-related, developmental factors in the five areas mentioned earlier that affect self-esteem. This realization means that it is necessary to tailor intervention strategies toward the cognitive and behavioral skill level of the client. At the same time, it is recognized that each individual is unique. Children and adolescents (as well as adults) have personal preferences, different environments, and individual talents or deficits that must be considered in creating an effective self-esteem enhancement program. In other words, the program depends heavily on rigorous psychological assessment.

System and Techniques

The program begins with a detailed assessment process aimed at identifying an individual's particular self-esteem problems, needs, and potentials. Interviews with the child and significant others, actual observations of the client in his or her natural environments while engaged in everyday activities, and psychological tests are all methods of gathering information that are recommended by the authors. The assessment process aims at identifying which basic type of self-esteem problem appears to be present and determining how serious it is, both of which involve a person's global self-esteem. The other four areas (social esteem, academic esteem, how one is esteemed as a family member, and one's feelings about body image) are evaluated as well, making the assessment comprehensive.

Pope et al. recommend using standard tests, such as the Piers-Harris (1969), to assess general self-esteem problems and issues. They also recognize that assessing specific areas like those mentioned earlier is often difficult because it involves finding or creating specific age-based norms for each domain, and because human development can vary considerably in any one of them. The authors are also sensitive to such factors as gender and self-esteem, as well as cultural diversity (although that term is not used) and self-esteem. Hence, they strongly recommend talking to others involved in the child's life. Such sources of information, especially those obtained from family and teachers, can reveal important things about how a child lives out academic, social, familial, and physical issues that may not be apparent in the therapy hour.

In addition to identifying self-esteem problems, a good assessment includes understanding the individual's particular strengths (Fischer, 1986). This part of the process is important because it is easier to design activities or experiences that are more likely to be successful and rewarding if we work with existing skills. Finally, the authors suggest that the clinician should assess and understand the individual's cognitive and self-evaluative styles. In other words, the therapist should develop a sense of the subject's "private speech" or habitual thinking patterns, especially those that concern the standards by which the person judges his or her behavior. In short, the assessment process is a crucial one for this enhancement approach. Not only does it let the therapist know with whom he or she is dealing so that the program can be individualized for the client, but accurate assessment also gives ideas about what is realistically possible.

This enhancement program aims to increase self-esteem by teaching the individual new, age-appropriate skills designed to help him or her handle the demands and problems of life more effectively. Pope et al. recommend that the clinician share this intent with the client in language that he or she will understand so the individual can be a partner in this process. The clinician and client contract to meet together on a regular basis to do this kind of learning. One or two 30-minute sessions per week are recommended for younger children, and one or two 60-minute sessions per week for older clients.

Pope et al. also point out that the program may be offered in group or individual settings. In either case, the therapeutic activity is structured in two ways. First, the process is broken up into eight segments, each of which focuses on a certain type of behavioral, cognitive, or social skill related to self-esteem. These skill areas are learning to solve social problems, developing positive self-statements, using a realistic attributional style, increasing self-control, setting appropriate standards, developing social understanding and social skills, increasing communication skills, and improving body image. The authors make it clear that the eight areas are arranged in a particular order and that following this sequence is a crucial part of the program. So important is this point that it is stressed in the introduction to the program and then again as the major point of the book's afterword.

Second, the format for all the activities associated with any of the areas is structured in a consistent way. In other words, each area becomes a program module. These modules always begin with an assessment of the individual's skills, abilities, and potential in each particular area so that the therapist knows what is needed and what is possible. Once the needed skills are identified, they are acquired by completing specific exercises. Then, the "homework" is assigned to the client, a technique that reinforces the new material and helps transfer it to the real world.

Although all the modules are structured in the same way, an individual may need less time in one area and more in another until a satisfactory degree of progress occurs, so help is individualized. Note that this program relies heavily on what behavioral therapists call "homework," which means that problems are identified, clients are given new alternatives to try, they receive feedback about their attempts, and then apply the new alternatives to real life until the new abilities become habitual. Such techniques make good theoretical and practical sense in a learning-based program because skill acquisition takes time and practice. Including real-life experiences into treatment means that learning may occur even after the program ends. In fact, "booster" sessions are recommended to "meet with the child to reassess his ability to use his new skills in a way which enhances his self-esteem" (Pope et al., 1988, p. 139).

Summary

There is also much to be said for this self-esteem enhancement system. First and foremost, it possesses what computer programmers call "transparency." The steps and procedures are extraordinarily systematic in that there is a clear, logical connection between the recommended exercises or activities and the well-respected cognitive-behavioral therapeutic techniques, such as using positive reinforcement, teaching problem-solving, and modifying self-talk. In addition, the program is structured in a stepwise fashion. This process makes it possible to track progress by comparing initial base ratings with final outcomes. A final strength of this approach is that it is designed to make a difference early in life, which could make it more effective in the long run because of the potential for prevention and treatment. However, it does need to be "translated" into the world of working with adults if it is to be used with that population, which is central for our purposes.

Bednar, Wells, and Peterson: Enhancing Self-Esteem Cognitively

Basic Ideas

The self-esteem enhancement system found in *Self-Esteem: Paradoxes and Innovations in Clinical Theory and Practice* by Bednar et al. (1989) is based on two perspectives. The first consists of concepts found in modern information-processing psychology and that distinguish the cognitive approach. The second set of ideas concerns a theory of psychopathology and its treatment that is based on a combination of cognitive and existential thought. After defining self-esteem as a feeling of self-approval, they go on to say that self-esteem is a dynamic phenomenon that develops as a result of the cognitive processes of feedback, circularity, and self-regulation. "Our model of self-esteem is based on four underlying assumptions, each of which involves *feedback* about personal and interpersonal acceptability" (p. 91). Later on the same page, it is noted that the feedback involved in self-esteem is such that it has the power to influence behavior.

Two types of feedback seem to be most important in relation to the development of self-esteem. Information about our behavior and selves that comes from others (or the social environment in general) is called external or interpersonal feedback. This type of information includes many of the social factors affecting self-esteem we found in reviewing self-esteem research, such as cultural influences. The other form, called internal feedback, comes from our own experience, especially from the evaluations we make of our own behavior and of ourselves. Both types of information play a role in regulating our actions, but internal feedback is seen as more important because it is affective, stronger, more direct, and difficult to dismiss.

Bednar et al. also maintain the position that the sad reality is that most of us face more negative sources of feedback about ourselves than positive ones. Because it is less frequent, they maintain that positive feedback is more important than negative. This internal/external, positive/negative feedback system is constantly operating and continually provides information to us about ourselves and what we are like. At some point in the developmental process, however, these feedback systems become self-regulating and, therefore, relatively stable. At that time, we achieve a degree of positive or negative self-esteem and seek to maintain it as a part of the self-system.

Another major process affecting the development of self-esteem is the individual's "response style," or how a person characteristically responds to psychological threat or conflict. According to this view, such stress (or what other theories call "anxiety") is an inevitable part of life. Although they can vary in terms of intensity and frequency, there are two opposing ways to deal with these stressors: People can respond to psychological threat by attempting to avoid it or by trying to cope with it. Each alternative has powerful consequences for self-esteem. Avoidance, for instance, is a defensive maneuver, a form of denial, which makes it an immature response when compared with coping, which is mature and realistic. Probably because it seems to promise less pain initially, avoidance is the path of least resistance in dealing with threat and anxiety. However, avoiding conflict is more costly in the long run because doing so cuts us off from valuable information concerning ourselves and the world around us.

In addition, excessive avoidance leads to chronic defensiveness, which creates its own burden: In turning away from the truth, we are trapped by it because now we must manage both the conflict and the false solution we offer it. Ultimately, habitual avoidance results in a phenomenon the authors call "impression management," which means having to maintain a facade as well as continuing to avoid the threat that gave rise to it. This stance toward the world and others requires a massive expenditure of perceptual, psychological, interpersonal, and behavioral energies. The more we choose avoiding over coping, the more likely serious distortions and unrealistic behaviors are to occur. If impression management continues long enough, then low self-esteem develops and with it comes an increased sensitivity to threats or even the possibility of threats. Eventually, this self-fulfilling prophecy leads to more serious difficulties, including the development of abnormal or pathological behavior.

Of course, the healthy way to deal with conflict is to cope, and coping works the same way: Conflicts arise, we respond, and sooner or later these patterns also become self-fulfilling. The difference is that these dynamics are based on facing the problem honestly, tolerating discomfort and uncertainty while doing so, taking psychological risks associated with being open to one's shortcomings, and, above all, taking responsibility for one's actions. Either way, Bednar et al. make it clear that most of us eventually tend in one direction more than the other and the patterns become set.

From this position, changing self-esteem must be based on the laws governing feedback, circularity, and self-regulation. The authors point out, for instance, that to survive, complex systems can never really be completely closed; they must always maintain the ability to adapt to changes in the environment because change is an environmental fact. Hence, new kinds of feedback can affect old patterns so that significant changes may occur. It is even possible for new homeostatic balance to be reached. In this case, the most effective way to increase self-esteem is quite clear: Stop avoiding conflicts and begin to face them. If this new and positive information is entered into the self-esteem frequently or powerfully enough (feedback), then the system ought to respond (circularity). Such an adjustment (self-regulation) would change the self-fulfilling nature to a more virtuous cycle of higher self-esteem instead of the vicious one associated with lower self-esteem.

System and Techniques

The central task in enhancing self-esteem is to reduce the degree to which a person engages in behavior (including thoughts and feelings) that promotes avoiding problems and to simultaneously strengthen the individual's capacity to cope with them. Because Bednar et al. (1989) recognize that there are affective, behavioral, and cognitive factors that make up experience, they structure clinical activities so that intervention occurs on all three levels: "The easiest way to do this is to deal with psychological events as they occur in the 'here-and-now,' which allows immediate access to the thoughts and feelings that accompany behavior as it occurs" (p. 173). This present-centered focus is characteristic of existential encounters.

In short, the therapeutic methods used to enhance self-esteem in this approach emphasize "experiential learning," which means that the therapy focuses on how the client avoids conflicts and problems, especially as they arise in the actual therapy session. Accordingly, the clinician is trained to focus on identifying opportunities in the actual therapeutic session to "catch" an individual engaging in conflict avoidance and to therapeutically confront these moments with the client. "Our assumption is that when personal learning takes place simultaneously at a cognitive, behavioral, and affective level, it has more psychological impact than when these domains are insulated from each other" (p. 174).

The process of change this program offers involves mastering four reasonably specific, indispensable steps. First, it is necessary to identify the client's dominant avoidance patterns of dealing with conflict, anxiety, or psychological threat, especially by observing how the client engages in avoidance while in the sessions. The aim is to assist the person in seeing these patterns for what they are: impediments to a better life. The therapist then asks the client to identify honestly and name the ways in which he or she closes off dealing with conflict. Each such pattern is uncovered in this way, as they occur, so that the client develops a sense of ownership for his or her own ways of avoiding dealing with conflict.

Second, the therapist moves the client toward discovering all the thoughts and feelings that accompany these avoidance patterns. This step is taken by asking the person to describe in as great detail as possible such things as the actual behavior involved in a particular way of avoiding, what he or she feels when turning away from reality, and the kind of thinking that goes on for him or her at these times. Although painful, this step is also best done in the here-and-now with the therapist because the material is psychologically fresh.

The third and critical phase is to help the person face the avoidance patterns he or she characteristically uses and to confront the negative self-evaluations that accompany them. In other words, the client is asked to face underlying fear, cowardice, or self-loathing, and so forth head on. Once again, this part of the process is done most effectively in vivo or with real conflicts that emerge in the actual sessions. The aim is for the client to encounter his or her own modes of avoidance as they are actually being lived. The authors stress that the act of making this realization and accepting responsibility for it is often painful, but also maintain that this pain is a necessary step toward coping. This new and honest behavioral response is also highlighted and examined in great detail. The therapist takes care to have the individual identify, explore, and label positive responses and self-evaluations because doing so is reinforcing and because it helps break old cognitive and behavioral patterns. The final step is one of continued learning or "gradually learning how to cope with personal conflicts" (1989, p. 140). This one is mastered when the client repeats the process of identifying, labeling, and experiencing the positive nature of coping until it becomes the primary response style, a process, of course, that requires considerable time.

Bednar et al. (1989) offer specific technical suggestions concerning timing and methods of facilitating this process at each step of the way. For example, they divide therapeutic work into two basic kinds of activity. The first, called "remediation," constitutes the bulk of the program and is aimed at breaking the negative avoiding patterns. The other work involves strengthening what they call the client's "disposition to cope" (p. 209). This process is less strenuous and demanding on the client because it involves conflict-free learning. Timing work in such a way as to alternate between remediation and this healthier disposition may help the process move at an optimal therapeutic pace.

It is also important to note that Bednar et al. (1989) specify that their program requires skilled assessment and that they identify two types of essential assessment activities. The first is called "process evaluation," which aims at determining "the client's capacity for a candid and realistic conversation about the meaning and significance of personal problems with a nonpunitive, reasonably astute professional person" (p. 188). Because the therapist is looking for limits and ability, he or she is active in this assessment. For instance, the therapist makes it clear that it may be necessary to actually push the client toward sensitive or painful material. In such work, the focus is on what makes *this* particular person defensive, the degree to which the patterns of avoidance are ingrained, and how well the individual can tolerate looking honestly at himself or herself. The other form of assessment focuses on what the authors refer to as an evaluation of "content and substance." This type of evaluation is more analytical than experiential, and focuses more on understanding the specific patterns of coping and avoiding that a person characteristically uses. For instance, it includes assessing which specific issues trigger these responses in a given individual and which behaviors he or she uses to avoid facing the conflicts involved in his or her responses.

Finally, Bednar et al. (1989) unequivocally indicate that the role of the therapist and the abilities of the person in that role are vital to this self-esteem enhancement program. In fact, it may be said that the entire process hinges on the ability of the therapist because he or she actively seeks to "make things happen" in the therapeutic encounter. For it to work, this approach to enhancing self-esteem depends on an intense personal encounter right in the office and on client risk-taking, both in and out of the session. Indeed, the authors say that, "Psychological anguish induced in treatment is the first sign of personal change in the direction of coping" (p. 134). Experiencing the full effect of one's own negative self-evaluation is a necessary but tricky part of treatment. Accordingly, Bednar et al. clearly emphasize the need for the program to be offered by a highly skilled, experienced therapist. He or she is admonished to make sure that things do not happen too quickly or too intensely in the process, as either of these two possibilities could be harmful to the client.

Summary

Perhaps the most important and distinguishing feature of this approach is that it is an explicitly clinical program. This highly individualized approach requires professional assessment and intervention by a well-trained individual who is capable of handling an intensive treatment process that involves risk-taking by the client both in and out of the sessions. However, an advantage the program offers is that it is capable of addressing more serious self-esteem problems: The combination of intensive individual work coupled with a high degree of clinician expertise allows other conditions, such as clinically significant depression or character pathology, to be treated at the same time as work is done on self-esteem.

Harter's Developmental Approach

Basic Ideas

It will be remembered that Harter (1999) offered an approach to understanding self-esteem based on two developmental factors that work together. These two "general antecedents" (p. 312) of self-worth are competence and what she calls social approval, which I refer to as worthiness. Being competent in the domains of life that are important to individuals personally plays an important role in fostering self-esteem and reflects the Jamesian approach to understanding self-esteem. Acceptance and approval from others, particularly significant others, also feeds into the self-esteem picture in terms of worth and is emphasized by the social learning tradition we saw earlier. Typically, the two forces interact with each other to produce a normal or healthy level of self-esteem that follows the usual developmental patterns for various age groups. Like all developmental phenomena, however, multidimensional developmental processes also mean that individual variation is the rule rather than the exception. In other words, we all have to "find" our own way to self-esteem in a manner that reflects individual temperament and circumstances.

However, sometimes the road through development is not smooth, which means that various types of difficulties may occur. In general, they include such possibilities as insufficient success in important domains, a lack of social approval at particularly significant times, and unfortunate mismatches between domains that are important to a particular person and the degree of approval that is received in relation to them. Such events can affect an individual in a negative way, depending on the meaning the domains hold at the personal level. When that happens, self-esteem problems are likely to occur. Depending on the directionality of the interaction of self-esteem and behavior for a given individual, the difficulties may then play a role in such phenomena as insecurity, anxiety, depression, and a whole host of problems, identified in the *Diagnostic and Statistical Manual of Mental Disorders, Fourth Edition* (2000) and mentioned earlier, that are connected to self-esteem. Fortunately, according to Harter's theory, if the lack of competence or worthiness is related to such difficulties, it should also be possible to work on problematic domains and thereby alleviate many self-esteem-related problems.

System and Techniques

Harter begins by noting that, historically, there are two general approaches to enhancing self-esteem. One is to focus on increasing a sense of worth as a person. In this case, the aim is to help the person find ways of feeling better about himself or herself in the hope that he or she becomes better able to tolerate such things as stress, disappointment, or criticism from others. The other approach, called "skills enhancement," focuses on helping people to acquire the skills that are necessary to be effective in various domains of life, which, in theory, leads to degrees of competence. Harter combined the two possibilities and built her program around three things: assessing the individual, tailoring interventions to behavioral and interpersonal domains that are important for the client's self-esteem, and using various cognitive and social learning techniques to enhance competence and worth or self-esteem.

Assessment plays a key role in this approach for reasons that are similar to those that influenced the program developed by Pope et al. If self-esteem is understood as being connected to various domains of living, then it is necessary to have an idea of how a particular individual is functioning in them to identify areas of difficulty. It is also important to note domains in which the individual is doing well, because in this approach, working with strengths is just as important as working on weaknesses. Similarly, if self-esteem is seen as being influenced by social forces and significant others, then it is helpful to know the major characters in a person's life, especially who is helpful and who is not. In short, a multidimensional model of self-esteem that is tied to development requires a multidimensional assessment of the individual, which is based on norms for a given major stage of life. Once assessment is complete, areas of concern are identified and potential strengths are clarified. Then, this information is used to develop a treatment strategy that is tailored to the person's specific needs. The clinician may select from a number of treatment techniques depending on what assessment reveals, but they can generally be divided into two categories that reflect the basic structure of self-esteem.

The first set of techniques is termed "Intervention Strategies Directed at Cognitive Determinants" (Harter, 1999, p. 316). The general strategy is to reduce major discrepancies between the ideal and real self. One way to accomplish this goal is to identify areas of life that are important to the individual but in which he or she is not doing well. Then, it is possible to direct work at increasing skills that are necessary for success in those areas. As success increases, the discrepancy should decrease, thereby making self-esteem rise. If that route is not possible, one may also focus on the importance of each area and reduce the significance of the ones in which an individual has little chance to succeed. Similarly, if such a tactic proves to be less than helpful, it is possible to increase the importance of another area that is more promising. Other, more cognitively oriented, techniques include encouraging the development of a more realistic image of the self, which allows one to use a host of techniques from attribution theory, narrative therapy, and so forth. All variations of this technique should aim at reducing the discrepancy, thereby altering the self-esteem picture in a positive way.

As might be expected from her approach, the other set of interventions is more social in nature. This approach requires an accurate sense of the client's social world, the people in it, and what roles they play in terms of offering positive or negative social support or influence. Once this information is established, it may be used to develop realistic intervention strategies that increase social support and, therefore, the individual's sense of social worth. For example, it might be possible to help a child see the support that is being given to him or her more clearly, which could help him or her feel less isolated. In another case, it might be helpful to encourage the individual's significant others to be more supportive or to at least reduce negative interactions. In other situations, it may even be necessary to help find new social sources of approval from which to internalize positive identifications. Finally, of course, Harter makes it clear that both cognitive and social interventions can and should be used together to create an optimal plan. She termed her approach the "case-formulation method" (Shrik & Harter, 1996) and concluded that aged-based assessment is the key to the process of designing appropriate interventions.

Summary

What is especially remarkable in Harter's approach is that she is one of the very few who have done major work in all three areas (theory, research, and practice), thereby giving her approach a high degree of consistency. In addition, the theory is powerful because it is based on two factors of self-esteem rather than one, which means that it can draw from both the Jamesian and social learning traditions. The approach is also highly developmental in character, which gives it the potential to apply to a wide range of people. Although not normed against large numbers of subjects, Harter has also developed assessment instruments that are both multi-dimensional and span the entire life cycle. Finally, she has combined theory with assessment to offer an approach to enhancing self-esteem in the clinical setting that is extremely individualized to the needs of the client. Unfortunately, these tests do not include norms for detecting self-deception and the ceiling effect, meaning that many false positives and negatives may slip by them in clinical work.

A Note on Burns' *Ten Days to Self-Esteem*

Although often referred to as a self-help program, and even though it is based on a worthiness definition of self-esteem, there are two good reasons David Burns' cognitively oriented *Ten Days to Self-Esteem* (1993a) and *Ten Days to Self-Esteem: The Leader's Manual* (1993b) deserve attention. First, this program is a systematic approach to dealing with self-esteem defined in terms of feeling worthy as a person and with various problems related to self-esteem, especially anxiety and depression. This 10-session approach is aimed at enhancing self-esteem using a variety of cognitive techniques. These steps are arranged in a sequential order and may be followed in the self-help or group settings. Each step involves specific activities, including assessment and enhancement techniques, that help prepare the individual for the next level. This program is highly structured through the use of a manual that includes specific guidelines for practitioners and clients. This "manualized" approach increases the program's reliability when compared with others, a characteristic that makes researching program effectiveness relatively straightforward. Also, the program seems to be more thoroughly tested than others: It has been used with various mental health populations and has been the focus of a longer term research project (1993a, 1993b) aimed at testing its efficacy, something that is very rare in this field.

Second, the approach also brings up a self-esteem issue that most scientific research and practices tend to avoid. We encountered this question in Chapter 3 when we looked at the humanistic approach to defining self-esteem in regard to the spiritual possibilities associated with its transpersonal school of thought. Burns (1993a) talked about this issue using the metaphor of a ladder. In particular, he envisioned self-esteem as a stagelike process. Beginning from the position of little or no self-esteem, the first step on this ladder is what he calls "conditional self-esteem." Next, there is "unconditional self-esteem," which is described as a type of self-esteem that we all have at birth and to which we are entitled as human beings. Finally,

> You can adopt the even more radical position that there is no such thing as self-esteem, just as there is no such thing as a worthwhile person or a worthless person. . . . This solution to the problem of self-esteem is in the Buddhist tradition because self-esteem is rejected as a useless illusion. (pp. 186–188)

Note that I am not necessarily agreeing with the position that "egolessness" is the ultimate goal of a search for self-esteem, and I certainly do not think self-esteem is useless. However, such a concern does raise some important self-esteem questions, such as how one understands it in relation to approaches that de-emphasize the importance of the self, or even see it as an obstacle to reaching "higher" levels of functioning. Crocker and Park (2003, 2004) and Crocker and Nuer (2003, 2004) made mention of this dimension of self-esteem when they showed how contingent self-esteem leads to a psychological dead end. Harter (1999) noticed this issue in relation to Zen.

Having done some work in that area (Mruk & Hartzell, 2003), I think some insight may be gained by considering the possibility that when defined in terms of two factors, self-esteem is a basic existential condition. In addition, the psychological and linguistic space created by the interaction of competence and worthiness is not necessarily inconsistent with various concepts of spirituality. For example, the most "spiritual" people I have met in the Eastern and Western traditions are not concerned with conditional self-esteem as Rogers or Burns described it. However, when it comes to dealing with the challenges of living in ways that are both competent and worthy, I cannot think of anyone who does that which is "just and right" much better than such people. In other words, although they may not call it self-esteem, the relationship between these two factors is still lived as such. This point is an important one because it takes away the negative connotations of self-esteem when seen from a theological rather than scientific view.

Summary of Findings About Enhancement Programs

At this point, the question becomes what do these major self-esteem programs show us about how to design a good program? In other words, is there a general structure that underlies scientific approaches to increasing self-esteem? Knowing about the essential components of such a process is important in two ways: This kind of information may be helpful in developing a phenomenological or meaning-based program, and such findings may help us evaluate the quality of a program in regard to existing standards of practice in the field.

For one thing, it now seems clear that the more sophisticated approaches to enhancing self-esteem have solid psychological roots good enough to stand the tests of time in scientific disciplines. For example, Frey's and Carlock's approach is based on a definition of self-esteem that is compatible with Branden's humanistic formulation, and many of their growth-oriented techniques are humanistic. Pope et al. clearly build on practices that are seen in the social learning approach developed by Rosenberg and Coopersmith. Bednar et al. identify their program as being cognitive and existential in nature, and the techniques they suggest for enhancing self-esteem seem to be compatible with both points of view. Finally, Harter's work has its roots in the two oldest traditions in the field. The point is that major self-esteem enhancement programs tend to have logical, identifiable ties to general theories of self-esteem, which, in turn, are connected to even larger theoretical perspectives in social science. A good self-esteem enhancement program is, then, set within *the context of a general theory of human behavior and is based upon competence, worthiness, or both.*

Second, an examination of data presented in this chapter suggests that *self-esteem enhancement programs are systematic.* Good programs appear to be structured in a programmatic or stepwise fashion. In each case, the system is organized according to clearly defined stages. Furthermore, these steps are always arranged sequentially to produce a cumulative effect when executed properly. Moreover, each phase is organized in a particular way: Any given step in any particular program aims at a reasonably clear goal and includes a relatively specific set of therapeutic activities designed to help the client reach it. In addition, major programs involve common processes. The more notable ones include increasing awareness of the importance of self-esteem, dealing with defensiveness and resistance to change, changing self-defeating behaviors, and acquiring new competencies. In short, enhancing self-esteem can be a specific, perhaps even specialized, therapeutic enterprise.

Third, each major self-esteem enhancement program recognizes the *importance of assessment.* This component can be included as an informal process as seen in Frey and Carlock or in Bednar et al., or as a formal one as found in Pope et al. and Harter. Identifying the significance of a person's self-esteem issues, knowing what type of self-esteem problems are being presented, and being able to adjust the pace and intensity of techniques to the needs of a particular person all involve assessment skills and procedures. Moreover, assessment usually works hand in hand with therapeutic work so that they strengthen each other. In short, assessment is an important part of enhancing self-esteem in two ways: It tells us what is needed for a given individual and helps prevent us from harming people.

Fourth, self-esteem enhancement programs do not rely on theory and technique alone. They all recognize the *importance of the role of the therapist or facilitator and his or her presence as a person* in enhancing self-esteem. Moreover, much of the process and outcome depends on the usual therapeutic intangibles, such as being reasonably caring, providing a certain degree of nurturing or warmth and acceptance, and being able to listen well, as well as other common factors (Arkowitz, 1997; Prochaska & Norcross, 1994; Seligman, 1995a) in the therapeutic process. However, each program also requires learning various skills, so the role of the clinician or facilitator in enhancing self-esteem is also that of teacher, coach, and champion, as the case may be. This dimension of enhancing self-esteem means that in addition to having a scientific background, those who run such programs should also offer encouragement when necessary, be as genuine as possible without becoming overly involved, and watch for the "teachable moment" (Havighurst, 1972) while doing this type of work.

The fifth and final finding about self-esteem enhancement programs is that there is a useful degree of *clinical diversity* present among these systems. For instance, Frey's and Carlock's program is extremely flexible. It may be used with many kinds of individuals providing they are basically healthy and may be offered in group or individual formats. Pope et al. and Harter offer ways to set up highly structured programs, which are helpful in dealing with special populations such as children or specially challenged individuals. And Bednar et al. offers a structured path to dealing with more serious self-esteem problems that require intensive and lengthy treatment. In short, solid programs are ones that are built on a certain type of fundamental structure that is especially helpful for enhancing self-esteem. Now, let us see how this search through the research and theory of self-esteem takes us to a more integrated position.

5

An Existentially Based Two-Factor Theory of Self-Esteem

The investigation of major definitions and theories in this field found that a good theory of self-esteem is likely to be characterized by at least four key features: basing the theory on a standard definition of self-esteem, grounding the theory in at least one of the major perspectives within psychology, accounting for the major (quantitative and qualitative) findings in the field, and offering empirically based ways of testing the theory in real-world settings. In other words, "good" self-esteem theories do not just pop up out of nowhere. These criteria are important because they not only provide clear guidelines for theory building but also enable us to validate its claims. We have already seen that the two-factor approach meets two criteria: It is based on a long-standing definition that has generated a body of supportive work over time and is grounded in a major psychological tradition, namely the humanistic-existential position. Now we must turn to the third requirement and show how an existential or meaning-based theory can deal with major self-esteem findings and integrate them in a unified, comprehensive fashion.

THE FUNCTION OF SELF-ESTEEM AS MEANING MAKING

The two-factor approach allows us to begin by understanding self-esteem in terms of a matrix of meaning, one that is created by facing various developmental and existential challenges in ways that are competent and worthy, and doing so over time. The term matrix is chosen because, by definition, a matrix is something that gives rise or birth to something else, in this case self-esteem and what it means about us as individuals. In addition, we saw research indicating that self-esteem serves two functions, namely self-protection and self-expansion. Therefore, both functions must be accounted for by this approach if it is to be comprehensive. Such a "meaning matrix," as it were, can be easily represented visually as seen in Figure 5.1.

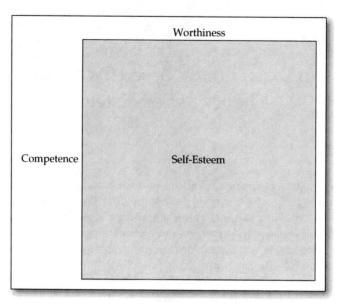

FIGURE 5.1
Two-factor self-esteem matrix.

The simple diagram shows how competence and worthiness interact with each other to create the psychological and linguistic space of self-esteem. Like Tafarodi's and Vu's (1997) analogy of a rectangle, it is possible to identify one factor as "height" and the other as "width." However, any combination of length and width creates any number of rectangles, and we know that competence and worthiness interact with each other as equal partners in regard to the formation and function of self-esteem. Thus, the analogy must be modified to accompany this aspect, something that is achieved by selecting the only rectangular form in which length and width are equal, namely a square.

In addition to accommodating these very basic dimensions of self-esteem, we can also use the analogy to map out more of the theory based on what the research showed us about competence and worthiness in the previous chapters. For example, it is possible to place competence on one axis of the matrix to represent the efficacy of behavior as seen in Figure 5.2. The horizontal axis is selected for this factor because behavior is easier to measure or observe than an internal state, and individual abilities are well disposed to being described in terms of a standard distribution that is often represented by a horizontal line indicating a continuum of performance from poor to good, or even exceptional. It is also possible to account for individual differences in this fashion. For instance, good or superior performance at a particular task, skill, or activity may be represented numerically with a positive value from 0 to 10, which is found on the right side of the line. Inferior or poor performance is placed on the other

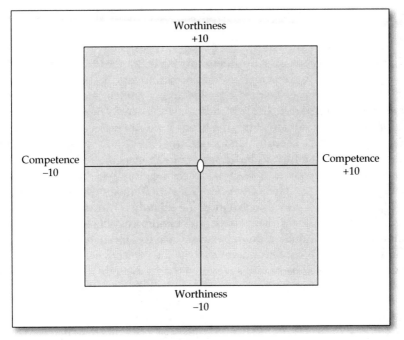

FIGURE 5.2
Self-esteem matrix and basic divisions.

side, starting with 0 and extending to −10. The result is a continuum of competence ranging from low, through average, to high. Global or general competence would be represented in the same fashion.

There is also good reason to represent the other factor, worthiness, with the vertical axis of the matrix. In this case, recall that self-worth involves values, such as general social values concerning what is desirable, being valued in a relationship, individual self-values related to worthiness as a person, and intrinsic and perhaps even cross-cultural or basic human values. Values are often arranged in terms of hierarchical importance or desirability, such as "superior and inferior," "higher and lower," "good and bad," and so forth. Thus, it is more descriptively analogous to illustrate worthiness with the vertical axis as presented in Figure 5.2. Those who have higher levels of feeling accepted, virtuous, or worthy would be found at the upper end, which is represented by the number 10. Those who live in a chronic state of self-loathing or demonstrate a lack of worthiness through their actions would be placed in the lower region, which ranges all the way to −10. Most of us would be somewhere between the two extremes, which would be represented by an area closer to the zero point. However, because research shows that most people say they are at least somewhat happy (Diener & Diener, 1995) and 0 is the middle of a standard deviation scale, it is important to realize that 0 does not mean none.

THE BASIC TYPES OF SELF-ESTEEM

In Chapter 3, we saw that there are several types and levels of self-esteem. High and low types of self-esteem are fairly standard descriptions that have been used by researchers and practitioners in the field from its beginning. However, the next type has many names, such as contingent, fragile, insecure, paradoxical, pseudo, unstable, and defensive self-esteem. I employ the term defensive self-esteem for two reasons. One is that this phrasing was first used by Coopersmith (1959, 1967) when he began to research the possibility of basic types of self-esteem. Second, no matter what term is offered as a way of describing this type of self-esteem, it always involves a state of vulnerability that results in some form of defensiveness as a way of regulating the self when threatened.

In words more consistent with our definition of self-esteem, this type of self-esteem is founded on an imbalanced relationship between competence and worth. Such a configuration weakens the protective ability and buffering functions of self-esteem in a way that makes the individual more vulnerable to perceived threats. Such increased vulnerability, in turn, creates a state of conscious or unconscious vigilance and an accompanying readiness to defend oneself from the instability generated by a lack of balance. Focusing on self-protection has the important side effect of diminishing the other function of self-esteem, which can limit the possibility of self-expansion.

What differentiates this type of self-esteem from simple, low self-esteem is that part of it is based in reality. In other words, defensive self-esteem involves the presence of genuine competence or a sense of worth, but not both. This condition makes defensive self-esteem difficult to dislodge. Consequently, rather than dealing with the imbalance, defending against the deficiency of a component is motivationally appealing: Such a response only requires deceiving one's self, which also seems to reduce tension and is therefore reinforcing. However, such a pattern can be maintained only by the frequent use of personal or interpersonal defensive modalities. These mechanisms may be mild ones, such as self-handicapping or relationship withdrawal, but can range to more severe levels, such as classical forms of denial, rationalization, projection, and the like.

Of course, any effective theory of self-esteem must be able to account for such a basic fact as the finding that there are types of self-esteem and how such a thing is possible. Once again, the two-factor fundamental structure rises to the occasion. Figure 5.3 shows that when competence and worthiness are placed in a dynamic relation to one another as required by this version of the two-factor approach, the result is the natural formation of basic self-esteem types, each of which reflects a unique combination of competence, worthiness, and whether they stand in a balanced relationship to each other. As the diagram indicates, these types clearly emerge from the two factors and their relationship. Indeed, this theoretical model

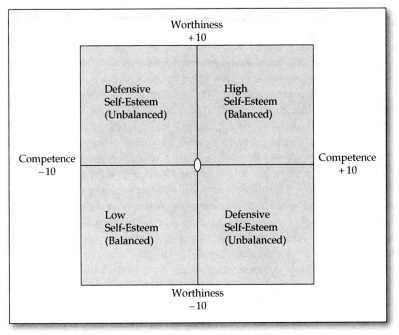

FIGURE 5.3
Self-esteem matrix and basic types of self-esteem.

even predicts that the relationship between competence and worthiness is such that basic types of self-esteem *must* be possible if the definition is valid. Having established this condition as the case, the next step is to examine whether the characteristics associated with the four types of self-esteem necessitated by the fundamental structure are also consistent with major research findings in the field.

Low Self-Esteem

According to the two-factor theory, low self-esteem involves living a perceived or actual lack of competence and a lack of perceived or actual worthiness. Such a configuration only occurs in the lower left quadrant of the matrix, where it is easy to see that the combination of fewer or weaker coping skills (less competence) and a shallow or low reservoir of positive self-feeling (lack of worth) makes people more vulnerable. In this case, the self-regulatory function of self-esteem would be reduced, which means, among other things, that the ability of self-esteem to buffer an individual facing stress would be diminished. As a result, self-protection would have a higher priority than self-expansion. We might also expect to see a number of the characteristics we saw associated with low self-esteem in Chapter 3 to occur under this condition, depending on how weak an individual's self-esteem shield happens to be. For example, this condition could easily result in such things as increased levels of caution, negative thinking, timidity, dependency, anxiety, depression, and so forth, just as was noted in that literature on low self-esteem covered in Chapter 3.

In addition, it is important to note that the relationship between the two factors is balanced in this quadrant of the diagram. Low competence often begets a weak sense of confidence or efficacy, which, in turn, may result in a diminished ability to initiate or sustain one's capacity to deal with a challenge. Often, the result is that it makes much more sense to focus on maintaining what little self-esteem one does have than it does to risk losing any of it. Therefore, such self-esteem management strategies as self-handicapping, avoiding loss, being sensitive to rejection, or settling for lower levels of personal or relationship satisfaction may seem "worth it." Notice that this type of dynamic is also consistent with the self-fulfilling tendency that we saw in the research on self-handicapping and in the work on low self-esteem in relationships. In short, a number of the major research findings associated with low self-esteem are compatible with the stable but unfortunate condition generally known as low self-esteem.

High Self-Esteem

According to the self-esteem meaning matrix, people with high self-esteem should typically exhibit a positive degree of competence and worthiness. This configuration is only found in the upper right quadrant. Once again, it is easy to see how much of the literature we reviewed on high self-esteem is consistent with this part of the matrix. For example, we would expect people who experience a high degree of worthiness to feel good about themselves in general, to have a sense of being acceptable and accepted in relation to others, to be relatively secure, to have reasonably satisfying lives, and so forth. Similarly, people who are high in competence in its various forms, which is also characteristic of this quadrant, would be likely to have the ability to be relatively open to new experiences, to engage in the risk-taking necessary for self-expansion, to deal with problems in a relationship instead of avoiding them, and to succeed more often in general. Once again, note that these characteristics are consistent with the literature on high self-esteem presented earlier and with work in positive psychology that links high self-esteem and higher life satisfaction (Diener & Diener, 1995). Clearly, the stability created by a synergistic relationship between the two factors not only buffers the individual against stress, but also facilitates such desirable phenomena as personal development, relationship growth, self-expansion, and overall well-being, just as the research indicates.

In addition, the matrix also allows us to appreciate the complexities of another important issue that is now often connected to high self-esteem. From a two-factor perspective, it is very difficult to understand how the negative or "dark" qualities associated with high self-esteem described by critics could exist in this quadrant. For example, it is true that people who have high degrees of narcissism, egotism, or antisocial traits often feel good about themselves and even score high on many self-esteem measures. However, it is also important to note that such studies are based on unidimensional definitions and measures of self-esteem that have little means to control for such things as the ceiling effect or self-deception. In addition, there is no good reason to think that they are associated with high self-esteem as the two-factor approach understands it. Given the theoretical and practical limitations, it is necessary to consider other possibilities before reaching the conclusion that self-esteem is as heterogeneous as some make it out to be. One important possibility arising from a two-factor point of view is that instead of self-esteem being the problem, the real issue stems from the lack of balance between feeling good about oneself and earning that feeling through such things as facing the challenges of living in ways that are both competent and worthy.

Defensive Self-Esteem

Research clearly supports the position that there are several forms of self-esteem that can be problematic. For instance, some people may look at first glance like they have high self-esteem, but further examination clearly reveals that they do not (Deci & Ryan, 1995; Greenier et al., 1995; Jordan et al., 2003; Kernis, 2003a; Tafarodi et al., 2001). Other work noted that people who live contingent self-esteem based on either success or being valued by others are quite capable of going to extremes to defend their unbalanced pursuit of self-esteem (Crocker & Park, 2004). Those who study what is called "relationship-contingent self-esteem" make the point that a certain type of self-esteem is characterized by a strong need to be accepted by others and by being more sensitive to rejection than others (Knee et al., 2008). In this case, self-esteem may be functional when an important relationship is stable, but when difficulties arise, such self-esteem shows itself in various forms of instability, such as intense feelings of insecurity, dramatic shifts in a sense of self, withdrawal from others, failed or poor relationships, and other forms of fragility.

According to our approach, defensive self-esteem stems from an unbalanced relationship between the two factors. The diagram suggests that there should be two ways of living this type of self-esteem. For example, although one may report an average or even high degree of feeling worthy or good about one's self, his or her sense of competence or history of actual achievements could be low. The result of this imbalanced state is likely to be a certain degree of vulnerability to anything that forces one to face such a personal deficiency. Therefore, the individual may readily engage in defensive behaviors. For instance, they may exaggerate the success they have had to feel more competent or they may deny their lack of competence by blaming others for failures. Such worthiness-based self-esteem occurs only in the upper left quadrant of the matrix, where a sense of worthiness is high but competence is low.

Conversely, others with unbalanced self-esteem may demonstrate average or even extraordinary degrees of competence in certain domains of life, such as work, but also experience an abiding lack of worth for various reasons. They, too, may be inclined to base their self-esteem on the one component that they do have and defend against the lack of the other when necessary. Focusing on achievements is often sufficient for a person in our culture to feel worthy, because it values success so highly. However, in addition to being driven in this fashion, sometimes failure occurs, in which case there is little to fall back on to protect the self. Thus, this configuration of factors also results in a state of vulnerability, vigilance, and readiness to defend one's self. Again, there are various modes of defensiveness that are likely to occur. Because competence is at least adequate over time, they range from simply being driven, such as an overachiever might be, all the way to the forms of psychopathology we saw associated with contingent self-esteem. Such competence-based, unbalanced self-esteem is found only in the lower right quadrant of the matrix.

The model suggests that extremes may also occur. For example, when people base their sense of self and self-esteem largely on either worth or competence, threats to the one factor they depend on should seem doubly powerful. In this case, it is conceivable that an individual could even react violently in a desperate attempt to push away a threat to preserve or reestablish some degree of esteem and related stability. Consequently, the two-factor approach also gives us a way to understand a connection between self-esteem and very dark phenomena, such as suicide or homicide, which some have found difficult to understand in regard to self-esteem.

Finally, it is important to note that the two-factor model does not necessarily maintain that these two ways of living defensive self-esteem are mutually exclusive. Remember, both types are inherently unstable, which means that it is also possible for an individual to slip back and forth between these two quadrants under certain conditions. People with highly fragile or very unstable self-esteem (Kernis, 2003a) seem particularly vulnerable to this condition. However, the point is twofold. First, it is no accident that the matrix readily accommodates the work we have seen on contingent, fragile, paradoxical, or unstable self-esteem, no matter what it is called: The two-factor approach actually requires such a condition. Second, it should also be clear that this view clearly differentiates defensive forms of self-esteem from healthy or positive high self-esteem, which means there is little problem dealing with the so-called heterogeneity of self-esteem in this model compared with others.

REFINING THE TYPES: INTEGRATING LEVELS OF SELF-ESTEEM

So far, we have seen that it is possible for the two-factor matrix to accommodate research concerning basic types of self-esteem. However, the careful reader will note that this typology does not integrate other research we encountered in Chapter 3 concerning different levels of self-esteem that occur within the same basic types. On one hand, for example, clinical work found low self-esteem to be associated with considerable human suffering and many disorders. On the other hand, more social psychological work on such things as self-handicapping and self-protective strategies in relationships made it clear that low self-esteem may reduce total satisfaction to some degree, but does not necessarily create such things as self-loathing, depression, and so forth. A comprehensive theory of self-esteem must integrate these seemingly contradictory phenomena, and a meaning-based, two-factor approach accomplishes this goal by making a distinction between different types of self-esteem and different levels of self-esteem within each type.

A similar issue was encountered in the development of the newer editions of the *Diagnostic and Statistical Manual of Mental Disorders* (American Psychiatric Association, 2000), which we will refer to collectively as *DSM*. The problem was addressed by using a prototypical method. According to this approach, one classical way of classifying human behavior diagnostically is to develop qualitatively distinct categories that are clearly distinguishable from one another. Such a categorical system is helpful in dealing with phenomena that are substantially distinct, such as an infection versus a broken bone. However, a diagnostic system concerning human behavior must also address the fact that most of it occurs on a range of possibilities, a characteristic that is called "dimensionality." For example, on one hand, anxiety is often useful when one is preparing for an important examination, looking out for danger in a combat situation, and so forth. In these instances, anxiety is not clinically significant and could even be a sign of mental health. On the other hand, anxiety that interferes with behavior or that causes undue distress, such as that which occurs in an anxiety disorder, is clinically significant and stands as a clear problem. The same is true with many other emotional states and personality characteristics.

The *DSM* uses a combination of categorical and dimensional features called a "prototypical" system to distinguish between types and levels of nonclinical and clinical conditions. For example, anticipating an examination, acting conscientiously, and being cautious are at one end of behavior associated with anxiety, whereas defensiveness, compulsiveness, and paranoia are at the other end. Although the ends of such continua are connected in terms of forming a range, they also differ qualitatively. Although no one knows the exact point at which nonclinically significant anxiety becomes clinically significant on the continuum, it is possible to differentiate between such states on the basis of a prototype. With no intention of oversimplifying the process, the prototype is based on a few key indicators or symptoms plus a number of dimensional indicators concerning the degree of difficulty or impairment that is present. When both criteria are met, clinical significance is said to occur. If we wish to use the analogy of a line ranging from 1 through 10 to illustrate the point, this cutoff would be somewhere around 7.

Perhaps the study of self-esteem can be approached in the same way. For example, each quadrant may be seen as a group of related self-esteem characteristics that are qualitatively distinct enough to be distinguished from one another as types, much like the major diagnostic groups. Yet, it is also possible that *within* a given type, there are significant differences concerning degrees of impairment between people at the high and low ends of a range. This dimensional aspect of self-esteem may be represented by an imaginary diagonal line that runs through the middle of each quadrant from 0 to its most extreme corner.

High self-esteem, then, is found in the upper right quadrant and ranges from the coordinate of 0 to the coordinate of +10 for competence and the coordinate of +10 for worthiness. Low self-esteem is found in the lower left quadrant and runs from the coordinate of 0 to the coordinate of −10 for competence and the coordinate of −10 for worthiness. Because defensive self-esteem is unbalanced, one of the two factors can be high, while the other is low. Such a pattern is found in two quadrants. The lower right quadrant, for example, runs from the coordinate 0 to the coordinate of +10 for competence and the coordinate of −10 for worthiness. Such competence-based self-esteem suggests problems concerning feeling worthy or doing worthy things and compensating for that by emphasizing one's success. The upper left quadrant runs from the coordinate 0 to the coordinate of −10 for competence and the coordinate +10 for worthiness. Such worthiness-based self-esteem indicates problems dealing with challenges competently but feeling worthy anyway, which results in defensiveness when threatened.

The next three diagrams show how an existentially based two-factor meaning matrix allows us to readily accommodate, if not predict, the existence of nonclinical and clinical (or statistically infrequent) forms of self-esteem using a method that is conceptually similar to that found in the *DSM*. Making this distinction allows us to integrate the research concerning different levels of self-esteem that were identified by researchers and presented in Chapter 3. This goal is accomplished by creating two levels of self-esteem within each type. The cutoff between levels within a type is represented by the coordinate 7 or –7 to show that one level is much more infrequent, extreme, uncommon, or clinically significant than the other.

The only other clarification to make concerns a need to distinguish between the two forms of defensive self-esteem. Both are based on an unbalanced relationship between the two factors, so the same general term of defensive self-esteem applies to them. However, because each type represents the presence of one factor and some sort of deficiency in the other, we must also have a way of differentiating them from each other. This distinction is made by simply using the Roman numeral I to identify worthiness-based unbalanced self-esteem and II to represent competence-based unbalanced self-esteem. Finally, the personality and behavioral characteristics associated with each type and level of self-esteem are summarized in chart form to help make the connections between the research on self-esteem we encountered and make the matrix clear.

As an aside, readers of the previous editions will note that I have altered some of the terms used in this edition from previous ones. Personally, I always find it distressing to see changes in models, as they may give the appearance of inconsistency or create a certain degree of stress for some people, especially students. Thus, I apologize. However, progress has been made in the field and in the development of this theory, which means that the diagrams must be adjusted to reflect these advances. Otherwise, the theory would not be a robust one. To sum up these relatively minor changes, I use the term defensive self-esteem to describe unbalanced types, as mentioned above. Also, the names of the nonclinical levels of self-esteem have been changed to be more descriptive of the research literature. Finally, I moved the cutoff between levels within the types from 5 or –5 to 7 or –7 to represent the distribution more accurately and because some researchers have been interested in exploring the possibility of merging elements of this theory with the scales of the Multidimensional Self-Esteem Inventory (MSEI) (O'Brien & Epstein, 1988). The use of 7 and –7 might increase compatibility with the t-scores used to differentiate types of self-esteem.

First, let us consider what the nonclinical forms of self-esteem look like using the diagram to represent the matrix. As seen in Figure 5.4, each basic type of self-esteem has such a level and it uniquely corresponds to the particular configuration of competence and worthiness that constitutes any given type. Thus, there are four distinct but "moderate" levels of self-esteem.

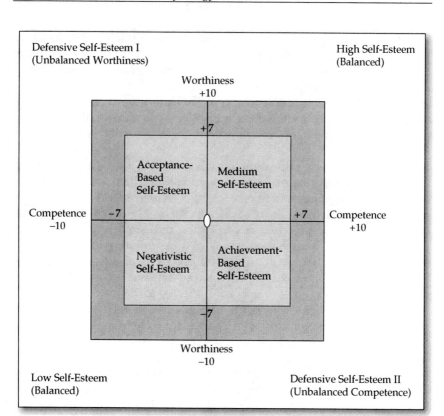

Defensive Self-Esteem I
(Unbalanced Worthiness)

High Self-Esteem
(Balanced)

Worthiness
+10

+7

Acceptance-
Based
Self-Esteem

Medium
Self-Esteem

Competence
–10

–7

+7

Competence
+10

Negativistic
Self-Esteem

Achievement-
Based
Self-Esteem

–7

Worthiness
–10

Low Self-Esteem
(Balanced)

Defensive Self-Esteem II
(Unbalanced Competence)

FIGURE 5.4
Self-esteem matrix and nonclinical levels of self-esteem.

Next, Figure 5.5 demonstrates how the matrix handles clinically significant levels of self-esteem characteristic of a given type. Of course, it is important to realize that the level called authentic self-esteem is *not* a clinical phenomenon, as it is the healthiest and most desirable level. However, authentic self-esteem is statistically infrequent because it is difficult to achieve or to maintain, much in the way an outstanding athlete's performance deviates from the norm in a positive direction. Thus, authentic self-esteem is only found in the upper portion of the positive quadrant and should not be mistaken for anything else.

Finally, it becomes possible to bring all the diagrams together in Figure 5.6 to demonstrate how well the matrix and the theory on which it is based integrate the information we have gathered about self-esteem so far. Of course, although these visual displays of the theory provide a good cognitive map for understanding self-esteem, it is still necessary to demonstrate how the levels and types work together in the ways that are depicted.

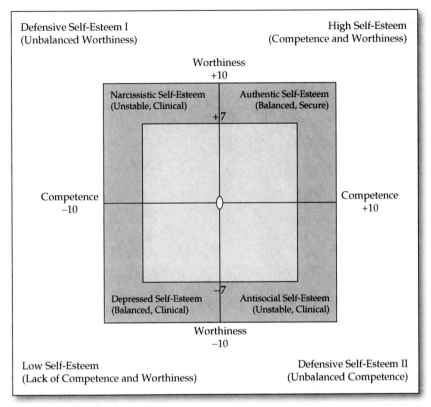

FIGURE 5.5
Self-esteem matrix and clinical levels of self-esteem.

Low Self-Esteem

Let us begin with describing the two levels of low self-esteem, because this type receives the most attention in the field. Brockner et al. (1993) and Rosenberg and Owens (2001) offered one clue to this aspect of self-esteem when they pointed out that many of the characteristics that have been attributed to low self-esteem actually exist as a continuum or range of experiential and behavioral possibilities, which is to say that it is dimensional. Both levels, of course, will be characterized by lower levels of competence and worthiness, which is indicated by the negative numbers in the diagram. Thus, the coordinates of –7, –7 are used to represent the cutoff differentiating the two, although there is no hard and fast line.

The Negativistic Level of Low Self-Esteem

Contrary to popular opinion, the research on self-handicapping and on self-esteem in relationships showed us that many people with mildly low

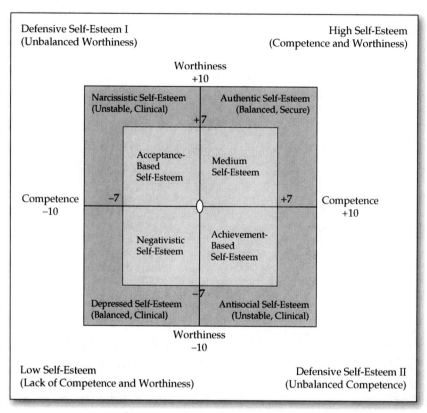

FIGURE 5.6
Complete self-esteem matrix: types and levels.

self-esteem do not hate themselves or even feel badly about themselves. Rather, they use various self-protective measures to regulate existing levels of self-esteem by keeping it stable rather than incurring the possibility of losing it that comes with taking the risks associated with self-expansion. For instance, the idea of a failure may be threatening enough to such an individual's existing sense of competence that it seems better to engage in self-handicapping by holding back on one's effort instead of giving one's best (Brockner et al., 1993; Snyder, 1989). That way, such individuals have an excuse for failure: He or she simply didn't care that much or try that hard, which makes failure quite understandable, but in a way that does not threaten self-esteem. Similarly, research showed that such people might prefer to miss an opportunity to initiate a relationship or to take a proactive stance when a relationship is in trouble in order to protect themselves, rather than risk rejection, which would lead to a loss of self-esteem (Downey & Feldman, 1996).

Some authors use the word "neutral" to describe milder levels of low self-esteem (Tice, 1993). However, the condition is still clearly negative because it limits possibilities for self-expansion and often diminishes a sense of happiness that positive psychologists associate with what they call "subjective well-being" (Baumgardner & Crothers, 2009). I prefer the word negativistic because it better captures the attitude that often accompanies this condition. In other words, people with mildly low self-esteem are quite capable of functioning adequately in life, sometimes even very well. However, they also routinely use self-handicapping strategies, negative thinking, pessimism, self-protective interpersonal behaviors, and so forth to maintain a sense of stability and self-feeling. This level may be barely noticeable in some people, such as those who demonstrate "healthy" pessimism, which might be represented by the coordinate of −1, −1 on the diagram. However, negativistic self-esteem becomes more problematic personally or relationally as it nears the −7, −7 level, where the pattern becomes clinically significant.

The Depressed (Classical) Level of Low Self-Esteem

In addition to mild forms of low self-esteem, we also saw that some 24 clinical conditions are associated with it in the *DSM*. Many of these conditions involve some sort of depression, which is why I use the name depressed self-esteem for this level. Depressed self-esteem is represented at the −7, −7 coordinate in the diagram, in contradistinction to its milder cousin, and offers little in the way of redeeming features: Few strive to be here because it is a painful place as well as one that is disruptive to behavior and relationships. Depression is most commonly associated with this level of self-esteem diagnostically, but depressed self-esteem is also a significant factor in other diagnoses, such as anxiety disorders and certain personality disorders.

Although desirable, it is not possible to discuss in this book how self-esteem plays a role in all these conditions, because we must stay focused on the central topic, which is the nature of self-esteem and its relationship to positive psychology. However, much of the literature on those disorders covers the clinical implications of low self-esteem, and the main point for our purposes is quite clear: Many studies suggest that low self-esteem increases an individual's "susceptibility to a wide range of problematic outcomes and experiences such as depression, eating disorders, teenage pregnancy, victimization, difficulty sustaining and forming close relationships, involvement in antisocial behavior, substance use, and suicide ideation and attempts" (DuBois & Flay, 2004, pp. 415–416). Note that some research is beginning to show the importance of dealing with low self-esteem in relation to the effective management of serious chronic mental disorders, such as schizophrenia (McReynolds, Ward, & Singer, 2002; Silverstone & Salsali, 2003). Similarly, low self-esteem has also been shown to play a role in regard to such things as alcohol abuse in the relational context (DeHart et al., 2008).

Defensive Self-Esteem I

If the matrix is correct, it should be possible to differentiate between the two imbalanced types of self-esteem that are inherently unstable but might be mistaken for genuinely high self-esteem because one component or the other is positive. For instance, Defensive Self-Esteem I, in the diagram, is unstable because of a deficiency in a sense of competence. If a person does not experience himself or herself as dealing with challenges competently, or even if the individual is competent but largely in domains of life that hold little meaning for him or her, then the person may suffer a self-esteem problem. However, people with this type of defensive self-esteem do have a sense of worth and could depend on the feelings associated with this component to compensate for the lack of competence. Unfortunately, this psychological maneuver comes at a cost: The individual is especially vulnerable to situations that require competence or that question his or her sense of worth. In other words, they are defensive, vigilant, and ready to respond to perceived threats in any number of ways.

Acceptance-Based Self-Esteem

In this model, people who live milder levels of this type of defensive self-esteem tend to rely on sources of worth and worthiness to feel good about themselves and maintain their identity in a stable way. Because we saw acceptance by others to be a key source of worth, we can refer to this level with the word "acceptance." Acceptance-based self-esteem also captures the type of behavior Crocker and Park (2004) noted when describing people whose self-esteem was contingent upon such things as being accepted by others, seeking approval from others, depending on others, and so forth, for their self-esteem. For example, such an imbalance may take the form of striving to meet a parent's or partner's idea of perfection, trying to please others even at the cost of displeasing one's self, maintaining a particular social image no matter what the cost, soliciting love and attention through subservience or sexuality, and consistently being dependent on others in a variety of ways.

As with negative self-esteem, at mild levels, acceptance-based self-esteem is not necessarily problematic. People may live their entire lives pleasing others by being a good spouse or partner, colleague, citizen, and so on. However, the defensiveness is likely to emerge under certain conditions, such as when feeling criticized, being sensitive to rejection, and the like. In addition, the lack of a sense of competence may be associated with underachievement in the workplace, avoiding confrontations, making excuses, blaming others, and so forth. Other acceptance-oriented behavior may manifest itself in such things as constantly soliciting positive interpersonal feedback, bragging, and the like. Such "normal narcissism," as Sedikides et al. (2004) called it, appears to have certain benefits at first glance. However, they also pointed out very clearly that narcissism in general does not correlate positively with genuine self-esteem. In short, such self-centered people are often inconvenient or annoying if, for instance, one has to work or live with them, but they do not necessarily suffer a diagnosable condition because behavior in this part of the quadrant does not reach clinical significance.

Narcissistic Self-Esteem

If such behavior is enduring, inflexible, and a source of impairment, which, not so coincidentally, are three main indicators of a personality disorder according to the *DSM* system, then the area of clinical significance has been reached. On the matrix, this configuration of self-esteem is represented by the −7, +7 position and beyond on the diagonal of the quadrant. At this point, a worthiness-based individual crosses the line to well-known clinical self-esteem problems (Crocker & Park, 2004; Deci & Ryan, 1995). For example, people who demonstrate a greatly exaggerated sense of their own importance, those who seem to expect others to automatically recognize their special character or abilities, and individuals who react far too strongly when someone questions their contributions or accomplishments may be demonstrating self-esteem problems severe enough to warrant the diagnosis of a narcissistic personality disorder (Raskin, Novacek, & Hogan, 1991). In addition, it may be possible to place delusional grandiosity and even certain aspects of mania here (Epstein, 1980).

The particular imbalance between competence and worthiness associated with this quadrant can be so severe that the individual becomes quite vulnerable to relatively mild challenges, ordinary social slights, or even to imagined injury. If one's vulnerability is acute, then the entire self-structure may become insecure, unstable, or even fragile. In such cases, lowering the sense of worth even further could lead to a strong negative reaction because there is little left with which to buffer threat. After all, a fall from a perceived high place is a frightening possibility and people react strongly when in danger. Thus, verbal aggression may be used to protect the self from further injury or collapse. In addition, when emotions are flaring strongly, it is easier to give in to negative impulses in the form of acting them out.

In extreme cases, this type and level of self-esteem might even be so fragile that the individual could resort to something like reactive aggression (e.g., revenge or violent acts) to soothe a narcissistic injury. Thus, this level of worthiness-based unstable self-esteem seems to account for a significant portion of the literature linking the so-called dark side of self-esteem with psychopathology and aggression. By the same token, this understanding of narcissism and related behavior is consistent with the clinical literature indicating that increasing genuine self-esteem is necessary in the treatment of narcissistic or borderline personality disorders (Levin, 1993). That is, if we can help such individuals achieve a more balanced type of self-esteem, then the problematic behaviors often associated with this condition would no longer be as likely.

Defensive Self-Esteem II

At first glance, the self-esteem diagram suggests that the two types of defensive self-esteem mirror each other, and, to be sure, there are many parallels. The main reason for this phenomenon is that both configurations of self-esteem are based on an unstable relationship between competence and worthiness. This condition manifests itself as a vulnerability to self-esteem threats, which means that the individual must spend psychological energies on being vigilant, consciously or otherwise. Such an insecure state is accompanied by a readiness to respond defensively in a number of ways identified earlier. A key difference, of course, would be that in the case of competence-based self-esteem, people are more easily threatened by feeling unworthy because they lack a basic sense of being valued or meeting standards of worth.

Accordingly, we can expect such individuals to be more vulnerable to failure, should it occur, because they have little to fall back on when this possibility arises. This situation might be likened to fighting a battle with half a shield. Further, because competence is very different from worthiness, the types and patterns of defensive maneuvers may vary from their worthiness-based counterparts, especially for those in the clinical range. Instead of pulling back and looking toward others for support, for example, those with competence-based defensive self-esteem may employ their skills and abilities to defend themselves more vigorously, either directly or indirectly. For example, instead of withdrawing, they may use their competence to push forward or act more assertively. After all, their competencies better equip them to move against a threat rather than away from it, and sometimes a good offense is better than a good defense.

Achievement-Based Self-Esteem

Because personally significant successes were identified as a major source of self-esteem, and because this quadrant emphasizes competence over worthiness, it makes descriptive sense to call lower levels of this type of defensive self-esteem "achievement-based self-esteem." The word achievement is also appropriate because it captures one of the primary ways in which people live this type and level of unbalanced self-esteem: Competence feels good, and success is often valued by others. Hence, in a certain sense, it is possible to treat success not only as a goal in and of itself but also as a substitute for worthiness. The result of this pattern could easily manifest in such things as competitiveness, perfectionism, a high need for achievement, or combinations of these characteristics because they all facilitate being successful in one way or another.

However, this self-esteem pattern is a double-edged sword. On the one hand, basing one's sense of self and value on success could help an individual adopt, strive toward, and even meet high expectations. As long as such individuals maintain this type of "devil's bargain" with self-esteem, they may look good in this regard and even test high for it on unidimensional measures. On the other hand, we also saw that such contingent self-esteem comes at a price. For example, those who are called overachievers often pursue success at the cost of such things as relationships or their own physical and mental well-being. Remember, Crocker and Park (2004) found that high-achieving college students who suddenly found themselves unable to get into a highly ranked graduate program reported significant decreases in self-esteem and other signs of distress far beyond those whose self-esteem was not contingent on success. Perfectionism, the inability to let go, and other forms of psychological rigidity may also reach problematic levels, because striving toward, driving at, and focusing on success make other things difficult. Such things as accepting criticism, failing to win recognition through achievements, or surrendering enough control to be open to the type of dynamics necessary for establishing and maintaining relationships could all be difficult for someone with competence-based self-esteem.

Antisocial Self-Esteem

As we near the point of clinical significance in this quadrant, the behaviors associated with this configuration may become more severe. Now competence-based defensive self-esteem could easily be associated with more serious behavior in the clinical and descriptive sense. For example, eating disorders, which are known to involve a high degree of perfectionism and a low degree of authentic self-esteem, become a possibility for some people (American Psychiatric Association, 2000; Baumeister et al., 2003; Crocker & Park, 2004; Harter, 1999; Rosenberg & Owens, 2001). Also, depending on how clever, creative, or talented one is, an individual may become very good at achieving success or acquiring power, which is the other source of competence. Such "acceptable" social aggression, for example, may be seen in certain business men and women who reach high levels of success or power. If the lack of worth is great enough, an individual's sense of conscience may become impaired. Then, people risk becoming "snakes in suits" as Babiak and Hare (2006) described it.

When threatened by failure, humiliation, or anxiety, the capacity to be assertive and a corresponding weakness of conscience, or even just a lapse in it, could result in more aggressive forms of acting out. Thus, it is not surprising to find defensive self-esteem, as I would call it, involved in such things as bullying (Thomaes, Bushman, Stegge, & Olthof, 2008) or workplace aggression (Harvey & Keashly, 2003). Indeed, in its most extreme form, antisocial self-esteem may be a factor in various forms of human brutality, such as that exhibited by some ruthless dictators. Such individuals wield much power but demonstrate little worthiness. Thus, the matrix once again accounts for another portion of the so-called dark side of self-esteem. However, now we know that, from a two-factor point of view, these phenomena are not really associated with self-esteem at all: Authentic self-esteem might even act in a way that limits such negative possibilities.

A Final Word About Defensive Self-Esteem

For the most part, people with defensive self-esteem manifest it in one of the two basic types presented above. However, it is important to remember that the essential characteristic of both forms is the unbalanced combination on which they are based, a condition that makes them inherently unstable. Also, because one factor is high, self-expansion is more important to such individuals than to those with low self-esteem. However, this motive conflicts with the self-protective function, which may create additional instability. Taken together, this configuration of factors means that under certain conditions, especially those involving stress, it is possible for people to slip back and forth between the two types of defensive self-esteem.

Like the others, this behavior may also vary in intensity, from mere ambivalence and uncertainty to extremes, such as narcissists who engage in antisocial behavior to protect their fragile sense of self-esteem (Levin, 1993; Thomaes et al., 2008) or antisocial individuals who also exhibit a narcissistic sense of their own value or importance. Thus, it is helpful to think of types I and II as variations on a theme, something that might actually be necessary if future editions of the *DSM* (or other major diagnostic systems) should drop the diagnostic name of a condition mentioned here, such as narcissistic or antisocial personality disorder.

Finally, it is humbling to remember that, under certain circumstances, such as ones involving high stress, prolonged strain, and great threat, anyone's defenses can be overwhelmed, thereby making self-regulation more difficult and behavior more likely to be reactive or impulsive.

Thus, all of us are vulnerable to at least temporary fluctuations in self-esteem, although those who suffer difficulties to begin with are at a much higher risk.

High Self-Esteem

Now that the more problematic issues associated with defensive types of self-esteem have been accounted for in the matrix, it is possible to look at the remaining quadrant, which consists of positive competence and positive worthiness. The chief characteristic of this type of self-esteem is that it is the only one in which both factors are positive and balanced. A positive plus a positive, as any schoolchild knows, is a very stable condition. Other connotations of positive apply here as well, such as a positive balance, positive affect, positive attitude, positive relationships, and so on. In a word, even though there are two levels of this type of self-esteem, balanced self-esteem in the two-factor model is healthy self-esteem, which means that it is a desirable psychological and behavioral state and trait.

Medium Self-Esteem

It would be a sad comment on human affairs if the types and levels of self-esteem identified so far constituted the entire self-esteem picture. Fortunately, there is good reason to believe that most of us have some degree of competence and worthiness compared with the other types, even when they are combined. After all, the major self-esteem instruments, including the MSEI, find that most people score somewhere in the middle of the range of possible scores, which is to say that this area is normative, if not normal. In other words, although what has been called medium self-esteem is seldom discussed in the literature these days, it is probably where most of us lie, especially when defining self-esteem in terms of two factors rather than one.

Some researchers suggest that self-esteem is rapidly rising across American youth today (Dingfelder, 2011). However, it is important to remember that such findings are based on the result of unidimensional measures, usually those that involve feeling good about oneself, which lack a way of detecting false positives. Whether research on a two-factor assessment would lead to the same results is very questionable. In short, although an increase in healthy self-esteem is desirable when defined in terms of two factors instead of one, it is more likely that medium self-esteem still stands as the most common type and level.

The dominant view on the character of medium self-esteem is represented by Coopersmith (1959, 1967) and Rosenberg (1965), who were among the first to use the term. This perspective holds the position that medium self-esteem results from enough exposure to positive experiences to avoid problems in this area, but not enough to reach an unusually high level. Fortunately, medium self-esteem is also anticipated by the matrix. Possessing some, but not an unusually high degree of, competence, and having a solid but not elevated sense of worth definitely place such people in the upper right quadrant. Because medium self-esteem is normal or average and ranges all the way up to the coordinates of +7, +7 in the diagram, it has plenty of room for this population.

This position also suggests that medium self-esteem is reasonably stable and secure or balanced, but still has the potential to move up to a higher level. Thus, unlike the other types and levels, the self-expansion function of self-esteem becomes very important here. Hence, such individuals are likely to appreciate opportunities to take the risks associated with actualizing themselves or with initiating, sustaining, and enhancing relationships more often than others. Similarly, those with medium self-esteem are more inclined to face the challenges of living in ways that reflect both competence and worthiness than any type or level we have seen to this point. In other words, medium self-esteem seems to be associated with a good or meaningful life, just as the early humanistic psychologists said.

Authentic Self-Esteem

Last and far from least important, we come to the final portion of the diagram. According to Kernis (2003a, p. 23), the highest form of self-esteem is characterized by four main qualities. To paraphrase, genuinely high self-esteem is *secure* enough to allow the individual to perceive and admit personal faults or limitations; *consistent* across conscious (explicit) and nonconscious (implicit) levels; *true* in that it does not require continual validation of worthiness from others or endless success to sustain itself; and *stable,* which is to say that it is largely balanced over time. These characteristics certainly warrant being placed in the upper section of the right quadrant. However, one should not confuse such "optimal" self-esteem, as Kernis called it, with lived realities. In real life, we could expect the individual with this kind of self-esteem to be *usually* secure, as people always have bad days; *mostly* uniform, because learning about oneself always takes time; *generally* true, as we all encounter challenges of living from time to time and cannot be expected to handle all of them perfectly; and *largely* stable because we all undergo periods of uncertainty in life.

The confusion generated by the so-called heterogeneity of high self-esteem makes it impossible to use that term to describe only one type or level anymore. Consequently, other words have been used to identify this form of self-esteem in the last decade, including "healthy," "optimal," "genuine," "true," "real," and "authentic" self-esteem. Of the options, I think authentic self-esteem is the most descriptive in relation to a two-factor theory for three reasons.

First, it was mentioned in Chapter 3 that the term authentic is now being used in qualitative and quantitative research on healthy or positive forms of self-esteem. Indeed, it was noted that there is even a growing body of literature based on using the experimental method to research authenticity, which marks a huge turning point in this area (Greenberg et al., 2004). For instance, although not defined in the same way we are using the term, self-determination theory differentiates between the protective and the enhancement functions of self-esteem based on experimental research concerning intrinsic motivation and authenticity (Ryan & Deci, 2004). Kernis (2003a, 2003b) found empirical support for the relationship between self-esteem and what I have called "self-esteem moments." Also, humanistic and existential psychologists have used the word authenticity to describe healthy behavior from their beginnings. Thus, this term is accompanied by more supportive work than the others appear to muster.

Second, the phrase authentic self-esteem also helps us make clarifications in other areas of the matrix. For example, the authentic–inauthentic distinction can be applied to all the types of self-esteem that we have encountered so far, especially to both types of defensive self-esteem as they are filled with self-deception or denial, which are common forms of inauthenticity. By the same token, all the varieties of what Kernis (2003a) called "fragile" self-esteem can be understood as being inauthentic because they crumble in the face of adversity. In other words, self-esteem that is defensive, paradoxical (differing at the explicit and implicit levels), contingent, or unstable cannot stand up because they all involve an imbalance of competence and worthiness: In a word, they are "fake" or inauthentic in essence, as well as by contrast.

Finally, the word "authentic" has strong existential connotations—connotations that take us back to the real life where self-esteem is lived by actual people in concrete situations. In this sense, self-esteem is tied to the existential question that each one of us faces every day: Are we going to act in ways that are authentic or inauthentic? How well or poorly we do so matters in regard to self-esteem because it reflects our ability to competently meet the challenges of living in a worthy way over time, which is at the existential heart of authenticity. Having arrived at this conclusion, we can now summarize the material that we have covered concerning the various types and levels of self-esteem, as well as how they are often lived, in a way that integrates this information into chart form as seen in Table 5.1.

TABLE 5.1
Integrating Research on Common Characteristics of
Types/Levels of Self-Esteem

Defensive Self-Esteem I: (Worthiness-Based)	High Self-Esteem
A. General Type: Unstable or fragile self-esteem characterized by a low sense of competence compensated for by focusing on or exaggerating one's sense of worthiness or importance, sometimes at others' expense.	A. General Type: Relatively stable or secure self-esteem characterized by higher degrees of self-awareness and openness to experience. Realistic optimism and lower levels of defensiveness. Usually satisfied with life and relationships.
B. Levels 1. Acceptance-seeking: Self-esteem often contingent on approval or acceptance from others. Prone to being dependent, sensitive to criticism and rejection. 2. Narcissistic: Exaggerated sense of worth regardless of competence level, sense of entitlement, and very reactive to criticism. Vulnerable to defensive acting out when threatened personally or socially.	B. Levels 1. Medium: Stable sense of adequacy in terms of competence and worthiness, interested in more. Future oriented. Easily the most common type and level of self-esteem. 2. Authentic: General sense of realistic competence and solid worthiness. Actively concerned with living out positive, intrinsic values. Relationships likely to be characterized by openness, mutual respect, and support.
Low Self-Esteem	Defensive Self-Esteem II: (Competence-Based)
A. General Type: Relatively stable reduced level of self-esteem characterized by a concern to avoid further loss of competence and worthiness. Often involves lower levels of relational or life satisfaction.	A. General Type: Unstable, often fragile self-esteem characterized by low sense of worthiness that is compensated for by focusing on competence and success, sometimes even at the expense of others.
B. Levels 1. Negativistic: Generally cautious style of self-regulation, focuses on self-protection. May be negativistic or pessimistic but is generally functional in life and in relationships. 2. Depressed: Impaired functioning due to a low sense of ability and worth. Often in poor relationships. Vulnerable to depression, giving up, various forms of dependency, self-abuse, or suicide.	B. Levels 1. Achievement-seeking: Self-esteem contingent on garnering successes or achievements. Anxious about and sensitive to failure. Often rigid, may seem perfectionistic, and driven toward goals at cost of self or relationships. 2. Antisocial: Exaggerated need for success or power. Self-esteem easily threatened when faced with loss or criticism. Can involve very aggressive forms of acting out in order to succeed or defend fragile sense of worth.

A Word About Self-Esteem "Profiles"

There are several factors that make it difficult to talk about levels and types of self-esteem in regard to a particular person. For example, the fact that self-esteem typically acts as a trait, but can fluctuate from time to time as a state, makes pinpointing where any given individual actually lies on the matrix challenging, not to mention that we all have good and bad days in life. Similarly, although we all move through the various domains associated with self-esteem as we age, some of them will be tied more to one person's identity than another's, which creates even more complexity.

One way to attempt such a fine-grained understanding is that rather than depicting any given individual in terms of a simple type or level, we may instead talk about the *area* of the matrix that a person's self-esteem picture would occupy. Thus, any particular individual may live mostly one type and level of self-esteem, but it is also likely to have "fingers" of it that extend into other levels or types in regard to certain domains, issues, or circumstances. After all, none of us is perfectly stable and balanced. Thus, when we state that he or she has medium self-esteem, for example, we mean to say that *most* of the time his or her self-esteem is medium, but that it may also vary in relation to stress or to certain domains of competence and worthiness, depending on the individual case.

It is possible to represent this dimension of self-esteem on the matrix by seeing a person's self-esteem pattern or profile as a "map" rather than a simple point created by the intersection of two coordinates. Thus, the matrix allows us to accommodate the lived reality that we all have unique self-esteem "fingerprints," although their outer ridges are likely to be in more than one type and level. One could even attempt to represent this aspect of self-esteem by sketching it as an area on the full image of the matrix, as in Figure 5.7, for any given individual. Such a practice is mostly representational but does show us the descriptive power of the matrix once again, and could even have some practical value, such as when working with clients.

In this section, it is worthwhile to note that this theory of self-esteem is reasonably consistent from beginning to end. In addition, the view accommodates a great deal of information uncovered by many years of qualitative and quantitative work. Moreover, the model has the capacity to move from the general level to the specific case. Of course, it still remains to show how such a meaning-based existential approach generates testable hypotheses and the results of such work, but that is the subject of the next chapter.

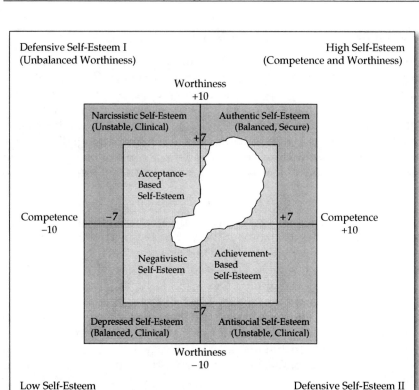

FIGURE 5.7
Individual self-esteem "map" (medium self-esteem pattern).

THE DEVELOPMENT OF SELF-ESTEEM

As discussed earlier, self-esteem must be understood as a developmental phenomenon and much work has been done in this area (Coopersmith, 1967; Rosenberg, 1965; White, 1959). However, to date, no one seems to have done as much as Harter (1999, 2003) in this area. As mentioned earlier, she tied the development of self-esteem to cognitive and social growth and traced these connections throughout the entire life cycle. Also, as noted earlier, Harter's multidimensional approach is compatible with a two-factor definition of self-esteem. Most of her work is dedicated to understanding the development of self-esteem in childhood and adolescence and stands as a classic in the field. Therefore, it is only necessary for us to mention a few points concerning those periods and then focus on how an existentially oriented, meaning-based approach to self-esteem understands the development of self-esteem in adulthood.

Childhood Precursors of Self-Esteem

Erikson (1983) pointed out that identity is the central task of adolescence, and Piaget (Harter, 1999) found that this is also the time when formal operational thinking begins. Because both a sense of identity and advanced cognitive abilities are needed when it comes to talking about the "self" in self-esteem, I am reluctant to use that term in regard to early childhood. In addition, the character of development is so fluid at this time of life that it might not even be possible to talk about such things as global self-esteem during the first years.

However, worthiness and competence are aspects of life that are important regardless of one's age and level of awareness, so it is necessary to consider these childhood precursors of self-esteem as "antecedents," to use Coopersmith's (1967) term. After all, time must pass before individuals come to the point at which they consciously "have" self-esteem in a way that also means they are responsible for managing it. Using Erikson as a precedent in terms of the formation of identity and Piaget's formal operations as being necessary for an appropriate degree of self-reflection, I would generally identify the period of late childhood and early adolescence as the point at which the psychological space formed by competence and worthiness begin to solidify into what we know as self-esteem. In other words, although it is important to talk about self-esteem in childhood, it is also necessary to remember the developmental fluidity of this time.

Although both traits are connected to each other throughout development, it is convenient to start with the worthiness dimension of self-esteem because in some ways it precedes competence. For example, even before an infant is born, he or she is already surrounded by a value-laden environment that structures in general what is to be perceived as good or bad, desirable or undesirable, attractive or unattractive, worthy and unworthy, and so on. In addition, parental attitudes are already at work in the form of hopes and fears, name selection, and in modern culture can even be seen in choosing things such as room colors and decorations. Although each perspective understands the development of worthiness from a different angle, it is usually emphasized early in the process of growth. For example, White (1959) talked about "loveworthiness" and identification with parental figures or objects. Coopersmith (1967) connected worthiness to various patterns of parenting. Rosenberg (1965) spoke of "reflected appraisals," humanists focused on being accepted "unconditionally" (Rogers, 1961), and so forth. Thus, the first source of worthiness we encounter, and perhaps also the first source of self-esteem, may be being accepted and valued by others.

Middle Childhood and the Emergence of Self-Esteem in Adolescence

Competence is also a part of infancy, but it usually takes longer to develop a clear sense of personal intentionality. Although parents and families are typically accepting of children and their abilities in the early years of life, the world of middle childhood is an unforgiving place by comparison. It is filled with constant evaluations of motor, social, intellectual, personality, and behavioral abilities as well as the lack of them. The classroom, playground, and neighborhood, as well as many peer-related activities are all arenas for a comparison of abilities and traits according to the external (and usually less accepting) standards of siblings, peers, teachers, and others. After all, who has not experienced the effect of being picked first or last for a team? Although Freud (1914/1957) depicted this "latency period" as a quiet time of psychological life, it may be the most foundational one for the development of a sense of competence.

For example, Erikson's (1983) well-known stage of "Industry vs. Inferiority" is descriptive of what goes on for the development of this time of life. First, being industrious involves both initiative, which requires a sense of agency, and the skills necessary to see something through to completion, which pertains to mastery. Both are necessary for competence. Second, inferiority accurately describes the psychological impact of excessive failure at this stage and very much speaks to the sense of insecurity that often accompanies defensive or low self-esteem. Harter's (1999) work goes one important step further and details the actual domains in physical, cognitive, and social life that generate the typical challenges involved in reaching a reasonable level of self-esteem.

At this time of life, each year seems to bring with it a new range of challenges and higher standards of worth to meet in regard to play, peers, school, and so on. The typical child has many successes and failures both great and small during this period. Eventually, however, steady patterns develop and individuals begin to find themselves being relatively competent in certain areas and less so in others. Some of these skills are valued as being more worthy than others, which means that there is plenty of individual variation in what could otherwise seem like a regimented process. Competence and values concerning that which are desirable or worthy begin to work hand in hand as equal partners during this time and eventually form the matrix for self-esteem described above. Thus, at some point in this "additive" process, as Harter (1999) called it, the individual comes to have what the literature refers to as basic or global self-esteem. In addition to being high or low in general, the two-factor model would add that such general self-esteem would also begin to take on the character of one of the four basic types.

By now the developing person is well on the way to acquiring his or her own self-esteem type and level. However, Harter's work also pointed out that the particular domains of life that are important for the development of self-esteem evolve over the life cycle. In other words, we always face the same basic self-esteem issue concerning the need to competently face life's challenges in a worthy way, but the domains that present them may change with age. Other research may take a slightly different approach and point out that certain domains remain consistent in life, but the nature of the challenges within them changes over time. Either way, change is part of the picture and it is one that evolves over a lifetime. The one exception seems to be physical appearance. Apparently, being accepted in this way stands as a lifelong self-esteem theme for reasons discussed in Chapter 3.

In short, the material we considered about the development of self-esteem indicates that there are at least three groups of factors that can have a negative impact on what appears to be a universal attempt to reach healthy self-esteem in childhood. First, a child may encounter major obstacles or problems in the early development of worthiness or competence. For example, such variables as genetic dispositions, learning disabilities, unsupportive or abusive parenting, and socioeconomic deprivation may affect the development of self-esteem in ways that impede its movement in a positive direction (Harter et al., 1998). Second, the degree of person-environment fit between a child's natural competencies and those that are valued in a particular family, neighborhood, or culture may be poor. For instance, being too different from others could act in a way so as to increase the chances of failure or rejection instead of success or acceptance, and thereby negatively affect the development of self-esteem. Third, the developing individual may encounter a conflict between intrinsic and extrinsic values that could make actualization difficult, because realizing intrinsic values is necessary for having authentic self-esteem (Deci & Ryan, 1995; Ryan & Deci, 2003).

Self-Esteem in Adulthood

The development of self-esteem is very dynamic early in life. Even so, its formation is largely reactive in the first two stages because of the biological and cognitive constraints of childhood and early adolescence. However, the research on self-esteem revealed that the processes associated with self-esteem can become quite conscious and thematic in adulthood. In addition to continuing to master new types of social relationships and acquiring the competencies that are necessary for adulthood, for instance, we know that there are special times when our self-esteem is challenged directly by adult life. These self-esteem moments are particularly useful for helping to understand other important processes associated with both developing and managing self-esteem.

As indicated in Chapter 3, Epstein (1979) has probably done the broadest work on the full range of self-esteem moments in adult life. Perhaps the most dramatic example of his research occurred when he took advantage of the "natural laboratory" of life and asked participants to keep a record or journal of the events that they experienced in a given period of time and to monitor themselves for fluctuations in their self-esteem. The data were then analyzed according to certain parameters of experience, such as the type of situation that triggered the response, the kinds of emotions experienced during the event, their relative intensity, and the behavioral manifestations of the experience.

As already noted, Epstein found that two such experiences seemed to affect self-esteem most directly: ones involving "success-failure" and "acceptance-rejection." These situations affected self-esteem in the expected directions. In addition, Epstein also found that 10 dimensions describing feeling states were significantly associated with changes in self-esteem. On one hand, an increase in self-esteem was found to be associated with "happiness, security, affection, energy availability, alertness, calmness, clear-mindedness, singleness of purpose, lack of restraint, and spontaneity" (p. 62). On the other hand, "when self-esteem was lowered, high levels were reported for unhappiness, anger, feelings of threat, weariness, withdrawal, nervousness, disorganization, conflict, feelings of restraint, and self-consciousness" (p. 62).

It is important to note that these and other findings are consistent and compatible with our more existential and phenomenological framework. If we examine his findings in terms of the self-esteem meaning matrix, for instance, it is clear that the success–failure experiences are competence-based and therefore can be located on the horizontal axis. In this case, we would also expect to find success to be associated with self-expansion and related positive affect. Similarly, we would predict that negative affect of one sort or another would accompany failure as well as various forms of self-protective behavior. The model would accommodate the ways that acceptance–rejection affects self-esteem by placing it on the worthiness–unworthiness dimension of the matrix in the same fashion. The beginning of a love relationship, for example, would enhance a sense of worth along the vertical axis of the matrix, stimulate positive affect, and help to expand the possibilities of the self in an interpersonal direction. Rejection or loss would move in the opposite direction, be accompanied by negative affect, and constrict the self interpersonally to help protect it.

In addition, we also noticed that the matrix can readily accommodate cultural factors as well. That is to say, more collectivistic societies could emphasize the value of social relationships, whereas individualistic ones could prioritize personal achievements more, although both factors would always be involved according to the two-factor research (Tafarodi & Swann, 1996). The same may be said in regard to gender differences associated with traditional patterns of gender identity formation, in which women might emphasize worthiness more than competence and where men might rate competence more highly, although, once again, both genders would value both factors (Epstein, 1979; Harter, 1999; Tafarodi & Swann, 1996). Note that the two-factor matrix would also be better prepared to handle such things as changes in cultural attitudes or values than unidimensional approaches in the same way, should they occur.

Self-esteem moments that involve both competence and worthiness are especially important because they show us how significant life events can affect self-esteem, regardless of gender. For example, researchers have examined particularly intense self-esteem moments that only seem to occur in situations characterized by two key features. First, these self-esteem moments begin with a fairly ordinary conflict in the everyday life and world of a given individual. Second, these conflicts quickly and deeply mobilize problematic self-esteem themes that begin early in life and then follow one into adulthood. When both types of conflict are activated by the same set of circumstances or event, they put self-esteem "at stake" in a way that means it can be either won or lost, depending on the outcome of the situation. Jackson (1984) likened these self-esteem conflicts to Freud's notion of the repetition compulsion, meaning that we are doomed to repeat them until we get them right. However, we can also understand such existential challenges in terms of the meaning-making function of self-esteem and its relation to related research on authenticity.

For example, as mentioned in Chapter 1, I investigated the phenomenon of problematic self-esteem themes using 20 subjects who represent a fairly stratified sample of American adults (Mruk, 1983). Let me briefly elaborate on this work to help understand the importance of these naturally occurring moments for self-esteem in adulthood, as they most clearly reveal the existential nature and importance of self-esteem. The participants were asked to describe two experiences in detail: a time when they were pleased with themselves in a biographically crucial way and a time when they were displeased with themselves in this fashion. The experiences spontaneously chosen by all of them can be described as breaking through a personal difficulty or limitation (which resulted in being pleased) and failing to do so (which resulted in being displeased). Three of the subjects were then extensively interviewed about their descriptions, a procedure that resulted in six research protocols (three instances of both being pleased and being displeased with oneself in this biographically crucial fashion).

The transcripts were then subjected to a phenomenological analysis based on Giorgi's (1975) version of the method described in Chapter 2 for two reasons: This technique is probably the most standardized format in phenomenological psychology and, more important for scientific purposes, it is a step-by-step process, which means that independent researchers can use the method to verify or dispute the findings. The complete sets of data (description of the experience plus the interview about it), which are called extended narratives, were then examined in terms of meaning units (meaningful transitions in the narrative data) depicted in the subjects' descriptions of their experiences. These units, in turn, were analyzed for similarities across the subjects, and the resulting empirical regularities were then used to identify essential components of the phenomenon or its "constitutive" elements. Such findings became the building blocks for developing the underlying structures of each type of experience, and eventually led to my first articulation of the fundamental structure of self-esteem (Mruk, 1983).

Examples of men and women dealing with certain self-esteem-related problems in their lives were presented in Chapter 1. All of them showed how certain situations challenge an individual's current configuration of competence *and* worthiness, which is to say self-esteem, in a way that reopens the individual's history concerning one or more unresolved biographic self-esteem themes. Another example not mentioned earlier concerns a person who is desperately afraid of leaving the safety of the first floor in a building and will not go to higher floors under *any* circumstances. One day this individual's best friend suddenly comes down with a particularly life-threatening illness and is being treated on the 38th floor of a large medical facility. The research participant describes driving around the hospital for hours before making a decision about whether to "do the right thing." Because the individual cannot continue to drive forever, as the end of the visiting hour approaches, his or her sense of competence and worthiness is challenged by the situation. In other words, the person is existentially staked to the situation because the impending decision holds meaning for both factors that determine self-esteem, and he or she cannot get out of the dilemma without making a decision.

In this case, like many others, what initially appears to be a simple problem turns out to be an existential challenge, because making the visit also requires facing a personal limitation that has a long history of difficulty. In this particular situation, for instance, having a loved one in a hospital was challenging enough because the individual facing the dilemma had a history of childhood experiences associated with sudden deaths. Even worse, some of them were traumatic, as one of this individual's parents literally dropped dead and suddenly fell to the ground right in front of the person as a child. Thus, the potential death of a loved one and riding an elevator, which may suddenly drop, are themes that invoke and characterize both the immediate and the historical dimensions of this situation. Consequently, this suffering soul drives and drives and drives until the moment of decision arrives.

Notice, however, that I did not identify the person's age, gender, cultural background, or even the outcome of this self-esteem moment, because I want to emphasize that these conflicts are painful regardless of such variables. The point is that if the details were changed in appropriate ways, then the person could be you, me, or anyone at all. These are human dilemmas because, in them, we have a strong desire to do that which is worthy, but we also seem to lack the competence to do so, often because of fear, past pain, or a strong lack of self-awareness. In one way or another, we all "drive around" these problems, not knowing what the outcome will be until we actually enact our decision and face the challenge of living authentically—or not.

The identifying characteristic of these self-esteem moments is their dual nature: A situation that requires some degree of competence and worthiness in the present (the surface conflict) also opens up an unresolved conflict involving a deeper challenge from the past (the source conflict). In addition, both conflicts seem to involve a single solution that is clearly "better," that is, more mature and authentic at both levels of the experience. For example, it is usually more worthy to stand up for one's rights, overcome a fear, treat one's body with respect, face loneliness, or be there for loved ones than it is to avoid these things. Yet, the underlying source conflict goes beyond the immediate situation and challenges the person to do precisely what he or she has become skilled at avoiding due to a historically painful lack of competence, worthiness, or both.

In short, the individual finds himself or herself at a crossroads of self-esteem. It is one in which he or she is confronted by an unknown, risky, and difficult, but self-expanding and authentic path leading in one direction. The other involves a familiar, secure, easy, self-protective, but inauthentic road leading away from the situation toward relief. All the while, the surface conflict relentlessly demands making a decision, right now. The study found that there are six steps or stages that a person must live through to resolve such self-esteem dilemmas. The first three are the same for both outcomes, so I only describe them once. The last three are different for each experience, so I present them separately.

Being pleased or displeased with oneself begins when a person comes to a situation that can be described as a biographical *fork in the road.* Typically, it begins when life forces the individual to choose between two alternatives. One of them is clearly worthy but requires a certain degree of competence, often a form of it that requires some courage to execute. The other is less worthy or even unworthy but does not involve demonstrating new forms of competence, actually facing a personal fear, or dealing with some form of danger. The person hesitates to make the decision because, in addition to the fact that one alternative is more difficult to execute than the other, he or she also faces a personally troublesome, historically significant self-esteem theme concerning competence and worthiness that has been mobilized by the situation. This development means that the person's history becomes a key component of the challenging situation, even though the surface nature of the problem may not seem terribly difficult.

The second stage involves a growing awareness of a particular combination of *choice and conflict*. Here, the individual becomes acutely, but not fully, aware that he or she cannot escape making a choice that affects both levels of the conflict. Consequently, this stage also involves the arousal of strong but opposing effect, such as desire and hope accompanied by fear and uncertainty, and other forms of approach-avoidance conflict or being torn in two directions. Often an individual may become confused as to what is "really" going on in the conflict because it has several complex dimensions to it. Now we can see the nature of the self-esteem conflict in familiar terms: The self-enhancing function of self-esteem conflicts with the self-protective function. The result is a unique type of self-esteem conflict where self-esteem is, as it were, at odds with itself. Imagine the affective and information processing conglomeration that such a state would create in any complex adaptive system, let alone a self-aware one that is based on meaning making. It is no wonder that such challenges are powerful self-esteem moments.

The third stage is one of *struggling, movement, and action*. It is by far the most complex part of the process, primarily because the individual now finds himself or herself engaged in two conflicts at the same time, one of which is situational and one that is autobiographical. Moreover, the alternatives involved in creating the conflicts have competing motivational structures. One solution is positive and worthy because it calls the individual forward both in terms of handling the immediate situation competently and in terms of wanting to expand beyond merely repeating the unworthy and incompetent patterns of the past and thereby self-actualize in important ways. These forces are counterbalanced by a desire to escape the situation and protect one's self from the past, both of which have a negative value because they require avoidant, defensive, or inauthentic behavior. Here, the individual is "pulled" back toward historically familiar but ultimately constricting domains of incompetent behavior or unworthy experience. In some sense, the two functions of self-esteem collide in a way that requires the person to quite literally make the existential decision of whether to expand and be freer or to be safer but constrained instead.

As the individual struggles between the options, he or she becomes more inclined toward one choice. However, it is clear that the outcome could go either way until the last moment, at which time the individual begins to act and starts to make, as well as live, one reality over the other. In existential terms, the person deals with the time constraints of the situation until it forces the individual to stake himself or herself on a "free" choice. Although either outcome occurs after a painful period, coming to the more positive resolution seems to be associated with how long and how deeply the individual engages in the process of struggling. It is here that such things as intrinsic values, self-awareness, honesty, and courage, all of which are involved in authenticity, come into play in regard to the situation and to self-esteem. Although it is difficult to penetrate the inner workings of such a decision any further without resorting to metaphorical or poetic language, it seems that the more the person understands what is actually at stake at the deeper level of the conflict, the more he or she is inclined to take the pro-self-esteem, self-expanding path. We shall see that aspect of this stage also presents important possibilities for therapeutic interventions.

The fourth stage in making an authentic and biographically crucial transformation of competence and worthiness involves moving into what I describe as *release, relaxation, and being pleased*. This one is characterized by immediate feelings of release (a pleasurable affective response), relaxation (a more bodily positive reaction signaling the release of stress), and becoming aware that one has "done it," so to speak (a cognitive recognition of success), concerning one's performance in the face of this particular challenge. This step gradually gives way to the fifth stage, called *meaning and affirmation*, where the individual understands and experiences the meaning of making an important authentic choice in regard to his or her competence and worthiness as a person. In other words, here, the individual realizes that by having done the "right thing," he or she is *already* more competent at living and is *unquestionably* more worthy as an individual because both have been undeniably actualized and demonstrated in the here and now of real life. In two-factor terms, the individual experiences more self-esteem because he or she *earned* it.

Finally, *learning and settling* occurs in the sixth stage, when life moves on, and the entire situation becomes a part of the person's history in a way that alters the story of the individual's problematic self-esteem theme in a positive direction. Although personal history can never be erased, it is important to remember that the meaning of the past can be modified, sometimes even transformed, and therefore be lived in a more positive fashion in the future. In the end, the self-esteem matrix is affected by the meaning of this event, and this type of existential response is "added" to the individual's current status concerning competence and worth. The experience also stands as a motivational landmark indicating the value of such things as the connection between authenticity and growth or expansion for the future.

Although the first three stages are the same, the fourth stage of an individual becoming displeased with himself or herself as a result of such a challenge begins when a person ends the struggling, makes the decision, and acts in an unworthy way, including failing to act at all. Such existential incompetence occurs when the motive to protect the self is stronger than the desire to expand by dealing with the challenge. The result is *relief, tension, and being displeased*, which means that instead of being freed from the conflict, the individual only experiences a temporary reduction of tension from the underlying issues. Rather than the relaxation and open-ness to life that accompany being pleased, the person remains cognitively and behaviorally confined to a familiar but constricted psychological and behavioral space. Often the disappointment, shame, or guilt associated with failure is met with defensive measures, so such displeasure may be buried, suppressed, denied, rationalized, or acted out in some negative way, none of which is to any avail in the long run and some of which can even make things worse.

The fifth stage of this path involves *meaning and disaffirmation*. As the individual re-engages the ordinary tasks of living, this particular situation and its challenge to self-esteem begin to fade. However, instead of being transformative, the inauthentic decision and experience may actually reinforce the underlying problematic self-esteem theme by becoming yet another part of it. Usually, the individual tends to report genuine remorse or at least regret over the missed opportunity. However, sometimes pain-ful effect is avoided through defensive maneuvers. Finally, as time moves on to the sixth stage, this negative self-esteem moment becomes one of *learning and settling*. This final transition in the process is similar to its more positive counterpart in that the event also stands as a self-esteem landmark. Yet, an important difference does occur: The event and experi-ence recede from awareness, but they can remain alive as a signpost or reminder of how important it is to act differently—the next time. Be that as it may, no corresponding modification of the self-esteem matrix occurs. In fact, if the action was incompetent or unworthy enough, some self-esteem may even be lost.

In addition to qualitative work, researchers are also conducting traditional quantitative investigations of the relationship between authen-ticity and self-esteem, as mentioned in Chapter 3. For example, the self-determination theory offers considerable experimental support for a strong connection between them. In particular, this material focuses on a process that involves awareness, especially self-awareness, action, and authenticity (Pyszczynski et al., 2004a) that is not uncharacteristic of how they work in the self-esteem moments described above. Similarly, Kernis (2003b) made the link between actualization, another process that involves authenticity, and self-esteem quite explicit when he said,

> Depending on how these challenges are resolved, individuals may proceed further down the path toward either optimal or frag-ile (or low) self-esteem. No matter whether these "moments" are challenges or affirmations, they provide significant opportunities for growth and self-understanding. (p. 89)

Kernis (2003b) then went on to discuss a key mechanism in this process that is consistent with work on self-esteem moments: The decision is best made when one "consults" one's feelings and motives. "Ultimately, their responses may follow social dictates, but if they are freely chosen and fully informed by their true self, they reflect authenticity. Authenticity, in turn, is a vital ingredient in promoting optimal self-esteem" (p. 89). We saw this relationship as playing a central role in the third and pivotal stage of the existential challenges described above. In a certain sense, then, authenticity may be said to be at the heart of self-esteem, something that is completely consistent with an existential approach to it.

Of course, there are negative and positive implications in the fact that such self-esteem moments are a part of adulthood. The bad news is that most of us have to deal with these types of problematic self-esteem challenges repeatedly in life: We cannot escape the psychological vulnerability they create because it comes from who each of us is as an individual. Thus, for those of us who have particularly poor self-esteem developmental histories, self-esteem becomes a heavier existential burden. The bad news is made worse by the additional fact that there is no guarantee we will resolve our self-esteem issues, as indicated by the relationship between self-esteem and various mental disorders in the *DSM*.

Still, the good news is just as potent. For one thing, this aspect of being human is like psychological karma. We do indeed reap what we sow in terms of competence and worthiness. In other words, self-esteem helps us to be psychologically and existentially honest: Like the movie *Groundhog Day* (Ramis, 1993), we are bound to encounter our self-esteem mistakes again and again until we do the right thing in regard to the underlying problematic theme. Thus, authentic self-esteem acts as an existential compass because the relationship between competence and worthiness at least points behavior toward its "true north" during difficult times. In short, self-esteem, authenticity, and various challenges of living work together to create self-esteem moments that act as developmental opportunities throughout the entire life cycle.

Sometimes, when I discuss this more existential aspect of self-esteem, students appreciate what I call the "bucket analogy." In other words, self-esteem may be likened to a bucket of water carried on a long desert journey. The water, of course, represents self-esteem because it is vital for survival. Wise travelers strive to refresh that vessel each time they encounter a potential source of self-esteem. The more often we are genuinely valued by significant others, act in virtuous ways, use influence in a positive fashion, or reach a psychologically healthy personal goal, the farther we can walk. Such a resource is precious on a long journey, so it also behooves the traveler to remember that managing self-esteem is equally important. After all, a stumble can cause a spill that slows a journey down, and too many falls can lead to a premature end.

REEXAMINING THE LINK BETWEEN SELF-ESTEEM AND BEHAVIOR

The last area to tackle in developing an existentially based, meaning-centered, two-factor theory of self-esteem is to articulate the link between self-esteem and behavior from this point of view. Looking back, it appears that there are three basic approaches to understanding the connection between self-esteem and behavior. The first one is to minimize the importance of self-esteem altogether due to what initially looks like only a weak statistical relationship (Baumeister et al., 1996, 2003; Damon, 1995; Emler, 2001; Seligman, 1990). However, we saw that there are several problems with this conclusion, especially the possibility that much of the statistical weakness might arise from defining self-esteem in a lopsided or unidimensional fashion and from the difficulties associated with attempting to quantify or to measure meaning.

Second, it is also possible to see self-esteem as a type of self-fulfilling process, one that is based on the idea that self-esteem acts as feedback for a self-system that seeks to maintain a high degree of stability while simultaneously attempting to maximize its potentials (Baldwin, 2006; Berenson & Downey, 2006; Bhatti et al., 1989; Coopersmith, 1967; Epstein, 1980, 1985; Leary, 2008; Murray, 2008). More sophisticated versions of this approach are found in the literature on complex adaptive systems (Johanson, 2009) concerning how large, complex systems with multiple feedback pathways may operate, such as in the case of global organizations.

However, as tempting as it might be to embrace this approach, there is a fundamental problem with it, namely that information-processing views are highly reductionistic (Costall & Still, 1987; Dreyfus & Dreyfus, 1986). That is, likening a human being to a computational system, even a sophisticated one, reduces the richness of human experience by making lived processes merely mechanical ones. For example, making a choice implies a certain degree of free will. However, a mere "decision" can be the result of logic trees, parallel processing, and probabilistic calculation that is sterile by comparison. Although such an approach may sound more "scientific" in the natural science sense, it fails at the lived level because it does not have any way to talk about explicitly human factors, such as meaning. In other words, from an existential point of view, the self-esteem matrix does not merely "process" information. Rather, it makes information *meaningful*, and meaning, as Jackson pointed out earlier when discussing methods, is beyond reduction.

The Alternative: Reciprocal Determinism, Directionality, Equifinality, or Co-Constitution

The third major approach to understanding the connection between self-esteem and behavior involves some form of reciprocity. For example, Bandura (1986) used the concept of "reciprocal determinism" to characterize the development of individual personality. In this case, causality is a process that is based on the interaction of two sets of variables, one from the person toward the environment and another from the environment toward the person. Over time, these factors influence and shape each until they result in the relatively stable patterns we call an individual's personality. We saw that Harter (1999) described the way in which the person and the world interact to form self-esteem in terms of "directionality," meaning that one's level of self-esteem may influence the outcome of a situation, and vice versa. People who specialize in integrating the biological, psychological, and social factors that interact in ways to create various mental disorders talk about causality in terms of "equifinality" (Durand & Barlow, 2013). This concept attempts to describe how complex behavior is the result of several types of multiple, interacting variables that cannot be traced to a single causal pathway.

Some phenomenologists base their understanding of causality on the process of constitution (Husserl, 1970b), which is often discussed by using the more contemporary term of *co-constitution*. This process consists of three elements: the person, the situation in which he or she currently finds himself or herself, and the relationship between the two. The term "self-world relationship" is used to refer to these three fundamental aspects of behavior. On the "self" side of the existential picture, each person faces the world and its situations, which includes others as well as objects, on the basis of the meanings that the individual brings to them. These meaning-making factors include a tendency to perceive events in ways that are compatible with one's cultural heritage, social background, personal identity, individual preferences (including one's genetic predispositions and intrinsic values), current degree of self-awareness and sense of agency (purpose, motivation, and free will or intentionality), and in situations that involve competence and worthiness, one's self-esteem.

The "world" side concerns what a particular situation brings to a person in terms of objects, people, possibilities, and limitations. After all, free will is always constrained by reality, which is why some prefer the term "situated free will" to a more open-ended understanding of the concept. The third term of "relationship" pertains to behavior and is represented by the hyphen in the self-world relationship because it expresses the interaction between the two co-constitutive dynamics and the behavioral and situational outcomes of such an exchange. Phenomenologists fully appreciate that neither side is more important than the other. Thus, we cannot rely on mere phenomenalism because it tends to emphasize the role of the subject in behavior too much to be faithful to reality. Nor can it be said that any situation announces endless possibilities: We are limited by the structure of our bodies, brains, and so forth. Consequently, it is also not possible to say that interpretation is everything, as many postmodernists tend to do. Rather, both sides of the interface between person and world interact to organize, form, create, or cooperatively constitute (hence, co-constitute) human realities.

The dynamic exchange between the self and the world (including the social world) is more like a dialectic or a conversation than a feedback loop because both sides allow certain possibilities to occur, or not, and both forces shape them over time until these possibilities have either played themselves out or flowed into new ones. In contrast, those who insist on a lineal cause-and-effect approach seem stymied when it comes to complex interactive processes. Perhaps insisting on a billiard-ball view of the world, where A strikes B in a way that predictably results in C, is simply not up to the task. The fact of the matter seems to be that "no global measure of adjustment (e.g., self-esteem, optimism, depression) shows promise as a strong single predictor or causal agent with regard to specific adaptive behaviors" (O'Brien, Bartoletti, Leitzel, & O'Brien, 2006, p. 29). However, longitudinal work indicates that self-esteem is more predictive of such things as "major depressive disorder, anxiety disorder, tobacco dependence, criminal convictions, school drop-out, and money and work problems, than other global indicators" (Swann, Chang-Schneider, & McClarty, 2007). Thus, to paraphrase Swann et al. (2007), it is clear that self-views, including self-esteem, matter statistically as well (p. 84).

The motivation to preserve a stable sense of self (self consistency or protection theory) and to maximize our potentials (self-expansion or enhancement theory) is what connects self-esteem to behavior, both motivationally and behaviorally. Because the dynamics of the situation are co-constituted by individuals and the situation in which they find themselves, cause and effect inevitably flow in both directions. It is difficult to measure such directionality statistically because, in addition to being based on meaning, it is also fluid. Yet, as Harter (1999) pointed out, there can be little doubt that self-esteem is *at least* phenomenologically important to the experiencing person who is trying to manage the realities of life at the lived level.

Finally, it is possible to illustrate the link between self-esteem and behavior in terms of self-esteem moments, as seen in Figure 5.8. Although this interaction may at first look like a feedback system that perpetuates itself in the form of a self-fulfilling prophecy, information should never be confused with meaning. The diagram is organized by time, so let us examine the relationship between self-esteem and behavior as it is lived chronologically.

The diagram is roughly broken into three sections based on the passage of time. They are labeled "past development," "present situations," and "future life." Along with many other things, the first part of

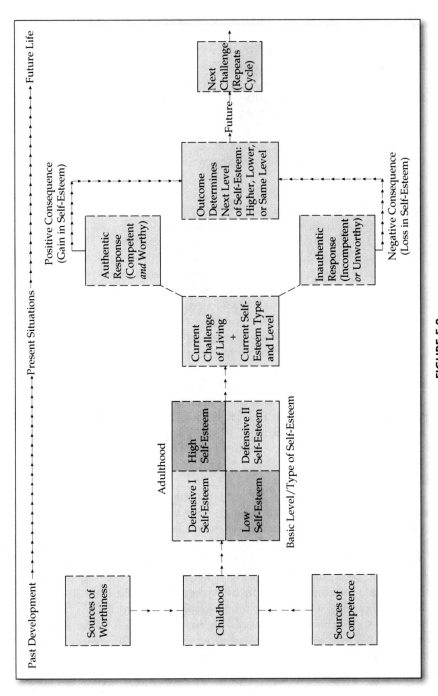

FIGURE 5.8
The relationship between self-esteem and behavior.

the diagram indicates that part of an individual's childhood includes his or her history concerning competence and worthiness as related, but distinct, developmental themes. Slowly, these antecedent processes become increasingly tied to one another during middle childhood so that they become intertwined dynamically in a relationship characterized by the set of checks and balances described earlier. During adolescence, self-esteem matures to the point that it begins to take on the character of one of the basic types and levels of self-esteem. From that point on, self-esteem emerges as a distinct phenomenon that is tied to identity. As the individual becomes increasingly capable of independent decision making by late adolescence or early adulthood, he or she also becomes more responsible for managing his or her own self-esteem, which can be done well or poorly. This development brings us to the second section of the diagram, which concerns the "here and now" of everyday life.

Once an individual reaches this level and establishes a basic type and level of self-esteem, life's present challenges take on new importance because they create opportunities for self-esteem moments. It is at these times that self-esteem becomes extremely active as a "behavioral variable" because it co-constitutes the structure of the situation, which means that it both influences and is influenced by whatever happens there. Through the complex interactive and dynamic process described above, the individual resolves the situation authentically or inauthentically. When the challenge is handled in a competent and worthy fashion, which is represented in the upper box to the right of the middle of the diagram, it has a positive meaning for the self and results in an increase in self-esteem. If self-esteem is already secure, then it is maintained at that level because it was reaffirmed. If the type or level was not especially secure, then an increase in self-esteem actually occurs, because it moves the matrix in a more balanced, which is to say secure, positive, healthy direction.

If the challenge of living is faced inauthentically, which is not to be confused with failing in an authentic attempt to deal with a challenge because no outcome is ever guaranteed when facing them, we move to the lower box of the diagram. If competence should occur without worthiness, then the outcome has little importance for self-esteem: Each of us is competent at many things that have little bearing on our self-esteem because they are not important to us in this way. Similarly, if worthiness is felt without earning it through exhibiting appropriate forms of competent behavior, then self-esteem is not likely to be affected for long either. However, if the challenge is handled inauthentically, which is to say without competence, worthiness, or both, then the outcome is likely to be a loss of self-esteem, as suggested by the diagram.

Finally, the last area of Figure 5.8 is labeled "Future" because the positive or negative effect of a current challenge of living is meaningfully added to the matrix, which continues with the person to the next challenge. In other words, the self-esteem moment is over and we return to the ordinary tasks of living, but the results of this existential encounter with ourselves is added to the self-esteem matrix and carried into the future as a co-constitutive element along with many others. The fact that life never stops bringing us new challenges means that self-esteem will always be a variable in our lives, sometimes weakly so, but other times quite strongly, as indicated by the qualitative and quantitative research on self-esteem moments.

The Fundamental Structure and Stability Versus Change

The last issue we need to address before moving on to showing how a two-factor meaning-based theory can be applied and tested at the practical level concerns understanding how self-esteem can be both relatively stable and yet open to change. We know that research concerning the development and assessment of self-esteem indicates that, once established, it becomes fairly consistent. At the same time, we also saw that self-esteem changes fairly dramatically under certain circumstances, such as when large-scale change occurs in a person's life or in regard to certain kinds of challenges. By this point, it should be clear that a two-factor definition of self-esteem captures both possibilities, but now we know why. The existential nature of the relationship between the regulatory functions of self-esteem, the challenges of living, and the dynamics of authenticity are such that self-esteem works in this fashion by design.

Thus, although self-esteem is primarily stable, it is theoretically possible to alter it in two ways. One is that small self-esteem moments could have a cumulative effect over time. In fact, we saw that some people advocate taking this approach with those who have low self-esteem because their focus on self-protection makes taking the risk for larger change unacceptable (Marigold et al., 2007). The other is to concentrate on larger challenges of living to create a more dramatic shift (Jackson, 1984). Some even advocate using both approaches at appropriate times (Bednar & Peterson, 1995).

In concluding this chapter, it is important to note that a two-factor, meaning-based approach seems to meet three of the requirements for a legitimate theory: It is based on a standard definition, is grounded in a tradition of work, and, as we have just seen, accounts for a great deal of research on self-esteem, some of which other theories cannot. Indeed, this approach describes how self-esteem is lived (in terms of competence and worthiness), shows how it works (on the basis of meaning), and describes the link between self-esteem and behavior (a co-constitutive process involving authenticity). Now let us turn to the task of moving from theory to practice in order to test this theory and the definition on which it stands.

6

Competence and Worthiness Training (CWT)—A Two-Factor Enhancement Program

In Chapter 4 we saw that self-esteem enhancement programs have something of a basic pattern or loose general structure. One logical way to develop an existentially oriented, meaning-based enhancement program, then, is to use those same general design principles in a way that is consistent with the fundamental structure of self-esteem. Accordingly, this approach must include working with competence and worthiness, assessing participants in order to individualize the program, enhancing self-esteem through the use of established techniques, proceeding in a systematic fashion, and helping the participant to maintain self-esteem gains after the program ends.

There are good clinical and research reasons for building a program on these foundations. For instance, a theoretically consistent, well-structured approach gives the client and facilitator common ground for their work together. Such a format protects the client because it requires the facilitator to offer a specific set of guidelines and procedures instead of offering a collection of techniques and calling them "self-esteem enhancing." In addition, unlike more open-ended or general therapies, the steady focus provided by a structured program helps us to avoid becoming bogged down in various clinical or developmental issues that could take us far afield in the practical setting. Hence, although a good program is flexible enough to allow us to deal with issues like depression or defensiveness along the way, it is sequenced clearly enough to keep the sessions moving in a specific direction from beginning to end.

One advantage of such consistency is that it allows us to observe how people move through the process and its procedures. This feature of the program means that a facilitator can develop a sense of what to expect, when to expect it, and sometimes from whom it may come. Such information can be useful in making groups run much more smoothly. There are, for example, certain types of people, interpersonal response styles, learning styles, or personality characteristics that can interfere with the group process (Burns, 1993b; Vinogradov & Yalom, 1989). In such cases it is advantageous to anticipate when that interference is likely to happen or to plan for what might work best in a particular situation based on past experience with the program. Similarly, running a reasonably well-structured program has teaching value. A structured approach allows us to identify common stumbling blocks to learning in advance of when they are likely to occur, thereby helping us to offer suggestions to practitioners for dealing with them from the outset.

In addition, the consistency of a well-structured program has research value: It allows others to use and evaluate the program in a reliable, consistent fashion, which is something that I will talk more about later. In order to maintain this important feature, I have made only minor modifications to this chapter and the handouts that accompany it. The most significant one is a name change. In recent publications (Mruk & O'Brien, in press) I call the program "Competence and Worthiness Training," or CWT, for two reasons. First, CWT is a more accurate description of the approach and what goes on in it. Second, changing the name this way helps to avoid some of the negative connotations that people still have concerning enhancing self-esteem due to the criticism it received in the more recent past. Finally, this title is more consistent with work in positive psychology that I will talk about in the next chapter. All of the other changes are too minor to comment on and should not affect research or practice.

Finally, if structured activities are a clear path for the facilitator, providing a look at them in advance is like having a map for the participants. Thus, I give people an outline for the program at its beginning. This cognitive map takes the form of a handout and lets them know where they are going and what self-esteem challenges they will face along the way. In addition, such a simple courtesy seems to help both the facilitator and participants begin to see each other as partners interested in the same journey, even though they play different roles in it. In the following pages, then, we walk through each part of the program as it is sequenced from beginning to end. Every step is accompanied by appropriate handouts to be used in this way of searching for self-esteem. They are all found in the Appendix so as to facilitate easy access, but the handouts should also be examined when they are discussed in this chapter so as to maximize one's familiarity with this material, especially if the intent is to offer or research CWT.

ENHANCING SELF-ESTEEM IN THE GROUP SETTING

Although I discuss enhancing self-esteem in an individual setting later, the group version of the program is the major format for this form of positive therapy. It should also be noted that CWT may be offered as either a therapeutic group for clinical populations or as a psychoeducational group for non-clinical populations. I will point out distinctions between the two when necessary and then offer guidelines to help structure them in appropriate ways. Both forms of the group are designed for about 6 to 12 people, plus a leader or two co-therapists, if desired. It is a good idea to keep a group designed to enhance self-esteem for clinical populations near the middle of this range, as other treatment issues are likely to crop up more frequently with this population. Combining non-clinical and clinical populations into one group is not recommended because the latter population often moves at a much slower pace than the former. CWT is designed to be an interdisciplinary approach and various forms have been used by counselors, psychologists, social workers, substance abuse specialists, and educators. I have found that a female and male co-therapist arrangement adds a potentially useful gender balance to the group, but this practice is not necessary in order for the program to work.

There are two other general program parameters to consider. First, its basic structure consists of a series of five meetings, each of which is about two hours long. The two-hour group format was selected because this period is a fairly standard recommendation for doing group work (Vinogradov & Yalom, 1989): Two hours is long enough to allow people to warm up to the session comfortably, engage in some real encounters or dialogue, and accomplish some "working through" issues. Each session is divided into approximately two 1-hour blocks with a short break between them, if necessary. I have neither run the group with people under 16-years-old, nor have I run it with clients who have less than average intelligence. It may be that such populations would do better with shorter and more frequent sessions, as Pope et al. (1988) and Shrik and Harter (1996) found with their programs for children and adolescents. Second, since practice is a part of the program, pacing it matters. The standard form of CWT is one 2-hour session a week for 5 consecutive weeks.

How long a program should be is always an important question. The 5-week period seems to be optimal in terms of making a compromise between having enough time to work on self-esteem in a way that allows for some change to occur and for maximizing attendance in an outpatient or educational setting. On one hand, for example, we know that changing self-esteem takes time and effort. On the other hand, the simple fact is that most adults have busy lives, and going beyond a limited number of sessions is likely to create problems with attendance, something that would impede the group processes and could diminish results for everyone in the program. Thus, although it is possible to offer a sixth or follow-up session, the program is presented as 5 weeks long.

It is important to realize that although CWT may seem rather short in terms of time or length, its 10-hour treatment requirement is supported by the literature and research on short-term or time-limited therapy (Wells, 1982). Moreover, we will see that the program generates statistically strong positive results when offered in this way (Bartoletti, 2008; Hakim-Larson & Mruk, 1997). In addition, I see no reason that people should not go through the program more than once if they have such a need or interest. Thus, any criticism that CWT is "too short to help" reflects a basic misunderstanding of the program and the evidence that supports it, which I will present at this chapter's end.

For most populations, it is more realistic to create a self-esteem program that is relatively brief and well-structured instead of long and open-ended. This framework is best served, then, by using a few solid therapeutic activities rather than a large range of them, especially because there simply are not many proven self-esteem enhancement activities to consider in the first place. It takes time to learn anything well, so marathon or weekend workshops are not recommended unless, perhaps, one is dealing with a motivated, high-functioning audience. Also, I have learned the hard way that care should be taken to do some pre-screening, even if it is just a referrals-only approach. Self-esteem and positive therapy are popular topics and such programs can draw people with much more serious issues than may meet the eye. Such individuals may slow down or disrupt a general population group, so it is more appropriate to refer them to a clinical or individual offering of the program, which will be described later. For example, it would not be helpful to place someone with an anti-social or histrionic disorder in a group for depression. Finally, clinical groups often move at a slower pace and go on for a longer time. Thus, working with inpatient or partial hospitalization groups may proceed at a slower pace.

With these general comments out of the way, we can now go through each of the five two-hour sessions individually. For every one, I present the basic *goal* for a given week, identify what *materials* are to be used during that period, and then present a step-by-step *procedure* to use as a method of reaching those goals. All of the required materials are presented in the Appendix, with the exception of the Multidimensional Self-Esteem Inventory (MSEI), which must be ordered separately. At the time of this writing, the address to obtain the instrument is: Psychological Assessment Resources Inc., 16204 North Florida Ave., Lutz, FL 33549, Tel: 800-331-8378. Its website address (URL) is http://www4.parinc.com. The standard form is normed for those between 18 and 65 years old, but its author is working on such things as a form for adolescents, expanding the normative base, collecting work using the inventory with various clinical populations (O'Brien, 2010), and translating the test into other languages, including Spanish. Pricing is modest compared to other professional instruments.

Sometimes I am asked questions about using other instruments or what to do if the MSEI becomes unavailable for one reason or another. In theory, there is some justification for considering the use of Harter's (Messer & Harter, 1986) scales because they at least examine specific domains of life that are relevant to competence and worthiness, especially if one is interested in a particular age range not covered by the MSEI. Moving down the list, it is also possible to consider using a basic instrument, such as Coopersmith's Self-Esteem Inventory (1981) or Rosenberg's (1965) scale, because their questions can be divided by hand into those that assess competence and those that evaluate a sense of worth. In the worst empirically supported case, it might even be possible to dispense with formal testing and simply ask subjects to rate themselves on the 8 basic self-esteem scales of the MSEI after explaining its domains to the group. However, it should be clear that none of these alternatives includes a defensiveness scale, which is a crucial one, and using other approaches would certainly require modifying some of the handouts in the program in ways I have not tested. Thus, I would consider alternatives only if absolutely necessary and would not present such results as being empirically sound.

WEEK 1: FOCUSING PHASE

Goal

The first week is the most important for two reasons: It sets the general tone for the entire program and people usually make the decision about whether to come back after this session. Therefore, we have two objectives here. One is building the foundation for a focused and supportive group. This aim involves facilitating a sense of interest, comfort, and purpose so that individuals feel *safe but ready to work*. The goal represents quite a clinical challenge because it requires facilitators to have the skills necessary to quickly achieve rapport with others. The other aim is to raise consciousness of self-esteem and its role in our lives because we found that this task is a focal point in all systematic self-esteem enhancement programs. Ideally, the result of this initial meeting is to come to a common ground in terms of what definitions are being used in the program, what kinds of work the group will be doing together, and sufficient motivation to attend the next session.

Materials

Taken together, all of the handouts in the Appendix form the basis for a self-esteem workbook. Thus, while I do hand them out session by session, I also provide each participant with a folder, ask them to keep their material in it, and request them to bring the packet to each session. It is advisable to have spares because inevitably someone forgets.

1. Week 1—Handout 1: Program Announcement. This statement simply makes it known that the program is available. It may be circulated among colleagues, to potential clients, or to general populations, depending on the setting in which one is going to be working. The announcement also makes it clear that the group is working on self-esteem and not on other issues. Naturally, the information may be modified as needed.
2. Week 1—Handout 2: Activity Schedule. This handout is the basic road map of the program and allows people to see where they are going if they participate in the program.
3. Week 1—Handout 3: Group Guidelines and Expectations. This handout consists of the rules governing the group and the interaction among its members. The guidelines are intended to help establish a supportive, respectful group code of conduct. The information is intended to facilitate the group process, encourage pro-self-esteem behavior, and address some potential ethical issues in advance. These principles can also be helpful in confronting and limiting inappropriate behavior if that happens to emerge in a group, though it rarely does.
4. Week 1—Handout 4: Defining Self-Esteem. The first stage of a standard enhancement program concerns increasing awareness about self-esteem. This exercise assists that process by helping us to think about the definition of self-esteem by taking some time to focus on competence and worthiness as we actually live these factors in daily life.
5. Week 1—Self-Esteem Journal. The facilitator may offer a spiral notebook or suggest that participants buy one to use exclusively for this purpose. I recommend providing a notebook to the clients in the folder mentioned above, because giving people "official" material tends to make the program seem more professional and could help motivate people to actually keep a self-esteem journal.
6. Week 1—Multidimensional Self-Esteem Inventory (MSEI). As mentioned earlier, this instrument is currently available through Psychological Assessment Resources Inc. This test, or something like it, is essential to the program. The leader should order this instrument well in advance. The cost for the test is relatively low and its format can easily be worked into a group setting, as the test booklets are reusable. The fact that it is not a self-help instrument makes the program a bit more demanding on the clinician, but it also helps to distinguish it as being more empirically based.

Procedure

This session is a busy one because it serves several important functions, including organizing the group, taking care of various administrative tasks, and beginning the program. I usually find it helpful to develop a brief program announcement, such as the Competence and Worthiness Training Program Announcement (Week 1—Handout 1). This simple device is a convenient way of letting an agency or other professionals, such as therapists, know that I am starting a new group and when it will be running so that they can refer appropriate patients for participation. The handout may also serve as something of a "recruitment" tool in the private practice setting.

After the group has been announced and is gathered together for the first time, I ask everyone to sit in a semicircle so that we can see each other. The materials are then distributed to each person. The room is always equipped with an overhead projector, chalkboard, whiteboard, flip chart, or the like, as some sort of public workspace is needed to demonstrate several of the activities and exercises. I typically introduce myself first and offer participants a warm welcome to the "exciting search for self-esteem that we will embark upon together over the next five important weeks." This introduction includes letting them know a little about my credentials, background, and preference for a scientific approach to enhancing self-esteem. I usually close with some information about my own self-esteem issues and the work I am doing on them, so they can know that I struggle with self-esteem too. The use of humor whenever possible and appropriate is beneficial. However, it is important to remember that humor must be used tastefully, especially in regard to such things as age, gender, and cultural diversity.

Step 1: Introducing the Program

We begin by sitting in the semicircle and looking at the Activity Schedule (Week 1—Handout 2). This outline is used to preview the program, a practice that is beneficial in several ways. In addition to providing a lay of the land, so to speak, an overview can put people at ease. Many individuals are a little apprehensive, even anxious, about being in the group. Sometimes, for example, they have outdated ideas of what to expect from a psychotherapeutic or psychoeducational group. Conversely, more experienced participants can expect too much from a group and need to allow others to catch up. Another important point is that many people who attend such groups usually have self-esteem problems. They may feel unworthy of group attention or may feel that their social skills are limited, so it often helps them to know in advance what to expect and what is expected of them.

Part A is a general introduction to the psychology of self-esteem. I usually begin by sharing some of the more important research findings concerning self-esteem and enhancing it. The aim is to dispel some of the myths that are a by-product of the popularization of self-esteem and to give the participants a few key findings they may trust. Although any facilitator is free to select the findings he or she feels are most important, it is often useful to talk about the "self-esteem fallacy" so that participants do not develop false expectations about rapid transformations in their self-esteem, general behavior, or personal happiness. The fallacy is, of course, that people often see self-esteem as though it is a magic bullet for transforming problems, creating mental health, or engendering superior performance in virtually any area of life.

While commonly held, this way of viewing self-esteem is simply incorrect and could lead to difficulties if left unaddressed. First, I point out the bad news: The research findings showing that self-esteem is only one factor affecting any given situation or behavior. This comment tends to capture the group's attention because self-esteem has become another buzzword, and I appear to contradict my own purpose. Then, I quickly follow up with the good news: Although perhaps small in effect, self-esteem is a constant force, which means that although increasing it may not make a great difference right now, even a small gain can have tremendous power over the course of time, especially a lifetime. The participants usually get this point without much difficulty and have already begun thinking about self-esteem more realistically.

It is not a good idea to spend a long time going over the research information on self-esteem. Although tempting, doing so takes too long, the exercise is too academic, and a few solid findings are easier to remember than a long list of weaker ones. Focusing on the work showing that the better self-esteem programs are systematic can create a good lead-in to the next part of the outline labeled B. This section of the material allows me to emphasize that it is possible to divide a good self-esteem enhancement program into several distinct parts and identify them on the handout. I also quickly point out the major activities that we will be doing for each stage, which are included on the handout. This procedure helps participants to understand the specific steps that they make from week to week and that the steps are linked together to produce a cumulative effect.

This approach also helps people begin to understand that enhancing self-esteem is a process rather than an event. In addition, seeing that no threatening activities are involved in the program, and assuring them that they do not have to do anything that makes them feel uncomfortable, seems to help calm those who have performance or social anxiety, a phenomenon that is to be expected in a group that consists of people who have difficulties with self-esteem. I always end this step by pointing out that we are already in the focusing phase because we are working on our awareness of self-esteem *right now.*

The next part of the introduction focuses on Group Guidelines and Expectations (Week 1—Handout 3). This material lays the foundation for how we treat one another in the group. I always try to read the guidelines and expectations aloud to stress the seriousness of the enterprise on which we are about to embark. This practice also ensures that everyone is familiar with the basic rules that govern the group, and even reinforces them to some degree. The voluntary nature of the program and a statement concerning confidentially are mentioned in the introductory paragraph. However, it is important to remember that the therapist, not necessarily the client, is the only one legally obligated to maintain confidentiality. Therefore, it is prudent to make group members aware that although you must maintain confidentiality, other group members are not obliged in this way as a part of informed consent. Similarly, respecting limits and differences is absolutely essential to our work because recognizing the rights and dignity of each human being is already self-esteem enhancing. The same applies to the issues concerning gender, age, culture, and so on.

The comments about attendance are important because the program is designed in a stepwise fashion and it is difficult, though not impossible, to recover from missing even a single week. In fact, if people anticipate missing even two weeks I suggest that they wait until another time to take the program. I also encourage people to participate actively in these groups, as learning and growing usually occur as a function of how much effort one puts into the process. However, it is important to remind participants that they are not required to do anything that feels uncomfortable to them, and that they should let the facilitator know when they feel that way so alternatives can be offered.

By now, the participants are likely wondering if they are just going to be lectured for 5 weeks, so at this point it is useful to engage in some basic ice-breaker activity to help them feel more comfortable and to help them see themselves as a group instead of as a collection of individuals. I typically ask participants to introduce themselves to the other members of the group by stating their first names and their interests in enhancing self-esteem. There are other standard getting-to-know-you activities that can be used here, but simple ones seem to be less threatening. After all, it is important to remember that some people are likely to be there because they have difficulties feeling comfortable in social situations. This entire step takes about 30 to 40 minutes to cover. A break can be given if necessary, but it should be a short one.

Step 2: Becoming Aware of Self-Esteem

We found that a good enhancement program begins by increasing awareness of the importance of self-esteem in our lives. An excellent way to begin focusing on self-esteem, and to achieve a common ground from which the group can work, is by defining it. The first experiential activity of the program is guided by the material found on the handout, Defining Self-Esteem (Week 1—Handout 4). It is designed to help the group do its own mini-phenomenology of self-esteem, though I seldom use that term because it is too technical for lay audiences. I begin by presenting and explaining a simple definition of self-esteem based on competence and worthiness, which is at the top of the handout.

In part I-A of the activity, participants are asked to examine their own biographies, both recent and past, for experiences in which they found themselves being competent, and to briefly describe one of them on the handout. Then, they are invited to examine this experience and ask themselves what it shows about the relationship between self-esteem and competence. Next, a key component of the exercise is taking the time to ask the group members to share these experiences and to ask what can be learned from them about self-esteem. I usually start by offering an example of my own recent experience and then ask for volunteers to do the same.

This activity helps people to see the connection between competence and self-esteem. In addition, the experiences are by and large positive, and sharing them is usually enjoyable. This work tends to help participants relax and brings the self-esteem–enhancing principle of positive feedback into play. The same procedure is repeated for worthiness in part I-B of the exercise. This one can be more difficult because worthiness is more abstract, which is why we begin with the competence dimension. Usually someone gives an example, such as an experience of helping someone, and the ball starts rolling. If not, then I again offer something to consider.

Often, the effect of this activity is surprisingly strong. First, tying experience to a definition makes it more meaningful. Second, having participants share some of what they experienced or discovered helps those who might be having a hard time with this exercise, or with understanding self-esteem in terms of a relationships between competence and worthiness instead of either one alone. Third, this activity makes people think about self-esteem and self-esteem moments in their own lives. Finally, this process of identifying, describing, and thinking about self-esteem is important because it prepares the group to write something in what will become a personal self-esteem journal. As a matter of academic honesty, I also let them know that there are other ways of defining self-esteem but might add something about the problems they create.

So far, in one session we have shown participants that they can identify, describe, and learn from experiences of competence and worthiness in their own lives. We have also helped them to see that these experiences are connected to self-esteem and to various challenges of living. The group is now ready for its first homework assignment, which is starting the self-esteem journal, as mentioned in part II of the handout. There is usually some resistance to this activity at first, probably because it requires work, and most people do not write regularly. Once again, I find it helpful to give the group members a blank notebook or at least an attractively bound packet of papers for the journal. This courtesy facilitates taking the journal seriously and adds a professional touch to the program. I also point out that the group has just shown they can do this kind of work because they have already described two relevant experiences.

Be sure to tell the group that they should write about any *positive* experiences with competence and worthiness they have during the next week. In keeping with what we will see as a principle of positive therapy, it is much more helpful to focus on positive experiences than on negative ones. After all, positive reinforcement is usually more effective and people with self-esteem problems often don't receive much of it. However, the rule is not hard and fast because "forbidding" people to write or talk about certain experiences is probably not a good idea. The importance of the journal is emphasized, but it is also helpful to let them know that although they are keeping one for all the sessions, the journals will not be collected or "graded" in any way. This step usually takes about 40 minutes.

Step 3: Administering the MSEI

Now we are at the end of our first meeting. Sometimes, depending on how large the group is and who is in it, participants either want to continue discussing their experiences or just end the session, feeling that they have worked hard enough for the first meeting. Either way, I tell them about the research findings concerning the need to assess self-esteem. At this point, O'Brien's and Epstein's MSEI (1988) is administered *but not scored*. The form can be filled out in about 20 minutes, but some people take longer, which is why it is good to give the test at the end of the session, when such differences do not require group members to wait for others to finish.

As an aside, I have found that it helps to make sure that the room being used is reserved for at least 2.5 hours to avoid any time crunches, especially for those who read or take tests slowly or who suffer from various learning disorders. Allowing people to take a little longer to fill out the form prevents them from feeling rushed, and if someone else is trying to access the room, the situation may become awkward. In addition, it is important to have the testing done the first week because it stimulates participants' curiosity about themselves and encourages them to come back, if only to find out their results! We do a lot of work in this session, but people also tend to be highly motivated at this point and usually manage to complete the tasks without difficulty.

WEEK 2: AWARENESS PHASE (APPRECIATING SELF-ESTEEM)

Goal

The second week continues the process of increasing awareness as a first step toward enhancing self-esteem. The goal is to raise consciousness concerning the nature of self-esteem, its value, and the sources of this vital psychosocial resource. Our objectives in this work include becoming aware of the basic types and levels of self-esteem, appreciating their related problems, and identifying individual self-esteem strengths and weaknesses based on the MSEI results.

Materials

1. Week 2—Handout 1: Self-Esteem Types, Levels, and Problems. This handout is used as a general introduction to the self-esteem meaning matrix (or cross of self-esteem, depending on which metaphor is more suitable for a particular group). It is designed to introduce how self-esteem works, especially in regard to how problems with competence and worthiness affect self-esteem.
2. Week 2—Handout 2: Applying the Multidimensional Self-Esteem Inventory Scales. This handout is designed to help participants make sense of their scores on the MSEI, especially as the scores apply to the program.
3. Week 2—Handout 3: Finding Sources of Self-Esteem. This worksheet is based on the research findings concerning the four major sources of self-esteem. It is set up to help people get in touch with how the sources are potentially available to them.

Procedure

Step 1: Review

I begin sessions by creating an opportunity for group members to share experiences and reflections from their self-esteem journal of the past week. Someone always seems to get the ball rolling, but sometimes it is helpful to model by sharing my own experience. Modeling, it will be recalled, is an established self-esteem enhancement principle. Reviewing in this way reinforces the importance of focusing on competence and worthiness as components of self-esteem, and going over material like this allows the group to see that these themes really are alive for themselves and others. All sessions begin with a review of the previous session because the process facilitates the development of a cohesive group and offers an opportunity to clarify and reinforce previous material.

Step 2: Determining Self-Esteem Issues

Becoming genuinely aware of the importance of self-esteem in human behavior also means knowing that there are problems associated with the lack of it. Although it is not necessary to go into great detail, it does help the group members to become aware of how deficiencies in competence or worthiness can have a negative impact on self-esteem. The basic version of the self-esteem matrix is used to do such work, which is why it is included in the handout Self-Esteem Types, Levels, and Problems (Week 2—Handout 1, part I). In working with non-clinical or psychoeducational groups, it is important to stress authentic self-esteem as well as achievement-based, acceptance-based, negativistic, and, especially, medium levels of self-esteem.

Although classically low, narcissistic, and anti-social levels of self-esteem may be mentioned to complete the diagram, it is usually not necessary to dwell on these types. Instead, I tend to focus on high, low, medium, and defensive self-esteem with most groups. However, in working with some clinical populations, such as those who abuse substances or sophisticated clinical groups, the more extreme areas should also receive considerable attention. Thus, the facilitator is free to use other diagrams from Chapter 5, including the chart on all of the levels and types of self-esteem, if the group is sophisticated enough.

In any case, it is extremely important to emphasize that medium self-esteem is preferable to all types and levels except authentic high self-esteem. For many clinical groups, the information lets them know that medium self-esteem is a step along the way and a worthy goal in its own right. This information is important because oftentimes people will aim at lofty goals which, under the circumstances, can be an invitation to failure. In other words, for some people, reaching the level of medium self-esteem is a significant achievement in itself and cannot be bypassed. This practice is also important for non-clinical or psychoeducational groups because it allows them to think about the process of moving toward authentic self-esteem.

The aim is to show how competence and worthiness are related to self-esteem and problems with it, but to do so in a way that addresses learning styles, such as that of visually oriented participants. Sometimes there is considerable value in asking people if they can recognize these kinds of self-esteem problems in themselves or in others, and to list the more common ones, as indicated in part II of the handout. Since the goal is to increase self-esteem and not to reinforce problems with it, I avoid dwelling on negative experiences too long. After all, group members usually are already quite good at focusing on negative phenomena and positive therapy works, in part, by accentuating healthy behavior. Finally, it is important to try to limit parts I and II to the first half of the session, so the best guideline to remember is to keep one's explanations clear, short, and to the point. Once again, if breaks are necessary, they should be brief.

Step 3: Interpreting the MSEI

We know that a good self-esteem enhancement program involves assessing self-esteem and that this process can be complex. Fortunately, the MSEI is easy to administer and interpret in a group setting, providing one has the proper credentials and practices the procedures in advance. *However, scoring the results and writing profiles does take time and should be done by the clinician, not the participants, between the first and second sessions.* The MSEI provides percentages and t-scores on the 11 scales for each gender, and the test manual shows how to interpret them. Remember, the normative samples are limited, and age and various cultural factors might affect scores (Sue & Sue, 1990), so I recommend a simple interpretive procedure as described below when working in the group format.

The handout that I have designed for this purpose is labeled Week 2—Handout 2: Applying the Multidimensional Self-Esteem Inventory Scales. The form is constructed so that it presents the 11 scales at the top of the page, which allows me to explain each one at the beginning. However, the "report" each individual receives after I score their results involves only four scales: the two highest and the two most problematic. This streamlined presentation of results allows me to individualize the scores in a way that is meaningful for the participant without having to explain t-score conversions or go over the complete profile for each person, either of which would be unwieldy in a group setting.

Next, I hand people their "profiles" and ask participants to look at their "results" (parts A and B of the handout). Notice that writing in the actual scores is not necessary. To save time, I begin the interpretive process by going over all 11 scales in front of the group. I also group them into three clusters: general self-esteem indices, those that are related to competence, and those that are connected to worthiness. One may even develop a brief handout that explains all the scales, if that approach is helpful. Finally, I answer questions to make sure that everyone has the opportunity to clarify what the results are suggesting for them and sometimes then ask if they can identify with the findings. Usually most people say "Yes," which makes the test seem more credible to the group. The individual practitioner is free to present the results in other ways or to use other forms, but I caution against becoming overly technical with the reports, providing all the scales, or listing actual scores, because it is easy to become bogged down with too many details.

The MSEI provides several kinds of information about an individual's self-esteem that can be useful in the program. The Global Self-Esteem Scale, for instance, is a composite figure that tells us something about the individual's general level of self-esteem. Another general scale called Identity Integration is less useful because identity is such a complex, abstract topic. However, elevated scores here can give some indication about the likelihood of other psychological issues that may have to be dealt with before self-esteem can become an appropriate project. For example, I have found this scale to be helpful when the individual does not find that any of the others speak to their experience of themselves. In this situation, for example, a person might report that he or she is going through a major crisis or life transition and simply does not know well enough who he or she currently is to render a valid profile. Showing them that such a phenomenon can be helped by the program gives them more confidence in the program itself, and if it does not, a referral may be made to a more appropriate treatment program.

Perhaps the most useful and fascinating scale is the one for defensiveness. It is crucial to remember that scores on this scale are arranged in a way that is opposite of the others. Whereas high scores on the other scales are generally positive, high scores on the defensiveness scale usually indicate that there is likely to be a problem with self-esteem. Such scores suggest that the individual is anxious about his or her self-esteem, often in ways that are difficult to detect upon first glance, as in the case of the successful overachiever. This scale is also useful in detecting various forms of unstable or fragile self-esteem, such as being too moralistic, rigid, or self-deceptive. Thus, it is important to remember that when the score for the defensiveness scale is numerically high, it is considered a self-esteem issue. In fact, in some ways this response is the "least positive" score possible and usually needs to be identified as a weak area on the results form. Occasionally, people present themselves this way and have enough insight to know about such things, but often they do not. Therefore, it is necessary to treat interpreting this scale, as well as those who score high on it, with as much sensitivity as possible.

At first, such people might be difficult to reach, but sometimes asking if they tend to have trouble admitting to mistakes, or if they are easily hurt by criticism even though they may not show it, allows them to get past this level of resistance. Occasionally, such individuals even become the most appreciative participants as the group moves on, because they begin to make insights that bring them a sense of relief. If the person does not respond favorably, at least the scale alerts us to the need to be cautious when interacting with him or her so as not to make the person more defensive or disrupt the group process.

The heart of the test consists of eight subscales that assess various domains of self-esteem. These basic self-esteem scales can be grouped together as reflecting either competence or worthiness. On the one hand, what the test calls Competence, Personal Power (or influence), Self-Control, and Body Functioning are behaviorally based or action-oriented qualities. Each one concerns an individual's ability to perform certain identifiable skills that can be evaluated to yield some measure of competence (or the lack of it). On the other hand, the qualities of Lovability,

Likability, Moral Self-Approval, and Body Appearance are more value oriented, and they range in importance in terms of being worthy (or not). Once again, I always close this part of the session by offering participants the opportunity to ask questions about their results.

Requiring people to consider both the areas in which they are strong as well as the areas in which they are weak is useful because there is a tendency for participants to pay too much attention to the negative aspects of their self-esteem assessment. Indeed, allowing such a negative drift to occur too often or too long in the group can actually reinforce self-esteem problems. Also, we saw that increasing success is a valid route to self-esteem and it is sometimes better to focus on this possibility by working with a client's strengths rather than with his or her weaknesses. Furthermore, some people suffer such serious self-esteem problems that they can only afford to work on increasing what little strength they have before they can address more difficult challenges. Participants are then instructed to start tracking the positive, but not negative, self-esteem themes in their journals, which should help them increase their awareness of self-esteem as they live it.

There is one additional possibility to consider that is of special interest. Once in a while, someone will present a profile in which many of the scores for the scales are in the low or very low range. Usually this event indicates low self-esteem in many domains as well as globally. However, I have had some individuals who presented such a profile that I personally knew to be very honest, rather humble, and even genuinely spiritual. Although it does not change presenting their self-esteem strengths and weaknesses on the profile, such a response presents some interesting things to consider. One is that the person may simply be psychologically secure or authentic enough to be very open about himself or herself. Another is that the individual may come from a cultural or religious background that deemphasizes the self enough to affect one's ability to rate oneself highly, though he or she may actually rate such rankings by external reviewers. This type of issue reminds us that a test is just a test—in this case, a rough indicator that is subject to many factors, which is why I recommend avoiding taking the results too literally.

Step 4: Finding Sources of Self-Esteem

Now that we have assessed self-esteem, it is important to be aware of its potential sources, especially those that are most readily available within the context of our own lives. The handout for this activity, Finding Sources of Self-Esteem (Week 2—Handout 3), lists each major source of self-esteem we found in the research, namely, personally significant achievements or successes, evidence of influence or power, acceptance or being valued by others, and virtue or acting on beliefs. It is helpful to point out that two sources of self-esteem are based on competence (achievements and influence) and two reflect worthiness (acceptance and virtue). After I describe the characteristics of each source, I include an example of a recent experience I have had in each of the two groupings to model them. Then, the participants are asked to try and identify a recent experience of their own in any of the four areas.

Some people complete this activity quite easily, but others have a hard time with it because they tend to look for only major achievements, influence, actions, or acceptance. Occasionally, people worry that they do not seem to have much material to put into one or more of the categories, so there is some value in having members share their work. Sooner or later, a person says something like, "It makes me feel good about myself when I find my child waiting for me at the door when I come home from work, " or "Someone was having a problem doing his job at work today and I was able to show him how: That made me feel that I have something to offer." Usually, others in the group then begin to look for small, but readily available, potential sources of self-esteem in their own lives and complete the activity.

Another factor to be aware of while working with groups is that self-esteem environments vary considerably between people. For instance, some life situations make one or another source of self-esteem more or less accessible than others, and not everyone is going to be able to readily find all four sources. The point is to let people know that these four basic sources of self-esteem really do exist and that they need to be aware of which ones are most likely to be available *in their own set of circumstances*. It is good practice to take some time to make sure that each member of the group becomes aware of at least one realistic source of self-esteem in his or her life, because having access to one of them is necessary for the program to work. In some cases, it helps to present the self-esteem bucket metaphor mentioned in Chapter 5. The point to stress is that all that the bucket needs to be "good enough" is for "water" to be put into it from at least one source of competence and one source of worthiness with some degree of regularity. Finally, we turn to the journal and ask participants to track the ways in which these potential sources of self-esteem manifest themselves during the next week. This information is used again at the end of the program.

WEEK 3: ENHANCING PHASE (INCREASING WORTHINESS)

Goal

As before, the third week begins with a review of the previous week's homework to reinforce the material that was learned and the need to sustain awareness concerning the importance of self-esteem. Once again, participants are asked to share their experiences in the form of an open discussion, but it is important to be mindful of the fact that this session involves learning new skills, so time is important. By now, the participants are usually comfortable enough with each other and with the group as a whole, so I may start to encourage individuals who seem to need a little help to participate more actively. Basically, the group typically starts to come together as a therapeutic enterprise at this point, just as it becomes time for members to start taking some small risks by participating in activities designed to increase worthiness and competence, and therefore self-esteem.

Materials

Note that all materials for this stage of the program come from our findings concerning the most valid self-esteem enhancement techniques.

1. Week 3—Handout 1: Enhancing Worthiness Through Positive Feedback
2. Week 3—Handout 2: Increasing Worthiness Through Cognitive Restructuring
3. Week 3—Handout 3: Cognitive Pattern-Breaking Outline

Procedure

The major activity this week is to work on what I sometimes euphemistically call self-esteem "gumption traps" (Pirsig, 1974), which is a phrase describing how we often create self-esteem problems that are vexing because they lessen our sense of worthiness. If the phrase "gumption trap" seems awkward, then "self-esteem trap" may be used. As we saw in the analysis of problematic self-esteem themes, these traps often act as powerful, co-constitutive processes. For example, they help us to experience ourselves as being less worthy than we are, thereby keeping us locked into our own negative self-esteem themes and actions. Note that these times in life do not include situations in which we face a challenge, try our best, and still fail. Those events may feel bad, but having tried our authentic best, we at least maintain our worthiness.

In this session we ask people to identify the *habitual and unnecessary* ways that they consciously or unwittingly work to maintain low or defensive self-esteem. Two activities are offered in this regard. The first one is more humanistic and involves fostering the experience of worthiness, even though we may tend to hide such knowledge from awareness. The second one is based on the principles of cognitive therapy. It involves learning how to identify and disrupt the habits of mind often called "thinking patterns" that lead to a lower than appropriate sense of worthiness.

Step 1: Enhancing Worthiness

This exercise is usually a surprisingly meaningful activity that is designed to help participants get in touch with their positive (worthy) qualities and to do so in a supportive environment where others are genuinely accepting of them. The exercise involves asking participants to fill out the Enhancing Worthiness Through Positive Feedback form (Week 3—Handout 1, part A), which involves writing down 10 positive qualities or attributes about oneself.

Occasionally, a person is unable to complete the list. There are two common reasons this event tends to occur. First, people often look for unusually significant achievements or outstanding qualities. Many of us would have a hard time coming up with 10 of those. Therefore, it is important to tell participants that things we easily overlook may also be indications of worth, such as being a good parent, being faithful to one's word, engaging in the virtuous act of fulfilling one's duties as a citizen by voting, and so on. Second, low self-esteem and competence-based self-esteem can interfere with a person's ability to perceive worthy things about himself or herself. Sometimes the individual may even feel so unworthy that he or she thinks there is *nothing* good to say about himself or herself.

For example, I still remember one woman who dropped out of a group because she felt unworthy of feeling worthy! Fortunately, she went back to individual therapy. However, this experience taught me that worthiness is more of an issue than sometimes meets the eye, especially when working with someone who may have led a lifestyle that incurred considerable social disapproval, such as addiction, prostitution, and so forth. Offering the group a small number of realistic examples and giving time to reflect on their positive qualities seems to help them complete the activity. Occasionally, some still do not fill in all the blanks. When this happens, it can be helpful to ask if they heard anything on someone else's list that applies to them and, if so, to add it to their own list.

Then, in part B of the handout entitled "Group Sharing," the lists are read out loud. This part of the activity should be done with considerable sensitivity because some people learn that saying positive things about themselves is "wrong" (e.g., a sign of a being a braggart or a violation of the principle of humility), or they are only accustomed to vocalizing their negative qualities. I usually begin by reading my own list to show participants that it is all right to say positive things about oneself and to get the ball rolling. Then, I ask for volunteers and try to make sure everyone has an opportunity to participate. It is easy to dismiss this exercise as a popularistic psychology gimmick, such as reading the list every morning while standing before a mirror. However, there is little evidence that such methods work, and it is important to make sure people know they are *not* being asked to do that. Instead, the exercise is designed to be done once, as part of the group, and for two good reasons.

First, although this activity has less empirical support for its effectiveness than others, it is actually a variation of the established self-esteem enhancement techniques we discuss in Chapter 3. Remember, we saw that being accepted and valued by others was a source of worthiness, and all of the major enhancement programs include this factor as a part of the program. The same may be said for the use of positive feedback that is at the heart of this activity. In addition, the exercise helps make the transition from mere learning to what positive psychology might call "deep" learning (Duckworth, Steen, & Seligman, 2005).

Second, some people feel so unworthy about themselves or come from environments that affirm so little about their value as a person that they weep when they realize that they actually have a number of real, identifiable, positive qualities. At such times, the rest of the group members may see how special the moment is and respond with comments of genuine affirmation and authentic appreciation. They may, for instance, even give a soft round of applause for the person or begin to share their own difficulties in thinking or speaking well of themselves. These self-esteem moments are also unique to the group process, and because they spontaneously emerge from others, the feedback may be more valuable than that which the facilitator could offer.

Step 2: Introducing the Concept of Cognitive Restructuring

The first part of the session usually takes about a half hour. Then, we turn to the handout Week 3—Handout 2: Increasing Worthiness Through Cognitive Restructuring. Most mental health professionals are familiar with this technique, and in Chapter 4 we found that some variation of it is often used in self-esteem work. However, it is important to remember that this practice is often new to clients. Therefore, it is best to present information about it clearly and walk them through the process step-by-step.

Consequently, part A of the activity involves explaining the basic idea behind this type of cognitive intervention and how it applies to self-esteem. The procedure usually involves a discussion about self-talk, self-fulfilling prophecies, and self-defeating behavior. I tend to use those terms instead of meaning-making or co-constitution because most people are more familiar with them. The important things to emphasize are: (1) the idea that distorted, irrational, illogical, or unwarranted thinking, or whichever term one prefers, leads to unwarranted perceptions, negative feelings, or dysfunctional behavior; and (2) if we correct such mistaken cognitive or information processing patterns, then our perceptions, feelings, and actions are more likely to change as well.

Next, we turn to part B, where I explain the terms I have chosen to describe these mental self-esteem traps and define them. After going through the definitions with the group, I attempt to illustrate the process in part C by giving an example of how they have worked in my life. For instance, I might begin by telling them about a time when a romantic partner of mine ended our relationship, and how my "self-talk" (meaning-making) at the time helped create (co-constitute) a higher degree of pain for me than was actually necessary. "There I sat in my lonely apartment," I might say, "convinced that no one would ever love me again because I was such a loser." Then, I ask participants to identify which "traps" I had fallen into as they look over the list of common mistakes presented in the handout. Usually, there are several possibilities to consider.

In this example, labeling often comes to mind fairly quickly, which suggests that the group is learning to use the terms in an appropriate way. I take some time to point out that it is usually necessary and appropriate for a person to be sad over a loss; otherwise, participants may develop exaggerated expectations about the value or effectiveness of this technique. After all, cognitive therapy is not magic. Then, I emphasize that the point is that one does not have to suffer *unduly* over an event, even a genuinely negative one. In other words, rather than become stuck in dejection or depression, it is also possible to experience the sadness of a loss as a part of accepting it. Though not easy, sadness is much healthier than refusing to deal with reality rationally, because being sad is a normal part of grieving and helps us move on to other possibilities.

This activity may be done with some good humor and fun. Indeed, sometimes the session becomes quite lively as we all learn to laugh at ourselves a bit more easily. Be careful about what is disclosed, however, because it may be similar to what someone in the group is currently working on, which means that you may fall prey to a transference situation. One time, for instance, I used this example, and a person in the group who had just left someone reacted poorly to the anecdote. Though relatively easy to deal with, working through that issue with the individual did take up valuable group time for the others.

It is also important to help people become aware of the negative cognitive patterns or worthiness traps they happen to use most often. In earlier editions, I limited myself to 10 "standard" terms associated with well-known approaches to show that the technique is supported by clinical literature. Since then, this practice has become so well accepted that it is not necessary to proceed in that way. In fact, when I compared several of the major lists available (Burns, 1980; Ellis & Harper, 1977; Leahy, 2003; McKay & Fanning, 2000) I found that there are over 20 terms used to describe cognitive errors, flaws, or distortions that concern the ways in which these destructive habits of mind get in the way of realistic perception and healthy experience.

Although it might be helpful to list all the terms, the same item is often defined in different ways by different authors, and keeping all of them in mind would be quite a task. A more useful approach is to look for those that run across the major lists. The result of my analysis is as follows: With minimal modification, five basic terms were used in all three approaches: Labeling, Filtering, Overgeneralizing (which also showed up in the research on self-esteem in Chapter 3), Personalizing, and Emotional Reasoning. Some version of several more terms also showed up on at least two lists: Mind Reading, Fortune Telling, Catastrophizing, Dichotomous Thinking, and Should Statements. In other words, there are a number of good, standard terms from which to choose.

The list I offer in the handout consists of the first set of five for two good reasons. First, these terms are the most universal, which makes them something of a standard. Second, they happen to be negative in a way that tends to undermine a sense of worthiness more than competence, which is, of course, what makes them most appropriate to this part of the program. However, a number of lines are left blank in the handout so that a clinician can add ones that he or she is comfortable with too. For example, I usually include catastrophizing because it is a common cognitive distortion and people seem to relate to it well, including the author. Once again, it is helpful to go over each term, give examples of each one, and allow the group members to ask questions to ensure that everyone understands what is meant.

Step 3: Cognitive Restructuring

Now comes the time to show the group how to use the technique to alter patterns that help to co-constitute a life of low or defensive self-esteem. Once again, there are several systems from which to choose (Freeman et al., 1990), including those mentioned earlier. The main differences between them are slightly different terms and the number of steps they use to reduce the negative effects of such mental habits.

In any case, the general idea is straightforward. First, it involves teaching people how to examine situations that bring them pain and to note the thoughts they have during those times. Then, the individual looks for cognitions that seem to cause discomfort and analyzes them for errors by comparing them with a list of common dysfunctional thoughts. Each such mistaken cognition is identified, named, and then corrected by restating the thought in more realistic terms. At the end of the process, the individual re-evaluates his or her feelings or experience to determine whether he or she is being more rational. The procedure is then repeated until the person's reactions correspond to the events as realistically as possible. For our purposes, the aim is to help the group understand how human beings trap themselves in ways that unnecessarily lessen their sense of worth, how to break out of those negative cognitive patterns when they occur, and how to start building new and healthier mental habits.

Whatever version of this approach is selected by the therapist, it is *essential* to walk people through the process step-by-step and to do so several times if possible. Thus, at this point we turn to the material labeled Week 3—Handout 3: Cognitive Pattern-Breaking Outline. There are shorter versions of this process and facilitators familiar with them are free to select one. I have kept the longer step-by-step version found in the previous edition in this one because it presents smaller steps, which might be helpful for novices. First, it is important to identify and explain the steps presented in the handout in part A. Then, it is possible to go to part B and demonstrate using the steps to disassemble a cognitive self-esteem trap and how to restructure cognitive patterns.

Typically, I begin by drawing a long horizontal line across the board, flip chart, or screen in front of the group and create sections numbered 1 through 7. Shorter formats would have fewer steps, but the procedure is the same. Then, I select an example that seems appropriate from my own life and take it through each of the seven parts of the process in a way that is as genuine as possible. For example, I describe the situation, identify my strongest negative feelings, and genuinely share my negative thoughts without overdoing it, which concludes the third item on the list. When it comes to the fourth point, however, I ask the group to help me identify my thinking mistakes or self-esteem traps. Then I request their assistance to help me reword my thoughts to reflect reality more accurately in the fifth part. Next, I assess my own feelings and usually have to admit some degree of positive change has occurred. Again, I point out that there is no magic in this process, but that dealing with reality is usually better than dealing with distorted versions of it. Occasionally I will do the seventh part as well, but not often, as I want to move on to volunteers.

It is also important to emphasize, as most of these programs do, that it is necessary to write out every step as we do them, because we can easily fall into these worthiness-eroding self-esteem traps and because we can fool ourselves by thinking it is sufficient to do the steps mentally. It is also helpful to point out that, like any bad habit, these cognitive patterns have been learned over the course of a lifetime and are therefore difficult to unlearn quickly: They are so well-practiced and ingrained quite literally in our brains that it takes something like writing to slow down cognitive and perceptual patterns enough to identify, let alone disrupt, them. Changing such habits of mind may even involve the process of neural sculpting, meaning that the process usually must be repeated many times before change occurs (Johanson, 2009).

To make sure the participants get the point and know how to use the program, I turn to part C. Here, I ask a participant to allow me to help restructure a negative experience that made him or her feel less worthy by working it through the process. It is, of course, important to get permission and to make sure that the experience is not too personal or powerfully overwhelming. All the work is shown on the board, in front of the group, and in an accepting fashion. After one or two times, the group typically becomes relaxed and people begin to volunteer to have their own experiences processed in this way. Eventually, I have the group tell me what to put on the board as we go through each of the steps. This part of the process is crucial to the program's success and can be fun. Finally, the last part of the activity involves a homework assignment, which is to continue practicing the technique during the next week and record results in their self-esteem journals.

WEEK 4: ENHANCING PHASE (INCREASING COMPETENCE)

Goal

The fourth week continues the enhancement phase of the program, but the focus shifts from working on worthiness to developing competence. In theory, this phase may be lengthened to include more activities than I offer here. If, for instance, we were working in a long-term group situation, then we could focus on learning to stand up for ourselves through assertiveness training. However, learning such sophisticated skills usually takes several weeks (Rakos, 1990). Therefore, the fourth session aims to round out the enhancement phase by increasing competence in other ways.

Materials

These materials are designed to aid the group's work on skills and abilities. Focusing on the competence factor in this way also helps to differentiate the program from the "feel-good" approaches mentioned earlier that received so much criticism. Since this program is based on two factors, the next set of activities focuses on the behavioral dimensions of self-esteem, or how we *earn* it.

1. Self-esteem journal data
2. Week 4—Handout 1: Enhancing Competence: Problem-Solving Method
3. Week 4—Handout 2: Enhancing Competence: Problem-Solving Worksheet

Procedure

Step 1: Review

The session begins with a review of the cognitive restructuring technique. I start by asking the group to share examples from their journals. However, instead of explaining the technique again, I ask permission to diagram a situation on the board from the group, and then have them work through it with me from beginning to end. I repeat this procedure until I am sure everybody knows how to use the technique. There are several reasons for beginning this way. One is that we are trying to help people acquire a new skill that must become a habit to work effectively. Such learning takes time and people often make mistakes in the early stages, just as any novice might. Also, the old habits are so powerful and so automatic that people are likely to be trapped by them again and again, despite attempts to intervene. Repeating the process reinforces new ways of dealing with these old self-esteem traps. Finally, it is not uncommon when going over them publicly for participants to see that someone else in the group actually found relief using this method. Often, hearing others talk about how they broke out of a trap, even if momentarily, lends credibility to the technique, gives hope for the future, and underscores the program's value.

It should be noted that some of the cognitive (co-constitutive) distortions we commit are trickier to deal with than others. Working through participants' problems on the board allows us to use our professional expertise to help with some of the more subtle self-esteem traps. For instance, I find that one of the most difficult distortions with which to deal occurs when a person co-constitutes a situation through what Burns (1980) called "emotional reasoning." I like to call this particular distortion "Yeah, but," which is a phrase a student of mine coined when she noticed that those are the very words people tend to use most often when they are engaged in emotional reasoning. Let me illustrate this phenomenon, because it can be disruptive to the group process if it is not dealt with successfully.

Typically, those who reason emotionally begin by presenting a situation that is genuinely unpleasant. They work what happened through the steps but see only a slight reduction in feeling intensity. Rather than trying to accept the fact that the situation is simply an uncomfortable one, or instead of being satisfied with a realistic reduction in negative affect, they start up all over again. Usually, such individuals offer superficial agreement by saying something like "Yes, I see what you mean, but. . .," then slip right back into reasoning illogically by letting feelings of discomfort replace reason. Although it may take several repetitions of going through the steps, having the individual work on each "Yeah, but" as it occurs often helps them to understand how they are distorting the situation in ways that keep it more painful than it needs to be. "If only this . . . or if only that. . ." is another variation on this theme that can be used to achieve the same distorted end. When a participant manages to realize the nature of this particular trap in the session, the event can be a powerful lesson for the individual as well as for the group, because it shows that even the most stubborn distortions can be broken.

Step 2: Enhancing Competence Through Problem-Solving

The second activity of the session, which usually comes after the break, continues to follow the two-factor, meaning-based theory of self-esteem by building on the connection between self-esteem and competence. The goal is to help participants learn a skill that increases their ability to better deal with the challenges of life. The single most powerful tool for this purpose is learning to solve problems effectively. After all, increasing this ability should enhance an individual's chance of success in a variety of situations, which, in turn, could lead to a greater demonstration of competence over time.

D'Zurilla and Goldfried (1971) helped to pioneer work in this area and D'Zurilla and Nezu (2001) refined it later. Pope et al. (1988) applied this technique to helping children enhance self-esteem. Like correcting mental errors, problem-solving has evolved into several different types of formats. However, the ideas and practices remain fairly standard: Learning how to solve challenges of living more effectively involves understanding that something is a problem, developing a plan of action to solve it, and then taking the necessary steps. This technique is chosen here because it is theoretically sound, nicely compatible with a theory of self-esteem based on competence and worthiness, reasonably well-researched, and relatively easy to both demonstrate and use.

We begin by turning to the first handout for this session, Enhancing Competence: Problem-Solving Method (Week 4—Handout 1). Although the temptation is to go directly to the problem-solving steps listed in part B, it is important to spend some time on the theory behind good problem-solving, which is found in part A. This practice helps participants appreciate that feeling, thinking, and behaving are distinct parts of the process, which is important because sometimes they have trouble distinguishing between one or more areas. For instance, I still find that males tend to have more difficulty than females with recognizing feelings, which often means that men have more trouble detecting early signs of a developing problem. All too often this tendency results in things having to get worse before they can get better. Thus, taking the time to explain the value of being able to identify and listen to feelings is helpful for many clients who have not been socialized in this way.

Then, I turn to part B and simply describe the eight steps identified there. This overview prepares the group to move through the next part of the session, which consists of walking the participants through the steps and procedures of the problem-solving process format presented in the handout for this activity. Next, we use the Week 4—Handout 2: Enhancing Competence: Problem-Solving Worksheet and move through it much in the way that we did with cognitive self-esteem traps. I usually begin by listing in order all the steps and procedures from part A on the board, which may be done in a vertical or horizontal fashion, although I find the latter more useful. Next, I take a problem I am facing in my own life that is not too personal or overly complex and work it through the process step-by-step. In other words, I first identify a problem and list it. Then, as step 2 indicates, I stop and think (aloud) about the difficulty and try to articulate what is really bothering me about this difficulty so that we are able to take the third step, which is to decide what an appropriate or effective goal would be in dealing with this particular issue. Note that each step in the handout is accompanied by a brief suggestion concerning how to go about completing the step, which is why it contains two columns, namely, "Step" and "Procedure."

Next, we think about and identify potential solutions to this particular problem and do some group brainstorming to generate a number of possibilities. This fourth step may be a little tricky because people tend to want to evaluate the relative merits of each possible solution as it is offered. Someone, for instance, often says, "Well, that sure won't work," and I have to remind the group that we are not yet evaluating solutions, just trying to list as many possibilities as we can. After writing a reasonable number of possible solutions on the board, we move to the fifth step, where we evaluate the alternatives individually. The typical approach is to think about the likely consequences for each one. Sometimes thinking in terms of what a given solution "gets me" versus what it will "cost me" is helpful.

In the sixth step, I select the best alternative listed earlier. Notice that what makes this step "best" is that it is the one that offers something of a real solution (what it "gets" me), but at a cost an individual is willing to pay (what it "costs" me). In other words, the most effective solution is sometimes not chosen because it requires more work than the individual is willing to do. Usually, however, the alternative that is selected in this situation does having something to offer. Then, of course, it is important to take the time to make a realistic plan of how to implement the decision I made. Paying close attention to detail is important because people usually make plans that are doomed to fail. Therefore, in this seventh step I ask the group to help me identify each specific activity that must be completed to implement the solution and to assist me in placing them in the order that is necessary for them to take me to the goal. Finally, I add another step that is not on most of the other versions of the technique, which is the need to practice problem-solving before deciding on whether or not it works. Many people try the method, find that it did not make the problem go away, and give up on the technique. Reminding them of this aspect of the learning process helps reduce this type of behavior.

After going through this practice run, we make the exercise more realistic by asking people to volunteer problems for part B. Of course, we work each one out on the board by asking the group to process the problem each step of the way. As the facilitator, I clarify their responses and write them on the board for all to see. The same procedure is repeated until we run out of time, and then the whole group is instructed to practice using this technique for the next week and to record their experiences in their self-esteem journals. Participants often seem pleased to receive training in problem-solving and even skeptical group members tend to see it as a tangible benefit of the program that is readily transferable to real life. Sometimes a participant agrees to think about what has been done here, use the technique on a particular problem, and report back to us on his or her experience of the problem at the next meeting during the review period.

There are some points to remember in working through both the cognitive restructuring and the problem-solving activities. For one thing, it is helpful to model them for the group, which is done both by the facilitator's working through his or her own problem and by working through problems from the group. Modeling not only shows each step of the process more clearly, but, as we have already seen, is itself a valid self-esteem enhancement technique that is tied to competence.

Trying things out also allows us to help dispel certain kinds of difficulties, such as the mistaken belief that these techniques make one feel great or that they will work overnight. For example, participants might say that even though their pain or uncomfortable feelings have been reduced by this or that technique, they still feel bad. At this point it is necessary to emphasize that the goal is to be realistic, which includes understanding that sometimes circumstances are simply uncomfortable. Then, it is helpful to point out that even a reduction in pain or anxiety is a net gain in these situations, which fully justifies using the technique. Even so, some participants say something like "OK, I've done what you want, but I still have a problem," or "None of the alternatives are good ones." Again, it is helpful to remind people that these techniques are not magical, just rational, and that they at least help us find the best ways to deal with problems or challenges of living.

Finally, we must consider the fact that the principle of practice is an important part of the entire program. By this time, people tend to groan about journal writing (and sometimes that does fall off, as is often the case with the journaling technique in general). However, now participants also see the value of doing the actual work, so I often try to reinforce the benefits of practicing by using the following analogy. The idea is to compare learning how to restructure one's thinking and response patterns with other forms of learning that participants can relate to more easily, such as weight lifting or joining an exercise class: One starts out slowly, and the first few attempts are clumsy and uncomfortable. However, if one sticks with the activity for a reasonable length of time, it usually results in clear gains. In other words, increasing self-esteem is just like any other complex learning activity—it takes time and work. I conclude by asking once again, "Why should you expect anything else when so many years have gone into learning to develop a self-esteem problem?"

WEEK 5: MANAGEMENT PHASE (MAINTAINING SELF-ESTEEM)

Goal

The fifth week deals with two related issues. First, the group meetings are coming to an end. Any experienced clinician knows about the importance of dealing with issues such as termination, separation anxiety, and the like. Second, and more important, ending the group means that its members no longer are able to count on the discipline offered by weekly meetings to help them focus their awareness or to reinforce the gains that have been made during the program. Thus, the finding we uncovered concerning the fact that good programs must deal with the problem of maintaining self-esteem turns out to be important enough to be the focus of the last regular meeting. Note that I use the term *managing* instead of maintaining self-esteem because management is much more active, dynamic, and future oriented than is maintenance, which, by contrast, implies holding steady rather than making advances.

Materials

The fundamental structure of self-esteem was found to consist of competence, worthiness, and the relationship between them. We will see in this phase that the relationship between the two factors is just as important as the factors themselves, because keeping them balanced is the key to managing self-esteem throughout the life cycle.

1. Self-esteem journal data
2. Week 5—Handout 1: Building a Self-Esteem Enhancement Project
3. Week 5—Program Evaluation Sheet (clinician's design or simple discussion)

Procedure

Step 1: Review

As usual, the session begins with a review of what the members of the group did with the problem-solving homework from the last session. Often, one person presents a positive experience and another presents an example in which the technique failed. Both experiences are good grist for the therapeutic mill: The former reinforces, as any testimonial tends to do, and the latter gives us an opportunity to practice once again. However, this time, when I ask for someone to volunteer material for us to examine, I make it a point to have the group tell me what steps to take as we walk the problem through the method. Such active engagement reviews the method but also stands as a practice session. This step should take no more than a half hour or so.

Step 2: Introducing the Concept of Managing Self-Esteem

Remember, self-esteem involves competently facing the challenges of living in worthy ways over time. The key, then, is to help people find ways of building on the work done to date so that they are better enabled to take advantage of new self-esteem opportunities in the future. The critical aspects of such a project include: helping people continue to be aware that self-esteem is a vital resource, finding ways to increase competence or worthiness, or both, and remembering how important it is to manage self-esteem effectively so that more authentic self-esteem is earned over time. One way to help participants in all three areas is to show them how to make self-esteem an ongoing personal project, something that can be done by developing a "self-esteem action plan."

The activity for this week, which is presented in Building a Self-Esteem Enhancement Project (Week 5—Handout 1), is divided into two parts. Part I is a visual representation of the idea of a self-esteem action cycle. This information is presented as a cycle for several reasons. One is that a dynamic view of self-esteem helps people understand how it works. Another is that many researchers routinely talked about self-esteem in terms of a cycle—a self-fulfilling one. In addition, such a straightforward presentation of a complex process helps people make sense out of the steps that are necessary to increase self-esteem. Finally, viewing self-esteem as a cycle makes it possible to connect some important aspects of increasing it to Fredrickson's (2002) Broaden and Build theory of positive emotions. However, we will explore the relationship between self-esteem and positive psychology in the next chapter.

As the chart indicates, participants are told that the *current* (or lived) status of their self-esteem is where we must start, no matter where it is, because that constitutes their existential situation. Moving clockwise, the next step is to identify one self-esteem *issue* to work on that is especially important right now in one's life. Once such a goal is identified, we can use the information acquired from other parts of the program to build an individualized self-esteem *project*. In other words, participants use their problem-solving skills to develop a clear behavioral plan to follow after the group is over, a plan that is connected to at least one source of self-esteem. Ultimately, of course, reaching the goal involves work and . *practice*, another theme we have stressed throughout the session.

Over time, such work results in new *learning* as well as an increase in one or both of the factors that affect self-esteem. Because acquiring more competence and more worthiness is additive (Harter, 1999), completing the cycle in this way shifts our position on the self-esteem matrix to some degree and thereby *changes* it in a positive direction, which establishes a new *current* level in a cyclical fashion. This form of progress is consistent with the diagram found in the handout and with the one concerning the development of self-esteem in adulthood (Figure 5.8), though I do not necessarily present the latter in this session. I also point out that one may always repeat the process, one project after another, until he or she is satisfied with the results.

Step 3: Building a Self-Esteem Action Plan

Now we move to part II of the handout and walk participants through the steps one at a time in a way that requires them to build an actual plan in the session. There are two reasons for doing so. First, this practice allows us to check work to see if participants really understand the cycle. Second, the exercise is designed to move into the future with them: If done correctly, the plan that is developed here also becomes the first self-esteem project that participants can work on to manage their self-esteem effectively when the group is over. Once again, the worksheet for this step is set up to be done in a stepwise fashion under the direction of the facilitator, who acts as teacher, coach, and troubleshooter for this process.

First, in part II-A, group members are asked to identify a self-esteem area that they wish to improve. Our work with the MSEI on identifying self-esteem strengths and weaknesses is very helpful here. For example, a person whose self-esteem is relatively healthy may be best served by building a project around a domain that scored low on the test. Such an individual is likely to be able to tolerate looking at shortcomings without becoming defensive or discouraged, which helps him or her to take a "fast track" toward increasing self-esteem. However, a person with a more serious self-esteem problem already focuses on his or her vulnerabilities, so that participant may be better served by taking a slower, gentler approach. In this case, working to improve functioning in an area where one is already doing at least moderately well may be more effective. Success could also help a person gain enough confidence to move on to more complex tasks. Selecting a goal in which one is likely to be valued by others may be appropriate for someone who suffers from a lack of worthiness. I usually leave the choice up to the members, but do suggest these basic guidelines to them as they are selecting an area for improvement.

Next, members are instructed to match the nature of their self-esteem project with an appropriate source of self-esteem by using the four basic sources they worked with in Week 2—Handout 3. This information is to be written in part II-B on the worksheet for the current step to help focus awareness. The activity also helps participants build an efficient program because they can begin to look for the kinds of self-esteem opportunities they need to make a given project successful. Individuals who suffer from difficulties with competence, for instance, might think about increasing various skills that could help them to have more achievements or influence. Some relevant possibilities in this regard include learning how to speak more effectively by taking a training course, or one that improves communication skills. Those who score lower on worthiness scales might seek out interpersonal opportunities that could lead to being accepted or valued more, such as doing volunteer work. They could also look for ways to act more virtuously, even if it is just to work on reducing a bad habit.

Notice that although either competence or worthiness may be emphasized in any given project, the other component is active as well. When encouraging the individual to increase competence, we also want him or her to do that by reaching worthy goals, not unworthy ones. When helping people to increase their sense of worthiness, we want them to do so by being virtuous or by behaving in ways that facilitate being valued for positive qualities that they actually demonstrate. In this sense, we are always balancing the relationship between the two factors and, therefore, self-esteem.

The next part, labeled II-C on the activity sheet, brings into play the problem-solving skills work done during the last session. Here, we ask individuals to examine their self-esteem needs, to consider the ways in which the source of self-esteem upon which they are focusing manifests itself concretely in their own lives, and then to generate some goals that are realistic in terms of their own situation and abilities. Once again, the tendency is for people to set their sights a little too high, so I help by asking them to decide on one or two goals that are meaningful but realistic. Sometimes it is helpful to go around the room asking participants what they are targeting as a goal so that others get some ideas too. It is also possible to ask participants to work in pairs to help in this fashion, which is a technique that can be quite useful because it tends to increase a sense of ownership in both individuals. Once again, the qualities of group work may be put to good use.

The final part, II-D, is the most important one and relies on the problem-solving skills learned in the last session. The task is to help members create a practical program; one that involves clear, realistic steps that result in reaching a reasonable self-esteem-enhancing goal. A good self-esteem project is, therefore, highly individualized. It must take into account various individual qualities and fit well with the individual's current environment or unique circumstances. For instance, a self-esteem enhancement project aimed at increasing competence for an individual who is challenged mentally would look different from one for a person who was doing reasonably well in life but who wishes to do better. In the first case, the goal of learning how to find the right bus to take home from work might be a major achievement. In the second, aiming for an award or promotion might be fitting. In all cases, developing a self-esteem project is like preparing for a trip in that the more planning one does, the more likely one is to reach the destination, though there is never a guarantee.

Now, we ask people to write down each and every step they must take to reach the goal they have identified. If the aim, for instance, is to work on body functioning by developing an exercise program, then the individual is asked to be specific about how this will happen. It might, for instance, mean trying out several sports. If so, the individual must indicate the initial steps needed to experiment in this way, such as calling the YMCA/YWCA, joining a club, or finding a friend involved in a relevant activity. If the individual decides to join the "Y," then he or she must find out how much the program costs, set aside a day to go to the gym, talk with a trainer, try a certain number of activities until one feels right, and so on. Similarly, if someone makes becoming more likable the goal, then he or she needs to consider such things as becoming involved in a worthwhile community activity or volunteering more at work. Depending on which activity is selected, there is often a need to develop a list of organizations, contact friends, make phone calls, meet with a few groups, and try out the activity until something suitable is found.

Focusing on these mundane details is positive for a number of reasons, ranging from such platitudes as "a journey of a thousand miles begins with a single step," or "inch by inch, it's a cinch," to the simple fact that small successes are often necessary in order to reach larger ones. To underscore the importance of detailed planning, I may present my own self-esteem enhancement goals and ask members to help me develop the specific action steps necessary to improve in this area so that they can see how it is done through modeling. Then, I encourage volunteers to present their plans to the group. As before, I put the steps on the board and walk the group through a volunteer's plan so that we can help improve it and so that I can reinforce the need for the plans to be detailed. This process is repeated until about the last 10 or 15 minutes of the session.

Finally, as the end of the session nears, I use the remaining time as an opportunity for members to share their experience about the 5 weeks, mention their plans for the future, and assess the value of the group. This evaluative moment may be done with a form if that is required, but I have found ordinary group discussion about what worked for them a pleasant and meaningful way to end the group. Not surprisingly, I remind them one more time about the crucial roles that hard work, practice, and time play in increasing self-esteem. Therefore, the last step in the activity is to point out to participants that the journal is a way of keeping these important ingredients in mind.

WEEK 6 (OPTIONAL): FOLLOW-UP SESSION

One last possibility needs to be mentioned. There can be value in adding a sixth session after the group has ended as a kind of follow-up or "booster" meeting. We know that increasing self-esteem requires hard work and that it can take a long time, but sometimes people start out well-intentioned and then become discouraged or bogged down for one reason or another. A follow-up meeting may help participants strengthen their resolve or see the progress they have made, either of which can powerfully reinforce positive change. It is possible to do several things to help such a session, if it is offered. For instance, the facilitator may ask participants to share their experiences about how they were successful and where they had difficulty, so that everyone can see how hard people have to work at managing self-esteem. Material from any of the sessions may be reviewed on request. Special group attention might be given to an individual self-esteem project or need. The follow-up session could also be used to remind people about the learning curve, how long they have had a problem with self-esteem, and the need to continue practicing.

Although most of my groups do not include this extra session, there is good reason to invest in this additional time upon occasion. This meeting may be included in the program from the beginning, by making it a 6-week program instead of 5. However, it is probably more effective to schedule a 1-month follow-up after the five sessions end. In fact, this arrangement is mentioned in the short-term psychotherapy literature and is purported to have an enhancing effect (Wells, 1982). The risk of going this route is that attendance is likely to be lower than the usual group meetings because of such things as time limitations, schedule conflicts, or the resurgence of old, poor self-esteem habits. Nevertheless, in general I have found that clients often seem pleased with the progress they have made and wish to share their success with others.

ENHANCING SELF-ESTEEM IN THE INDIVIDUAL SETTING

We saw earlier that self-esteem enhancement programs may be designed for the individual setting (Bednar et al., 1989; Pope et al., 1988; Shrik & Harter, 1996). It is also possible to organize CWT in a way that is compatible with individual work. This version is based on a planned short-term treatment model (Wells, 1982) that continues to be a common practice for at least two reasons: It reduces costs and the literature on the subject tells us that it is reasonably effective. However, another crucial distinction of modern time-limited therapies is that, unlike traditional psychotherapy, this approach is usually structured and focused. Typically, the client and therapist identify a particular problem or issue that is to be the center of their work and relationship. Long-term problems involving such goals as general personality reorganization or psychotic conditions are not well suited to short-term work (Mann, 1973), which means that careful screening and diagnosis are a part of the process. Finally, there are psychodynamic, behavioral, cognitive, and even humanistic approaches to short-term work, which means that such a format is compatible with a number of therapeutic orientations.

The general approach is to adapt CWT to fit the short-term framework without changing the essential character of the program. That is, we would begin a standard intake evaluation to make sure that this type of work is appropriate for the client and then use the same steps found in the group format to organize the treatment. Because most clinicians tend to work with individual clients in one-hour appointments, the program could be broken up into 10 one-hour periods instead of five two-hour meetings without much logistical difficulty. In short, one way of adapting the program to individual work is by making its steps the basis of a short-term therapeutic contract, the primary focus of which is to work on enhancing self-esteem. In fact, I have been interested in investigating this approach and have even developed a format for it that is found in the Appendix and labeled "Supplement I."

Just as there are some advantages to working in the group format, the individual setting offers its own unique possibilities. For one thing, it allows us to focus more directly on the client as a particular and special person, which, among other things, allows us to take better advantage of assessment. For example, in this setting we are free to use the MSEI to explore *all* the domains of self-esteem it evaluates, rather than just identifying the areas with the highest and lowest scores. Such work is likely to increase awareness of self-esteem in general, but it also allows us to develop a much better understanding of how the components and dimensions of self-esteem are alive in a particular person's life. Thus, this approach also allows us to expand the assessment to include identifying self-esteem themes that are especially important for a given individual.

Also, individual work is better positioned to use naturally occurring self-esteem moments, especially those involving problematic self-esteem themes. After all, the longer a client is in treatment, the more such opportunities are likely to arise. This aspect of individual work can be beneficial for two reasons. First, earlier we saw that a positive resolution of such self-esteem challenges can genuinely modify underlying problematic self-esteem themes in a positive direction.

Second, as Bednar et al. (1989) pointed out, individual therapy adds new elements to the situation that make a meaningful difference in their outcomes. For example, the client does not have to face the challenges of living alone in this therapeutic arrangement. Here, the therapist may help increase the client's awareness of what is really at stake and facilitate dealing with a challenge that involves significant biographic self-esteem themes. In fact, the clinician may even assist in navigating the six steps of this process so that it comes to a positive end. Moreover, even if a client fails, we can help the individual understand how that happened and think about ways to improve his or her chances the next time such a challenge occurs.

Given the nature of the relationship between self-esteem and authenticity, this work is much more existential than pedagogical, which, among other things, means that both client and therapist are more actively engaged with each other here. Therefore, it is important to realize that there are two limits to consider concerning this approach. First, the therapist should be well-acquainted with the program before beginning to use it in the individual setting. Second, clinicians should pay close attention to the usual possibilities that occur in more intensive therapeutic relationships, such as transference, counter-transference, acting out, and so forth, and be prepared to handle them according to the standards of practice. After all, because there is no one else to bring into the picture in this format, the relationship between the client and therapist is more intense than in the group setting.

One last word about formats and the program in general is in order. It should be clear that group and individual approaches have their respective strengths and weaknesses. For instance, the former has rich dynamics of the group process to rely upon, such as multiple perspectives, spontaneous opportunities, group affirmation, and reduced cost, whereas the latter offers more personal attention and more individualized support. However, the step-by-step character of either one may seem somewhat rigid to those who are more comfortable with a traditional humanistic or psychodynamic approach. If so, then it is important to realize that, although structured, the program cannot be successfully run in a mechanical fashion.

In other words, much of the program's effectiveness is likely to involve the same interpersonal attitudes of acceptance, care, and respect for others, or the so-called "common factors" of effective therapy (Arkowitz, 1997; Prochaska & Norcross, 1994; Seligman, 1995a). If the quality of interpersonal contact is poor, mechanical, or "manualized," then the effectiveness of the program is likely to suffer, perhaps even fail. In CWT, the therapist is not just a good technician or a skilled teacher: He or she also becomes an important source of worthiness through acceptance and of competence through modeling. Although the program's steps show people where to go, it is the therapist's unique and authentic presence, as well as the ability to connect with others (Mruk & Hartzell, 2003), that takes people there.

VALIDITY REVISITED

We are at the end of this existentially oriented search for self-esteem, which means that it is important to address one last issue. From the beginning, I have stressed the importance of basing the program on good research and sound theory. For example, I attempted to show how the program meets the criteria for construct validity in two ways. First, it was said that a comprehensive approach must be able to accommodate important insights and findings made by researchers, theoreticians, and clinicians from other perspectives. The idea was that validity increases in relation to the descriptive power of the theory, in this case the ability of a two-factor framework to integrate the major research findings on self-esteem. Upon reflection, it must be said that the approach actually seemed to do quite well in this regard. For example, the work on the definitions of self-esteem, the self-esteem paradoxes, and the research findings on self-esteem were all shown to be compatible with the fundamental structure of self-esteem and the meaning matrix.

Second, it was mentioned that a valid approach would be one that is theoretically consistent. This criterion seems to have been met as well, because we just saw how an existentially oriented two-factor approach to self-esteem is capable of moving from research through theory and to practice in an extremely consistent fashion. The self-esteem meaning matrix, for instance, was even able to predict the necessity of certain types of phenomena, such as types of self-esteem.

However, the practical aspect of the program means that we are also interested in applying its techniques to actual human life. This dimension raises standards to higher levels: After all, if we hold ourselves out as being able to help, we should be able to demonstrate the efficacy of our methods, especially in an evidence-based world. In general, validity in an applied setting is said to involve two criteria: clinical efficacy and clinical utility (Durand & Barlow, 2013). In other words, a legitimate therapeutic program should be accompanied by research demonstrating its effectiveness (clinical efficacy) and its practicality or usefulness in real-world settings (clinical utility). For example, a program that is valid but too cumbersome or expensive to use in real life is not helpful in the larger sense, and a program that is very easy to implement but that is not valid is even worse. Fortunately, a growing body of work indicates that CWT performs well at both levels.

The fact that CWT involves a structured process with clear steps and standardized materials is important because it means the program is easy to implement in the applied setting. In fact, any competent clinician or educator should be able to move through the process and materials without difficulty, which is one reason I detailed those procedures. This aspect of CWT gives it a solid degree of clinical or applied utility, thereby satisfying that requirement. The program is, indeed, practical. In addition, the fact that CWT is structured and standardized in this way also increases reliability in the research setting. The program, for example, even includes a respected assessment instrument that makes such things as pre- and post-testing research a logical way of testing its clinical efficacy.

In addition to using the program in my own applied work, I have trained graduate students, practicing mental health professionals of several types, and educators to use it. Thus, CWT has been offered to such populations as traditional and non-traditional college students, clients in mental health settings, people in counseling programs, and general audiences in the psychoeducational setting. The program has also been used by others who followed the book and then wrote or talked to me about their positive experiences afterward. All of these things are pleasant to hear and do suggest some degree of efficacy, especially since some of this type of feedback is in written form. For example, some educators expressed support for the psychoeducational aspects of the program (Jindal-Snape & Miller, 2008) and another has used it with groups of women at a major university (Hunt, 2010). Even so, applied social scientists and the concept of evidence-based treatment expect more.

Fortunately, CWT is being used and studied in various applied settings, and some results have been published. For example, the program was first evaluated in a community mental health setting by Hakim-Larson and Mruk (1997). This pilot study involved using CWT with over 30 participants in several groups: those suffering from anxiety or depression, people with substance-related disorders, a group of people who were co-dependent, and a non-clinical group that acted as something of a control. The design of the project involved using the MSEI assessment as a pre- and post-testing instrument. I collected the data and then submitted it to my colleague who worked at another university. Then, Hakim-Larson independently analyzed the data in order to, among other things, control for bias on my part. She found that participant scores changed in the expected positive direction and that the size effect was a large one, indicating that CWT "really works." All of these groups received the treatment, so there was no control in the classical sense. However, Kazdin (1992) and Seligman (1995a) pointed out that this situation often occurs in real-world settings and does not necessarily have a negative impact on results.

Bartoletti and O'Brien (2003) developed a more rigorous and tightly controlled study of CWT's efficacy that also involved a pre- and post-test design. Bartoletti (2008) then extended the work by comparing three groups: one from a community mental health setting, another from a college counseling center, and the third as a control group that did not receive treatment. Once again, this line of work resulted in the expected positive change and was accompanied by a significant size effect. More recently, Haringsma (2011) conducted a much larger study that involved training facilitators for groups as well as many more participants. This study also investigated whether or not CWT is effective with healthy or "normal" populations to assess its value as a form of positive therapy, something I will discuss in the next chapter. As one might expect with a healthy population, the magnitude of change was smaller for this group, but it was still significant and in the desired direction.

Although a handful of studies may seem like a small body of work, it is important to realize some other things about it before drawing conclusions. Chief among them may be that research on CWT is unusually diverse, which attests to its utility: The program has been run in several clinical, college, and psychoeducational settings. Second, the fact that there is a body of work supporting the program's efficacy is unusual in this field. Most self-esteem enhancement programs have not been scrutinized in this way. In short, there does appear to be good reason to take the position that a two-factor, existentially oriented, meaning-based approach to the research, theory, and practice of self-esteem stands up to major qualitative and quantitative indices of validity. Thus, it can be said that not only does CWT appear to meet or exceed the standards of practice for enhancing self-esteem as they exist today, but it also satisfies those of an evidence-based approach as well.

7

Self-Esteem and Positive Psychology

What is positive psychology? Is there only one form of it? What does positive psychology study? Does that material include self-esteem? If there is a relationship between what is called positive psychology and self-esteem, how do these fields interface with each other in terms of research, theory, and practice? Because the answers to these questions were still unclear at the time, the last edition of this book argued for the position that self-esteem *should* have a place in positive psychology. However, new developments in positive psychology make it possible to talk about the place that self-esteem now *has* in that field. Thus, in addition to creating the need for another edition, it is important to address these questions anew.

When Seligman (1999) first announced the birth of positive psychology during his presidential address to the American Psychological Association in Boston in 1998, I was in the audience. Although very appreciative of the many opportunities his inaugural vision offered psychology, I was surprised that the importance of healthy self-esteem and the negative impact of unhealthy forms of it were not discussed. The surprise changed to disappointment when self-esteem did not emerge as a topic in what many would consider to be the first major description of positive psychology, written by Seligman and Csikszentmihalyi and published by the prestigious American Psychological Association (2000). Similarly, it was disconcerting to find that only one chapter addressed self-esteem in what is probably the first major handbook on positive psychology 2 years later (Snyder & Lopez, 2002). Sadly, that piece largely treated self-esteem as a cultural artifact of the West, albeit an important one. Finally, it became clear that something was amiss when self-esteem was not even mentioned as a character strength or virtue in one of the first major books on this important dimension of positive psychology (Peterson & Seligman, 2004).

In short, until recently, self-esteem seemed to be missing the boat of positive psychology, or perhaps it was the other way around, given that the field of self-esteem preceded that of positive psychology by over a century. Of course, there may be several reasons why such a glaring omission occurred. Remember, for example, that self-esteem underwent a period of severe criticism just before positive psychology emerged. Perhaps, then, positive psychology evolved in such a way so as to avoid such controversy while attempting to establish itself in the field, and simply dropped the topic as a matter of expedience. It could also be that the tendency to use unidimensional definitions of self-esteem was an issue. After all, when seen this way, it is difficult to determine whether self-esteem should be seen as a factor affecting behavior or as a result of it, thereby reducing the importance of self-esteem. It is even possible to attribute this oversight to the mere youth of positive psychology, as it is not realistic to expect an emerging area to identify all of its important themes at once. Whatever the cause or causes, the point of the last edition was that the absence of a major place for something as positive as healthy self-esteem in a field called positive psychology had to be addressed, especially if self-esteem is defined in terms of two factors instead of one.

Fortunately, what I call second-generation positive psychologists have moved well beyond this early point. No longer primarily concerned with defending the legitimacy of a new field, these researchers and clinicians now routinely include self-esteem as an important topic. For example, Carr (2011) devoted an entire section to self-esteem when covering such things as positive selfhood in his textbook on positive psychology. This section even included a lengthy review of the two-factor approach presented in an earlier edition of this book. In addition, a number of positive psychologists talk about self-esteem in relation to positive behavior and other topics of interest to positive psychologists. For instance, self-esteem is often discussed in relation to happiness and well-being (Baumgardner & Crothers, 2009), relationships (Mruk, in press), and psychotherapy (Linley & Joseph, 2004; Mruk, 2008a). Therefore, it is clear that it is no longer necessary to justify a relationship between the fields. Instead, it is important to understand and perhaps advance the growing interface between the two fields. To proceed in this direction, however, it is first necessary to examine what is meant by positive psychology and the areas it studies, especially as they pertain to self-esteem.

WHAT IS POSITIVE PSYCHOLOGY?

Those who are new to the field may be surprised to know that the term "positive psychology" can be traced to at least 1882 (Taylor, 2001). Those who are new to psychology in general may be surprised to know that there are actually two major forms of positive psychology active today. Because we have used history as a guide in defining self-esteem, it makes sense to continue in that fashion. Understanding the historical evolution of a field also provides other insights concerning such things as the emergence of similarities and differences that occur within given schools and approaches.

The Original (Humanistic) Positive Psychology

Decades ago, a few individuals realized that the social sciences were failing to live up to an important aspect of their commitment to study the full range of human behavior, particularly its richer and higher dimensions. Initially, some of them attempted to focus on things such as positive subjective experience, human potential, and facilitative social institutions, which would foster healthy experiences and development, all of which are a part of positive psychology today. For example, Adler (1927) was interested in the concept of *community* mental health and Horney (1937) declared a "war" on neurosis. Later, several psychologists, such as Gordon Allport and Gardner Murphy, addressed similar themes in a more academic context (Taylor, 2001). However, the first organized positive response was offered by humanistic psychologists around the early 1950s.

Basic Humanistic Ideas and Characteristics

Like most movements, humanistic psychology began as a core of ideas around which an identity forms. One part of the nexus concerned the reductionistic philosophical foundations of the psychological perspectives that were dominant at the time, especially the psychodynamic and behavioral points of view. Both of these mainstream positions were based on the logical positivism of psychology practiced as a natural science. From the beginning, humanistic psychologists saw such mainstream or traditional approaches as too limited to understand the full richness of human experience, especially its more positive possibilities. To them, we are more than just the results of our past histories, our bodies, or our environments.

Thus, humanistic psychology began as a protest, one that was "directed against the entire orientation of psychology since Hobbes and Locke, against its Newtonian and Darwinian models of man, and against its mechanistic, deterministic, and reductionist character" (Misiak & Sexton, 1973, p. 115). Taking issue with standards that characterized nearly all of psychology and psychological research at the time, the editor of the *Journal of Humanistic Psychology* is quoted as having said that humanistic psychology is:

> Primarily an orientation toward the whole of psychology rather than a distinct area or school. It stands for respect for the worth of persons, respect for differences of approach, open-mindedness as to acceptable methods, and interest in exploration of new aspects of human behavior. (Maslow, 1964, p. 70)

Sutich went on to identify some of the topics that this new form of psychology should prioritize.

> As a "third force" in contemporary psychology it is concerned with topics having little place in existing theories and systems; e.g., love, creativity, self, growth, organism, basic need-gratification, self-actualization, higher values, being, becoming, spontaneity, play, humor, affection, naturalness, warmth, ego-transcendence, objectivity, autonomy, responsibility, meaning, fairplay, transcendental experience, peak experience, courage, and related concepts. (pp. 70–71)

Finally, Maslow even talked about positive psychology as such: For example, the title of an entire appendix to one of his books reads "Problems Generated by a Positive Approach to Psychology" (Maslow, 1954/1970). Of course, the problems he talked about are all "good" ones in that they are positive, not problem or disease based. In other words, it is clear that he intended this form of positive psychology to investigate topics such as positive emotions, experiences, characteristics, motivations, relationships, organizations, and so on, all of which are of interest to the new positive psychology of today.

For those who are less familiar with it, humanistic psychology continued its original mission but has matured to the point that now includes a general set of positive psychological themes, issues, and concerns that carve out a reasonably clear, although certainly not dominant, place in psychology. Tageson (1982) identified seven of them. First, this perspective is characterized by a phenomenological approach, which is to say that it focuses on human life as it is actually lived and experienced in the real world by real people making real decisions. Thus, although much of standard or traditional psychology practiced as a natural science prioritizes research done in laboratories or statistical correlations of behavior, such work is often seen as marginally relevant or sterile compared with the richness of real life. Next, humanistic psychology is characterized by a holistic approach to understanding the person and behavior. This view rejects those that reduce us to mere biological organisms, prisoners of the past, complicated products of environmental forces, or some sort of wet computer as we see in the evolutionary, psychodynamic, social learning, and cognitive perspectives, respectively.

Third, humanistic psychology is concerned with appreciating, understanding, and facilitating the basic human tendency to grow, actualize, and live the good (i.e., rich and meaningful) life. Consequently, this approach also emphasizes self-determination, which includes such things as intrinsic motivation and autonomy, or "free will" over the more deterministic factors of biology or learning. Fifth, humanistic psychology is an active psychology. It is one that focuses on authenticity as a key to healthy psychological functioning, as opposed to inauthenticity that is characterized by poor choices and an unwillingness to accept responsibility for one's action and life. Self-transcendence is next, particularly the human capacity to grow beyond the self and form a larger sense of community or connectedness. Finally, humanistic psychology is person-centered, which is to say that, although it is not necessary to embrace every choice that a person makes in life, it is still important to treat people with respect, dignity, and some degree of compassion or at least understanding.

In addition to Tageson's list, I would add an eighth defining characteristic based on Maslow's words, namely, those concerning being open minded about methods: Humanistic psychology values methodological diversity. Instead of eschewing the methods of traditional empirical psychology, the humanistic approach accepts the full range of methods seen in the continuum in Chapter 2 as being potentially useful. For example, we found that only methods associated with the qualitative paradigm are capable of accessing the data of human experience as it is actually lived. Consequently, it is not surprising to find humanistic research being done with phenomenological, interview, case study, and narrative techniques. However, we also saw that it is possible to use quantitative methods, such as in the case of integrated description, in a way that strengthens either end of the methodological continuum. What could be more sensible?

Like traditional psychology, contemporary humanistic psychology involves developing more sophisticated methods for researching human experience and behavior (Greenberg et al., 2004), including mixed methods, those that integrate qualitative and quantitative work, and even multiple methods (Wertz, 1984). Indeed, Taylor (2001) found that many of the over 2,700 articles on self-actualization "refer to the measurement of self-actualization as a personality construct using Shostrom's Personal Orientation Inventory, obviously now a well-established research tool in psychology" (p. 21). Moreover, this approach is represented in the field by the usual bodies. For example, humanistic psychology has given rise to several longstanding refereed scientific publications, such as the *Journal of Humanistic Psychology* and *The Humanistic Psychologist*. Similarly, humanistic psychology has spawned a number of professional organizations that support its efforts, including a division in the American Psychological Association. In short, there can be very little doubt that the humanistic approach was and still stands as the first organized form of positive psychology.

Finally, it is important to point out that humanistic psychology is not monolithic. Just like any other major scientific perspective on human behavior, humanistic psychology may be grouped into a number of schools. For example, we have been using the existential–humanistic position in this book because it emphasizes the individual and authenticity while facing the challenges of living. This person-centered approach has dominated the field for quite some time. Another smaller branch is the transpersonal school that focuses more on such things as interpersonal, cultural, and perhaps even spiritual ways of transcending individual experience. As an aside, for those who feel that investigating such aspects of being human is nonscientific, I offer the following thought: Although investigating such material is difficult, if psychology is to be charged with the mission of understanding human behavior, and if human behavior actually does involve such a "spiritual" dimension, then any psychology that does not study such phenomena may have failed its goal *in principle* and in practice.

The Place of Self-Esteem in Humanistic Psychology

Those familiar with this approach to psychology know that from the beginning, self-esteem is seen as one of the most basic and important dimensions of human life. For example, we saw in Chapter 3 that both of its major founders, Rogers and Maslow, held self-esteem to be a central factor in human development and behavior, although in somewhat different ways. Because humanistic psychology is often given limited attention in psychology textbooks and programs today, there is some value in covering these points at the risk of being repetitive, especially for those who are newer to the field.

Maslow clearly saw self-esteem as a need, one that is basic enough to organize an entire stage of human development in his well-known hierarchy of needs (1954/1970). A classical definition of needs in psychology is to say that they arise from states of deprivation, which, in turn, create drives that propel organisms toward goals (Rathus, 2007). Maslow called such basic needs deficiency needs, or "D-needs," and identified physiological needs, safety needs, needs for love and belongingness, and the need for self-esteem. Because humanistic psychology focuses on positive dimensions of human life, he also identified a second set of needs that shape motivation in this more self-actualizing direction. These needs motivate the organism to reach for higher levels of being and are thereby called "B-needs." They include such things as the ability to actualize possibilities that lie within the self and perhaps in some ways even transcend it through such acts as creativity.

The perspicacious reader might notice that self-esteem occupies a curious place in this well-known hierarchy of needs, which includes five stages of development: physiological needs, safety needs, needs for loving and belongingness, self-esteem, and self-actualization, in that order. On one hand, self-esteem is a basic or developmental need, which means that we are driven toward satisfying it. Like most developmental tasks, this one builds upon the accomplishments of previous stages and then becomes heightened at a certain time of life. Thus, self-esteem becomes a central organizer of experience and behavior after the individual achieves some degree of worth in the previous stage of loving and belongingness.

In the framework of the two-factor model, the stage of love and belongingness may be said to focus on developing a sense of being accepted and valuable or worthy as a person, whereas the stage of self-esteem completes the process by resulting in a sense of competence and self-respect. Like life in general, most developmental models make plenty of room for the fact that growth is never guaranteed. In other words, people who fail to grow for one reason or another become stuck or fixated in the stage where problems arise and then go on to manifest its characteristics in negative ways. In this case, self-esteem may become contingent on approval or success, as Crocker and Park (2004) described.

On the other hand, self-esteem stands just below the B-needs or the higher needs for being, especially those concerning self-actualization. This position is unique in the hierarchy and suggests that self-esteem occupies a crucial point in growth. In other words, the ability to stand up for that which is "just and right," as Milton said, is necessary for development. From a humanistic point of view, then, it makes sense that self-esteem is an important factor in regard to a host of positive experiences and characteristics such as subjective well-being, healthy relationships, optimal functioning, and especially actualization. In other words, when defined in terms of two factors instead of one, self-esteem may well be the "pivotal variable" that Rosenberg (1965) thought it to be. In this case, the function of self-esteem is clear: It is what determines whether an individual moves toward expanding the self and reaches toward higher possibilities, or focuses on protecting the self and settling for less.

As discussed at some length earlier, Rogers' (1951, 1961) understanding of the role of self-acceptance (which is a way he often talked about self-esteem) in growth and development gives it a more central place. For example, where Maslow's view of self-esteem centers its importance at a certain time of life, Rogers saw self-esteem as emerging much earlier and as playing a continuous role in development that works hand in hand with the central tendency of an organism to grow. If one is fortunate enough to have parents who offer disciplined (i.e., well structured and authoritative) unconditional positive regard, then the pathway toward healthy self-esteem is more readily available to the individual. Once a person has such a basic level of healthy self-esteem, he or she feels worthy and competent enough to take the risks associated with self-expansion and actualization. Those without healthy self-esteem still attempt to grow because that drive is inherent to life. However, their journey is much more difficult and may be characterized by self-protection and inauthenticity instead.

In other words, being accepted by others and accepting one's self help with the worthiness component of self-esteem. Being able to take reasonable risks necessary to acquire competence when facing normal developmental challenges facilitates the emergence of this component. Having at least medium self-esteem, in turn, allows one to continue to address the challenges of living, including those that involve finding relationships and meaning in life, in ways that are more worthy over time. Thus, self-esteem is necessary for the process of becoming, as Rogers said, "fully functioning" (1961) as a person.

Perhaps due to his clinical background and interest, Rogers also saw the development of self-esteem as being much more active in terms of mental health and illness. In this case, the lack of authentic self-esteem is seen as resulting from conditional parental regard and authoritarian, permissive, or uninvolved parenting, as discussed in Chapter 3. These factors may inhibit the development of self-awareness, diminish self-acceptance, and obscure intrinsic values, all of which make authentic self-esteem difficult. From a humanistic perspective, being out of touch with one's self in these ways may also contribute to other more serious problems, such as making poor career choices, selecting unsatisfying relationships, and anxiety or depression.

Fortunately, Rogers (1951) also suggested that if a lack of authentic self-acceptance or esteem is at the core of these problems, then increasing it can reinvigorate the growth tendencies central to all human beings. Thus, humanistic therapies often focus on helping individuals to increase self-awareness, accept themselves more fully, experience their feelings, and act in ways that are consistent with their intrinsic values through appropriate risk-taking. Such psychological realignment or "congruence" (1961) allows the organismic character of the self to re-establish the possibility of continued growth and actualization. In short, for much of humanistic psychology, self-esteem, or some form of it, is a central factor all the way from theory to practice.

The New (Positivistic) Positive Psychology

It is well known that Seligman and Csikszentmihalyi (2000) are two of the founding fathers of what is today called positive psychology. Rather than focusing on reductionism as the main problem, they presented positive psychology as a reaction to another aspect of contemporary psychology. In this case, the objection centers on the ways in which psychology was influenced by certain events associated with the aftermath of World War II. In particular, the negative effects of the war on various soldier and civilian populations, coupled with a huge influx of federal and academic money aimed at treatment, are seen as shifting the very foundations of psychology. Consequently, it moved from a traditional academic footing to a more applied one that is based on the problem and disease models.

Positive psychology's intent to address this situation is apparent in the first attempts to define the field. To paraphrase Seligman and Csikszentmihalyi (2000), for instance, positive psychology can be seen as a science of positive subjective experience, positive individual traits, and positive social institutions (p. 5). However, we have seen that definitions often evolve over time, and now most positive psychologists understand positive psychology as "an umbrella term for the study of positive emotions, positive character traits, and enabling institutions" (Seligman, Steen, Park, & Peterson, 2005, p. 410). This broader definition is important because it means that positive psychology can include work done by other social scientists who come from different areas but who happen to be concerned with positive phenomena.

Basic Ideas and Characteristics

To examine the place of self-esteem in positive psychology, we must first understand its character as an emerging field. Fortunately, the general intent of this approach is very clear:

> The message of the positive psychology movement is to remind our field that it has been deformed. Psychology is not just the study of disease, weakness, and damage; it also is the study of strength and virtue. Treatment is not just fixing what is wrong; it is also building what is right. Psychology is not just about illness or health; it is also about work, education, insight, love, growth, and play. And in this quest for what is best, positive psychology . . . tries to adapt what is best in the scientific method to the unique problems that human behavior presents in all its complexity. (Seligman, 2002, p. 4)

Thus, the primary aim of positive psychology is to offer a corrective balance to traditional psychology. This effort begins with reminding psychology that although it should be concerned with more negative behavior to help ease humanity's suffering, it is at least as important to keep the other, more positive, end of the continuum in mind. For those who are more historically oriented, I should say that a more accurate way of describing this field is to call it "new positive psychology" because humanistic psychology used the term earlier. For those who are more technically exacting, it is also possible to describe it as "positivistic positive psychology" because of its underlying philosophy of science (Mruk, 2006, 2008b). However, let us stay with the term positive psychology because it is the one that is used more often today.

Positive psychology then takes this message to the research and applied levels by encouraging psychologists and others to study the positive aspects of human behavior more vigorously than in the past. They seem to be doing just that. For instance, various handbooks (Snyder & Lopez, 2002) and textbooks (Baumgardner & Crothers, 2009; Carr, 2011; Compton, 2005; Peterson, 2006) on positive psychology clearly cover a wide range of positive behavior. This work includes studying things such as happiness, positive emotions, positive states of being, health and longevity, positive self-regulation, optimal functioning, positive traits, meaningful work, healthy relationships, and institutions that foster them, including healthy families, schools, and workplaces. The similarity between topics of interest between the two positive psychologies is clear, striking, and important.

The core characteristics of positive psychology center around three global pillars or concerns (Compton, 2005). The first is a focus on positive subjective experience, such as "well-being, contentment, and satisfaction (in the past); hope and optimism (for the future); and flow and happiness (in the present)" (Seligman & Csikszentmihalyi, 2000, p. 5). Thus, the general tone of positive psychology is true to its stated intent: to balance traditional psychology's emphasis on illness and problems by concentrating on understanding positive human phenomena. Second, positive psychology focuses on identifying, researching, and facilitating the development of positive human qualities and characteristics, including "the capacity for love and vocation, courage, interpersonal skill, aesthetic sensibility, perseverance, forgiveness, originality, future mindedness, spirituality, high talent, and wisdom" (Seligman & Csikszentmihalyi, 2000, p. 5). Again, in just a few years, the new field has already produced several impressive works on these topics (Aspinwall & Staudinger, 2003).

The third core characteristic of positive psychology concerns understanding the relationship between group or social behavior and basic human values, especially "the civic virtues and the institutions that move individuals toward better citizenship: responsibility, nurturance, altruism, civility, moderation, tolerance, and work ethic" (Seligman & Csikszentmihalyi, 2000, p. 5). This dimension expands the scope of positive psychology beyond that of much traditional psychology because to achieve healthy human functioning, people need to live in societies that are actively concerned with fostering optimal growth and development. Thus, positive psychology is a social and psychological project.

However, it would be a mistake to see positive psychology as a monolithic discipline. Like most fields, it is characterized by different schools of thought that share the same core. For example, the hedonic approach focuses on what is called subjective well-being and tends to study such things as pleasant experiences or happiness in general. The other, or eudaimonic, approach concentrates on what is described as psychological well-being and gravitates toward researching the good life in an Aristotelian sense of the term (Baumgardner & Crothers, 2009).

In summary, Seligman and Csikszentmihalyi (2000) acknowledge that positive psychology is "not a new idea" (p. 13) and it is easy to see a number of similarities between the two types of positive psychology. For example, they both arose as a reaction to the traditional, mainstream, and dominant psychologies of their respective days. Similarly, both of them emphasize the importance of studying the same general domains of human behavior, namely, positive emotions, higher forms of motivation, healthy relationships, and growth-promoting institutions, including families, workplaces, governments, and societies. Finally, both fields have developed to the point where they are now characterized by differing, and sometimes even competing, schools of thought within their respective disciplines.

Given these solid core similarities, the question becomes, how do the two approaches differ? The answer seems to be found in one very large and overarching distinction concerning the scientific method. One of the reasons I talked about scientific paradigms in Chapter 2 is that appreciating the full range of the methodological continuum is important for understanding the difference between the two positive psychologies. Remember, the qualitative and quantitative branches of this range stand as very different views of science and how to do it. Maslow's (1964) point mentioned earlier, namely, that humanistic psychology "stands for respect for . . . differences of approach, open-mindedness as to acceptable methods" (p. 70) makes it absolutely clear that humanistic psychology is open to both ends of the methodological continuum. In fact, this approach is well known for its qualitative orientation and highly values it. However, positive psychology strongly embraces traditional psychological research methods, which are solidly grounded in the logical positivism of the quantitative end of the methodological continuum.

Although I would regard it as an oversimplification of the humanistic approach, the early founders of positive psychology make this distinction unequivocally important and clear. For example, in what may be the first major publication on the approach, it was said that,

> Unfortunately, humanistic psychology did not attract much of a cumulative empirical base, and it spawned myriad therapeutic self-help movements. In some of its incarnations, it emphasized the self and encouraged a self-centeredness that played down concerns for collective well-being. Further debate will determine whether this came about because Maslow and Rogers were ahead of their times, because these flaws were inherent in their original vision, or because of overly enthusiastic followers. However one legacy of the humanism of the 1960s is prominently displayed

in any large bookstore: The "psychology" section contains at least 10 shelves on crystal healing, aromatherapy, and reaching the inner child for every shelf of books that tries to uphold some scholarly standard. (Seligman & Csikszentmihalyi, 2000, p. 7)

While we shall see that what can be called second-generation positive psychology is more flexible in this regard, this methodological difference is what differentiated the two psychologies in the beginning and is still very much present today in some quarters.

Self-Esteem and Positive Psychology

In the last edition of this book, it was necessary to argue the position that it is possible to achieve common ground between the two psychologies in relation to the psychology of self-esteem. Although perhaps not yet a major theme, enough progress has occurred in this regard that we can now move beyond mere potential and talk about the actual connections between the two fields.

Self-Esteem and the Hedonic School. In general, this type of work in positive psychology focuses on happiness and includes such things as satisfaction with life and relationships (especially marriage), positive attitudes (such as optimism), positive experiences (including flow), and positive effect (hence, the word "hedonic" or pleasurable). All these things are collectively referred to as "subjective well-being" (Baumgardner & Crothers, 2009). The hedonic approach to positive psychology also tends to be highly empirical in the traditional, positivistic sense of the term, and most of its research is based on correlations, surveys, and other objective methods. A substantial body of work on self-esteem now exists in relation to this type of positive psychology.

As a case in point, work in positive psychology found a strong positive correlation between greater levels of self-esteem and higher degrees of general happiness with life. For example, Diener and Diener (1995) conducted a study involving some 13,000 college students from over 30 nations and found a correlation of 0.47 between self-esteem and life satisfaction. In addition, although it is difficult to establish clear cause-and-effect relationships for reasons discussed in Chapter 5, this type of positive psychology has little difficulty with the buffering effect of self-esteem, because it reduces the impact of things that may decrease subjective well-being such as stress (Baumgardner & Crothers, 2009, p. 187). Consequently, work on the protective self-regulatory function of self-esteem is important for positive psychologists. Thus, because research on happiness and life satisfaction is a major theme in the hedonic school of positive psychology, it is fair to say that related work on self-esteem occupies a real place in the general field of positive psychology.

Some positive psychologists take the position that healthy self-esteem is related to a positive sense of self (Carr, 2011), which is related to a number of topics of interest to positive psychology, such as optimal functioning, positive affect, and healthy relationships. Work on the self-expansion regulatory function of self-esteem becomes very relevant in this regard. For example, we saw that self-esteem plays a significant role in relationships. Although low self-esteem was shown to interfere with subjective well-being in relationships, high self-esteem actually facilitates its development and may even be necessary for it to occur. How healthy or authentic self-esteem fosters such things as initiating, healing, sustaining, and enriching or expanding relationships should be of acute interest to positive psychologists concerned with relationship satisfaction, happiness, and well-being.

Both the self-expansionary function of self-esteem and the fact that it feels good or has positive hedonic affective qualities represent another set of important tie-ins between the two fields that has not been touched on before. It will be recalled that several self-esteem researchers pointed out the self-fulfilling character of self-esteem. For example, Bednar and Peterson (1995) talked about self-esteem and feedback in this fashion, and several researchers on self-esteem in relationships described both high and low self-esteem as generating positive and negative affective and behavioral cycles. Researchers also characterized the role of self-esteem in relationships as positive and negative self-fulfilling prophecies (Baldwin, 2006; Berenson & Downey, 2006; Leary, 2008; Murray, 2008). It happens that Fredrickson's (2002) Broaden and Build theory of emotion, which may stand as the single most important theory and body of research on affect that has emerged so far in positive psychology, appears to work in the same fashion.

This positive approach to emotions and behavior suggests that just as negative emotions such as fear, anxiety, and anger evolved to help our species survive, so did positive feelings and affect. Negative emotions and related behavior tend to be highly focused, involve strong bodily reactions, and narrow attention to the immediate danger or situation. In other words, negative emotions evolved to help us concentrate our resources on such things as staying alive in dangerous situations. This type of affect and its accompanying physiology are readily observable because it often activates the sympathetic nervous system. Thus, negative emotions are often relatively easy to observe, measure, and study.

By contrast, positive emotions are often subtle, bring few visible signs of excitation to the body, and allow attention to relax, which enables it to be more open to new or even distant possibilities. For example, positive emotions such as interest, curiosity, aesthetic perception, or contemplation are often pleasant in very refined ways that are difficult to detect or study. However, all of them tend to expand attention in a way that might also have survival value in regard to the process associated with such things as discovery or creativity, which have a different type of evolutionary survival value for individuals and groups.

Fredrickson (2002) also developed a very convincing method for studying positive emotions in controlled situations. Very briefly stated, the experimental design involved establishing physiological baselines for control and experimental subjects, and then exposing both groups to negative emotional stimulating scenarios. Next, the experimental group was presented with positive emotional stimuli to consider, while the control group received affectively neutral stimuli. In each variation of the design, those who were exposed to positive stimuli seemed to recover baseline functioning much more quickly, suggesting that positive affect is beneficial because of an "undoing effect" (p. 127) created by positive emotions.

In addition, she went on to note that just as negative affect can cycle downward under prolonged conditions to produce such undesirable phenomena as depression, positive affect may create a corresponding upward cycle that broadens or expands perception and builds behavior in a healthy direction over time. Hence, positive emotions are important because they lead to new or more adaptive behaviors under certain conditions. Further, positive emotions seem to work in much the same way that all emotions do: through the mechanisms of reinforcement, in this case positive reinforcement. If so, the theory concludes, then positive emotions may help reduce the detrimental impact of negative ones and even facilitate upward emotional and behavioral cycles toward well-being in general.

What connects the two fields is that it is possible to integrate this type of work in positive psychology with the motivational dimensions of self-esteem. For example, the downward spiral sometimes created by negative emotions could be a mechanism that contributes to the negative self-fulfilling prophecy often referred to by those who study self-esteem and self-esteem in relationships. In this case, we would expect perception to be narrowed just as it is with such things as vigilance, self-handicapping, or withdrawal in the personal or interpersonal spheres. Conversely, the broadening and building aspects of positive emotions could contribute to the motivational and affective nature of the self-expansionary function of self-esteem. In this instance, we would expect to find perception broadening out in a way that includes new possibilities, which, in turn, may facilitate taking reasonable risks to reach more positive hedonic or eudaimonic goals, just as we saw with work describing high healthy self-esteem. The point is that, once again, there is new work in both fields that indicates the existence of important connections between them.

Finally, it is important to note that this type of self-esteem work is characterized by the types of methods this branch of positive psychology values most: those that involve surveys, experimental manipulation, and statistical tests of significance. In short, this branch of positive psychology clearly identifies self-esteem as an important topic in relation to subjective well-being, and there is every reason to believe more could be done in this part of the interface between the two fields.

Eudaimonic Positive Psychology and Self-Esteem. The other major school to emerge so far in positive psychology is the eudaimonic approach. This somewhat abstract Greek word is also connected to happiness and satisfaction with life, but in a very different way from its hedonic counterpart: It is concerned with what positive psychologists call psychological well-being, which may be defined as "engagement with and full participation in the challenges and opportunities of life" (Linley & Joseph, 2004, p. 5). In other words, from this point of view, psychological well-being is founded on the good life in an Aristotelian sense (Baumgardner & Crothers, 2009, p. 18): one that is based on meaning, the process of self-realization, and virtue.

Positive psychologists sometimes make this point by using an analogy called the "experience machine" (Nozick, 1974). This theoretical device allows a person to be hooked up to a machine that will allow him or her to experience any type of feeling, behavior, or state imaginable. If happiness and satisfaction were the main or only goals in life, then experiencing endless pleasure, intense satisfaction, or pure joy in this fashion would be very appealing to most people and they would often agree to live this way. However, when most people are asked if they would like to be hooked up to such a device and live this way, they almost invariably say "no" (Peterson, 2006). The point is that there is more to life than pleasure. In contrast to the hedonic nature of subjective well-being, psychological well-being involves meaning, such as that which is found in deep relationships, significant work, or as a result of dedication to a cause or purpose, such as helping others.

This type of meaning is the ground for a deeper sense of happiness and well-being than that which can be found through the senses, enjoyable moments, and so forth. In fact, sometimes pursuing such meaning comes at considerable cost and even suffering, as in the case of sacrificing one's life for a worthy cause. However, it is also true that researching meaning is much more difficult than measuring degrees of happiness because meaning is never tangible. Consequently, this approach to positive psychology requires more methodological flexibility. For example, because meanings reside in people, such work often involves asking them questions and using more qualitative methods, including narratives and interviews. This type of work is very compatible with much of the experientially based research we saw on self-esteem.

Authenticity, Self-Esteem, and Positive Psychology

Psychological well-being is a major focus of both positive psychology and the field of self-esteem. For example, self-realization is necessary for the good life. This process involves such things as the discovery, expression, and fulfillment of inner potentials, all of which were found to be associated with the self-expansion function of self-esteem. However, work on authenticity may show more specific and far-reaching connections between self-esteem and this branch of positive psychology.

Authenticity is at the very foundation of humanistic psychology in theory and practice. Just as existential philosophers made authenticity a major component of this view, humanistic psychologists, such as Rogers, did the same with psychology. Medlock (2012) reviewed the literature on authenticity very carefully and identified six key characteristics that can be adapted to a discussion on self-esteem. First, authenticity involves being oriented to a "higher" (although not necessarily spiritual) self that is based on positive processes and values. Next, these intrinsic values are self-defining in that we make existential choices based on them (a process that requires self-exploration and self-knowledge). Third, authenticity involves being grounded in a here-and-now sense of self and experience (which is congruence in Rogers' sense of the term).

In addition, authenticity occurs as an expression of personal autonomy that is realistic within various social and historical constraints (we are free to act within the bounds created by the constraints of any given situation and are responsible for those choices). Fifth, authenticity occurs in a cultural context, especially in regard to our relationships with others (human beings are social creatures). Finally, authenticity involves an individual authoring a narrative of his or her life and identity that is constructed by the self and others (which brings modern cognitive discoveries into the picture of authenticity). Medlock also fully appreciates the inherent connection between the words "authoring" and "authenticity," which has to do with being an authority, creating something, and legitimizing it, in this case a life.

Research on Authenticity

However, as insightful as it may be, such philosophical and literary support concerning the importance of authenticity for self-esteem and the eudaimonic good life are unlikely to work well for the more empirically oriented positive psychologists. Fortunately, sufficient methodological advances have been made so as to generate this type of research on authenticity that is of interest to both groups, and therefore constitutes another interface between self-esteem and positive psychology.

For example, self-determination theory (SDT) operates from an explicitly existential and organismic, which is to say humanistic, point of view. SDT holds that there are three most basic human needs: autonomy, competence, and relatedness. To paraphrase Ryan and Brown (2003, p. 73), this view understands autonomy as a combination of "volition and ownership, and initiative," competence at being "able to effectively act on, and have an impact within, one's environment," and relatedness as "feelings of belonging and connection," which I characterize in terms of providing a sense of acceptance or worth.

Although SDT does not see self-esteem as one of the most basic human needs, it is still regarded as an important phenomenon because an individual's self-esteem affects such things as self-regulation and authenticity, both of which are vital to this view. For example, if a person suffers from low, fragile, contingent, paradoxical, or unstable self-esteem, then much of self-regulation will be defensive. Understanding oneself as having a poor degree of competence impairs, among other things, autonomous functioning because such a perceived deficiency makes it difficult to take the risks associated with acting on the basis of one's intrinsic values. Similarly, basing one's sense of worth on external rather than internal standards creates a condition of dependence on others that constrains one's ability to function on the basis of intrinsic motivation. Thus, the lack of competence, autonomy, and relatedness to others are conditions that decrease self-esteem and one's ability to function authentically.

In contrast, having a good sense of oneself as being fairly competent, autonomous, and connected results in what SDT calls "true self-esteem" (Deci & Ryan, 1995). In this case, defensiveness is minimal, which allows the individual to get in touch with intrinsic values more easily. This awareness helps the person know what to actualize and to take appropriate risks in that direction. In other words, self-esteem is important because, depending on whether it is positive or negative, self-esteem helps create a cycle of authenticity or inauthenticity.

In addition to offering important insights into the nature of self-esteem, one of the most important things about SDT is that it is an existentially oriented approach to understanding human behavior *that is supported by just the type of empirical studies and methods that appeal to positive psychology.* For example, some experimental and longitudinal work has been done showing that people work longer, harder, and with more enjoyment when pursuing intrinsic goals rather than extrinsic ones (Sheldon & Kasser, 2001). Indeed, most major principles of this approach are supported by such research. In fact, empirical work on authenticity has now reached the point where its accumulated mass is substantial enough to be recognized by mainstream psychology. For instance, the

Handbook of Experimental Existential Psychology (Greenberg et al., 2004) contains many examples of traditionally based research on humanistically oriented topics, such as terror of death, the importance of meaning, choices-making motivation, authenticity, and so forth, which are important to the new positive psychology as well.

Notice that I am *not* saying that work of SDT on self-esteem necessarily supports the view that is presented in this book. For instance, I argue that self-esteem is a basic human need when it is defined in terms of competence and worthiness. SDT does not, even though self-esteem shows up among the top three basic human needs in a study performed by Sheldon et al. (2001), which both positions use to make their points. However, it is quite clear that findings on the relationship between self-esteem and authenticity should be highly valued by eudaimonically oriented positive psychologists because this work involves several processes related to their view of the good life, such as the value of "knowing one's self" and that of acting with integrity.

As noted earlier, Michael Kernis (2003b) may have made even more headway into the interface between self-esteem and authenticity while using very traditionally empirical methods. His work begins by identifying four basic components of authenticity. They are *awareness*, especially of feelings, thoughts, values, hunches, and the ability to trust them; *unbiased processing*, which involves a certain degree of openness to internal and external realities; *action*, or the ability to function in ways that are consistent with one's authentic self; and *relatedness*, which includes awareness of the importance of others. When added together, "authenticity can be characterized as reflecting the unobstructed operation of one's true, or core, self in one's daily enterprise" (p. 13). Koole and Kuhl (2003) found that Kernis was able to "operationalize" high, secure self-esteem based on this approach and did so in ways that resulted in traditionally empirical support for his work on self-esteem and authenticity.

Kernis' (2003b) work also illustrates a link between self-esteem and positive psychology in terms of optimal functioning, which is important for psychological and subjective well-being. As he said,

> I believe that optimal self-esteem involves favorable feelings of self-worth that arise naturally from successfully dealing with life challenges; the operation of one's core, true, authentic self as a source of input to behavioral choices; and relationships in which one is valued for who one is and not for what one achieves. . . . Moreover, it is characterized by favorable implicit feelings of self-worth that stem from positive experiences involving one's actions, contextual factors, and interpersonal relationships. (p. 13)

Operating from one's intrinsic self, authentically dealing with life's challenges, and affirmative relationships all pertain to a two-factor approach to self-esteem. For example, they were found to be involved in certain types of important self-esteem moments, namely, those that involved acting in virtuous ways, such as when overcoming fear to respond appropriately to a stricken friend or standing up for that which is good and right. However, these processes are also important for positive psychology because they are necessary for living a good life in the Aristotelian sense. In fact, we shall see more of this connection when we look at self-esteem in relation to his discussion of virtue near the end of this book.

The point of reviewing empirically based self-esteem work on authenticity from these two sources (SDT and Kernis) is twofold. First, it demonstrates that authenticity is directly tied to self-esteem in ways that are compatible with the two-factor approach. Second, if authenticity is conceptually connected to the good life, it would stand to reason that this area of self-esteem work should be of genuine interest to positive psychology. Because positive psychologists are interested in cataloging positive experiences, for instance, they could examine self-esteem moments in this way. Such a list could increase our ability to understand important existential situations and how decisions are made in them. This type of information could even lead to practical applications of the type desired by the core concerns of positive psychology. For example, knowledge about the types of situations that can affect authentic self-esteem should be useful in helping parents create environments that foster positive development, help people live more meaningful lives, and perhaps even facilitate the creation of healthy work and other social environments. In a word, both disciplines share an interest in understanding what it is to live optimally and help people get there.

Positive Psychology, Self-Esteem, and the Good Life

Another connection between eudaimonic positive psychology and self-esteem concerns the study of positive human characteristics and virtue. The general idea powering this dimension of positive psychology is that if we know which human characteristics are positive, healthy, and virtuous, then we also know which types of traits to target, nurture, and support. This aim is also a part of the positive psychology's third core focus concerning the development of healthy people, institutions, and societies. Consequently, some positive psychologists are very actively attempting to develop a nosology of positive characteristics, although each such project has its own criteria for identifying a basic strength or virtue.

One of the best known and most highly developed positive classification systems was pioneered by Peterson and Seligman (2004) and is aimed at creating a type of positive diagnostic system. To this end, they reviewed research related to happiness, optimal functioning, and well-being, but also examined philosophical and religious values from many cultures to give their approach depth and empirical breadth. The positive values and characteristics culled from both bodies of material were then subject to an evaluation process involving 10 criteria that were thought capable of determining whether a particular trait, quality, or characteristic is a genuine positive strength. One result of this is the identification of 24 positive characteristics that reflect six basic or universal human virtues.

Not so coincidentally from the two-factor point of view, it turns out that their list of strengths that the positive psychology classification system has rendered so far includes the quality of *integrity*. This character strength, as it is called, is placed under the virtue of *courage* because establishing and maintaining one's integrity as a human being often requires facing fear and accepting responsibility for one's actions. However, integrity is a complex quality and comes in many forms, so this characteristic is bracketed in Peterson and Seligman's list to include authenticity and honesty. Consequently, the phrasing for this desirable trait or quality actually reads, "Integrity [authenticity, honesty]" (Peterson & Seligman, 2004, p. 29). We saw that all three of these qualities are connected to self-esteem and vice versa in the more intense types of self-esteem moments and in the research on authenticity. In other words, when self-esteem is defined as competently facing life's challenges in a worthy way over time, then self-esteem is very much connected to "integrity" or that which is "just and right" in Milton's sense of the term. At the very least, then, it seems reasonable to suggest that the classification should be modified to read "Integrity [authenticity, honesty, authentic self-esteem]" or perhaps simply "Integrity [authentic self-esteem]."

Additional evidence for understanding self-esteem as a positive characteristic in this model comes from the fact that, when defined in terms of two factors, self-esteem may stand up on its own right. For example, Peterson and Seligman stated that a given human quality or characteristic must meet "most" of 10 criteria to qualify in this regard, although it is not certain whether that means six of them or more (Peterson & Seligman, 2004, p. 16). Perhaps briefly taking a two-factor–based understanding of self-esteem through this "test" will help us determine whether it is possible to argue that this characteristic merits such consideration.

The first criterion concerns fulfillment: whether a quality fulfills an individual in a way that is consistent with an Aristotelian view of the good life. This indicator is also known as the "deathbed test" (Peterson & Seligman, 2004, p. 17). The test is that if a person was dying, would the individual be likely to wish, in the face of death, that he or she would have spent more time living in a particular way (or exhibiting a particular characteristic), if he or she had not done enough of it already in life? It seems to me that the powerful self-esteem moments we examined would suggest an affirmative answer. In other words, competently facing such major challenges of living certainly would be something that people would hope to be able to say that they had done enough of at the end of life. If not, it seems just as likely that they would say that they wish they had, either of which meets this test.

The second criterion focuses on whether a particular strength or quality is morally valued in its own right. The type of worth that comes with acting in a way that is virtuous, which constitutes an entire source of self-esteem, clearly seems relevant in this regard. The third criterion is the stipulation that a true human strength does not diminish other people in any way. In this case, it is possible to argue that authentic self-esteem qualifies because, unlike other ways of defining it, worthiness balances action in a two-factor view, which means that behavior that diminishes others would be unlikely to occur from this definitional perspective.

The fourth criterion is more difficult to consider because it may be less clear or straightforward than the others. It concerns the degree to which "being able to phrase the 'opposite' of a putative strength in a felicitous way counts against regarding it as a character strength" (Peterson & Seligman, 2004, p. 22). This statement may mean that the opposite of authentic self-esteem needs to be examined for certain types of contradictions. If they occur, then the quality cannot be considered desirable in this way. Although they do make it clear that certain qualities, such as those that are "bipolar," cannot be compared against this criterion, it is very clear that low self-esteem does not have many characteristics that are desirable, at least according to the self-esteem matrix and the *Diagnostic and Statistical Manual*. Thus, self-esteem musters acceptance when assessed this way.

The fifth criterion is that the characteristic or quality must occur in a range of situations or behaviors, much as a trait would. Self-esteem certainly meets this measure: We saw in Chapters 3 and 5 that self-esteem may be stable, low, unstable, fragile, secure, and so forth, but tends to be reasonably consistent, much like a personality trait, and can even be measured like one. The sixth criterion is that a positive strength must be "distinct from other positive traits in the classification and cannot be decomposed into them" (Peterson & Seligman, 2004, p. 24). In this case, we saw that breaking self-esteem down into its components of competence and worthiness actually destroys something quite valuable, because it is the relationship between the two factors that creates self-esteem, not the components alone. The seventh criterion is that a character strength is "embodied in consensual paragons" (Peterson & Seligman, 2004, p. 24), such as stories, fables, and so forth. One would be hard-pressed to talk about self-esteem "fables." However, it is possible to point to any number of stories about individuals who struggled to do the right thing in trying circumstances, and we know that such virtuous behavior is tied to self-esteem.

It is said that the eighth criterion does not apply to all strengths, but some of them involve young people who demonstrate extraordinarily high degrees of a particular characteristic. We do not, of course, speak of self-esteem prodigies and ask them to perform for us. Yet, most parents, teachers, coaches, counselors, and so forth have said that a particular child seemed to have unusually good self-esteem and consider such a remark to be a compliment. Thus, this criterion could be met, although by definition, that is not necessary in this system. The ninth criterion defines a positive characteristic by noting whether or not negative behavior is present when the quality is absent. In this case, it is difficult to imagine anyone praising the virtues of having classically low self-esteem or of any form of defensive self-esteem as defined here, so it certainly passes muster in this regard.

Finally, the tenth criterion concerns whether social institutions foster the development of the positive characteristic in question. To this end, I would point out that most parents work hard to let their children know that they are accepted and loved as worthy individuals. In addition, many teachers struggle daily to help their students gain competence in ways that will serve them well. After that, we are on our own. Even so, as adults, we often admire people who display a balance of competence and worthiness at the workplace, in relationships, while recreating, or when dealing with a challenge. It is, after all, a question of integrity, of being willing to stand up for that which is just and right or good.

It is possible to further develop each point of the above argument supporting the position that when defined as a balance of competence and worthiness, self-esteem "passes the test." However, I think it is clear that we have seen enough evidence to say that authentic self-esteem stands up to the criteria necessary to be considered a positive human strength or characteristic from the perspective of positive psychology itself, just as it does for the humanistic perspective.

The reader, of course, is invited to perform his or her own analysis based on the criteria. Even so, some may see this book as being biased in this situation. Therefore, it is also necessary to point out that there are other powerful reasons that self-esteem should be understood as a positive strength according to the tenets of modern positive psychology. In this case, it is helpful to remember that the eudaimonic branch of positive psychology bases its view of the good life on Aristotelian foundations (Jorgensen & Nafstad, 2004, pp. 16–17). Students of philosophy know that this perspective, which is one of the most influential in the entire history of the world, includes a specific view of virtue and virtuous characteristics.

Although it is not possible to present Aristotle's entire line of reasoning here, he does make it clear in Book II, Chapter 6 of *Nicomachean Ethics* that every virtue "both brings into good condition the thing of which it is the excellence and makes the work of that thing be done well" (McKeon,

1941, p. 957). When defined in terms of competence and worthiness, self-esteem certainly seems to demonstrate this aspect of virtue. When someone deals with a challenge of living in a worthy fashion, we saw in the step-by-step analysis of powerful self-esteem moments that he or she actually does "bring into good condition" (make positive) their "excellence" (worth as a human being) by doing something "well" (resolving a challenge competently).

Aristotle also developed one of the earliest sets of criteria to evaluate whether a particular characteristic is virtuous. According to this classificatory system, many aspects of life may be lived in terms of excess (too much), defect (too little), or in terms of an intermediate (balance) between the two.

> Virtue, then, is a state of character concerned with choice, lying in a mean, i.e. the mean relative to us, this being determined by a rational principle, and by that principle by which the man of practical wisdom would determine it. Now it is a mean between two vices, that which depends on excess and that which depends on defect; and again it is a mean because the vices respectively fall short of or exceed what is right in both passions and actions, while virtue both finds and chooses that which is intermediate. (McKeon, 1941, p. 959)

The "intermediate," of course, is "that which is equidistant from each of the extremes" (p. 958) and provides the foundation for the Greek standard known as the Golden Mean. Aristotle went on to show how this approach to defining virtue may be applied to human characteristics. For example, he reasoned, as does positive psychology, that courage is a virtue because it is the intermediate of fear and confidence. In this case, the extreme of too much fear could take the form of such deficits of character or behavior as cowardice or panic, whereas an excess of confidence may result in such dangerous extremes as bravado or outright foolhardiness. However, courage is equidistant from both: It is a balance between the recognition of real danger and the willingness to act when necessary in spite of the risk.

Similarly and most importantly, Aristotle noted that "with regard to honor and dishonour the mean is proper pride, the excess is known as a sort of 'empty vanity,' and the deficiency is undue humility" (p. 960). In a real sense, the modern-day language for the psychological space he called "proper pride" may be nothing other than what we call authentic self-esteem. For example, we have seen that an excess of worthiness that is not balanced by competence results in problems associated with the most extreme form of vanity, which is narcissism. Similarly, we found that an abundance of competence without the counterbalance of worthiness is often characterized by a lack of honoring the value of the self, whether it be one's own or that of others, through negative behavior. Self-esteem, then, may be seen as the intermediate of competence and worthiness because it is the point where one balances the other.

In addition, this line of reason allows us to reconsider one final issue concerning the value and virtue of healthy self-esteem. It is crucial to remember that the two-factor approach to defining self-esteem is actually talking about the relationship between competence and worthiness, not either one alone. In this view, self-esteem is a semantic term, one that attempts to describe a particular psychological space. Although the name of this characteristic certainly reflects one's culture, the existence of the space seems to be universal. Perhaps this way of understanding self-esteem and the two-factor approach adds clarity to the earlier question concerning the relationship between self-esteem and culture.

APPLIED POSITIVE PSYCHOLOGY, SELF-ESTEEM, AND CWT

It was earlier said that after its core, the second distinguishing feature of positive psychology is its applied focus: Positive psychology is not just academic psychology, although it is concerned with those issues. This practical aspect of positive psychology focuses on developing empirically based ways to help people live better lives by focusing on positive experiences and traits, by developing positive interpersonal connections in social institutions, including the family or schools, and even by fostering the creation of healthier societies.

To date, this emerging discipline is actively pursuing at least two general strategies in this regard. One involves helping people deal with existing problems and issues in a positive way, which is sometimes called "positive clinical psychology" (Peterson & Seligman, 2004) or simply "positive therapy" (Seligman, Rashid, & Parks, 2006). This type of work involves "the application of positive psychology research to the facilitation of optimal functioning" (Linley & Joseph, 2004, p. 4). The other focus is on prevention and is concerned with supporting the development of various positive human qualities, such as resilience and the virtues mentioned earlier, as well as the types of social processes and institutions that foster them. Given the relationship between healthy self-esteem, authenticity, and optimal functioning, it stands to reason that work on increasing self-esteem should be of considerable interest to any form of positive psychology.

Perhaps the first thing to note about the clinical application of positive psychology is that it has become surprisingly friendly to humanistic psychology and psychotherapy compared to the harder stand Seligman and Csikszentmihalyi initially took. For example, in one of the first major books on applied positive psychology, Linley and Joseph (2004) said that while positive psychology and humanistic psychology are different,

> Humanistic psychology is a broad church, and there are parts of it we would not recognize as positive psychology; but in our view, the ideas of the main humanistic psychology writers, such as Rogers and Maslow, deserve to be set center stage within positive psychology. Theirs was an empirical stance, explicitly research-based, albeit lacking in the sophistication of current psychological research methods. We ought to respect this lineage, and we encourage those who are not familiar with this earlier work to visit it. (p. 365)

Even more to our point, such second-generation positive psychologists also take a positive stance toward self-esteem, which we have seen to be a central theme in humanistic psychology. For example, Heatherton and Wyland (2003) said that, "Perhaps it is appropriate in this time of positive psychology to reclaim the positive in self-esteem" (p. 39). Consequently, it is not unreasonable to ask whether positive therapy is another example of an area that both positive psychologies share. To answer this question, it is first necessary to examine what is meant by positive intervention, which consists of positive therapy and positive prevention. Then, we can address the final question of whether competence and worthiness training (CWT) may be considered as a form of positive, as well as existential, therapy.

Positive Intervention (Positive Therapy and Positive Prevention)

In reviewing the field, Duckworth et al. (2005) stated that positive intervention appears to be based on two principles that are solidly grounded in positive psychology's basic concerns as well as its vision of the "good" life; one that is characterized by three major attributes: pleasure (which is positive experience or hedonic happiness), engagement (which involves such things as commitment to work and satisfying relationships), and meaning (which is found by using one's signature strengths for projects or causes that are "bigger" than the self).

The first principle of applied positive psychology is the position that "positive interventions by definition build pleasure, engagement, and meaning, and we believe they are therefore fully justifiable in their own right" (Duckworth et al., 2005, p. 641). For example, some positive interventions, such as "savoring" (Peterson, 2006), tend to generate hedonic experiences that increase an individual's level of satisfaction with life and subjective well-being. Others, including well-being therapy (WBT) (Fava, 1999), are more eudaimonic in that they enhance a person's sense of engagement with life or its meaning. We will examine this type of thera-peutic activity shortly, but for now, the point is that positive strategies are understood as being healthy and acceptable in essence: They need no further justification.

Second, positive therapy brings something valuable to the table that is inherent to its orientation. As Duckworth et al. (2005) went on to say, "building positive emotion, engagement, and meaning may actually coun-ter disorder itself" (p. 641). For example, Fredrickson's (2002) work dem-onstrated that positive interventions may actually have the therapeutic effect of decreasing the impact of negative states through what she called the "undoing effects" of positive emotions. If so, increasing the frequency of pleasure, engagement, or meaning in someone's life is therapeutic and may even help create an upward positive cycle that could lead to a bet-ter life for anyone, even those who do not suffer a diagnostic condition. The connection we saw in Fredrickson's work between positive emotion and resilience, or the ability to bounce back after adverse conditions and return to baseline functioning, offers evidence for this position.

In addition, like all effective therapies, some positive interventions are connected to what are called the common or nonspecific factors, which have long been associated with positive therapeutic outcomes regardless of orientation (Prochaska & Norcross, 1994; Torrey, 1972). One such therapeutic "deep strategy," for example, is hope (Seligman, 2002), which is an implicit feature of the good life and of positive psychology in general.

I would add that a third distinguishing principle of positive practice is that it strives to be evidence based. This characteristic expresses positive psychology's strong acceptance of traditional scientific methodologies that differentiates it from humanistic positive psychology. Although such things as positive states and common factors seem right and feel good, applying such techniques and strategies to real human lives demands more evidence: Any scientifically oriented practitioner should be able to either demonstrate that what he or she does with people works, or at least be able to point to a reasonably solid body of work indicating that it does. After all, results that can be examined, duplicated, and tested are a hall-mark of the scientific method. Consequently, many positive interventions are highly structured or even "manualized," which is to say they are set up in a step-by-step fashion so that, in part, techniques can be assessed in this fashion.

Positive psychologists usually identify Fordyce (1977, 1983) as developing the first form of positive therapy. He worked with a substan-tial number of community college students in the 1970s who reflected a wide range of demographic, intellectual, motivational, and other char-acteristics, thereby giving his work a significant degree of generaliz-ability (Baumgardner & Crothers, 2009). His approach is based on the deceptively simple behavioral principle that actions precede feelings and thoughts. In this case, we would say that doing positive things that feel good or seem meaningful is likely to increase one's sense of well-being. Thus, he identified some 14 activities, attitudes, or behaviors that are associated with reducing negative affect, increasing positive affect, facilitating optimism, engaging in meaningful things such as relationships or work, and so forth.

Next, he created a simple assessment device to help an individual identify which of the 14 areas would be best to explore given his or her personality or circumstances. The program then assisted people in designing ways of implementing the items they selected into their lives to enrich them in those ways. This program was deliberately constructed to focus on developing positive experiences much more than eliminating negative ones. Finally, Fordyce tracked a number of individuals through his program with pre- and postmeasures to help validate its efficacy.

Fava (1999) is often credited with developing the first form of clinically based positive therapy. His "WBT," as it is called, was originally designed to deal with the problem of relapse, which is a major issue in the treatment of affective disorders. The approach is based on the finding that "psychological well-being could not be equated with the absence of symptomology, nor with personality traits" (Ruini & Fava, 2004, p. 371). Instead, psychological well-being is associated with the development of human potential, which both humanistic and positivistic psychologists would call self-actualization or self-realization, even if one only has brief episodes of it. WBT is a short-term approach that is based on the idea that people who suffer negative affective conditions tend to ignore positive ones, *even when they do occur.* Chronically low levels of satisfying experience increase the likelihood of negative responses to life, which, in turn, facilitates the occurrence of relapse. If so, breaking this cycle of negative affect and experience with positive ones may prevent relapse and thereby assist in recovery.

Ruini and Fava (2004) specify that the treatment consists of eight 30- to 50-minute sessions that are offered either once a week or once every other week. The sessions are roughly grouped into three sets or phases. The initial meetings focus on helping patients to identify episodes of well-being that they do experience, describing the circumstances that surrounded them when they occurred, recording the situations and experiences in a diary that is kept for this purpose, and then rating the degree of well-being they experienced on a scale of 0 to 100, with the latter being the highest. Note that realizing that one has moments of well-being in the midst of severe illness may be helpful in itself, which is consistent with the first pillar of positive psychology mentioned earlier. That is not even to mention the potential possibility of the "undoing" effects that such positive periods might offer.

The middle or intermediate sessions aim at identifying the ways in which people either short-circuit or prematurely end such experiences. This phase also involves teaching them how to avoid doing that, often through cognitive restructuring work. The last cluster of sessions focuses on helping the therapist and client identify specific problem areas that impair the client's ability to experience well-being so that special efforts can be made to address them. This aspect of the program's work involves more detailed assessment using the Well-Being Scales (Ryff & Singer, 2002).

The results of the scales are then used to focus on identifying areas of psychological well-being that may be especially helpful to a given individual. These target areas are environmental mastery, personal growth, purpose in life, autonomy, self-acceptance, and positive relations with others. The aim is to facilitate development in the selected areas so as to both counteract the depression and provide a sense of positive growth. Because it is used with clinically significant disorders, WBT may be a part of traditional therapy, including medications, as well. So far, research on WBT for this population generates considerable support as indicated by pre- and posttesting using the scale mentioned above (Ruini & Fava, 2004; Ryff & Singer, 2002).

A more recent trend in work on positive interventions involves identifying, testing, and evaluating specific positive therapeutic techniques, strategies, and activities (Duckworth et al., 2005; Seligman, Rashid, et al., 2006; Seligman, Steen, et al., 2005). Those that are determined to be efficacious may then be used in isolation, combined with more traditional therapies, or perhaps even be integrated in the form of an entire positive therapeutic or prevention program. For example, Seligman, Steen, et al. (2005) began by identifying approximately 100 therapeutic practices that could be evaluated for their efficacy in ways that were potentially measurable. Those that showed evidence of being useful were then further evaluated through the use of standard methodological procedures, such as control and experimental groups as well as pre-and posttesting procedures. This comprehensive, careful, and empirical process resulted in the identification of several positive practices that do, indeed, seem to increase happiness and well-being for sustained periods.

For example, the already well-known "Three Good Things" activity (Seligman, Steen, et al., 2005) seems to be especially powerful in these ways. The development of the technique involved assessing subjects' current level of happiness with a standardized instrument, having them write down three good things that happened during their day, and then having them describe what about each thing was good. Participants continued this practice for various periods of time and then their happiness levels were assessed again. Seligman, Steen, et al. reported that engaging in this practice for 1 full week resulted in substantial increases of happiness over time. Further, the research clearly indicated that the longer the technique is practiced, the longer its effects last over time. Another form of this technique is called "Count Your Blessings" (Lyubomirsky, Dickerhoof, Boehm, & Sheldon, 2011).

Similar work has been done with other positive techniques, such as expressing gratitude (Emmons & McCullough, 2003). Another one is based on helping people identify their own individual character strengths and then "exercising" them more often (Seligman, Steen, et al., 2005), which is something akin to identifying self-esteem strengths and building an enhancement program around them. Finally, positive psychologists have also investigated combining positive therapeutic activities with traditional ones to work on increasing subjective and psychological well-being by addressing both strengths and weaknesses. For example, Seligman, Rashid, et al. (2006) did careful research using both positive and traditional therapeutic practices, including the use of medications, with people who suffer unipolar depression. As with Fava's program, the results were positive.

In summarizing the literature on positive intervention, it is clear that such an approach is marked by three characteristics that, when taken together, differentiate it from other methods. First, positive practices focus on enhancing subjective and psychological well-being by increasing the likelihood of experiencing pleasure, being engaged with the world and others, and finding greater meaning in life. Second, positive practice brings something uniquely positive to the situation, such as positive affect or experience, and usually does so in a structured fashion: It usually involves active engagement from participants and is often time limited. Finally, positive intervention attempts to be evidence-based. The structured focus on positive affect and experience tends to increase user reliability and facilitates validation through such standard methods as pre- and posttest comparisons.

Although prevention is much more difficult to assess because it involves future outcomes instead of actual ones, positive prevention attempts to apply the same practices in, for instance, the educational or workplace setting (Peterson, 2006). In either case, the high degree of similarity between the three general principles of positive intervention mentioned earlier and these three practical characteristics is important: They systematically act together to constitute a reasonably identifiable set of criteria by which to evaluate actual applications.

CWT as a Positive, as Well as Existential, Approach

It is already clear that CWT stands as a humanistically based, existentially oriented practice because it involves helping people to face challenges of living, make authentic choices, and self-actualize in one context or another.

Further, this approach emphasizes self-esteem because when it is defined as a relationship between competence and worthiness, self-esteem is a central factor in all of those processes. The final question becomes, then, may CWT also be regarded as a type of positive intervention? Although there is an irreducible tension between the reductionistic foundation of positive psychology and the nonreductionistic underpinnings of CWT, there are at least two ways CWT is a positive practice, regardless of which definition of positive psychology one embraces. One of them is theoretical and the other is practical.

It is important to note that second-generation positive psychologists, particularly those who work in applied settings such as psychotherapy, are not opposed to humanistic psychology at the theoretical level like the first generation often seemed to be. Instead, more contemporary positive psychologists see a number of theoretical connections between the two approaches. For example, in the introduction to their book on positive psychology in practice, Linley and Joseph (2004) noted that there has been debate about the relationship between positive and humanistic psychology. However, they concluded that, "To be sure, there are differences between positive psychology and humanistic psychology, but we believe that these differences are far outweighed by their similarities . . ." (pp. xv–xvi). Consequently, they urge both fields to work together to advance science and enhance practice by focusing on similarities and by addressing common goals. They go on to do just that in their book.

Later, Linley and Joseph (2004) ask the question we are posing about CWT and then go on to answer it in a strikingly unambiguous fashion.

> Can some therapies be considered positive therapies? Our answer to this is yes. In particular, those therapies based on the theoretical premise of an organismic valuing process and an actualizing tendency appear to be most consistent with what the positive psychology research is now telling us. (p. 354)

Of course, CWT includes organismic valuing and self-actualization because this approach rests on humanistic theoretical foundations and because we saw them to be active processes in major self-esteem moments. Thus, the program aims at helping individuals get in touch with themselves organismically by valuing and experiencing positive self-esteem moments more fully. Similarly, CWT is clearly connected to the tendency to actualize, as seen in such things as helping people face life's developmental and existential challenges as authentically as possible. In short, there is little doubt that CWT meets the theoretical criteria that positive psychologists themselves offer for evaluating whether it may be regarded as a form of positive therapy or intervention.

The other way in which CWT would need to be compatible with positive intervention to be seen that way is based on its practical characteristics. Remember, a positive approach consists of focusing on the positive to enhance well-being, by bringing uniquely positive contributions to the applied situation in a structured or systematic fashion, and by using practices that are based on demonstrable evidence. Therefore, let us reach a final conclusion about CWT by examining it in terms of these three practical or concrete criteria.

First, there can be little doubt that CWT focuses on using positive affect and experiences to increase well-being. For example, the entire program consists of a series of activities centered on positive affect or experience, such as exploring being competent or describing one's worthwhile characteristics, to facilitate feeling better about one's self. Therefore, CWT aims at increasing subjective well-being. However, because only authentic self-esteem counts in this approach and because it is solely achieved by authentically dealing with the challenges of living, CWT also aims at increasing psychological well-being. After all, in this program, self-esteem is earned, not given. Thus, it affirms deeper eudaimonic values and meanings by helping the individual actually do that which is worthwhile in the first place. We could even say that authentic self-esteem feels good hedonically because it is also good eudaimonically. Even brief moments of authentic self-esteem that occur in the program feel good, reflect more active engagement with life, and are meaningful, especially to people who lack authentic self-esteem.

Second, it is very clear that CWT incorporates a high level of positive affect and experience into a well-structured therapeutic process in a way that involves the unique characteristics of positive psychology. For example, some more traditional approaches to enhancing self-esteem spend much time on exploring negative self-esteem moments or the reasons that one has come to have low or defensive self-esteem. CWT does not. Instead, like any positive approach, CWT asks participants to identify, focus on, explore, understand, and elaborate the character of positive experiences, events, and strengths, such as those that occur in positive self-esteem moments. In doing so, this approach incorporates the undoing effect of positive emotions emphasized in positive psychology. In addition, the self-esteem project offered at the end of the program is consistent with the positive position, that is, it is possible to create an upward emotional, behavioral, and interpersonal cycle.

Like positive intervention in general, CWT also goes to some length to remind therapists and facilitators about the importance of the common therapeutic factors, such as facilitator qualities or deep structures that characterize all effective therapies. It might be added that these general aspects of good therapy are just as likely to apply to good teaching as well, which is relevant to the psychoeducational aspects of CWT or prevention.

Not only were these factors present when discussing the program's steps, but they are actually built into some activities. For instance, asking facilitators to present examples from their own lives also gives them the opportunity to be genuine, warm, and open, all of which have been identified as common factors (Prochaska & Norcross, 1994; Torrey, 1972). Finally, the self-esteem enhancement project created at the end of the program is based on hope for the future.

The last point may be the most important, considering the contemporary movement toward evidence-based practice. It concerns the positive therapeutic practice of providing support for what we do with others. In addition to relying on evidence-based techniques whenever possible, CWT grew out of investigating self-esteem using the method of integrated description. This approach begins with the qualitative data of human experience, but ends by validating such results through the application of quantitative measures. The method allowed us to return to the facts themselves, to paraphrase a great phenomenologist (Husserl, 1970b), and to investigate the ways in which self-esteem is actually lived and experienced. Doing so made it possible to embrace Milton's original definition, see self-esteem as a relationship between competence and worthiness, understand the basic characteristics of self-esteem, such as its various types, and develop a highly structured, step-by-step, reliable enhancement program that has been tested and validated by standard quantitative measures. What more can be asked of any method of assisting others therapeutically or of helping people to prevent future problems?

In addition to meeting theoretical requirements, it is clear that CWT also meets the more objective or practical standards of positive intervention. Therefore, it seems reasonable to conclude that CWT is a type of existential therapy that also stands as a positive practice or intervention. Although it is difficult to predict the next steps in the development of CWT, it is possible to suggest some avenues that might be productive. For example, researchers could examine the use of CWT in the individual setting, which I think could be a very straightforward dissertation or publishable research project. In addition, there may be considerable value in asking the question of whether this psychological space we call self-esteem goes by different names in different cultures. If so, then the universal character of authentic self-esteem becomes clearer. If not, then at least we would know a limit of CWT, one that is common of many modern Western therapies.

In addition, there is no reason CWT could not be researched for use with other populations, such as adolescents in the school setting. Likewise, it is possible that CWT could be modified for the workplace environment in an attempt to increase a sense of well-being in that arena or for older adults to help them effectively manage self-esteem while aging. To the extent that so-called life coaching involves research, CWT could also be studied in regard to helping "normal" people get more out of life. Finally, I can only wonder about what it would be like to grow up in a home where parents value competence and worthiness enough to consider them as active guidelines. Dealing with these critical developmental and existential challenges in ways that demonstrate and reflect competence *and* worthiness would benefit society, as well as the individual, in ways that are consistent with the long-range goals of both positive psychologies.

Competence and Worthiness Training (CWT): A 5-Week Self-Esteem Enhancement Program

WEEK 1—HANDOUT 1: PROGRAM ANNOUNCEMENT

Competence and Worthiness Training Program Announcement

This 5-week program is a group experience designed to increase our understanding and awareness of self-esteem. Participants have the opportunity to assess their self-esteem, understand its basic components, and learn how to work on self-esteem issues. You also create your own self-esteem improvement program and use group exercises to help you work on increasing your self-esteem during the program and afterward.

The program is run by_____, who is credentialed as a_____, and who is interested in helping people to increase their self-esteem. The group sessions are based on a psychoeducational format, so learning is emphasized. The program is a focused one, meaning that we deal with one theme, self-esteem, as the main topic of all meetings and activities. Anyone currently involved in treatment for a mental health condition is advised to discuss with his or her therapist whether or not to be in this program.

We will meet for 2 hours on _____ from _____for 5 consecutive weeks. Attendance at all meetings is strongly encouraged because the program is designed to move in a step-by-step fashion. We hope to see you there, so please be sure that you reserve a place through_____, who may be reached at _____before _____, as there are a limited number of seats.

WEEK 1—HANDOUT 2: ACTIVITY SCHEDULE

I. Competence and worthiness training (CWT) program steps.
  A. Introduction to self-esteem and basic research about it.
  B. Procedure:
    1. Week 1: *Focusing phase:* Defining self-esteem
      a. Discussing basic concepts
      b. Assessing individual self-esteem
    2. Week 2: *Awareness phase:* Appreciating self-esteem
      a. Understanding common self-esteem problems
      b. Understanding the sources of self-esteem
    3. Week 3: *Enhancing phase:* Increasing worthiness
      a. Understanding cognitive restructuring
      b. Removing "self-esteem traps"
    4. Week 4: *Enhancing phase:* Increasing competence
      a. Introduction to problem-solving
      b. Practicing problem-solving techniques
    5. Week 5: *Management phase:* Maintaining self-esteem
      a. Planning your own self-esteem action programs
      b. Evaluating the approach: Strengths and limits

WEEK 1—HANDOUT 3: GROUP GUIDELINES AND EXPECTATIONS

Group Guidelines and Expectations

The CWT program is run by_____, who is credentialed as a_____. The group sessions are based on a psychoeducational format, so learning is emphasized. The program is a focused one, meaning that we will deal with one theme, self-esteem, as the main topic of all meetings and activities. Anyone currently involved in treatment for a mental health condition is advised to discuss with his or her therapist whether to be in this program.

We will meet on _____ from _____for 5 consecutive weeks. Some basic rules will help us create a positive, supportive group environment.

1. Confidentiality: Mutual trust among group members is important. Each of us has a right to privacy, and we all depend on each other to have it.
2. Respect: For the program to enhance your appreciation of self-esteem, it is important that all members treat each other with the respect that each unique human being deserves. Although we may have differences of opinion, it is essential that we welcome diversity.
3. Attendance: Attendance at all meetings is strongly encouraged because the program is designed to move in a step-by-step fashion. Also, group processes cannot work well if a large number of people are not present or if attendance is sporadic. Each of us depends on all the others in this regard, so do your best to be here for yourself and others.
4. Participation: The benefits of most therapeutic or psychoeducational activities are related to how much you participate in the process. However, other than following the previously listed rules, you are not required to do anything that you do not feel comfortable doing.

WEEK 1—HANDOUT 4: DEFINING SELF-ESTEEM

I. Self-esteem is based on facing life's challenges in ways that are competent *and* worthy.
  A. Experience of competence
    1. Briefly describe such an experience.

    2. What did the experience show you about competence?

  B. Experience of worthiness
    1. Briefly describe such an experience.

    2. What did the experience tell you about worthiness?

II. Keeping a self-esteem journal.

WEEK 2—HANDOUT 1: SELF-ESTEEM TYPES, LEVELS, AND PROBLEMS

I. Self-esteem matrix: basic types and levels

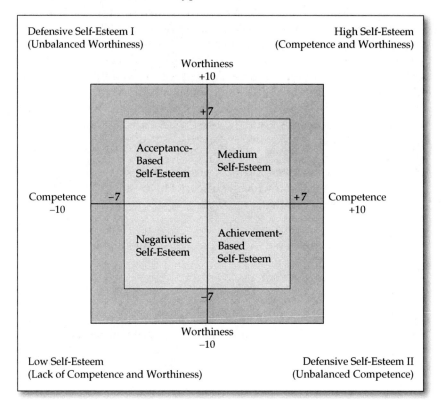

Defensive Self-Esteem I
(Unbalanced Worthiness)

High Self-Esteem
(Competence and Worthiness)

Worthiness
+10

+7

Acceptance-
Based
Self-Esteem

Medium
Self-Esteem

Competence
−10

−7

+7

Competence
+10

Negativistic
Self-Esteem

Achievement-
Based
Self-Esteem

−7

Worthiness
−10

Low Self-Esteem
(Lack of Competence and Worthiness)

Defensive Self-Esteem II
(Unbalanced Competence)

II. Common self-esteem problems (to be discussed)

WEEK 2—HANDOUT 2: APPLYING THE MULTIDIMENSIONAL SELF-ESTEEM INVENTORY SCALES

Self-esteem profile for _____ Date_____

    The Multidimensional Self-Esteem Inventory (MSEI) has 11 scales. The scales describing general levels of self-esteem are global self-esteem, identity integration, and defensiveness. Competence-related scales are competence, personal power, self-control, and body functioning. Worthiness-related scales are lovability, likability, moral self-approval, and bodily appearance. I will explain what all the scales mean in the group, but your test results focus on the two highest scores, which are your self-esteem "strengths," and the two lowest areas. At this point in life they are likely to be:

A. Current self-esteem strengths (most positive scores).
   1. The positive scale on which you scored highest is _____.
      This scale suggests that:

   2. The positive scale on which you scored second highest
      is_____.
      This scale suggests that:

B. Potential self-esteem growth areas (least positive scores).
   1. The scale on which your most sensitive score occurred is

      _____.
      This scale suggests that:

   2. The scale on which your second most sensitive score occurred is

      _____.
      This scale suggests that:

WEEK 2—HANDOUT 3: FINDING SOURCES OF SELF-ESTEEM

I. Personal achievements or successes.

II. Evidence of influence or power.

III. Acceptance or being valued.

IV. Virtue or acting on beliefs (doing the "right thing").

WEEK 3—HANDOUT 1: ENHANCING WORTHINESS THROUGH POSITIVE FEEDBACK

A. List positive features.

1. _____

2. _____

3. _____

4. _____

5. _____

6. _____

7. _____

8. _____

9. _____

10. _____

B. Group sharing (invitation to read aloud).

WEEK 3—HANDOUT 2: INCREASING WORTHINESS THROUGH COGNITIVE RESTRUCTURING

I. Common cognitive self-esteem traps.
   A. Concept: Mistakes in thinking and perceiving that keep us stuck or in pain.
   B. List of common self-esteem traps:
      1. *Emotional Reasoning*: Letting feelings overrule rational thoughts, such as frequently saying, "Yeah, but" or "If only."

      2. *Filtering*: Focusing attention on the negative aspects of a situation or event and ignoring or minimizing positive possibilities.

      3. *Labeling*: Using negative labels to describe self or others, such as calling yourself or others a "loser," a "wimp," or a "dummy."

      4. *Overgeneralizing*: Extending the negative meanings of an event beyond what is necessary so that it seems worse than it is.

      5. *Personalizing*: Being too sensitive about an incident or event so that it becomes more painful than realistically necessary.

      6. _____

      7. _____

      8. _____

      9. _____

      10. _____
   C. Facilitator's example of making an error.

WEEK 3—HANDOUT 3: COGNITIVE PATTERN-BREAKING OUTLINE

I. Implementation of the cognitive self-esteem restructuring process.
  A. The 7-step method:
    1. *Identify a situation, event, or interaction* that lessened your self-esteem.
    2. *Note the strongest negative feelings* you had in that moment and rate them on a scale, such as of 1–10.
    3. *Identify the primary negative thoughts* you were actually having in the situation.
    4. *Name ANY thinking errors* by examining your negative thoughts for those that reflect one of the mistakes people make in reacting to events on the list of frequent errors.
    5. *Make corrections* by substituting a realistic thought or reaction for each thinking error you made.
    6. *Reevaluate your feelings* about the situation, as they are now on the same scale, and compare them with the results of Step 2. You should note some reduction of intensity.
    7. *Repeat* the process until errors no longer occur.
  B. Facilitator's example of cognitive restructuring. (Work through all the steps on the board.)
    1.
    2.
    3.
    4.
    5.
    6.
    7.
  C. Participant's examples. (Work problems offered by the group on the board.)

WEEK 4—HANDOUT 1: ENHANCING COMPETENCE: PROBLEM-SOLVING METHOD

A. Basic problem-solving theory:
   1. Feelings often let us know that a problem is developing.
   2. Thinking helps us to understand the problem better.
   3. Actions allow us to solve the problem.
B. Basic problem-solving steps:
   1. Realize that there is a problem.
   2. Stop and try to understand it well.
   3. Decide on a goal.
   4. Identify possible solutions.
   5. Think about the likely consequences of each solution.
   6. Choose the best, most realistic solution.
   7. Make a detailed plan for carrying out the solution.
   8. Practice!

WEEK 4—HANDOUT 2: ENHANCING COMPETENCE: PROBLEM-SOLVING WORKSHEET

A. The problem-solving process: Facilitator example.

Step	*Procedure*
1. Identifying a problem:	Look for emotional cues.
2. Stop and think:	Ask yourself, "What is the problem?"
3. Decide on a goal:	Ask yourself, "What do I really want here?"
4. Identify possible solutions:	Use brainstorming to generate possibilities.

    a.

    b.

    c.

5. Think about likely consequences:	Ask yourself, "What happens if this occurs?"

    a.

    b.

    c.

6. Choose the best plan:	Ask yourself, "Which one am I willing to live with?"
7. Make a step-by-step plan:	Ask yourself, "What do I actually need to do next?"

    a.

    b.

    c.

8. Learning: Practice, practice, and more practice!

B. Client or participant example.

WEEK 5—HANDOUT 1: BUILDING A SELF-ESTEEM ENHANCEMENT PROJECT

I. Self-esteem action cycle:

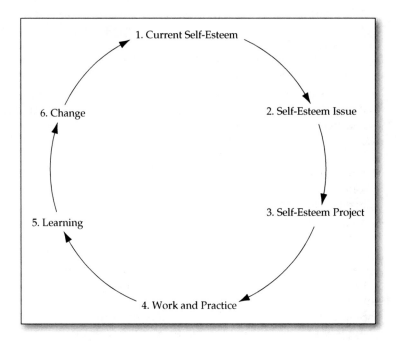

II. Self-esteem action plan: Increasing and maintaining self-esteem
   A. Identify a self-esteem strength or weakness to work on:
      _____
   B. Match the issue with at least one of the four sources of self-esteem: _____
   C. Identify a realistic goal or outcome: _____
      _____
   D. Write specific, workable action steps for the goal or outcome:
      1.
      2.
      3.
      4.
      5.

SUPPLEMENT 1: ACTIVITY SCHEDULE FOR RESEARCHING
THE INDIVIDUALIZED PROGRAM

A. Focusing phase: Defining self-esteem.
1. Step or Week 1: Introduction to the program.
To be done after screening, intake, and diagnostic work are completed. Build rapport and go over this program outline or use Week 1—Handout 2: Activity Schedule.
Use Week 1—Handout 4: Defining Self-Esteem. Set up the journal.
2. Step or Week 2: Understanding the self-esteem matrix.
Give the MSEI. Review journal work by exploring the client's experiences of competence and worthiness. Use Week 2—Handout 1: Self-Esteem Types, Levels, and Problems.
B. Awareness phase: Appreciating self-esteem.
3. Step or Week 3: Assessing self-esteem.
Use Week 2—Handout 2: Applying the MSEI Scales. Review the journal work. Go over MSEI Profile, but explore all the scales instead of just two.
4. Step or Week 4: Understanding the sources of self-esteem.
Review the journal work. Use Week 2—Handout 3: Finding Sources of Self-Esteem. Explore the sources of self-esteem as they were present in the past for the individual and the ways in which they might be present in the person's life today.
C. Enhancing phase: Increasing worthiness.
5. Step or Week 5: Introduction to cognitive restructuring.
Review the journal work. Explore worthiness by using Week 3—Handout 1: Enhancing Worthiness Through Positive Feedback; explore areas and feelings in some detail.
6. Step or Week 6: Removing cognitive "self-esteem traps."
Review Journal. Teach cognitive restructuring using Week 3—Handout 2: Increasing Worthiness Through Cognitive Restructuring; and Week 3—Handout 3: Cognitive Pattern-Breaking Outline.
D. Enhancing phase: Increasing competence.
7. Step or Week 7: Introduction to problem-solving.
Review journal work, use Week 4—Handout 1: Enhancing Competence: Problem-Solving Method. Use Week 4—Handout 2: Enhancing Competence: Problem-Solving Worksheet.
8. Step or Week 8: Practicing problem-solving techniques.
Review journal work; review previous lessons on cognitive restructuring and problem-solving.

E. Management phase: Maintaining your self-esteem.
   9. Step or Week 9: Planning your own self-esteem action programs. Review journal work. Use Week 5—Handout 1: Building a Self-Esteem Enhancement Project.
   10. Step or Week 10: Evaluating the approach. Strengths and limits. Deal with termination issues.
F. Optional follow-up: Booster session(s).

References

Aanstoos, C. (Ed.). (1984). *Exploring the lived world: Readings in phenomenological psychology* (Vol. 23). Atlanta, GA: West Georgia College.

Adler, A. (1927). *Understanding human nature.* New York, NY: Fawcett.

Alberti, R. E., & Emmons, R. L. (1982). *Your perfect right: A guide to rational living* (4th ed.). San Luis Obispo, CA: Impact Publishers.

American Association of University Women. (1991). *Shortchanging girls, shortchanging America.* Washington, DC: Author.

American Psychiatric Association. (2000). *Diagnostic and statistical manual of mental disorders* (4th ed., text rev.). Washington, DC: Author.

Arkowitz, H. (1997). Integrative theories of therapy. In P. Wachtel & S. Messer (Eds.), *Theories of psychotherapy: Origins and evolution* (pp. 227–288). Washington, DC: American Psychological Association.

Aron, A., Ketay, S., Riela, S., & Aron, E. (2008). How close others construct and reconstruct who we are and how we feel about ourselves. In J. Wood, A. Tesser, & J. Holmes (Eds.), *The self and social relationships* (pp. 209–229). New York, NY: Psychology Press.

Aspinwall, L. C., & Staudinger, U. M. (Eds.). (2003). *A psychology of human strengths: Fundamental questions and future directions for a positive psychology.* Washington, DC: American Psychological Association.

Babiak, P., & Hare, R. (2006). *Snakes in suits: When psychopaths go to work.* New York, NY: Harper.

Baldwin, M. (2006). Self-esteem and close relationship dynamics. In M. H. Kernis (Ed.), *Self-esteem issues and answers: A sourcebook of current perspectives* (pp. 359–366). New York, NY: Psychology Press.

Bandura, A. (1986). *Social foundations of thought and action: A social cognitive theory.* Englewood Cliffs, NJ: Prentice Hall.

Bandura, A. (1997). *Self-efficacy: The exercise of control.* New York, NY: W. H. Freeman.

Bartoletti, M. (2008). Effectiveness of Mruk's self-esteem change program on psychological and physiological measures of well-being. *Dissertation Abstracts International: Section B. The Sciences and Engineering, 68*(8-B), 5557.

Bartoletti, M., & O'Brien, E. J. (2003). *Self-esteem, coping and immunocompetence: A correlational study.* Poster session presented at the annual meeting of the American Psychological Association, Toronto, Canada.

Battle, J. (1992). *Culture-free self-esteem inventories* (2nd ed.). Austin, TX: Pro-ed.

Baumeister, R. F. (Ed.). (1993). *Self-esteem: The puzzle of low self-regard.* New York, NY: Plenum.

Baumeister, R. F., Campbell, J. D., Krueger, J. I., & Vohs, K. D. (2003). Does high self-esteem cause better performance, interpersonal success, happiness, or healthier lifestyles? *Psychological Science in the Public Interest, 4,* 1–44.

Baumeister, R. F., Smart, L., & Boden, J. (1996). Relation of threatened egotism to violence and aggression: The dark side of self-esteem. *Psychological Review, 103*, 5–33.

Baumgardner, S. R., & Crothers, M. K. (2009). *Positive psychology.* Upper Saddle River, NJ: Pearson.

Beane, J. (1991). Sorting out the self-esteem controversy. *Educational Leadership, 49*, 25–30.

Bednar, R., & Peterson, S. (1995). *Self-esteem: Paradoxes and innovations in clinical theory and practice* (2nd ed.). Washington, DC: American Psychological Association.

Bednar, R., Wells, G., & Peterson, S. (1989). *Self-esteem: Paradoxes and innovations in clinical theory and practice.* Washington, DC: American Psychological Association.

Bellavia, G., & Murray, S. (2003). Did I do that? Self-esteem-related differences in reactions to romantic partners' moods. *Personal Relationships, 10*(1), 77–95.

Berenson, K., & Downey, G. (2006). Self-esteem and rejection sensitivity in close relationships. In M. H. Kernis (Ed.), *Self-esteem issues and answers: A sourcebook of current perspectives* (pp. 367–373). New York, NY: Psychology Press.

Berger, P. L. (1967). *The sacred canopy.* New York, NY: Doubleday.

Bhatti, B., Derezotes, D., Kim, S., & Specht, H. (1989). The association between child maltreatment and low self-esteem. In A. M. Mecca, N. Smelser, & J. Vasconcellos (Eds.), *The social importance of self-esteem* (pp. 24–71). Berkeley, CA: University of California Press.

Block, J., & Robins, R. (1993). A longitudinal study of consistency and change in self-esteem from early adolescence to early adulthood. *Child Development, 64*(3), 909–923.

Block, J., & Thomas, H. (1955). Is satisfaction with self a measure of adjustment? *Journal of Abnormal and Social Psychology, 51*, 257–261.

Bradshaw, P. (1981). *The management of self-esteem.* Englewood Cliffs, NJ: Prentice Hall.

Branden, N. (1969). *The psychology of self-esteem.* New York, NY: Bantam.

Branden, N. (1983). *Honoring the self.* Los Angeles, CA: Tarcher.

Branden, N. (1994). *The six pillars of self-esteem.* New York, NY: Bantam.

Brockner, J., Wiesenfeld, B., & Raskas, D. (1993). Self-esteem and expectancy-value discrepancy: The effects of believing that you can (or can't) get what you want. In R. Baumeister (Ed.), *Self-esteem: The puzzle of low self-regard* (pp. 219–241). New York, NY: Plenum.

Brown, J. D., Cai, H., Oakes, M. A., & Deng, C. (2009). Cultural similarities in self-esteem functioning: East is east and west is west, but sometimes the twain do meet. *Journal of Cross-Cultural Psychology, 40*, 140–157.

Brown, J. D., Collins, R. L., & Schmidt, G. W. (1988). Self-esteem and direct versus indirect forms of self-enhancement. *Journal of Personality and Social Psychology, 55*(3), 445–453.

Burger, J. M. (1995). Need for control and self-esteem: Two routes to a high desire for control. In M. H. Kernis (Ed.), *Efficacy, agency, and self-esteem* (pp. 217–233). New York, NY: Plenum.

Burns, D. (1980). *Feeling good: The new mood therapy.* New York, NY: Signet.

Burns, D. (1993a). *Ten days to self-esteem.* New York, NY: Quill.

Burns, D. (1993b). *Ten days to self-esteem: The leader's manual.* New York, NY: Quill.

Butcher, J. N., Graham, J. R., Ben-Porath, Y. S., Tellegen, Y. S., Dahlstrom, W. G., & Kaemmer, B. (2001). *Minnesota Multiphasic Personality Inventory-2: Manual for administration and scoring* (Rev.). Minneapolis, MN: University of Minnesota Press.

Campbell, J. D. (1999). Self-esteem and clarity of the self-concept. In R. Baumeister (Ed.), *The self in social psychology* (pp. 223–239). New York, NY: Taylor & Francis.

Campbell, J. D., & Lavallee, L. (1993). Who am I? The role of self-concept and confusion in understanding the behavior of people with low self-esteem. In R. Baumeister (Ed.), *Self-esteem: The puzzle of low self-regard* (pp. 4–20). New York, NY: Plenum.

Campbell, W. K., Rudich, E. A., & Sedikides, C. (2002). Narcissism, self-esteem, and the positivity of self-views: Two portraits of self-love. *Personality and Social Psychology, 28*(3), 358–368.

Carr, A. (2011). *Positive psychology: The science of happiness and human strengths* (2nd ed.). New York, NY: Routledge.

Clark, J., & Barber, B. (1994). Adolescents in post divorce and always married families: Self-esteem and perceptions of father's interest. *Journal of Marriage and Family, 56,* 608–614.

Cole, C., Oetting E., & Hinkle, J. (1967). Non-linearity of self-concept discrepancy—the value dimension. *Psychological Reports, 21,* 56–60.

Compton, W. (2005). *An introduction to positive psychology.* Belmont, CA: Thomson.

Cooley, C. H. (1909). *Human nature and the social order.* New York, NY: Scribner.

Coopersmith, S. (1959). A method for determining types of self-esteem. *Journal of Abnormal Social Psychology, 59,* 87–94.

Coopersmith, S. (1967). *The antecedents of self-esteem.* San Francisco, CA: Freeman.

Coopersmith, S. (1981). *Adult form SEI Coopersmith Inventory.* Palo Alto, CA: Consulting Psychologists Press.

Costall, A., & Still, A. (Eds.). (1987). *Cognitive psychology in question.* New York, NY: St. Martin's Press.

Cramer, D. (2003). Acceptance and need for approval as moderators of self-esteem and satisfaction with a romantic relationship or closest friendship. *Journal of Psychology, 137*(5), 495–505.

Crocker, J., & Nuer, N. (2003). The insatiable quest for self-worth. *Psychological Inquiry, 14*(1), 31–34.

Crocker, J., & Nuer, N. (2004). Do people need self-esteem? Comment on Pyszczynski et al. *Psychological Bulletin, 130*(3), 469–472.

Crocker, J., & Park, L. E. (2003). Seeking self-esteem: Construction, maintenance, and protection of self-worth. In M. R. Leary & J. P. Tangney (Eds.), *Handbook of self and identity* (pp. 291–313). New York, NY: Guilford.

Crocker, J., & Park, L. E. (2004). The costly pursuit of self-esteem. *Psychological Bulletin, 130*(3), 392–414.

Damon, W. (1995). *Great expectations: Overcoming the culture of indulgence in our homes and schools.* New York, NY: Free Press.

Deci, E. L., & Ryan, M. R. (1995). Human autonomy: The basis for true self-esteem. In M. H. Kernis (Ed.), *Efficacy, agency, and self-esteem* (pp. 31–51). New York, NY: Plenum.

DeHart, T., Tennen, H., Armeli, S., Todd, M., & Afflect, G. (2008). Drinking to regulate negative romantic relationship interactions: The moderating role of self-esteem. *Journal of Experimental Social Psychology, 44*(3), 527–538.

Devos, T., & Banaji, M. R. (2003). Implicit self and identity. In M. R. Leary & J. P. Tangney (Eds.), *Handbook of self and identity* (pp. 153–175). New York, NY: Guilford.

Diener, E., & Diener, M. (1995). Cross-cultural correlates of life satisfaction and self-esteem. *Journal of Personality and Social Psychology, 68*, 653–663.

Diggory, J. C. (1966). *Self-evaluation: Concepts and studies.* New York, NY: Wiley.

Dijksterhuis, A. (2004). I like myself but I don't know why: Enhancing implicit self-esteem by subliminal evaluative conditioning. *Journal of Personality and Social Psychology, 82*(2), 345–355.

Dingfelder, S. (2011). Reflecting on narcissism. *Monitor, 2*, 64.

Downey, G., & Feldman, S. (1996). Implications of rejection sensitivity for intimate relationships. *Journal of Personality and Social Psychology, 70*, 1327–1343.

Dreyfus, H. L., & Dreyfus, S. E. (1986). *Mind over machine: The power of human intuition and expertise in the era of the computer.* New York, NY: Free Press.

DuBois, D. L., & Flay, R. R. (2004). The healthy pursuit of self-esteem: Comment on and alternative to Crocker and Park (2004) formulation. *Psychological Bulletin, 130*(3), 415–420.

Duckworth, A. L., Steen, T. A., & Seligman, M. E. P. (2005). Positive psychology in clinical practice. *Annual Review of Clinical Psychology, 1*, 629–651.

Durand, V. M., & Barlow, D. H. (2013). *Essentials of abnormal psychology* (6th ed.). Belmont, CA: Wadsworth, Cengage Learning.

D'Zurilla, T. J., & Goldfried, M. R. (1971). Problem-solving and behavior modification. *Journal of Abnormal Psychology, 78*, 107–126.

D'Zurilla, T. J., & Nezu, A. M. (2001). Problem-solving therapies. In K. S. Dobson (Ed.), *Handbook of cognitive behavioral therapies* (2nd ed., pp. 211–245). New York, NY: Guilford.

Ellis, A., & Harper, R. (1977). *A new guide to rational living.* North Hollywood, CA: Wilshire Book.

Emler, N. (2001). *Self-esteem: The costs and causes of low self-worth.* York, England: York Publishing Services, Joseph Rowntree Foundation.

Emmons, R. A. & McCullough, M. E. (2003). Counting blessings versus burdens: An experimental investigation of gratitude and subjective well-being in daily life. *Journal of Personality and Social Psychology, 2*, 377–389.

Epstein, S. (1979). The ecological study of emotions in humans. In P. Pliner, K. R. Blankstein, & I. M. Spigel (Eds.), *Advances in the study of communication and affect, Vol. 5: Perception of emotions in self and others* (pp. 47–83). New York, NY: Plenum.

Epstein, S. (1980). The self-concept: A review and the proposal of an integrated theory of personality. In E. Straub (Ed.), *Personality: Basic aspects and current research* (pp. 83–131). Englewood Cliffs, NJ: Prentice Hall.

Epstein, S. (1985). The implications of cognitive-experiential self-theory for research in social psychology and personality. *Journal for the Theory of Social Behavior, 15*, 283–309.

Epstein, S., & Morling, B. (1995). Is the self motivated to do more than enhance and/or verify itself? In M. H. Kernis (Ed.), *Efficacy, agency, and self-esteem* (pp. 9–30). New York, NY: Plenum.

Erikson, E. (1983). *The life cycle completed.* New York, NY: Norton.

Fava, G. A. (1999). Well-being therapy: Conceptual and technical issues. *Psychotherapy and Psychosomatics, 68*, 171–179.

Finkelhor, D., & Browne, A. (1985). The traumatic impact of child sexual abuse: A conceptualization. *American Journal of Orthopsychiatry, 55*, 530–541.

Fischer, C. (1986). *Individualizing psychological assessment.* Belmont, CA: Wadsworth.

Fordyce, M. W. (1977). Development of a program to increase personal happiness. *Journal of Counseling Psychology, 24*, 511–520.

Fordyce, M. W. (1983). A program to increase happiness: Further studies. *Journal of Counseling Psychology, 30*(4), 483–498.

Franks, D. D., & Marolla, J. (1976). Efficacious action and social approval as interacting dimensions of self-esteem: A tentative formulation through construct validation. *Sociometry, 39*(4), 324–341.

Fredrickson, B. (2002). Positive emotions. In C. R. Snyder & S. J. Lopez (Eds.), *Handbook of positive psychology* (pp. 120–134). New York, NY: Oxford.

Freeman, A., Pretzer, J., Fleming, B., & Simon, K. (1990). *Clinical applications of cognitive therapy.* New York, NY: Plenum.

Freud, S. (1957). *On narcissism: An introduction* (standard ed.). London, UK: Hogarth Press. (Original work published 1914)

Frey, D., & Carlock, C. J. (1989). *Enhancing self-esteem* (2nd ed.). Muncie, IN: Accelerated Development.

Frey, D. E., Kelbley, T. J., Thomas, J., Durham, L., & James, J. S. (1992). Enhancing self-esteem of selected male nursing home residents. *Gerontologist, 32*, 552–557.

Gecas, V. (1971). Parental behavior and dimensions of adolescent self-evaluation. *Sociometry, 34*(4), 466–482.

Gecas, V. (1982). The self-concept. *Annual Review of Sociology, 8*, 1–33.

Gecas, V., & Schwalbe, M. L. (1983). Beyond the looking-glass self: Social structure and efficacy-based self-esteem. *Social Psychology Quarterly, 46*(2), 77–88.

Gergen, K. J. (1991). *The saturated self: Dilemmas of identity in contemporary life.* New York, NY: Basic Books.

Giorgi, A. (1970). *Psychology as a human science: A phenomenologically based approach.* New York, NY: Harper & Row.

Giorgi, A. (1971). Phenomenology and experimental psychology: 1 & 2. In A. Giorgi, W. Fischer, & R. Von Eckartsberg (Eds.), *Duquesne studies in phenomenological psychology* (Vol. 1, pp. 6–28). Pittsburgh, PA: Duquesne University Press.

Giorgi, A. (1975). Convergence and divergence of qualitative and quantitative methods in psychology. In A. Giorgi, C. Fischer, & E. Murray (Eds.), *Duquesne studies in phenomenological psychology* (Vol. 2, pp. 72–79). Pittsburgh, PA: Duquesne University Press.

Giorgi, A. (1984). Towards a new paradigm for psychology. In C. Aanstoos (Ed.), *Exploring the lived world: Readings in phenomenological psychology* (Vol. 22, pp. 9–28). Atlanta, GA: West Georgia College.

Gottleib, L. (2012, July–August). How to land your kid in therapy. *Atlantic Magazine*, pp. 64–78.

Greenberg, J., Koole, S., & Pyszczynski, T. (Eds.). (2004). *Handbook of experimental existential psychology*. New York, NY: Guilford.

Greenberg, J., Pyszczynski, T., & Solomon, S. (1995). Toward a dual-motive depth psychology of self and social behavior. In M. H. Kernis (Ed.), *Efficacy, agency, and self-esteem* (pp. 73–99). New York, NY: Plenum.

Greenier, K. D., Kernis, M. H., & Waschull, S. B. (1995). Not all high (or low) self-esteem people are the same: Theory and research on stability of self-esteem. In M. H. Kernis (Ed.), *Efficacy, agency, and self-esteem* (pp. 51–71). New York, NY: Plenum.

Guindon, M. H. (2002). Assessment and diagnosis: Toward accountability in the use of the self-esteem construct. *Journal of Counseling & Development, 80*(2), 204–214.

Gurwitsch, A. (1964). *The field of consciousness*. Pittsburgh, PA: Duquesne University Press.

Hakim-Larson, J., & Mruk, C. (1997). Enhancing self-esteem in a community mental health setting. *American Journal of Orthopsychiatry, 67*, 655–659.

Haringsma, R. C. (2011). *Competence and Worthiness Training as a positive psychological intervention to enhance self-esteem: A randomized trial* (Unpublished doctoral dissertation). Department of Psychology, VU University, Denmark.

Harter, S. (1985). *The Perceived Competence Scale for Children* (Unpublished manuscript). Department of Psychology, University of Denver, Denver, CO.

Harter, S. (1993). Causes and consequences of low self-esteem in children and adolescents. In R. Baumeister (Ed.), *Self-esteem: The puzzle of low self-regard* (pp. 87–111). New York, NY: Plenum.

Harter, S. (1999). *The construction of the self: A developmental perspective*. New York, NY: Guilford.

Harter, S. (2003). The development of self-representations during childhood and adolescence. In M. R. Leary & J. P. Tangney (Eds.), *Handbook of self and identity* (pp. 610–642). New York, NY: Guilford.

Harter, S., & Whitesell, N. R. (2003). Beyond the debate: Why some adolescents report stable self-worth over time and situation, whereas others report changes in self-worth. *Journal of Personality, 71*(6), 1027–1058.

Harter, S., Whitesell, N. R., & Junkin, L. J. (1998). Similarities and differences in domain-specific and global self-evaluations of learning disabled, behaviorally disordered, and normally achieving adolescents. *American Educational Research Journal, 35*(4), 653–680.

Harvey, S., & Keashly, L. (2003). Predicting the risk for aggression in the workplace: Risk factors, self-esteem and time at work. *Social Behavior and Personality, 8,* 807–814.

Havighurst, R. J. (1972). *Developmental tasks and education* (3rd ed.). New York, NY: McKay.

Heatherton, T. D., & Wyland, C. (2003). Why do people have self-esteem? *Psychological Inquiry, 14*(1), 38–41.

Heidegger, M. (1962). *Being and time.* New York, NY: Harper & Row. (Original work published 1927)

Hernandez, L., & Blazer, D. (Eds.). (2006). *Genes, behavior, and the social environment: Moving beyond the nature/nurture debate.* Washington, DC: The National Academy Press.

Hewitt, J. P. (2002). The social construction of self-esteem. In C. R. Snyder & S. J. Lopez (Eds.), *Handbook of positive psychology* (pp. 135–158). Oxford, UK: Oxford University Press.

Hobbes, T. (1994). Part I, chapter 13. In Curley, E. (Ed.), *Leviathan: With selected variants from the Latin edition of 1668* (pp. 99–104). Indianapolis, IN: Hackett Publishing. (Original work published 1651)

Horney, K. (1937). *The neurotic personality of our time.* New York, NY: W.W. Norton.

Howard, G. (1985). *Basic research methods in the social sciences.* Glenview, IL: Scott Foresman.

Hunt, B. (2010). Women and self-esteem. In M. Guindon (Ed.), *Self-esteem across the lifespan* (pp. 191–204). New York, NY: Routledge.

Husserl, E. (1970a). *The crisis of European sciences and transcendental phenomenology.* Evanston, IL: Northwestern University Press. (Original work published 1954)

Husserl, E. (1970b). *Logical investigations II* (J. Findlay, Trans.). New York, NY: Humanities Press. (Original work published 1901)

Jackson, M. (1984). *Self-esteem and meaning: A life historical investigation.* Albany, NY: State University of New York.

James, W. (1983). *The principles of psychology.* Cambridge, MA: Harvard University Press. (Original work published 1890)

Jindal-Snape, D., & Miller, D. J. (2008). A challenge of living? Understanding the psycho-social processes of the child during primary-secondary transition through resilience and self-esteem theories. *Education Psychological Review, 20,* 217–236.

Johanson, G. J. (2009). Nonlinear science, mindfulness, and the body in humanistic psychotherapy. *The Humanistic Psychologist, 37,* 159–177.

Johnson, K. (1998, May 5). Self-image is suffering from a lack of esteem. *New York Times,* p. F7.

Jordan, C. H., Spencer, S. J., Zanna, M. P., Hoshino-Browne, E., & Correll, J. (2003). Secure and defensive high self-esteem. *Journal of Personality and Social Psychology, 85*(5), 969–978.

Jorgensen, I. S., & Nafstad, H. E. (2004). Positive psychology: Historical, philosophical, and epistemological perspectives. In P. A. Linley & S. Joseph (Eds.), *Positive psychology in practice* (pp. 14–34). Hoboken, NJ: John Wiley & Sons.

Kazdin, A. (1992). *Research design in clinical psychology.* Needham Heights, MA: Allyn & Bacon.

Kernis, M. H. (Ed.). (1995). *Efficacy, agency, and self-esteem.* New York, NY: Plenum.

Kernis, M. H. (2003a). Optimal self-esteem and authenticity: Separating fantasy from reality. *Psychological Inquiry, 14*(1), 83–89.

Kernis, M. H. (2003b). Toward a conceptualization of optimal self-esteem. *Psychological Inquiry, 14*(1), 1–26.

Kernis, M. H., & Goldman, B. M. (2003). Stability and variability in self-concept and self-esteem. In M. R. Leary & J. P. Tangney (Eds.), *Handbook of self and identity* (pp. 106–127). New York, NY: Guilford.

Kitano, H. H. (1989). Alcohol and drug use and self-esteem: A sociocultural perspective. In A. M. Mecca, N. J. Smelser, & J. Vasconcellos (Eds.), *The social importance of self-esteem* (pp. 294–326). Berkeley, CA: University of California Press.

Knee, R., Canevello, A., Bush, A., & Cook, A. (2008). Relationship-contingent self-esteem and the ups and downs of romantic relationships. *Journal of Personality and Social Psychology, 95*(3), 608–627.

Koole, S. L., & Kuhl, J. (2003). In search of the real self: A functional perspective on optimal self-esteem and authenticity. *Psychological Inquiry, 14*(1), 43–48.

Krauthammer, C. (1990, February 5). Education: Doing bad and feeling good. *Time Magazine,* p. 78.

Kuhn, T. (1962). *The structure of scientific revolutions.* Chicago, IL: University of Chicago Press.

Kwan, V. S. Y., Bond, M. H., & Singelis, T. M. (1997). Pancultural explanations for life-satisfaction: Adding relationship harmony to self-esteem. *Journal of Personality and Social Psychology, 73,* 1038–1051.

Leahy, R. L. (2003). *Cognitive therapy techniques: A practitioner's guide.* New York, NY: Guilford.

Leary, M. R. (2004). The sociometer, self-esteem, and the regulation of interpersonal behavior. In R. F. Baumeister & K. D. Vohs (Eds.), *The handbook of self-regulation: Research, theory, and application* (pp. 373–391). New York, NY: Guilford.

Leary, M. R. (2008). Functions of the self in interpersonal relationships: What does the self actually do? In J. Wood, A. Tesser, & J. Holmes (Eds.), *The self and social relationships* (pp. 95–115). New York, NY: Psychology Press.

Leary, M. R., & Downs, D. L. (1995). Interpersonal functions of the self-esteem motive: The self-esteem system as a sociometer. In M. H. Kernis (Ed.), *Efficacy, agency, and self-esteem* (pp. 123–144). New York, NY: Plenum.

Leary, M. R., & MacDonald, G. (2003). Individual differences in self-esteem: A review and theoretical integration. In M. R. Leary & J. P. Tangney (Eds.), *Handbook of self and identity* (pp. 401–418). New York, NY: Guilford.

Leary, M. R., & Tangney, J. P. (2003). The self as an organizing construct in the behavioral and social sciences. In M. R. Leary & J. P. Tangney (Eds.), *Handbook of self and identity* (pp. 3–14). New York, NY: Guilford.

Leo, J. (1990, April 2). The trouble with self-esteem. *U.S. News and World Report,* p. 16.

Leo, J. (1998, May 18). Damn, I'm good! *U.S. News and World Report,* p. 21.

Levin, J. D. (1993). *Slings and arrows: Narcissistic injury and its treatment.* Northvale, NJ: Aronson.

Linley, P. A., & Joseph, S. (2004). *Positive psychology in practice.* Hoboken, NJ: Wiley.

Lyubomirsky, S. (2001). Why are some people happier than others? The role of cognitive and motivational processes in well-being. *American Psychologist, 56,* 239–249.

Lyubomirsky, S., Dickerhoof, R., Boehm, J. K., & Sheldon, K. M. (2011). Becoming happier takes both a will and a proper way: An experimental longitudinal intervention to boost well-being. *Emotion, 11,* 391–402.

Mack, F. (1987). Understanding and enhancing self-concepts in black children. *Momentum, 18,* 22–28.

Maddux, J. E., & Gosselin, J. T. (2003). Self-efficacy. In M. R. Leary & J. P. Tangney (Eds.), *Handbook of self and identity* (pp. 218–238). New York, NY: Guilford.

Mann, J. (1973). *Time-limited psychotherapy.* Cambridge, MA: Harvard University Press.

Marcel, G. (1964). *Creative fidelity.* New York, NY: Noonday Press.

Marigold, D. C., Holmes, J. G., & Ross, M. (2007). More than words: Reframing compliments from romantic partners fosters security in low self-esteem individuals. *Journal of Personality and Social Psychology, 92*(2), 232–248.

Maslow, A. H. (1964). *Religions, values, and peak-experiences.* New York, NY: Viking.

Maslow, A. H. (1968). *Toward a psychology of being.* Princeton, NJ: Van Nostrand.

Maslow, A. H. (1970). *Motivation and personality.* New York, NY: Harper & Row. (Original work published 1954)

McKay, M., & Fanning, P. (2000). *Self-esteem* (3rd ed.). Oakland, CA: New Harbinger.

McKeon, R. (Ed.). (1941). *The basic works of Aristotle.* New York, NY: Random House.

McReynolds, C. J., Ward, D. M., & Singer, O. (2002). Stigma, discrimination, and invisibility: Factors affecting successful integration of individuals diagnosed with schizophrenia. *Journal of Applied Rehabilitation Counseling, 33*(4), 32–39.

Mead, G. H. (1934). *Mind, self, and society.* Chicago, IL: University of Chicago Press.

Mecca, A. M., Smelser, N. J., & Vasconcellos, J. (Eds.). (1989). *The social importance of self-esteem.* Berkeley, CA: University of California Press.

Medlock, G. (2012). The evolving ethic of authenticity: From humanistic to positive psychology. *The Humanistic Psychologist, 40*(1), 38–57.

Menard, A., & Offman, A. (2009). The interrelationships between sexual self-esteem, sexual assertiveness and sexual satisfaction. *Canadian Journal of Human Sexuality, 18*(1), 35.

Merleau-Ponty, M. (1962). *The phenomenology of perception.* New York, NY: Humanities Press. (Original work published 1945)

Messer, B., & Harter, S. (1986). *Adult self-perception profile* (Unpublished manuscript). Dept. of Psychology, University of Denver, Denver, CO.

Michel, W., & Morf, C. (2003). The self as a psycho-social dynamic processing system: A meta perspective on a century of the self in psychology. In M. R. Leary & J. P. Tangney (Eds.), *Handbook of self and identity* (pp. 15–43). New York, NY: Guilford.

Miller, R. (Ed.). (1992). *The restoration of dialogue: Readings in the philosophy of clinical psychology*. Washington, DC: American Psychological Association.

Miller, T. (1984). Parental absence and its effects on adolescent self-esteem. *International Journal of Social Psychiatry, 30*(4), 293–296.

Milton, J. (1931). Paradise lost. In F. A. Patterson (Ed.). *The works of John Milton*. New York, NY: Columbia Press. (Original work published 1667)

Milton, J. (1950). Apology against a pamphlet. In C. Brooks (Ed.), *Complete poetry and selected prose of John Milton*. New York, NY: Modern Library. (Original work published 1642)

Misiak, H., & Sexton, V. S. (1973). *Phenomenological, existential, and humanistic psychologies: A historical survey*. New York, NY: Grune and Stratton.

Mruk, C. (1981). *Being pleased with oneself in a biographically critical way: An existential-phenomenological investigation* (Unpublished doctoral dissertation). Duquesne University, Pittsburgh, PA.

Mruk, C. (1983). Toward a phenomenology of self-esteem. In A. Giorgi, A. Barton, & C. Maes (Eds.), *Duquesne studies in phenomenological psychology* (Vol. 4, pp. 137–148). Pittsburgh, PA: Duquesne University Press.

Mruk, C. (1984). Integrated description: A phenomenological technique for researching large scale, emerging human experience and trends. *Advances in Consumer Research, 3*, 566–570.

Mruk, C. (1994). Phenomenological psychology and integrated description: Keeping the science in the human science approach. *Methods: A Journal for Human Science* (annual edition), 6–20.

Mruk, C. (1995). *Self-esteem: Research, theory, and practice*. New York, NY: Springer.

Mruk, C. (1999). *Self-esteem: Research, theory, and practice* (2nd ed.). New York, NY: Springer.

Mruk, C. (2006). Defining self-esteem: An often overlooked issue with crucial implications. In M. Kernis (Ed.), *Self-esteem issues and answers: A source book of current perspectives* (pp. 10–15). New York, NY: Psychology Press.

Mruk, C. (2008a). Positive psychology and positive therapy: Implications for practitioners. *Ohio Psychologist, 55*, 16–17.

Mruk, C. (2008b). The psychology of self-esteem: A potential common ground for humanistic positive psychology and positivistic positive psychology. *The Humanistic Psychologist, 36*, 143–158.

Mruk, C. (2010). Integrated description: A humanistic method for an evidence-based world. *The Humanistic Psychologist, 38*, 305–316.

Mruk, C. (in press). Self-esteem, relationships, and positive psychology: Concepts, research, and connections. In M. Hojjat & D. Cramer (Eds.), *Positive psychology of love*. Oxford, UK: Oxford University Press.

Mruk, C., & Hartzell, J. (2003). *Zen and psychotherapy: Integrating traditional and nontraditional psychotherapies*. New York, NY: Springer.

Mruk, C., & O'Brien, E. J. (in press). Changing self-esteem through competence and worthiness training: A positive therapy. In V. Zeigler-Hill (Ed.), *Current issues in social psychology*. New York, NY: Psychology Press.

Murray, S. (2008). Risk regulation in relationships: Self-esteem and the if-then contingencies of interdependent life. In J. Wood, A. Tesser, & J. Holmes (Eds.), *The self and social relationships* (pp. 3–25). New York, NY: Psychology Press.

Neiss, M. B., Stevenson, J., & Sedikides, C. (2003). The genetic bases of optimal self-esteem. *Psychological Inquiry, 14*(1), 63–65.

Newman, B., & Newman, P. (1987). *Development through life: A psychosocial approach* (4th ed.). Chicago, IL: Dorsey Press.

Nozick, R. (1974). *Anarchy, state, and utopia.* New York, NY: Basic.

O'Brien, E. J. (2010). *Bibliography of references to the Multidimensional Self-Esteem Inventory MSEI.* Odessa, FL: Psychological Assessment Resources.

O'Brien, E. J., Bartoletti, M., & Leitzel, J. D. (2006). Self-esteem, psychopathology and psychotherapy. In M. Kernis (Ed.), *Self-esteem issues and answers: A source book of current perspectives.* New York, NY: Psychology Press.

O'Brien, E. J., Bartoletti, M., Leitzel, J. D., & O'Brien, J. P. (2006). Global self-esteem: Divergent and convergent validity Issues. In M. H. Kernis (Ed.), *Self-esteem: Issues and answers* (pp. 26–35). New York, NY: Psychology Press.

O'Brien, E. J., & Epstein, S. (1988). *MSEI: The Multidimensional Self-Esteem Inventory.* Odessa, FL: Psychological Assessment Resources.

O'Brien, E. J., Leitzel, J., & Mensky, L. (1996). *Gender differences in the self-esteem of adolescents: A meta-analysis.* Poster session presented at the annual meeting of the American Psychological Association, Toronto, Canada.

Orth, U., Trzesniewski, K., & Robins, R. (2010). Self-esteem development from young adulthood to old age: A cohort-sequential longitudinal study. *Journal of Personality and Social Psychology, 98*(4), 645.

Pallas, A. M., Entwisle, D. R., Alexander, K. L., & Weinstein, P. (1990). Social structure and the development of self-esteem in young children. *Social Psychology Quarterly, 53,* 302–315.

Park, L., Crocker, J., & Vohs, K. (2006). Contingencies of self-worth and self-validation goals: Implications for close relationships. In K. Vohs & E. Finkel (Eds.), *Self and relationships: Connecting intrapersonal and interpersonal processes* (pp. 84–103). New York, NY: Guilford Press.

Peterson, C. (2006). *A primer in positive psychology.* Oxford, UK: Oxford University Press.

Peterson, C., & Seligman, M. (2004). *Character strengths and virtues: A handbook and classification.* Oxford, UK: Oxford University Press.

Pettijohn, T. F. (1998). *Sources: Notable selections in social psychology.* Guilford, CT: Dushkin/McGraw-Hill.

Piers, E., & Harris, D. (1969). *Piers-Harris Children's Self-Concept Scale.* Los Angeles, CA: Western Psychological Services.

Pillemer, D., Ivcevic, Z., Gooze, R., & Collins, K. (2007). Self-esteem memories: Feeling good about achievement success, feeling bad about relationship distress. *Personality and Social Psychology Bulletin, 9,* 1292–1305.

Pirsig, R. (1974). *Zen and the art of motorcycle maintenance.* New York, NY: Morrow.

Pope, A., McHale, S., & Craighead, E. (1988). *Self-esteem enhancement with children and adolescents.* New York, NY: Pergamon Press.

Prochaska, J. O., & Norcross, J. C. (1994). *Systems of psychotherapy: A transtheoretical analysis* (3rd ed.). Pacific Grove, CA: Brooks/Cole.

Pyszczynski, T., Greenberg, T., & Goldberg, J. L. (2003). Freedom versus fear: On the defense, growth, and expansion of self. In M. R. Leary & J. P. Tangney (Eds.), *Handbook of self and identity* (pp. 315–343). New York, NY: Guilford.

Pyszczynski, T., Greenberg, J., Sheldon, S., Arndt, J., & Schimel, J. (2004a). Converging toward an integrated theory of self-esteem: Reply to Crocker and Nuer (2004), Ryan and Deci (2004), and Leary (2004). *Psychological Bulletin, 130*(3), 483–488.

Pyszczynski, T., Greenberg, J., Sheldon, S., Arndt, J., & Schimel, J. (2004b). Why do people need self-esteem? A theoretical and empirical review. *Psychological Bulletin, 130*(3), 435–168.

Rakos, R. F. (1990). *Assertive behavior: Theory, research, and training.* London, UK: Routledge.

Ramis, H. (Producer & Director). (1993). *Groundhog Day* [Motion picture]. USA: Columbia Tri-Star Films.

Raskin, R., Novacek, J., & Hogan, R. (1991). Narcissistic self-esteem management. *Journal of Personality and Social Psychology, 60*, 911–918.

Rathus, S. (2007). *Psychology: Concepts and connections, brief version* (8th ed.). New York, NY: Thompson/Wadsworth.

Regier, D. A., Narrow, W. E., Rae, D. S., Manderscheid, R. W., Locke, B. Z., & Goodwin, F. K. (1993). The de facto mental and addictive disorders service system. Epidemiologic catchment area prospective 1-year prevalence rates of disorders and services. *Archives of General Psychiatry, 50*(2), 85–94.

Rodewalt, F., & Tragakis, M. W. (2003). Self-esteem and self-regulation: Toward optimal studies of self-esteem. *Psychological Inquiry, 14*(1), 66–70.

Rogers, C. (1951). *Client centered therapy.* Boston, MA: Houghton Mifflin.

Rogers, C. (1961). *On becoming a person.* Boston, MA: Houghton Mifflin.

Roid, G. H., & Fitts, W. (1988). *Tennessee Self-Concept Scale.* Los Angeles, CA: Western Psychological Services.

Rosenberg, M. (1965). *Society and the adolescent self-image.* Princeton, NJ: Princeton University Press.

Rosenberg, M. (1979). *Conceiving the self.* New York, NY: Basic Books.

Rosenberg, M. (1986). Self-concept from middle childhood through adolescence. In J. Suls & A. G. Greenwald (Eds.), *Psychological perspectives on the self* (Vol. 3). Hillsdale, NJ: Lawrence Erlbaum.

Rosenberg, M., & Owens, T. J. (2001). Low self-esteem people. In T. J. Owens, S. Sheldon, & N. Goodman (Eds.), *Extending self-esteem theory and research: Sociological and psychological currents* (pp. 400–436). New York, NY: Cambridge.

Rosenberg, M., Schooler, C., Schoenbach, C., & Rosenberg, F. (1995). Global self-esteem and specific self-esteem: Different concepts and different outcomes. *American Sociological Review, 60*, 141–156.

Rosenberg, M., & Simmons, R. G. (1971). *Black and white self-esteem: The urban school child* [Monograph]. *Social Psychological Implications IX, Rose Monograph Series.* Washington, DC: American Sociological Association.

Ruini, C., & Fava, G. A. (2004). Clinical applications of well-being therapy. In P. A. Linley & S. Joseph (Eds.), *Positive psychology in practice* (pp. 371–388). Hoboken, NJ: Wiley.

Ryan, R. M., & Brown, K. W. (2003). Why we don't need self-esteem: On fundamental needs, contingent love, and mindfulness. *Psychological Inquiry, 14*(1), 71–76.

Ryan, R. M., & Deci, E. L. (2003). On assimilating identities to the self: A self-determination theory perspective on internalization and integrity within cultures. In M. R. Leary & J. P. Tangney (Eds.), *Handbook of self and identity* (pp. 253–272). New York, NY: Guilford.

Ryan, R. M., & Deci, E. L. (2004). Avoiding death or engaging life as accounts of meaning and culture: Commentary on Pyszczynski (2004). *Psychological Bulletin, 130*(3), 473–477.

Ryff, C. D., & Singer, B. (2002). From social structure to biology: Integrative science in pursuit of human and well-being. In C. R. Snyder & S. J. Lopez (Eds.), *Handbook of positive psychology* (pp. 541–555). Oxford, UK: Oxford University Press.

Salmivalli, C, Kaukiainen, A., & Lagerspetz, K. M. J. (1999). Self-evaluated self-esteem, peer evaluated self-esteem, and defensive egotism and predictors of adolescents' participation in bullying situations. *Personality and Social Psychology Bulletin, 25*(10), 1268–1278.

Sanford, L., & Donovan, E. (1984). *Women and self-esteem.* New York, NY: Anchor Press/Doubleday.

Sappington, A. (1989). *Adjustment: Theory, research, and personal applications.* Pacific Grove, CA: Brooks/Cole.

Scheff, T. J., & Fearon, D. S., Jr. (2004). Cognition and emotion? The dead end in self-esteem research. *Journal for the Theory of Social Behavior, 34*(1), 73–90.

Scheff, T. J., Retzinger, S., & Ryan, M. (1989). Crime, violence, and self-esteem: Review and proposals. In A. M. Mecca, N. J. Smelser, & J. Vasconcellos (Eds.), *The social importance of self-esteem* (pp. 165–199). Berkeley, CA: University of California Press.

Schneiderman, J. W., Furman, M., & Weber, J. (1989). Self-esteem and chronic welfare dependency. In A. M. Mecca, N. J. Smelser, & J. Vasconcellos (Eds.), *The social importance of self-esteem* (pp. 200–247). Berkeley, CA: University of California Press.

Sciangula, A., & Morry, M. M. (2009). Self-esteem and perceived regard: How I see myself affects my relationship satisfaction. *Journal of Social Psychology, 149*(2), 143–158.

Sedikides, C., Rudich, E. A., Gregg, A. P., Kumashiro, M., & Rusbult, C. (2004). Are normal narcissists psychologically? Self-esteem matters. *Journal of Personality and Social Psychology, 87*(3), 400–416.

Seligman, M. E. P. (1990). *Learned optimism: How to change your mind and your life.* New York, NY: Simon & Schuster.

Seligman, M. E. P. (1995a). The effectiveness of psychotherapy: The consumer's report study. *American Psychologist, 40*, 965–974.

Seligman, M. E. P. (1995b). *The optimistic child: A proven program to safeguard children against depression and build lifelong resilience.* New York, NY: HarperCollins.

Seligman, M. E. P. (1999). The president's address (annual report). *American Psychologist, 54,* 559–562.

Seligman, M. E. P. (2002). Positive psychology, positive prevention, and positive therapy. In C. R. Snyder & S. J. Lopez (Eds.), *Handbook of positive psychology* (pp. 3–9). Oxford, UK: Oxford University Press.

Seligman, M. E. P., & Csikszentmihalyi, M. (2000). Positive psychology: An introduction. *American Psychologist, 55,* 5–14.

Seligman, M. E. P., Rashid, T., & Parks, A. (2006). Positive therapy. *American Psychologist, 61,* 774–788.

Seligman, M. E. P., Steen, T. A., Park, N., & Peterson, C. (2005). Positive psychology progress: Empirical validation of interventions. *American Psychologist, 5,* 410–421.

Sheldon, K. M., Elliot, A. J., Kim, Y., & Kasser, T. (2001). What is satisfying about satisfying events? Testing 10 candidate psychological needs. *Journal of Personality and Social Psychology, 80*(2), 325–339.

Sheldon, K. M., & Kasser, T. (2001). Goals, congruence, and positive well-being: New empirical support for humanistic theories. *Journal of Humanistic Psychology, 41*(1), 30–50.

Shrik, S., & Harter, S. (1996). Treatment of low self-esteem. In M. A. Reineke, F. M. Dattilio, & M. Freeman (Eds.), *Cognitive therapy with children and adolescents: A casebook for clinical practice* (pp. 175–198). New York, NY: Guilford.

Sigelman, C. S., & Shaffer, D. R. (1995). *Life-span human development* (2nd ed.). Belmont, CA: Brooks/Cole.

Silverstone, P. H., & Salsali, M. (2003). Low self-esteem and psychiatric patients: Part I—the relationship between low self-esteem and psychiatric diagnosis. *Annals of General Hospital Psychiatry, 2*(2), 1–9.

Smelser, N. J. (1989). Self-esteem and social problems: An introduction. In A. M. Mecca, N. J. Smelser, & J. Vasconcellos (Eds.), *The social importance of self-esteem* (pp. 1–23). Berkeley, CA: University of California Press.

Snyder, C. R., & Lopez, S. J. (2002). *Handbook of positive psychology.* Oxford, UK: Oxford University Press.

Snyder, C. S. (1989). Reality negotiation: From excuses to hope and beyond. *Journal of Social and Clinical Psychology, 8,* 130–157.

Sommer, K. (2001). Coping with rejection: Ego defensive strategies, self-esteem, and interpersonal relationships. In M. Leary (Ed.), *Interpersonal rejection* (pp. 167–188). New York, NY: Oxford University Press.

Stinson, D. A., Logel, C., Zanna, M. P., Holmes, J. G., & Cameron, J. J. (2008). The cost of lower self-esteem: Testing a self- and social-bonds model of health. *Journal of Personality and Social Psychology, 94*(3), 412–428.

Sue, D. W., & Sue, D. (1990). *Counseling the culturally different: Theory and practice.* New York, NY: Wiley.

Sullivan, H. S. (1953). *The interpersonal theory of psychiatry.* Chicago, IL: University of Chicago Press.

Swann, W., Jr., Chang-Schneider, C., & McClarty, K. (2007). Do people's self-views matter? Self-concept and self-esteem in everyday life. *American Psychologist, 2,* 84–94.

Swanston, H. Y., Tebbutt, J. S., O'Toole, B. I., & Oates, R. K. (1997). Sexually abused children 5 years after presentation: A case-control study. *Pediatrics, 100,* 600–608.

Tafarodi, R. W., & Ho, C. (2003). In defense of insecurity. *Psychological Inquiry, 14*(1), 77–79.

Tafarodi, R. W., & Milne, A. B. (2002). Decomposing self-esteem. *Journal of Personality, 70*(4), 443–483.

Tafarodi, R. W., & Swann, W. B., Jr. (1995). Self-liking and self-competence as dimensions of global self-esteem: Initial validation of a measure. *Journal of Personality Assessment, 65*(2), 322–342.

Tafarodi, R. W., & Swann, W. B., Jr. (1996). Individualism-collectivism and global self-esteem: Evidence for a cultural trade-off. *Journal of Cross-Cultural Psychology, 27*(6), 651–672.

Tafarodi, R. W., & Swann, W. B., Jr. (2001). Two-dimensional self-esteem: theory and measurement. *Personality and Individual Differences, 31,* 653–673.

Tafarodi, R. W., Tam, J., & Milne, A. (2001). Selective memory and the persistence of paradoxical self-esteem. *Personality and Social Psychology Bulletin, 27*(9), 1179–1189.

Tafarodi, R. W., & Vu, C. (1997). Two-dimensional self-esteem and reactions to success and failure. *Personality and Social Psychology Bulletin, 23*(6), 626–635.

Tageson, C. W. (1982). *Humanistic psychology: A synthesis.* Homewood, IL: Dorsey Press.

Taylor, E. (2001). Positive psychology and humanistic psychology: A reply to Seligman. *Journal of Humanistic Psychology, 41*(1), 13–29.

Tennen, H., & Affleck, G. (1993). The puzzles of self-esteem: A clinical perspective. In R. Baumeister (Ed.), *Self-esteem: The puzzle of low self-regard* (pp. 241–263). New York, NY: Plenum.

Thomaes, S., Bushman, B., Stegge, H., & Olthof, T. (2008, November/December). Trumping shame by blasts of noise: Narcissism, self-esteem, shame, and aggression in young adolescents. *Child Development, 6,* 1792–1801.

Tice, D. (1993). The social motivations of people with low self-esteem. In R. Baumeister (Ed.), *Self-esteem: The puzzle of low self-regard* (pp. 37–54). New York, NY: Plenum.

Torrey, E. F. (1972). *Witchdoctors and psychiatrists: The common roots of psychotherapy and its future.* New York, NY: Harper & Row.

Tryon, W. (1991). Uncertainty reduction as valid explanation. *Theoretical and Philosophical Psychology Bulletin, 11*(2), 91–98.

Trzesniewski, K. H., Robins, R. W., Roberts, B. W., & Caspi, A. (2004). Personality and self-esteem development across the life span. In P. T. Costa & I. C. Siegler (Eds.), *Psychology of aging* (pp. 163–185). Amsterdam, The Netherlands: Elsevier Science.

Twenge, J. M., & Campbell, W. K. (2002). Self-esteem and socioeconomic status: A meta-analytic review. *Personality and Social Psychology Review, 6*(1), 59–71.

Twenge, J. M., & Crocker, J. (2002). Race and self-esteem: Meta-analyses comparing Whites, Blacks, Hispanics, Asians, and American Indians. *Psychological Bulletin, 128*(3), 371–408.

Vaillant, G. (1995). *The wisdom of the ego: Sources of resilience in adult life*. Cambridge, MA: Belknap Press.

Vinogradov, S., & Yalom, I. D. (1989). *A concise guide to group psychotherapy*. Washington, DC: American Psychiatric Press.

Waters, L. E., & Moore, K. (2002). Predicting self-esteem during unemployment: The effect of gender, financial deprivation, alternate roles, and social support. *Journal of Employment Counseling, 39*(4), 171–189.

Weissman, H., & Ritter, K. (1970). Openness to experience, ego strength and self-description as a function of repression and sensitization. *Psychological Reports, 26*, 859–864.

Wells, E. L., & Marwell, G. (1976). *Self-esteem: Its conceptualization and measurement*. Beverly Hills, CA: Sage.

Wells, R. A. (1982). *Planned short-term treatment*. New York, NY: Free Press.

Werner, E. E., & Smith, R. S. (1992). *Overcoming the odds: High-risk children from birth to adulthood*. Ithaca, NY: Cornell University Press.

Wertz, F. (1984). Procedures in phenomenological research and the question of validity. In C. Aanstoos (Ed.), *Exploring the lived world: Readings in phenomenological psychology* (Vol. 23, pp. 9–28). Atlanta, GA: West Georgia College.

White, R. (1959). Motivation reconsidered: The concept of competence. *Psychological Review, 66*, 297–333.

White, R. (1963). Ego and reality in psychoanalytic theory: A proposal regarding independent ego energies. *Psychological Issues, 3*, 125–150.

Winnicott, D. (1953). Transitional objects and transitional phenomena. *International Journal of Psychoanalysis, 34*, 89–97.

Wood, J. V., Giordano-Beech, M., Taylor, K. L., Michela, J. L., & Gaus, V. (1994). Strategies of social comparison among people with low self-esteem: Self-protection and self-enhancement. *Journal of Personality and Social Psychology, 67*(4), 713–731.

Wylie, R. (1974). *The self-concept* (Vol. 1). Lincoln, NE: University of Nebraska Press.

Zeigler-Hill, V., Campe, J., & Myers, E. (2009). How low will men with high self-esteem go? Self-esteem as a moderator of gender differences in minimum relationship standards. *Sex Roles, 61*(7/8), 491–500.

Index

Aanstoos, 50, 271
abuse, 4, 25, 76, 82, 89, 151, 160, 183, 193, 275
acceptance, 19, 31, 61, 62, 67, 68, 70, 71, 74, 77, 78, 96, 101, 108, 112, 116, 136, 152, 160, 165, 166, 193, 196, 197, 216, 227, 228, 237, 241, 246, 248
acceptance-based self-esteem, 148, 150, 152, 153, 160, 162
achievement, 34, 35, 72–74, 76–78, 81, 106, 144, 152, 154, 155, 160, 167, 196, 197, 199, 212, 213, 261, 281
action plan, 210, 211, 267
achievement-based self-esteem, 148, 150, 154, 155, 160, 162, 193
Adler, 4, 12, 34, 104, 223, 271
adolescence, 19, 68, 89, 93, 110, 112, 162, 163, 165, 178, 272, 276, 282
adulthood, 24, 33, 60, 88, 89, 100, 112, 162, 165, 167, 173, 178, 211, 272, 281, 286
aggression, 13, 16, 153–156, 272, 277, 285
Alberti, 99, 271
American Association of University Women, 68, 271
American Psychiatric Association, 3, 145, 155, 271
analogy, 11, 22, 28, 31, 77, 120, 138, 146, 173, 208, 235
antisocial, 38, 108, 143, 151, 156, 184
antisocial self-esteem, 149, 150, 155, 160, 162
anxiety, 3, 6, 15, 32, 36, 44, 49, 54, 79, 81, 82, 83, 89, 92, 106, 114, 115, 126, 128, 131, 133, 142, 145, 146, 151, 156, 176, 188, 208, 209, 218, 228, 233

applied, vii, xi, 4, 45, 53, 57, 59, 99, 105, 113, 117, 118, 122, 159, 179, 206, 217, 218, 229, 230, 243–245, 250, 251, 279
Aristotelian, 45, 46, 231, 235, 239, 240, 242
Arkowitz, 96, 136, 216, 271
Aron, 71, 79, 271
Aspinwall, 230, 271
assessment, v, 36–39, 85, 89, 94, 106, 112, 113, 121, 123, 124, 129, 130, 132, 133, 135, 136, 157, 179, 184, 196, 215, 218, 247, 248, 256, 268, 275
at-stake, 11, 12, 13, 25, 167, 171, 216
authentic self-esteem, 1, 6, 7, 18, 22, 28, 29, 57, 61, 62, 77, 78, 84, 87, 88, 100, 148–150, 155, 156, 158, 159, 160, 162, 164, 165, 173, 193, 210, 228, 233, 239, 240–243, 251, 252
authenticity, 4, 7, 23, 25–27, 67, 74, 83, 87, 118, 140, 159, 167, 171–173, 178, 179, 196, 216, 225, 236–240, 244, 278, 279
awareness, 61, 87, 98, 108, 113, 115, 120, 135, 160, 163, 169–172, 175, 186, 189, 190, 192, 196–198, 209, 212, 215, 216, 228, 237, 238, 255

Babiak, 156, 271
balance, x, xiii, 16, 28, 54, 78, 80, 109, 127, 140, 143, 157, 183, 209, 229, 230, 242, 243
Baldwin, 71, 174, 233, 271
Bandura, 20, 98, 174, 271
Bartoletti, xiii, 3, 7, 20, 101, 176, 184, 218, 219, 271, 281
Battle, 95, 271